THE FLIGHT OF THE ROMANOVS

Romanov patriarch Alexander III leading the family at military maneuvers

THE FLIGHT OF THE ROMANOVS

A Family Saga

JOHN CURTIS PERRY
CONSTANTINE PLESHAKOV

KONECKY&KONECKY

Konecky and Konecky
72 Ayers Point Rd.
Old Saybrook, CT 06475

Copyright © 1999 by John C. Perry and Constantine V. Pleshakov

Published by special arrangement with Basic Books, a member of
the Perseus Books Group

ISBN: 1-56852-397-1

Designed by Rachel Hegarty

Printed in the U.S.A.

FOR
BENJAMIN, ASA, JACK, THOMAS,
AND CHARLOTTE
AND ELZA

CONTENTS

Photographs appear after pages 126 and 238

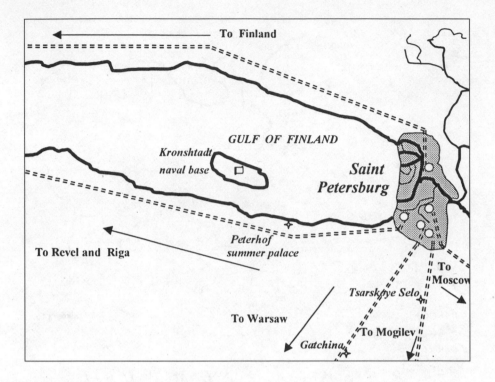

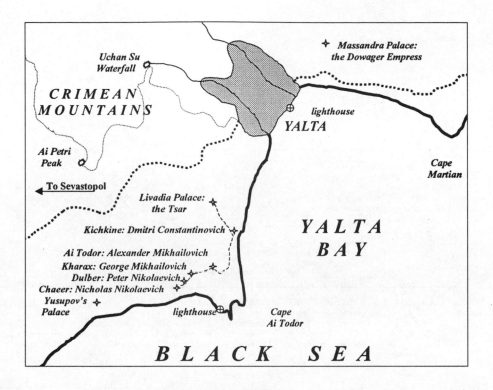

Uchan Su
Waterfall

✦ Massandra Palace:
the Dowager Empress

CRIMEAN
MOUNTAINS

lighthouse
YALTA

Ai Petri
Peak

Cape
Martian

◄ To Sevastopol

Livadia Palace:
the Tsar

YALTA
BAY

Kichkine: Dmitri Constantinovich

Ai Todor: Alexander Mikhailovich
Kharax: George Mikhailovich
Dulber: Peter Nikolaevich
Chaeer: Nicholas Nikolaevich
Yusupov's
Palace

lighthouse

Cape
Ai Todor

BLACK   SEA

THE ROMANOV DYNASTY
ABBREVIATED

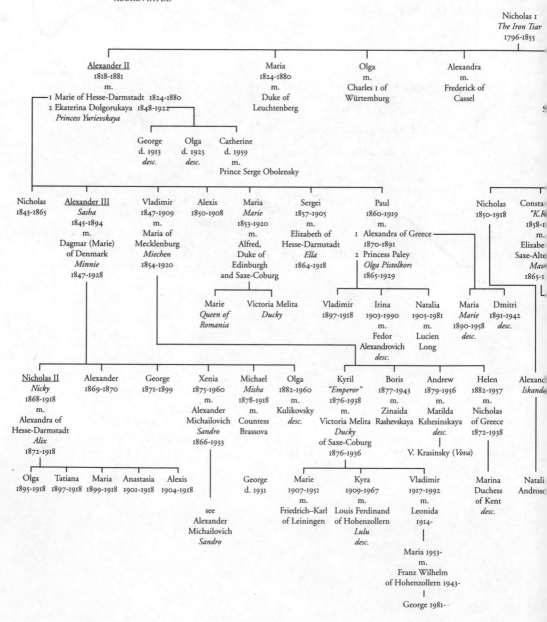

Nicholas I
The Iron Tsar
1796-1855

Alexander II
1818-1881
m.
1 Marie of Hesse-Darmstadt 1824-1880
2 Ekaterina Dolgorukaya 1848-1922
Princess Yurievskaya

Maria
1824-1880
m.
Duke of
Leuchtenberg

Olga
m.
Charles I of
Würtemburg

Alexandra
m.
Frederick of
Cassel

George
d. 1913
desc.

Olga
d. 1925
desc.

Catherine
d. 1959
m.
Prince Serge Obolensky

Nicholas
1843-1865

Alexander III
Sasha
1845-1894
m.
Dagmar (Marie)
of Denmark
Minnie
1847-1928

Vladimir
1847-1909
m.
Maria of
Mecklenburg
Miechen
1854-1920

Alexis
1850-1908

Maria
Marie
1853-1920
m.
Alfred,
Duke of
Edinburgh
and Saxe-Coburg

Sergei
1857-1905
m.
Elizabeth of
Hesse-Darmstadt
Ella
1864-1918

Paul
1860-1919
m.
1 Alexandra of Greece
1870-1891
2 Princess Paley
Olga Pistolkors
1865-1929

Nicholas
1850-1918

Consta
"K.K
1858-1
m.
Elizabe
Saxe-Alte
Mav
1865-1

Marie
*Queen of
Romania*

Victoria Melita
Ducky

Vladimir
1897-1918

Irina
1903-1990
m.
Fedor
Alexandrovich
desc.

Natalia
1905-1981
m.
Lucien
Long

Maria
Marie
1890-1958
desc.

Dmitri
1891-1942
desc.

Nicholas II
Nicky
1868-1918
m.
Alexandra of
Hesse-Darmstadt
Alix
1872-1918

Alexander
1869-1870

George
1871-1899

Xenia
1875-1960
m.
Alexander
Michailovich
Sandro
1866-1933

Michael
Misha
1878-1918
m.
Countess
Brassova

Olga
1882-1960
m.
Kulikovsky
desc.

Kyril
"Emperor"
1876-1938
m.
Victoria Melita
Ducky
of Saxe-Coburg
1876-1936

Boris
1877-1943
m.
Zinaida
Rashevskaya

Andrew
1879-1956
m.
Matilda
Kshesinskaya
desc.

Helen
1882-1957
m.
Nicholas
of Greece
1872-1938

Alexand
Iskand

Olga
1895-1918

Tatiana
1897-1918

Maria
1899-1918

Anastasia
1901-1918

Alexis
1904-1918

George
d. 1931

Marie
1907-1951
m.
Friedrich–Karl
of Leiningen

Kyra
1909-1967
m.
Louis Ferdinand
of Hohenzollern
Lulu
desc.

Vladimir
1917-1992
m.
Leonida
1914-

Marina
Duchess
of Kent
desc.

Natali
Androso

V. Krasinsky (*Vova*)

see
Alexander
Michailovich
Sandro

Maria 1953-
m.
Franz Wilhelm
of Hohenzollern 1943-

George 1981-

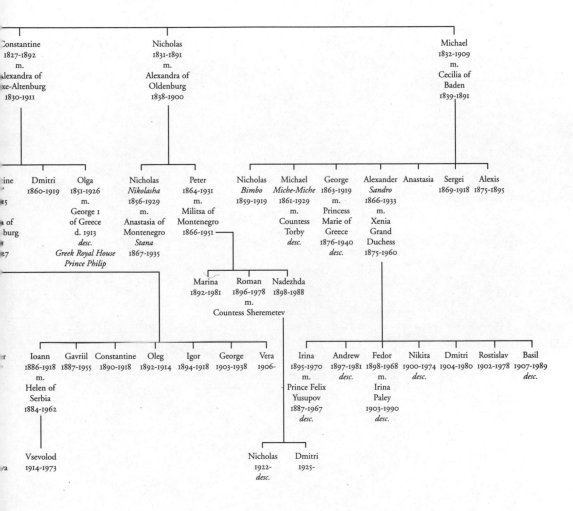

Constantine
1827-1892
m.
Alexandra of
[Sa]xe-Altenburg
1830-1911

Nicholas
1831-1891
m.
Alexandra of
Oldenburg
1838-1900

Michael
1832-1909
m.
Cecilia of
Baden
1839-1891

[...ine]   Dmitri   Olga   Nicholas   Peter   Nicholas   Michael   George   Alexander   Anastasia   Sergei   Alexis
[...]   1860-1919 1851-1926 Nikolasha   1864-1931   Bimbo   Miche-Miche 1863-1919   Sandro   1869-1918 1875-1895
           m.   1856-1929 m.   1859-1919   1861-1929   m.   1866-1933
[...a of]   George 1   m.   Militsa of   m.   Princess   m.
[...burg]   of Greece Anastasia of Montenegro   Countess   Marie of   Xenia
[...]   d. 1913   Montenegro 1866-1951   Torby   Greece   Grand
[...7]   desc.   Stana   desc.   1876-1940   Duchess
            Greek Royal House 1867-1935   desc.   1875-1960
            Prince Philip

                                Marina   Roman   Nadezhda
                                1892-1981 1896-1978 1898-1988
                                          m.
                                Countess Sheremetev

[...r]   Ioann   Gavriil   Constantine Oleg   Igor   George   Vera   Irina   Andrew   Fedor   Nikita   Dmitri   Rostislav Basil
        1886-1918 1887-1955 1890-1918   1892-1914 1894-1918 1903-1938 1906-   1895-1970   1897-1981 1898-1968 1900-1974 1904-1980 1902-1978 1907-1989
        m.   m.   desc.   m.   desc.   desc.
        Helen of   Prince Felix   Irina
        Serbia   Yusupov   Paley
        1884-1962   1887-1967   1903-1990
                                                                                   desc.   desc.

[...a]   Vsevolod   Nicholas   Dmitri
        1914-1973   1922-   1925-
                                                                         desc.

FOREWORD
THE FLIGHT OF THE ROMANOVS:
A FAMILY SAGA

CONSPIRACY AND MURDER, imprisonment, torture, flight, and abduction punctuate the story of the Romanovs, Russia's last imperial dynasty, during their last century. It is a chronicle of glittering sadness, of unfulfilled expectations and squandered opportunities. As with any family, the Romanovs provide a saga of love and lust, of personal tensions and rivalries, of antagonisms and even hatreds. But because of who these people were, issues of wealth and position permeated and complicated their personal relationships. Before the great revolution, the grand dukes and grand duchesses fled from reality at home, living sumptuous jewel-studded lives in palaces isolated from the harshness and brutality of Russia, or they retreated to luxurious vacations abroad. Probably no society has ever experienced a sharper contrast between privilege and poverty, with so few rich and so many poor. This huge disparity fed rage, hatred and ultimately revolution, forcing the Romanovs and all Russian aristocrats to flee for their lives.

Most of the Romanovs, like most royals, were ordinary people thrust by birth into extraordinary circumstances of opulence and power. In a nation of strong women, the Romanov women were characteristically stronger than the men, but, when the dynasty faltered, none emerged to seize the throne. The failure of the Romanov will and ability to lead caused many millions to die and shattered a brilliant culture; the misspent lives of the Romanovs brought a tragedy of monumental proportions to the people of Russia.

This book is the story of the last century of the Romanovs, from the youth of the future Alexander III in the 1860s to the death of his daughter, Olga, the last grand duchess, in 1960. Ours is the first book to look at the Romanov family at large when the dynasty was reaching its end. We ask what role the grand dukes and grand duchesses played in the events in Russia that changed world history, as well as explore what happened to those who fled and survived the Red Terror. Today, in Russia's desperate search for order, questions of leadership assume fresh importance.

Many Russians now blame the Romanovs, rulers of Russia for three hundred years, for a legacy of material poverty and political repression. Many other Russians now look back on the imperial era as a lost paradise, when a demigod presided over the nation, providing the daily bread and insuring the physical security of his—or her—people. How these starkly different interpretations will balance out remains to be seen. "Foretelling the future of any nation is impossible; foretelling Russia's past is impossible," the Russians say. Armed with this caution we begin our story.

ACKNOWLEDGMENTS

T his book is a project that has occupied the two of us for more than five years. In the course of pursuing research and writing we incurred obligations to many people whom we would now like to thank.

First of all we would like to thank staff members at a number of archives that have proved to be treasure vaults for our research: the Bakhmetieff Archives (Columbia University, New York), Connecticut College Archive (New London, CT), Fridjof Nansen Archives (University of Oslo), Gosudarstvenny Arkhiv Rossiiskoi Federatsii (State Archives of the Russian Federation, Moscow), the Hoover Institution Archives (Stanford, CA), Houghton Library (Cambridge, MA), Public Record Office (London) and Rossiisky Gosudarstvenny Arkhiv Voenno-morskogo Flota (Russian State Naval Archives, St. Petersburg). We are grateful for the gracious permission of Her Majesty, Queen Elizabeth II, to read and quote from archival materials at Windsor Castle.

For the illustrations our acknowledgments go to the Hoover Institution, Rossiiski Gosudarstvenny Arkhiv Kinophotodokumentov (Russian State Pictorial Archives, Krasnogorsk), Royal Library (Copenhagen), Grand Duchess Leonida Georgievna, Princess Natalia Iskander and Alexander Zakatov. Alexey Maslennikov and Natalia Piliguda have also rendered us great help in finding and handling illustrations for the book.

This book would have been impossible to write, had there been no oral history available. Among the Romanov family members we would like to thank Prince Alexander Romanov, Princess Irina Bagration, Marusya Chavchavadze, Prince Dmitri Romanov, Olga Kulikovsky, Grand Duchess Leonida Georgievna, Princess Natalia Iskander, Prince Nicholas Romanov and Prince Paul Ilinsky. Thanks are also due to a number of experts and witnesses interviewed—Paul Grabbe, Rosemary Kerry, Vladislav Kostin, Princess Tatiana Ladyzhenskaya, Mikhail Moliukov, Rev. Nikon, Andrei Shmeman, Betty Tobias, Kyra Volkova Robinson, Angela Winthrop and Alexander Zakatov. Precious oral history interviews and also invaluable research trips were arranged by Elza Bilenko, Stanislav Dumin, Valery Maksimenkov, Rev. Nikon, Alexander Radashkevitch, Andrei Shtorkh, Alla Solovieva, Alexander Sumerkin, Mikhail Trubetskoi and Elena Zelenina.

For digging in the libraries and quarrying information, we are deeply grateful to Jacek Bylica, John Fargis, Nick Gill, Stephen Halsey, Kirstin Hill, Tim House and Stephen A. Lambo. For help in a wide variety of other matters relating to this project, we would like to note the kindness of Lady Sheila de Bellaigue, Jane R. Bredeson, Oliver Everett, Dallas Finn, Donald Foreman, Inger Marie Kromann Hansen, Frances Haviland, Louisa Illum, Bodil Ostergaard-Andersen, Ilga Paddock, Diane Windham Shaw, Lee Stookey, Lis Tarlow, Renate von Bulow Wilson, Keiko Usami and Hugo Vickers. We would also like to thank the library of the Norwegian Nobel Institute for an altruistic book-search for our project.

The interest of several friends and colleagues in the project has helped to sharpen our argument and to locate new facets in the research. Our gratitude goes to Matt Auer, Lev Doubnitsky, Sergei Doubnitsky, Ekaterina Egorova, Vladimir Larin, Valery Petrov, Martin Sherwin, Bill Taubman and Igor Tchabanov.

For reading and commenting on various drafts of the text, we vastly appreciate the labors of Nick Dinos, Liz Perry, Carolyn Slayman and Bill Woerhlin. Our special thanks to Maria Perry Burtis for her painstaking execution of the genealogical chart.

Susan Rabiner gave us welcome and shrewd advice in shaping the manuscript in its early stages. Tim Bartlett saw a book in a pile of manuscript and his blue pencil skillfully guided our progress. Elisheva S. Urbas gave us valuable advice on structure as we brought the project to its close. Throughout, Gerry McCauley, our agent, sustained us with his cheerful optimism. To everyone, our profound thanks, but we must end with the usual disclaimer: All errors are the sole responsibility of the authors.

Last but not least, we would like to thank the Government of the Russian Federation for having invited us to the funeral of Emperor Nicholas II and his family at St. Petersburg in July 1998.

PART ONE

Pinnacle

"A Prophecy"

A year shall come of Russia's blackest dread;
Then will the crown fall from the royal head,
The throne of tsars will perish in the mud,
The food of many will be death and blood.

—Mikhail Lermontov (1830)
[Anatoly Liberman, translator]

❧

CHAPTER ONE

Death of a Tsar

MARCH 1, 1881

A T 1:45 ON SUNDAY AFTERNOON, MARCH 1, 1881, Alexis Volkov, a soldier of the Pavlovsky Regiment who was guarding the squat regimental barracks facing Aptekarsky Lane in St. Petersburg, heard an explosion from the direction of nearby Ekaterininsky Canal. Although not particularly alarmed, he shifted towards the canal as far as his position as a guard permitted. Within several minutes, a second and louder explosion shook the air. Volkov could see smoke slowly rising over the water and small knots of people rushing about. In several minutes two sledges, one bearing a mangled, mortally wounded Emperor Alexander II, passed by way of Aptekarsky and Millionnaya Street to the Winter Palace. Grand Duke Michael Nikolaevich, who before the attack had been following his brother, the tsar, at some distance, was now sitting next to the dying master of the world's largest empire, cradling his inert body against his chest, and fulfilling his imperial brother's murmured last command: "Quickly, home . . . to the palace . . . die there . . . "

Just the day before, Alexander, the liberator of the serfs, having recently changed his own life by marrying his longtime mistress, had decided to change Russia's political order. He had signed a manifesto declaring that a number of members of the state council would hereafter be elected. This would be the first, cautious step toward a constitutional monarchy. Emperor Alexander II had decided to yield full autocracy, the legacy of his imperial ancestors.

That night he had played cards with his wife. She asked him not to attend the military parade the next day, March 1st. "Why shouldn't I go?" the emperor said in a merry voice. "I cannot live in the palace like a hermit."

Now Cossacks carried the tsar up the great Palace's white marble staircase, leaving a trail of droplets of blood. Minutes later, the sovereign lay unconscious on a sofa facing the window of his first-floor study in the Winter Palace, heavily hemorrhaging: A grenade had crushed both of his legs below the knees. His right leg was still booted, his left, a shapeless bloody mess. Blood drenched Alexander II's face and his abdomen was torn open. So forceful had been the explosion that broken pieces of the tsar's gold wedding ring, a symbol of his notorious second marriage, had imbedded themselves in the flesh of his right hand, although the hand itself had otherwise been unhurt by the grenade. Grand Duke Michael Nikolaevich, in full parade uniform, stood at the head of the deathbed, looking at his brother and weeping. For a while, he was the only Romanov to watch the tsar's agony.

Despite many threats and attempts on his life over the past fifteen years, Alexander II had taken on no real cloak of security. He had chosen not to surround himself with bodyguards and detectives; he continued to enjoy long solitary walks along the Neva embankment, elbowing his way through his subjects when necessary, but always preserving a sense of dignity and calm. Six past attempts on his life had failed; the sovereign had seemed to enjoy the firm protection of God. Now Alexander's violent death forever shattered the likelihood of any tsar ever again mingling freely with his people.

In chaos and panic, people ran in and out of the emperor's increasingly crowded study where he lay prostrate, three doctors hovering helplessly nearby. Servants carrying basins of reddened water came out of the study, and people in the hallways and on the stairs stopped them in order to dip their fingers or moisten their handkerchiefs in the precious blood. The rigid protocol and organization of court life had momentarily collapsed. Young officers, complete outsiders, having received the news of the attack, rushed to the Winter Palace to peer in at the deathbed. Only their own sense of discretion and decorum prevented them from approaching the dying tsar.

One person stood in the chamber as solemn and solid as a rock, and everyone else there was eager to witness the exact magical moment when all the gigantic authority, both social and sacral, would flow from the agonized Alexander II into his son, who would thus be transfigured from the Grand Duke Alexander Alexandrovich into His Imperial Majesty, the Emperor Alexander III. When he had arrived on the scene, the heir asked the court physician, Sergei Botkin, how long the sovereign would live. "Ten or fifteen minutes," Botkin answered. Alexander Alexandrovich, his stoic composure momentarily shattered, exclaimed, "What have we come to!" He then sobbed and embraced his uncle, Michael Nikolaevich.

The heir had arrived at the Winter Palace as the terrible rumor was already spreading over the central blocks of St. Petersburg. Crowds already packed his route—the elegant Nevsky Prospect, the wide passage under the majestic arch of the General Staff building, and the huge semicircular Palace Square. Alexander Alexandrovich had heard the two ominous explosions while he and his wife, Maria Fedorovna, were going in to lunch at their Anichkov Palace residence. A Cossack, galloping into the courtyard of the Anichkov, quickly broke the news. "A sledge!" the grand duke roared, tearing down the stairs.

Silence had fallen over the center of the city, interrupted only by occasional outbursts against the "students," as terrorists were called. Women spat at officers, "You, the military! You've failed to save our tsar!" Alexander Alexandrovich, slowly driving through the crowds in his sledge, a huge figure next to his tiny wife, could not move any faster. When the officers in the mob solemnly saluted him, he returned the salute and his wife bowed.

A rare case of a son's conservatism and a father's liberalism alienated the two Alexanders. The son did not believe that the reign of Alexander II had been a model reign, nor that the life of Alexander II had been the model life of a Christian monarch. Standing by the deathbed of his father and ending the grand ducal stage of his life, Alexander Alexandrovich's grief undoubtedly fought with other, equally powerful, emotions.

Looking at his father's mangled body, Alexander Alexandrovich was sure of one thing: The hydra of the revolution must be crushed, if the Romanov dynasty were not to be extinguished. His father might be just the first victim of the fanatics. Alexander Alexandrovich must protect his family.

Yet almost everything Alexander II had done angered his son. His sweeping reforms—emancipating the serfs, shaking up the administrative apparatus, creating self-rule for territorial units—all seemed to be misconceived. In Russia, reform was taken by radicals as a sign of weakness, a faltering of the autocracy embodied by the imperial house. And a sign of weakness perhaps it was. Alexander II himself had declared, "Let us liberate the serfs from above or they will liberate themselves from below."

Alexander II's reforms had given Russia its first free press, trials by jury and limits on corporal punishment. They had also nourished an exuberant cultural life, with Tolstoy, Dostoevsky and Tchaikovsky its primary exemplars. Reform had brought railroads, the telegraph, steamships and factory machinery, with capitalism winning the country. But reform had also spawned the dragon of Russian revolution with its inflammatory leaflets, terrorist networks and bombs. Alexander II had met the challenge with dignity. He saw to it that the revolutionaries were pursued, but only within the limits of law.

To Alexander III the fruits of his father's rule were a lesson. His father had unleashed the vermin, had been too chivalrous to crush them, had been too proud to stop his daily walks. And now here he lay—the sacral monarch, the "tsar," or Caesar, something more than a European king, a quasi-divine figure—anointed by God, yet bleeding and dying. With the premature death of Alexander II, the first and only great reformer tsar since Peter the Great, the Romanovs would lose an opportunity to lead Russia into modern life.

The son stood beside the father's couch and scowled. A young woman ran into the study and fervently embraced the dying tsar, paying no attention to his brother or his children. She was his former mistress and new wife, Princess Ekaterina Yurievskaya. She administered some medicine to him.

The doctors pronounced the sovereign dead at 3:35 P.M. The esoteric status of tsar passed from father to son. As the imperial standard was slowly lowered, the great crowd massed outside the palace fell silently to its knees on the snowy pavements.

❧

The grand dukes of Russia hurried to the funeral from all over Europe. The emperor's sons, Vladimir and Alexis, were already in St. Petersburg. Two of Alexander II's other younger surviving sons from his first marriage, Sergei and Paul, had heard the news in Paris. Sergei was calm, but the emotionally fragile Paul, completely undone, had to be carried to the train. Alexander II's younger brother, Nicholas Nikolaevich Senior, with his own sons Nicholas and Peter, sped to Russia on an express train from Cannes. In Berlin, the Russian Embassy staff members met them on the station platform to demonstrate their grief, and the old German kaiser, William I, sent his aide-de-camp to represent him there. In Verzhbolovo, the frontier station, the grand dukes put on their gray military uniforms with black mourning bands. The train passed through the heavily guarded frontier, and pressed on into the great Russian plain, with sentries posted along the tracks emerging suddenly out of the spring mist.

Five days later, on March 6th, a memorial mass was held at the Winter Palace. The emperor's grief-stricken widow was hardly able to stand unsupported. When escorted to the open coffin, she discovered that the emperor's face was covered by a veil. She bent, abruptly tore the veil away and started kissing the face of her husband. On the evening of the same day she came again to the coffin, bringing a wreath made of her own hair, celebrated for its beauty, and put it into the hands of the corpse, her last gift to him. The body of the emperor then had to be taken to the small yellow-walled cathedral of Saints Peter and Paul, where every ruler since Peter the Great lay encased in his or her plain sarcophagus and where Alexander II would now have his final resting place.

The funeral itself, an affair of much greater pomp, took place two weeks after the emperor's death. On the day of the funeral, at the Saltykov entrance to the Winter Palace, two groups awaited the arrival of the new imperial couple, Emperor Alexander III and Empress Maria Fedorovna. On the right side of the wide staircase, the Romanov grand dukes and grand duchesses were assembling. On the left stood a tiny group of mourners, ignored as much as possible by the others: Alexander II's second wife, Yurievskaya, with her three children, ages nine, eight and three, all dressed in black, the princess hiding her face behind a black veil.

The doors of the Winter Palace now opened, and the imperial couple stood in the huge lobby, appearing to approach *their* own family, the grand dukes and duchesses. Then Alexander III, about to descend the stairs, looked back to see Princess Yurievskaya, his stepmother, raising

her veil. With the great steps of a giant, Alexander approached his father's widow and said something to her. Maria Fedorovna, the new empress, hesitated, not knowing whether it was appropriate in her new
role to talk to the controversial woman. If the empress chose to give a
hand to the princess instead of an embrace, the late emperor's young
widow would be obliged to kiss her daughter-in-law's hand. Princess
Yurievskaya then quickly approached her; they faced each other for a
moment and suddenly the empress embraced the princess, both crying.
The princess nodded to her children and they kissed the empress's hand.
But the emperor, unwilling to endorse the rapprochement, was already
in the doorway, and the empress hastily followed him.

The grand dukes left, and Princess Yurievskaya with her three children remained standing as if turned to stone. Another private memorial mass was planned for her to attend in the cathedral. A social leper,
she was not to mix with the rest of the royal family for the funeral.

All the churches of St. Petersburg now tolled their bells, filling the
air with their solemn mournful tones. A three-gun salute from the
cathedral of Sts. Peter and Paul signalled the mourners to assemble
there at half-past ten. Sleighs began to converge there. Thickly falling
snow blurred the outlines of the great buildings of the monumental
city. Wind piled the snow up against the legs of soldiers stationed
along the Neva; they shivered despite their fur caps and heavy overcoats. Cossacks on station, their horses half buried in the deepening
drifts, guarded the path cleared across the frozen surface of the river.
The temperature had plummeted to twenty degrees below zero.

The Romanovs intended the funeral to display the power and
majesty of the dynasty; within the cathedral the white marble tombs
of earlier Romanovs demonstrated its continuity as well. Flowers in
bunches and wreaths from the crowned heads of Europe—many of
them part of the Romanov extended family—and from all parts of the
empire, from rich and poor, high and low, old and young lay round
the glittering bier. Decorating the walls were emblems and symbols of
the provinces the "Tsar of All the Russias" had governed: Moscow,
Kiev, Vladimir, Novgorod, Siberia, Poland, Estonia, Finland, Georgia
and so on, from the Baltic to the Pacific and from the Arctic Ocean to
the Pamir Mountains. The cloth of silver that illuminated the dark ec-
clesiastical vestments and the brilliant sparkle of foreign military uniforms provided the only other color in a sea of black wool, fur, lace
and crepe.

The space was not enormous; aside from the imperial family, only the diplomatic corps, special foreign visitors and the greatest Russian dignitaries could be admitted. Britain's Prince and Princess of Wales (she the sister of the new empress) and the Crown Prince of Germany, the highest ranking foreigners, entered just after the Metropolitan (Archbishop) had begun to intone the requiem mass.

As the long service drew to its close, the priestly choir sang "Eternal Memory," the last hymn to accompany a tsar to the realm of the dead. Its richly textured sound seemed to soar to the very heavens. It was time for the family to bid their farewells.

First the emperor, then the grand dukes and grand duchesses, bent and kissed the slain sovereign. Foreign relatives followed suit. The ambassadors had started to approach the coffin to pay their respects when they were halted. From the depths of the cathedral, assisted by the Minister of Court, Count Alexander Adlerberg, a young woman under a long veil was coming: Princess Yurievskaya, defying convention by her presence. She knelt at the coffin and put her head against it, staying there for several minutes; then standing, leaning on Count Adlerberg's arm, she slowly withdrew. The diplomats moved forward.

After Alexander III folded the imperial cloak of gold and ermine into his father's coffin, eight aides-de-camp carried forward the lid which was covered with flowers and bore the late tsar's sword and helmet. The lid was then bolted on. The emperor, the grand dukes and the foreign princes raised the coffin, carried it a few paces to its final resting place, and the Metropolitan pronounced a benediction. The coffin was then lowered to the roaring guns of the fortress saluting the dead monarch six times, with the rolling fire of musketry filling the silence between the deep reports of the guns. During these military honors, the members of the imperial family filed past the open grave as they left the cathedral, tossing earth on the coffin as was the Russian custom.

Along Millionnaya Street the new emperor returned from Sts. Peter and Paul in an open sledge, with his petite empress Maria Fedorovna sitting next to him. Under minimal convoy the emperor was going to the Anichkov Palace, where he had lived as heir. The air in the Winter Palace still smelled of death. Alexander III wanted to start afresh. The first thing he would do would be to flee from the city founded by the greatest of his ancestors, Peter.

Much of the Romanov family drama unfolds in St. Petersburg, Peter the Great's city, created by his steely will, named for his patron saint, the apostle, a city of contrasts wrought by the interplay of water, sky, light, fog, clouds and earth, stone thrust into swamp. Peter chose a Dutch name as if to declare his intention of building a Western European city. The "Venice of the North," the "Palmyra of the Snows," foreigners called it with astonishment, responding to the city's monumental character. According to legend, Peter's ghost sometimes rises from his white sepulchre at Sts. Peter and Paul Cathedral to walk again through his city, built upon the bones of thousands of laborers who died at their task.

Water dominated the St. Petersburg of the Romanovs. The canals and the Neva flooded the city every year, and the salty spice of the sea, along with the richer odors of mud and tar, permeated the air. In winter, November to April, snow covered the ground, its whiteness constantly renewed. Workers scraped the icy pavements and cordoned off the streets to shovel the roofs. The jingling of troika harness, the whistling of the sea breezes and the solemn toll of church bells gave Petersburg its characteristic sounds.

The great squares afforded generous spaces for the play of light as well as for the passage of people. Pastel greens and creamy yellows gave color to the facades, especially nurturing to the eye during the long monochromatic winters. In June, the magic of the "white nights," when the sun sets for less than two hours, offered a sense of freedom, even abandon, but summer was offset by the grim harshness of January, with frigid winds sweeping in from the Gulf of Finland over the frozen rivers and canals, stinging the cheeks, driving people to huddle beneath their coats and caps and scurry for the warmth of shelter. The heat of summer, from which the rich and privileged sought refuge in their country houses and estates, would bring epidemics of typhus and cholera, especially to the city's dark corners, its hovels and tenements and overcrowded crime-ridden slums, where diseases festered and a street fight might erupt over a few rotten turnips.

St. Petersburg's classic severity, its majestic grandeur, made it seem almost un-Russian to those who did not live there, but its massive uniformity and disciplined regularity well expressed the autocratic spirit that Peter and his successors endeavored to implant in the realm. Being "new," the city lacked any sense of medieval Russia, and at its core at least it had none of the unplanned natural growth, the congeniality and warmth that age alone can give. Moscow symbolized Russia in a way that St. Petersburg never could. But the Romanovs after Peter did not identify with Moscow and spent little time there.

Under Alexander II, the Russian imperial court had reached the apex of its splendor, the most magnificent in Europe. The crown jewels were undoubtedly the world's richest; only the Persian and the British might even compare. The jewels were used by the sovereign and his consort but not personally owned by him, remaining the property of the state. The 194-carat Orloff diamond, the Polar Star, a pale red ruby of 40 carats, and the Imperial Diadem, which held 13 enormous pearls and many smaller ones, as well as 500 diamonds, were only some of the more notable pieces. These crown jewels were brought out only for state occasions, but personally owned jewels were another matter and some of them, too, were truly extraordinary. Empress Maria Fedorovna, wife of Alexander III, often wore a necklace made of 36 diamonds weighing a total of 475 carats. The center diamond of the string alone weighed thirty-two.

Russians had started mining their own precious stones in the seventeenth century when the Romanov dynasty was founded. Before that, gems came from southern Asia and elsewhere. European Russia, the heart of the nation, held no minerals. Even the pearls of the northern rivers were usually small, irregular in shape and dull in luster. But as Russians began to move eastward and to settle in the Urals, they discovered new sources of precious and semiprecious stones—first, in 1635, malachite; followed by jasper, sard, and agate, topaz, amethyst, and beryl. Peter the Great and Catherine both pressed for more, Peter to ornament his new capital city, Catherine in order to indulge herself in huge basins and urns carved from single blocks of jasper, porphyry or other exotic stones. Diamonds were not discovered in Russia until 1829; emeralds followed shortly, as did rare semiprecious stones like green garnets and alexandrite. The great Yakutia diamond mines which now figure so importantly in the world market were not opened until 1949. So despite the riches available from Russian mines, many of the Romanov jewels had therefore been collected at even more extravagant cost, over centuries and from all over the world.

Court rituals reflecting the ancient imperial and churchly traditions of Byzantium further enhanced the splendor of the jewels and the dress. To these Byzantine influences were added the personal taste of Catherine the Great and the style of eighteenth-century France.

Catherine created the patterns of the Russian imperial court, and after her no one dared or cared to attempt to change them. The furniture in the state rooms remained in the same arrangement; the footmen carried the same braziers of incense from room to room; messengers wore the same archaic red and gold liveries with ostrich-feathered caps; and, as one court lady remembered, "for all I know the same plates for hot bread and butter on the same tea table were traditions going back to Catherine the Great."

Perhaps it was comfortable to fall into the pattern, knowing that a page would always present a dish of sweets in the same fashion or that a card table would always be set in the same corner with a glass of wine on it because that was Catherine's wish. Everything in the palace that pertained to anything beyond the personal life of the monarch and his immediate family was prescribed and performed according to a rigid and intensely conservative etiquette.

Prince Christopher of Greece, a Romanov through his mother, Olga Constantinovna, remarked that

> the palace of Tsarskoye Selo [located outside St. Petersburg] was the most beautiful in Europe, a storehouse of treasures. Plates of old Chinese porcelain, whose value was literally beyond price and which formed part of a collection presented to Catherine the Great by the Emperor of China of her day, were inlaid into the solid amber walls of one room; another room was walled in rarest lapis lazuli. The great banqueting-hall which ran the whole width of the palace, two stories high, was of blue and silver and lighted only by thousands of candles. The picturesque Abyssinian guard always stood at the door on State occasions, six coal-black negroes presented to the Czar by Menelik, Emperor of Abyssinia. Tall, splendidly built, in their wide trousers and scarlet turbans, they stood immobile as though they had been cast in bronze.

The palaces, with their severe formality and cold splendor, resembled museums more than homes, the public spaces to be supplemented by private retreats where the monarch and his family actually lived. The Winter Palace where Alexander II died stretched for half a mile along the Neva, its size and opulence providing a material symbol of the power and wealth of the Romanov autocracy. Yet it represented fantasy, not reality, and what took place within was all carefully

choreographed and never left to chance; the setting and the ceremonies were intended to overawe both Russians and foreigners and to
impress upon them the majesty, power and taste of the Russian imperial institution embodied by the Romanovs.

Guests would arrive and enter the palace by one of a number of
great carpeted marble staircases. Huge windows opened onto the
river, admitting a flood of light enhanced by the reflections cast by the
sun dancing on the surfaces of the water. Winter froze the Neva into
a mass of ice, covered with snow. In daytime, light from out-of-doors
interplayed with the richly veined marble walls of the vast high-
ceilinged reception halls, cathedral-like spaces with gilded mirrors, in-
laid doors and highly polished parquet floors. An army of liveried
servants waxed the floors daily, skating along with a brush attached to
one foot. Imperial greenhouses supplied the great halls with orchids
and other flowers, sometimes brought by train from the Crimea. The
delicate fragance of orange blossoms sweetened the air. Palm trees
lined the main staircase and the corridors. A winter garden roofed
with glass provided a place where trees and shrubs could flower
throughout the coldest times and fountains soothed the ear with their
murmuring sounds. One empress even kept a cow in this space so that
she might enjoy fresh milk daily.

The Winter Palace also had its own theater seating several hundred
people. There the leading artists of the day, both Russian and foreign,
would sing, dance or act. Sometimes members of the imperial family
would themselves perform in the best tradition of private amateur theatricals which European royalty so much enjoyed. Using the pen name
"K.R." (he romanized his name with a "K" rather than a "C"), the
Grand Duke Constantine Constantinovich, an actor and playwright as
well as a poet, translated the plays of Shakespeare into Russian for
performance there. In a performance of Pushkin's *Eugene Onegin*, the
young future Nicholas II played the title role, other parts being played
by other members of the family.

Connected to the palace was a large building called the Hermitage
whose special purpose was to house the collections of paintings, sculpture and myriad objets d'art amassed by the Romanovs over three centuries. Today the whole building complex is known as the Hermitage,
and it houses one of the world's greatest art collections.

In the palace at night, illumination was provided by thousands of
wax candles placed in wall sconces and crystal chandeliers, an innun-

dation of light into a sea of darkness. Pillars of malachite, porphyry, onyx and jasper punctuated the wall spaces. Huge vases, specially made in imperial factories for imperial use, marble statuary, and finely fashioned chairs, tables and cabinets were generously scattered throughout, although the vast space left ample room for literally thousands of people to circulate. An imperial reception at the Winter Palace might have three thousand guests who ate, drank and danced. To this glittering setting the guests would bring their own colorful contribution, the ladies blazing with jewels, dresses cut low to display the bosom and shoulders, the married women wearing sparkling jeweled diadems, the girls wearing flowers in their hair. Military officers wore their richly decorated dress uniforms, often with crested helmets. Court officials wore short breeches, white silk stockings and much gold braid.

The tapping of an ivory-tipped ebony wand by the master of ceremonies signalled the appearance of the emperor and empress. First the imperial couple would be greeted in the Malachite Hall by the entire imperial family, the diplomatic corps and the highest court officials, and then perhaps receive presentations in the throne room. At a large event the imperial party, including perhaps a dozen or more grand dukes and grand duchesses, would process throughout the enfilade of great rooms, bringing momentary silence to the conversation, deep bows and curtsies, as the imperial party made its way slowly through the guests, massed tightly together. The opening dance, a polonaise, was always led by the emperor, but to call it a "dance" may be somewhat misleading—its stately tempo was more akin to a parade. Its measured dignity, though, seemed entirely appropriate to the occasion. "Our procession," one grand duke recalls, "had to pass through all the halls with six chamberlains in front of us announcing our approach. We circled the palace three times, after which the dancing began in every hall, quadrille, waltz and mazurka being the only dances approved by etiquette."

Supper would be served at midnight at small tables, the imperial couple themselves not sitting but moving from table to table to chat with the guests and perhaps to take a sip of champagne. Alexander II liked champagne but drank only moderately because he suffered from asthma. At a reception or a ball, the point was for the emperor to appear to drink and eat with as many guests as possible. A socially accomplished imperial person was not unlike an actor, always in control, fusing dignity with affability, authority with charm. A few well-chosen words could put anyone at ease and the trick was to move from one person to another with a remark that might bring both of them into the conversation. A highly trained memory was an immense imperial asset. But everything did not always go smoothly. One guest remembers that at all the great imperial banquets, "a court official stood behind the chair of every royal guest to hand the champagne for the toasts. This was a matter of solemn ritual. The wine was first poured out by a footman, then it had to be passed to a page who, in turn, passed it to the hander. . . . The hander was usually distinguished, aged and tremulous, so between them they managed, as often as not, to upset the contents of the glass all over you. I can still remember my sister's distress when her favourite pale blue velvet Court dress turned a vivid green in patches after her hander had spilt six glasses of champagne over it."

Amid the grandeur and formality of this glittering environment, Alexander II presided over a large extended family whose lives were predictably regimented and formal as well. Nicholas I, Alexander II's father, had sired a family of four boys and three girls. Had it not been for his fertility (and that of the empress, his dear "Mouffy"), the Romanovs would have become extinct well before the twentieth century. In the mid-eighteenth century, at one point there were only two Romanovs beside the ruler. All twentieth-century Romanovs are descendants of the awesome Nicholas I, the "Iron Tsar."

Of all ruling Romanovs, at least since Peter the Great, Nicholas most epitomized autocracy. Unusually tall, with an "Olympian profile" and piercing eyes making even brave men tremble, Nicholas seemed more monument than mortal man. Loving, perhaps, but stern, he treated his children as if they were raw recruits and he a drill sergeant. Although Nicholas sought to embody Russia, paradoxically his tastes were foreign and he and his court presented themselves as part of the greater European royal family, a way of enhancing the lordly separation between the tsar and his subjects.

The Romanovs were hardly even Russian in blood. In order to maintain a claim to the imperial succession, a grand duke was obliged to marry royalty. Mere nobility would not suffice. If he chose to marry outside royalty, the marriage was considered "morganatic," that is, his wife and their children would not enjoy his lofty status. The rest of the family judged morganatic marriage scandalous because the individual who did it obviously chose the gratification of personal desires over the retention of his place in the succession, love over duty, thus shattering his emotional as well as hierarchical relationship to the throne and to the rest of the family.

As a result, since Peter, most Romanovs had married foreigners. For generations the various small states of Germany provided Romanov brides, all of them born "royal." Each German princeling was proud of his status and would try to emulate, on as large a scale as he could afford, the splendors of the environment and routine of Versailles. "Pumpernickel courts," Thomas Carlyle, the Victorian essayist, called them contemptuously. But Protestant German royalty provided brides (and grooms also, when needed) not simply for Russia but for all the royal houses of northern Europe. Baden, Wurtemberg, Saxony and Hanover were all possible sources, but tiny Coburg took pride of place. Bismarck dismissed it derisively as "the studfarm of Europe." The result was that everyone in Europe who was royal, Romanovs included, was related, at least if they were not Roman Catholics, and the relationships were kept close by continued intermarriage. Northern European royalty comprised one large German extended family. The great poet Alexander Pushkin allegedly liked to illustrate Romanov intermarriage with foreigners with a bottle of water, some red wine and a few glasses. Setting the glasses in a row, he would fill up the first with wine, proclaiming "that glass is our glorious Peter the Great: it is pure Russian blood in all its vigor. Just look at the crimson glow!" In the second glass he mixed wine and water in equal amounts. In the third he put one part wine and three parts water, continuing in this fashion, mixing each new glass in the same inverse progression. If we were to take this beyond Pushkin's time, by the seventh glass, representing the blood of Alexander III, the "German" water was barely tinged by the "Russian" wine, now only one sixty-fourth of the contents.

In 1881, at the time of Alexander II's assassination, all of his male Romanov relatives—his three brothers and his nephews, his five surviving sons from his first (non-morganatic) marriage—all held the title of grand duke, and their wives, sisters and daughters were all grand duchesses. Like an emperor or empress, a grand duke or grand duchess was expected to patronize the arts and to support charities, and to live in a grand manner. The presence of a grand duke or grand duchess at any gathering, no matter how inconsequential, was enough to transform it into an event. The tsar's charisma extended to the whole family.

Although they might walk along the granite quays of Petersburg, even alone or accompanied only by a dog, grand dukes were conspicuous, always subject to popular scrutiny, and the tsar's secret police kept a careful eye on them. Their role was not easy. If they showed energy and eagerness to serve, that ambition might provoke jealousy and excite suspicion. If, on the other hand, they did too little, they might be judged self-indulgent and hedonistic. Though they were usually mere figureheads of army or navy administration, public opinion nonetheless would judge grand dukes harshly for anything that went wrong. Grand dukes had responsibility without authority. The real purpose of the grand duke was to stand by in case he should be called to the throne.

Family tradition dictated the pattern for the education of grand dukes. As imperial children they were educated by tutors and could not be sent to schools. Thus their exalted positions isolated them from other children of their own age. In his first years, a Romanov male spent his time in the hands of women, cared for by a procession of wet nurses and nannies with whom his emotional attachments could become strong, especially as he received little time or attention from his mother. Travel and court duties tended to separate imperial parents, mothers as well as fathers, from their children.

From the time of the Emperor Paul in the late eighteenth century, every grand duke was given nominal command of a guards regiment at birth. Real education for a Romanov boy thus began at age six or seven when he would be abruptly, and often painfully, thrust into an entirely male and military environment. The overwhelming importance of the military arts within grand ducal education reflects the centrality of the military to the Romanovs and throughout aristocratic Russian society.

The military prized physical fitness and the vigorous outdoor life. Military culture developed its own aesthetic, with brilliant uniforms and sparkling decorations, drills and maneuvers executed with choreographic flourish and mathematical exactitude, all conveying a sense of rationality and order, romance and heroism, but bearing little relationship to the brutal reality of war. But the purpose of this activity was to promote unthinking conformity, not to simulate the conditions of combat. Unlike the chaos of war or even of civil administration, the parade ground offered a mechanical elegance susceptible to tight control. The Romanovs loved it and even the flinty Nicholas I could weep at the sheer beauty of a skillfully performed lunge of massed bayonets or a thundering cavalry figure eight.

One of the Iron Tsar's grandsons, Grand Duke Alexander Mikhailovich (Sandro), recalls:

> to the age of fifteen my education resembled the training in a regiment. My brothers Nicholas, Michael, Sergei, George and myself lived as in barracks. We slept on narrow iron beds, only the thinnest possible mattress being allowed over the wooden planks. I remember that even in later years, after my marriage, I could not become accustomed to the luxury of a large bed with double mattresses and linen sheets, and ordered my old hard bunk to be put next to it.
>
> We were called every morning at six o'clock. We had to jump out of our beds immediately, for a severe punishment swiftly followed an attempt to sleep "just five minutes more."
>
> Kneeling in a row in front of the three ikons, we said our prayers, then took a cold bath. Our breakfast consisted of tea, bread and butter. Any other ingredients had been strictly forbidden, lest we should develop a taste for a luxurious life.
>
> A lesson in gymnastics and practice with firearms filled another hour, particular attention being paid to the handling of a mountain gun placed in the garden. . . . At the age of ten I would have been able to take part in the bombardment of a large city.
>
> From eight to eleven, and from two to six, we had to study and do our homework. . . . Our educational program, planned for eight years, consisted of lessons in religion (Old and New Testament, Divine Service, history of the Greek Orthodox Church, comparative history of other churches), Russian grammar and literature, foreign literature, history . . . , geography, mathematics . . . , natural history, French, German, English, calligraphy and music. On top of that we were taught the handling of all sorts of firearms, riding, fencing, and bayonet fighting.

Tutors punished poor performance: "The smallest mistake in spelling of a German word deprived us of dessert."

And this was not all. Training continued at the luncheon table when the children were interspersed with the guests and expected to converse with them. "Laughing at poor jokes and simulating a vivid interest in the political developments abroad entered into our obligations of hospitality, and developed in us a sense of self-relying resourcefulness." One was not to talk too much or too loudly and never across the table. Grand ducal children rarely saw their parents alone, especially at meals. Even without guests, people were always in attendance, equerries and ladies-in-waiting who lived in the palace and sat at table. Children lived in their own quarters separate from the adults, and they were not expected to leave that domain unless dressed properly and prepared to behave with decorum. This was then the usual pattern for royal and aristocratic children throughout Europe.

Royal children seldom had the opportunity to play with their contemporaries, with the exception of brothers and sisters or cousins. And so although constantly surrounded by people, they often suffered from loneliness. The fact that they were children, not adults, was usually given scant consideration.

On coming of age at sixteen, a grand duke swore an oath in the presence of the emperor to obey the laws of succession to the throne and to respect the institutions of the imperial family, although he would usually not gain full control of his wealth and income for another five years. The idea was to break him in gradually to this life of extreme privilege.

The education of grand duchesses was deemed far less important than that of grand dukes. They were brought up like royal women elsewhere in Europe, learning to sew, knit, and to embroider on silk and satin, to play the piano and perhaps the harp, to sing, to draw and paint, to recite, dance, and to take part in amateur theatricals. Learning how to enter and to leave a room was important, as was the ability to make conversation, and in several languages at that. Grand duchesses were brought up to be attentive to the sick and aged; organized work for charities would be an important part of their daily lives.

Obviously for anyone with any intellectual interests or abilities, the prescribed routine was inhibiting. To move outside it caused trouble; being conspicuous aroused envy and provoked criticism. One grand duchess declared that "an intellectual mediocrity was both a refuge and a protection; and this was true not only in Russia but in princely circles everywhere."

The grand ducal families and some other Russian aristocrats in the late 1800s developed a taste for things English, what Vladimir Nabokov called "the comfortable products of Anglo-Saxon civilization." Pear's soap and fruit cakes, playing cards and puzzles, striped blazers and collapsible rubber bathtubs were among the "snug and mellow" things to be acquired in the English shop on Nevsky Prospect. These English tastes were not confined to the Russian aristocracy; the daughters and granddaughters of Queen Victoria carried to their marriages throughout Europe chintz-covered furniture, vases full of fresh flowers, and a passion for opening the windows to fresh air. Their houses looked like Tudor manors or Mayfair mansions, and meals followed the English pattern of hearty breakfasts, family luncheons, afternoon tea, and dinner in the evening.

English nannies brought to Russia all the customs and crochets of their own country, indoctrinating their charges into the proper British way of doing things, injecting into the children's English the dropped aitches of cockney speech, and cowing all the other servants. Nannies are one reason why English became the favored second language among European royalty. Some of the Romanovs even learned English before they learned Russian. Outside the family they usually spoke Russian, inside the family more rarely.

Royalty does not use surnames; the Romanovs simply used Christian names and patronymics. Thus Alexander II was Alexander Nikolaevich, Alexander son of Nicholas; his father the Emperor Nicholas I was Nicholas Pavlovich, Nicholas son of Paul. Because the same names tended to be used over and over, nicknames supplanted them. Thus Alexander Alexandrovich was known generally to the family as "Sasha," at least until he became Alexander III, when few presumed any longer to call him anything but "Your Majesty."

Three of Alexander II's brothers, Constantine, Nicholas and Michael, each formed his own branch of the imperial clan, and these were known respectively as the "Constantinovichi," the "Nikolaevichi," and the "Mikhailovichi." Grand Duke Constantine Nikolaevich came to be well known both as the most politically liberal Romanov of his generation and for his interest in the navy. One of his sons, Constantine, would become the poet "K.R."; one of his daughters, Olga, would become Queen of Greece.

Alexander II's next younger brother, Nicholas Nikolaevich, the third son of Emperor Nicholas I, was a well-known gourmet and served in the Russo-Turkish War of 1877–78, commanding the Russian forces in the European sector with no particular distinction. After the war, he suffered the acute embarrassment of being charged with financial irregularities, of receiving bribes and embezzling money from the government. He had only two sons, but one of them was an army commander like his father; Nicholas Nikolaevich Junior, known in the family as "Nikolasha," would serve as commander-in-chief of the Russian armies during the early months of World War I.

The Mikhailovichi, a much larger group, were sometimes called "the Caucasians" by the rest of the family because father Michael spent much of his career as viceroy of that region of the empire, attempting to pacify its unruly and diverse nationalities. To be called "Caucasian" was something of a putdown, reflecting the attitude that people so distant from European Russia must be cultural barbarians. Furthermore the Mikhailovichi, it was commonly said, had Jewish blood on the maternal side, causing anti-Semites in the rest of the family to look down their noses at them.

During the war with Turkey, Grand Duke Michael Nikolaevich served with enthusiasm, if not with great success, as counterpart to his brother Nicholas, commanding the Russian forces on the Asian front of the conflict. Michael, in his absorption with military matters, was probably more like his father, Nicholas I, than were any of his brothers. Though the youngest of his generation, he would become the doyen of the grand dukes, the venerable family patriarch, living until 1909, dying at seventy-seven, an age old by Romanov standards.

Each of these brothers had his own career or material ambitions, and this posed a problem for the sovereign, especially as the family began to proliferate. Romanov family harmony suffered from the overlapping ambitions for office of its male members and from the social ambitions of its female members, also vying for opportunities for their menfolk upon which their own prestige ultimately rested. The heir to the throne and his offspring could enjoy the expectation of ultimate leadership. For the rest, the only open career was the military, either army or navy, with a limited number of top positions. As a result, cousin was obliged to compete with cousin. To these career rivalries could be added those emerging from the clash of personalities, making family politics potentially stormy. Only a strong tsar could maintain order within the family. Alexander II was not by nature that sort of personality. Furthermore, the family believed that he had compromised his moral authority.

For fourteen years Alexander II had enjoyed a passionate affair with the young Ekaterina Dolgorukaya. Ekaterina had begun to see the emperor in the Summer Garden facing the Neva River in St. Petersburg, where he enjoyed strolling like a simple mortal among the lime trees, clipped allées and white marble statues. The two began to meet frequently in the secluded paths of different parks, and within a year, on July 1, 1866, in the Babigon Pavillion at Peterhof Palace, they became lovers.

Then Alexander II began to realize that he wanted more and he promised to marry Ekaterina when he became free. He suspected that his ailing wife would not live much longer. Ekaterina began to come to the Winter Palace three or four times a week, opening a side door with her own key and going to a ground floor room to await the emperor. She was seventeen. He was forty-seven.

Alexander gave his mistress the title of Princess Yurievskaya, as well as three children, George, Olga and Catherine. By entitling Ekaterina, he provoked general dismay among the family, especially the imperial womenfolk. A steady flow of rumor maintained that the parvenu princess was venal, taking commissions for lobbying this or that project.

Terrorists, dissatisfied with the scope and tempo of the emperor's political reforms, had begun to pursue Alexander; he had several narrow escapes from violent death. Thus for security reasons, he brought his second family to the Winter Palace, to live under the same roof as his empress, Maria Alexandrovna. The empress's rooms lay directly below those of her rival, and the sound of children's footsteps overhead was a constant reminder to Maria Alexandrovna, now an invalid, of her husband's infidelity.

Clearly her husband had loved his future empress when they were first married. He had chosen her after their first brief meeting even though she was only fifteen, from a minor German state, and rumored to be the illegitimate fruit of her mother's liaison with a lowborn man. Alexander's parents thought he could have made a stronger match. But despite numerous children, over the years the couple drifted apart; she spent more and more time abroad.

Then tragedies ensued: first, consumption claimed their eldest son, Nicholas, and then the emperor became caught up in the romance with Ekaterina. Maria Alexandrovna proved to be unable to face these challenges directly. She retreated into religion and ill health. Alone, she died on May 22, 1880, and on July 6th, to the disgust of his first family, Alexander married Ekaterina.

The marriage was morganatic because the bride, although an aristocrat, was not of royal blood. This meant that her children had no succession rights and that, although she was the emperor's official wife, Ekaterina was not an empress. Nonetheless Alexander insisted that his grown children from his first marriage openly meet his second family.

Although the emperor could marry the woman he loved, he could not live a happy and quiet life because terrorists continued to stalk him. The irony was that Alexander II was genuinely willing to share some of his absolute power. "Am I a wild animal that I must be so hunted?" Alexander cried, after yet another unsuccessful attempt on his life. He was shot at; he was the target of bombs. Would-be assassins even stuffed dynamite beneath a dining room of the Winter Palace itself, though the explosion failed to catch the tsar. Old women predicted doom, whispering that the names of the emperor's first five sons when written in a column formed a prophetic acronym. Read down, the first letter of each name (Nicholas, Alexander, Vladimir, Alexis, Sergei) spelled "na vas," "at you," or, with some imagination, "get you!" When read up, "savan" or "shroud."

Now it seemed that the old women proved to have been prescient; Alexander II was gone. Russia needed new leadership to take it into the changes required if the nation were to compete successfully with its rapidly modernizing rivals, especially the newly united Germany. The House of Romanov needed another Peter the Great, a leader with intelligence, imagination and ruthless determination both to guide the nation and to govern the family.

CHAPTER TWO

⨎

The *Muzhik* Tsar

1 8 8 1 – 1 8 9 4

BEFORE HIS SUDDEN ASCENT TO THE THRONE, Alexander Alexandrovich, called "Sasha," had gone through a painful youth and early manhood. We know little of its details. Consensus has it that Sasha was a stolid, average, Russian male with a soldier's education and tastes. Certainly, he showed no serious interest in the arts or intellectual pursuits. His most striking characteristic was his 6'4" bull-like frame and great strength. His hands were so strong, it was said, that he could tear a pack of cards in two or bend a firetongs double. Yet he was clumsy.

The family did not anticipate that Sasha, being a younger son, would ever become emperor. His older brother, Nicholas Alexandrovich, was the heir. But Nicholas suffered from the great plague of the nineteenth century, tuberculosis, and, although he was sent to the south of France to recuperate, in the spring of 1865 the family received the news that Nicholas Alexandrovich had little time to live.

Sasha departed for France on April 4, 1865, to be followed two days later by his father, the Emperor Alexander II, and two of his younger brothers, Vladimir and Alexis. In eighty-five hours, Alexander and his boys reached the bedside of the dying Nicholas. By that time, the empress, the little brothers Sergei and Paul, and sister Marie had already gone to Nice, as had Dagmar, Princess of Denmark, the fiancee of the young dying *tsesarevitch* (heir to the throne). On his deathbed, Nicholas was thinking about his brother Alexander and whispered that he had an "honest and crystal soul." He told his mother, "I don't know whom I love more, Sasha or Dagmar."

On April 11th, at eight in the morning, the emperor and empress, the brothers, and Dagmar came into Nicholas's room. Sasha was standing to the right of the bed, Dagmar to the left. Nicholas held their hands and those present thought that before he breathed his last he made clear his intent that Sasha was to marry Dagmar.

A year and a half after Nicholas's death, on November 9, 1866, that marriage would take place. Individual feelings did not govern royal marriages; they were a dynastic matter. But Sasha seemed happy with the pretty and petite Dagmar. Danish-born Dagmar promptly converted to Orthodoxy and took a Russian name as was customary. Officially she became Maria Fedorovna, her patronymic derived from the name of an icon sacred to the Romanov family since the founding Romanov tsar, Michael, had been blessed by it in 1613. Fedor was also the name of Michael's father and therefore the progenitor of the dynasty. The family called Maria Fedorovna "Minnie."

Alexander's new life as heir and married man appeared placid and well-ordered: telegraphing the commander of his yacht *Tsarevna* with necessary instructions, attending his mother's musical parties at the Winter Palace, and enjoying life with Minnie at Anichkov Palace. Like his grandfather Nicholas I, who liked dances only to the extent that they compared to military maneuvers, Alexander Alexandrovich never liked balls, but he did like music and enjoyed playing musical instruments. One day on his yacht, the band finished playing and put down its instruments. The heir took them up, one by one, and played the Russian national anthem with each, much to the delight and amusement of everyone there. By 1881, Sasha and Minnie had five of their eventual six children.

Then, with unexpected suddenness, the responsibilities of rule thrust themselves upon Alexander Alexandrovich. He was no longer Sasha but "The Emperor."

No nineteenth century Romanov had come to the throne happy with the legacy of his predecessor. Alexander III believed that three sets of events during the previous reign had been disastrous. First, his father had started an unsuccessful war with the Turks in which Alexander

Alexandrovich himself had participated and from which he had emerged with a feeling of repulsion toward war. Second, the new freedoms introduced by Alexander II only seemed to inspire Russsian radicals to want more. Third, Alexander II had put his mistress in the Winter Palace and married her immediately after the death of the empress.

After his father's death, Alexander III removed from court all the closest associates of the late emperor. He established three priorities: to bring about internal security and political stability; to keep the nation at peace; and to restore respectability to the monarchy and the Romanov family.

Alexander II had firmly believed in the sacral bond linking dynasty and people. Writing to one of his sons who had just toured the countryside, he said, "I hope it will prove useful to you to have seen with your own eyes the devoted attachment of the Russian people to its imperial house. You will understand that this attachment obliges us to love our people and to strive to be useful to them." Alexander II's assassination had exploded the confidence of Alexander III in this "attachment," the unquestioning loyalty of his subjects; the murder shook the very foundations of the monarchy. Alexander III's first consideration therefore became security.

The first decision the new tsar had to make was where to live. The Anichkov Palace, where he had been living, was a spacious but rather modest edifice directly on the main street of the city, Nevsky Prospect. Peter the Great's daughter, Empress Elizabeth, had built the Anichkov for her secret husband Grigory Razumovsky, a former church choir singer from Ukraine. In the early nineteenth century, Nicholas Pavlovich, the future Nicholas I, had lived there, and since that time, all heirs to the throne had done so. As an integral part of the cityscape, the palace looked threateningly easy to attack. Any passerby could lob a bomb or shoot a gun from a cab, not to mention that the terrorists had become hellishly efficient at digging tunnels. For a reigning emperor, Anichkov was unsuitable.

Nor was the Winter Palace any too safe, built in the years when a potential threat against the emperor's life could come only from inside his own family and not from his subjects. Furthermore, for the simple tastes of the new emperor, his father's home was simply too stylish, too opulent, too grand.

Instead Alexander chose Gatchina, a remote country palace, about twenty miles outside of St. Petersburg, built in a semicircle by his great grandfather Paul I, with a large gravelled space in front where Paul could indulge his passion for military parades. A huge park with lakes adjoined the palace. Simple, even grim, rural, functional and, above all, easily protected, Gatchina was the ideal place for Alexander III to reside.

Yet Gatchina had a gloomy reputation among courtiers. As late as the 1850s, the bed in which Emperor Paul had been murdered, still stained by his blood, was kept in Gatchina, brought there from St. Petersburg. A tunnel leading from the palace to the lake was reported to have been a rescue passage directly from Paul's bedroom. The rooms looked "horrible and gloomy" and the ceilings were so low the new emperor was reported to scrape his head on them. When the royal family arrived, the building was so cold that they all had to wear overcoats. But the emperor liked Gatchina and that was all that mattered.

On March 14, 1881, only days after his succession, the emperor issued a manifesto explaining the succession procedure in case of his death. Until his eldest son, the heir, Nicky, came of age, Alexander's brother Vladimir would become regent with the title of "Ruler of State." If Nicky were to die young, he was to be succeeded by the next oldest surviving of his two brothers, George and Michael. No alternative regent was suggested for Vladimir. The Empress Maria Fedorovna was to remain the guardian of all their children until they came of age.

Even before that, the most pressing matter facing the new tsar concerned Alexander II's decree announcing the beginning of political reform, scheduled to be published March 2nd. The assassination had intervened on March 1st. Was it proper for the new monarch to destroy his father's political testament? Alexander III, though appalled at the upsurge of liberalism (which he saw as the source of terrorism), nonetheless hesitated. His decision, however, was shaped by his official tutor, Constantine Pobedonostsev, a staunch conservative, who preached the combination of Orthodoxy and autocracy. Alexander III cancelled his father's decree.

Pobedonostsev, a strange pale androgynous creature, with skin like parchment, his waxy ascetic face dominated by frighteningly large ears, often raised both arms and depicted the horrors awaiting the empire in case of further reforms. Romanov power and continuity depended, in his view, on "keeping Russia in a frozen state. The slightest warm breath of life would cause the whole thing to rot." Pobedonostsev's only close friend was the novelist Dostoevsky. A belief in mysticism, a deep interest in church affairs and Russian Orthodoxy as the core of Russianness in general, in opposition to the Europeanization of the country so favored by reformers, bound the two men together.

In 1865, Pobedonostsev had resigned as professor of law at Moscow University in order to concentrate on royal education, and he implored Alexander to demonstrate his firm will at all times, letting everybody know, "I want this or I don't want this and hence will not tolerate it." He begged the tsar to take good care of himself in the capital full of terrorists and to flee the "damned place" as soon as he could. He advised Alexander to lock all of his doors himself, the outside entrance included, and to search his bedroom before getting into bed, especially checking the space under the furniture.

Pobedonostsev argued that the previous liberal course of Alexander II could only "lead to collapse, the collapse of Russia and tsardom." Concessions would not appease the "villains" wanting change; only "iron and blood" could destroy them. Pobedonostsev insisted that the closest associate of Alexander II, Count Mikhail Loris-Melikov, who had urged the liberal reforms, should be fired immediately.

Alexander III checked the liberal course abruptly; extreme conservatism resulted. On June 11, 1881, he wrote to his brother Sergei that Loris-Melikov had "made such a mess by his flirting with the press and the game of liberalism that very soon we would have found ourselves on the verge of political revolution." This was the new tsar's final verdict. The game of liberalism was over. Period.

Five of the six assassins of Alexander II were hanged publicly. The sentence of the sixth was commuted to life imprisonment only because she was pregnant and a pregnant woman could not be executed for any crime. The victims at the scaffold all bore signs on their chests: "Tsar-killers." Mobs watched the protracted death process with grim satisfaction. Three died as planned, but the hangman was drunker than usual and the noose of the fourth criminal slipped. Twice he had to be hauled back up to the top of the gibbet before he could finally be dispatched. For the last criminal, the fumbling executioner thereupon tied a double knot, thus ensuring but protracting his strangulation.

To catch and kill the agents of terrorism was relatively easy; to cope with its root causes was a different matter. And Alexander III had other matters to deal with.

A staunch nationalist, Alexander III decided it was his duty to direct Russian foreign policy personally. He once said, "I am my own minister of foreign affairs." The tsar would meticulously read diplomatic correspondence and pertinent clippings from the foreign press. After his death he was given the title of "Peacemaker," and indeed his was the only Romanov reign without war.

Among Alexander's most important childhood memories were ones connected with war, when, in June 1854, during the Crimean War, a large British-French fleet, nine steamers and eighteen sail, under the command of Sir Charles Napier, approached the Russian island fortress of Kronstadt, only a few miles away from the capital. The young Alexander's parents took him, along with his brothers, to a hillside on the coast to see these enemy ships, boldly riding at anchor eight miles off the great Kronstadt naval base, flaunting Western naval power in the heart of Russian waters, taunting Russian inability to do anything to counter it, symbolizing the futility of Russia's war with Britain and France.

As a young man, Sasha participated in the Russo-Turkish War of 1877–78, initiated by his father in the hopes of achieving Slavic unity and Russian control over the coveted Black Sea straits. He came away from the experience with a strong aversion to war. Later, as emperor, Alexander III would say, "No person with a heart would like war."

This did not mean that he did not favor military preparedness. On the contrary, he saw it as the only effective deterrent to war. As early as 1870, in a letter to a friend, Alexander III remarked of the conflict then raging between Prussia and France, "One cannot help worrying about the future of our motherland, for the filthy Prussians will soon get her!" Alexander signed an alliance with France in 1892, and the delighted French subsequently named a bridge spanning the Seine in his honor. The tsar was happy to be able to curb the Germans, whom he identified with the Prussians and whom he and his wife hated with all their hearts. Minnie could never forget Prussia's brutal seizure of Schleswig-Holstein, a part of her beloved Denmark. But Alexander's true sentiments about foreign affairs are summed up in his remark that "we have only two allies in the world, our Army and our Navy!"

Widespread Russian resentment over German arrogance and condescension reflected both an atavistic fear of "the Teutons" and Russia's own cultural insecurities on the European frontier. Alexander III intensely disliked not only the Prussians but also Germanic influence in Russia generally. German names had come to dominate lists of high government officials and army officers. German names were promi-

nent among those who carried the Russian flag, exploring and con-
quering Asia. Throughout the nineteenth century, a consistent one-
third of high government officials were of German descent, even more
in the ministries of war and foreign affairs. All these leaders emerged
from less than one percent of the total population of Russia.

Alexander did not like the disproportionate German influence, perhaps because he sensed the danger of a popular perception that the
Romanovs and their court were under German influence, and in part
because he associated any foreign influences with political liberalism.
Once, when still the heir, receiving senior Russian officers and having
met a dozen whose names started with "von" and ended with "heim"
or "bach," Alexander finally encountered a man with the thoroughly
Russian surname of Kozlov. "About time, too," Alexander pronounced in his deep voice, and his remark became proverbial, quoted
with delight by many of his subjects who shared his feelings.

Meanwhile, in the weeks following the funeral, the new emperor
began to handle the fractiousness of the family by negotiating with his
young stepmother, Yurievskaya. The princess agreed to forego any
right to live at the Winter Palace or any other imperial residences elsewhere in Russia. In return she requested a separate house for her children and for herself. Her financial resources then amounted to 3.4
million rubles; she was advised to put that huge sum into the State
Bank of Russia in the names of her children. Finally, with all the procedures finished, the princess and her children moved to France, to di-
vide their time between Paris and the Riviera.

The emperor was glad to see them out of the country but continued
to regard Yurievskaya as a reminder of his father's embarrassing infatuation. As late as 1885, he was still getting secret reports about her
style of life and social connections, obtained through an agent in Paris.
The emperor would read and sort the intelligence reports attentively,
separating "nonsense" and "inconsequential" from "partial truth."

The emperor also made arrangements for his parents' tombs. He
decided that they were not to be white marble like the other tombs in
Sts. Peter and Paul Cathedral. Instead he chose blood-red rodonite for
his mother, green jasper for his father. Both were carved out of priceless single blocks of stone; the imperial order took sixteen years to execute. Alexander III wanted his parents to be remembered differently
from all other Romanovs: his father assassinated by terrorists, his

mother abused by her husband's infidelity. But she was designated as the martyr and lay in the red tomb, not he.

Alexander III worried about the moral fiber of the dynasty. His lenient father, before becoming an emperor, had allowed his own sister, Maria Nikolaevna, to marry her lover, thus legitimizing an illicit relationship. Alexander II had set very relaxed standards for others in the family as well, tolerating grand ducal relationships with ballet dancers, and the only time when he had acted decisively to discipline a family member was in a case of theft. Alexander II's nephew, Grand Duke Nicholas Constantinovich, a young guards' officer, had stolen a spectacular diamond necklace from his mother, Grand Duchess Alexandra Iosifovna. The same night the police spotted the missing diamonds on the neck of an American courtesan sitting in the box of a theater watching a ballet performance. When arrested, the young woman declared the necklace to be the gift of her lover, Grand Duke Nicholas Constantinovich. The grand duke was promptly declared "mentally ill," and he disappeared into the Central Asian steppes for a comfortable but unconventional exile.

Puritanical in his own tastes, Alexander III fought the decaying moral climate of the *fin de siècle* as hard as he could. Tolstoy's novella *The Kreutzer Sonata* was banned as offensive and dangerous in its discussion of sex, although ironically, Tolstoy actually condemned sexual passion even within marriage as degrading and a despoiler of human lives. Tolstoy's wife and manager, the resolute Sofia Andreevna, allegedly went to St. Petersburg to beg the emperor to cancel the ban. Alexander III said, "Before answering you, Countess, let me ask you one question. Have your children read *The Kreutzer Sonata*?

"Of course not, Sovereign," Sofia Andreevna exclaimed.

"In that case," said Alexander in a paternal manner, "why do you want to corrupt the children of others?"

Alexander III set his own standards of morality. When his trusted associate and protege, Sergei Witte, married a divorcee, she was not allowed to be received at the court for ten years. When a minor Romanov, Duke George of Leuchtenberg, already married to a Montenegrin princess, moved in with his French mistress, Alexander was infuriated. Told that the nobleman was spending his vacations in Biarritz, he exclaimed, "So the prince is washing his filthy body in the waves of the ocean."

Grand dukes often got into trouble for seeking out inappropriate mates. Alexander III denied his cousin Nikolasha the right to marry a merchant's daughter. Another cousin, Michael Mikhailovich— "Miche-Miche," as the family called him—is chiefly known for causing trouble on this score. Tall and handsome—like so many of the grand dukes—and rich of course, Miche-Miche was not allowed to marry the daughter of the former Minister of Interior, a commoner. Ultimately, without imperial approval, he married another commoner, a granddaughter of the poet Pushkin, and fled into permanent exile in Great Britain, safe from the consequences of the imperial wrath. Empress Maria Fedorovna, a strong upholder of family values, angrily referred to Miche-Miche as "swine." Alexander III would not forgive grand dukes who broke the rules.

From the beginning the Romanovs both respected and feared Alexander III as the stern patriarchal head of the family. Unlike his father, Alexander III did not allow anyone, even family members, to drop in on him without an appointment. On his part, he would send little notes asking whether he could come to visit a relative, even a brother. This protocol was calculated to set up a subtle barrier between him, as tsar, and everyone else. He was resolved that familiarity should not leech his authority, and he was determined to codify the relationships of the Romanovs with the state.

On July 4, 1886, the emperor issued a "Decree on the Imperial Family," sharply defining the privileges of the Romanovs, the first such ukase since that of Emperor Paul I, issued April 5, 1797. Alexander III's concern was understandable, because the descendants of Paul's son Nicholas I had started reproducing in prodigious numbers. Michael Nikolaevich had six sons. If the sons were as fertile as their father, this branch alone would have thirty-six grand dukes! Such proliferation would mean an enormous future financial burden to the crown, difficulty in finding suitable occupations for so many Romanovs and a consequent lessening of family prestige.

Though the imperial decree stated that a special commission chaired by Grand Duke Vladimir was responsible for its contents, clearly the document expressed the will of the tsar himself. Among the stipulations was that the title of grand duke and grand duchess would from now on belong only to the children, siblings and grandchildren through the male line of an emperor. Great-grandchildren and their eldest sons would receive the title of Prince of Imperial Blood and be addressed as Imperial Highness. Others more remotely related to an emperor were given the title only of Highness. Children born from marriages not approved by the emperor would not have any privileges of the Imperial House.

The decree provoked intense family resentment, especially among grand dukes whose offspring would not have their title and others whose privileges were curtailed by it. But no one dared speak out against the wishes of the tsar.

The matter was not simply one of prestige but also of money. Romanovs had private wealth; sometimes it was very large. A grand duke or a prince drew income from any lands he might personally own and enjoyed interest from bank deposits, or returns from stocks and bonds, if he had made such investments. The emperor had no control over this. But a special trust or appanage, the *udely*, paid grants to all the Romanovs. Alexander III's decree redefined the amounts and the conditions of each grant.

For example, under the new plan an empress would be given two hundred thousand rubles a year plus an annual allowance to maintain her court, but if in her widowhood she left Russia, that amount would be cut in half. The *tsesarevitch* (heir to the throne) would get money for the expenses of his court plus one hundred thousand a year. The state treasury would pay specified sums to the Romanovs as onetime payments: the daughters and grandsons of an emperor were to receive one million rubles, great-grandchildren and great-great-grandchildren, one hundred thousand, further generations, only thirty thousand. An emperor's sons, other than the heir, were to get one hundred fifty thousand rubles plus one million for "settling down" and, when married, two hundred thousand yearly, plus thirty-five thousand for maintaining their palaces annually. The daughters of an emperor would receive only fifty thousand a year.

Romanovs customarily spent both lavishly and thoughtlessly; it cut against the grain of royal culture to be frugal or even to take an interest in business matters. Household expenditures tended to be very high to support a style analogous to that of an emperor although on a reduced scale. Many people depended entirely upon each grand duke or prince. Masters of ceremonies, valets, grooms, maids, butlers, gardeners and cooks all expected not only wages but also presents, at least twice yearly, at Christmas and Easter, and perhaps on the occasion of the employer's saint's day as well.

What did a ruble buy in the late 1880s? One hundred kopecks equalled one ruble; a bottle of wine would be thirty-five kopecks, beef cost six to seven kopecks a pound. Renting a modest house in Ukraine for the whole summer cost one hundred rubles. In Moscow, a spacious downtown apartment would rent for seven hundred fifty rubles yearly; a farm in the fertile Poltava region cost three thousand to buy. In 1888 Anton Chekhov received one thousand rubles for his masterpiece "The Steppe" and wrote, "one should be a very great writer indeed to earn one thousand rubles in one month." Usually he was paid fifteen kopecks per line. These amounts offer perspective on the grants the state gave to the Romanovs, both their grandeur and also the speed with which prodigal living could dissipate them.

The Romanov family, notwithstanding Alexander III's emphasis on convention, retained their high-flying exuberance. Each adult grand duke kept his own court and his own palace. The Marble Palace of the Constantinovichi was the most splendid of all grand ducal residences. But the other grand dukes also did quite well for themselves, especially Vladimir Alexandrovich, the tsar's brother.

Vladimir was a man of considerable energies and some ability, a hard drinker, *bon viveur* and connoisseur of the arts. The story has it that as a young man when the subject of his marriage was brought up and the name of his potential mate mentioned, Vladimir said, "Poor girl!" When his imperial father inquired what he meant, Vladimir replied, "What sort of husband shall I make, Sire? I am drunk every night, and cure next morning's headache by getting drunk again!"

Vladimir served as commanding officer of the Imperial Guards and was appointed president of the Academy of Fine Arts; the latter responsibility he much preferred over the former. Despite his Romanov conservatism, Vladimir often sided with radical artists whose ideas were alien to the monarchy. He encouraged Ilya Repin to finish two challenging paintings, *Volga Boatmen* and *Farewell to a Recruit*, both depicting the utter misery of the people and loaded with the promise of revolution.

Vladimir himself painted well, and he was a significant patron of the ballet and an original backer of the great impressario Sergei Diaghilev. A hearty man with a big voice (unable to speak without shout-

ing, even at a dinner party), the grand duke was adored by Paris waiters and chefs. He would make a big fuss about the shortcomings of a
menu, as if to demonstrate his refined knowledge of cookery and
scorn for what was offered to him, but end up by tipping lavishly all
around. Not everyone appreciated Vladimir's exuberance. The visiting
American heiress, Consuelo Vanderbilt, who had married the Duke of
Marlborough, thought Vladimir "autocratic and overbearing," needing "only to have a knout in his hand to complete the perfect picture
of the haughty Russian aristocrat."

The Vladimir Palace stands on the Neva at Dvortsovaya Embankment, the closest any grand duke lived to the Winter Palace. The glass
of Vladimir Alexandrovich's front door reflected the gilded spire and
cupolas of the Peter and Paul fortress cathedral, directly across the
Neva. A Russian architect had designed the grand duke's residence,
but its exterior, a medley of granite, brick and stucco, was modeled
after a fifteenth-century Florentine palazzo. The rich textures make
the building look like a giant chocolate layer cake. Lion masks and
coats of arms cast in concrete ornament the facade. The interior reflects French and other, eclectic foreign influences. The deliberate mixture conveys a sense of newfound opulence, a taste very much
characteristic of the era of the 1880s, in the United States as well as in
Russia.

The white marble staircase of the main entrance to the Vladimir
Palace was always brightly lit; originally two stuffed bears stood at either side of the foot of the stairs, each holding a tray with the traditional greeting of bread and salt. Passing under an elegant low arch,
the visitor found himself overwhelmed by a spacious hall leading to
the main rooms, also done up in great style. The drawing room, commanding a spectacular view of the Neva, was in French, Louis XVI,
style, with large windows and mirrors enhancing the natural light.

Elsewhere stained glass windows gave one the impression of being
in a castle from a fairy tale. Window glass engraved with palm trees,
which Vladimir brought back from Maxim's, his favorite restaurant in
Paris, further added to the room's effect. The many paintings by all of
the leading Russian artists of the time reflected the grand duke's strong
interest in the arts. Everywhere were marble, rare woods and gilded
plaster. The golden monogram of the owner, a Kyrillic "B" standing
in Russian for Vladimir, with a flower inside at every turn, constantly
reminded the visitor of whose house it was.

The grand duke's wife had a Moorish boudoir built to her own tastes, its walls covered with elaborate designs of inscriptions from the Koran in gold. The background was red and blue, the windows shielded by golden-colored bars in a star-like Arabesque design. The folding wooden doors of her boudoir were arched and also decorated in the Arabic manner, reflecting the then current European fascination with the exoticism of Islamic culture. With rooms like these, the Vladimir Palace could easily compete with anything at the royal courts of the smaller European nations.

The careful attention paid to kitchen, pantries and wine cellars reflected the keen interest of both Vladimir and his wife in fine food and drink. The records of the house list thousands of bottles of hundreds of different wines. And every winter the grand duke ordered prime sturgeon, some weighing several hundred pounds, sent in blocks of ice from beyond the Urals. Half a dozen barrels of black caviar were also brought for the grand ducal table. The palace boasted three libraries, the collection including the personal library of Alexander II, who had bequeathed it to Vladimir. After 1917 these books were randomly sold off by weight, and now they enrich several American university collections.

Vladimir's wife, the formidable Grand Duchess Maria Pavlovna, "Miechen" as the family called her, was perhaps the strongest of all the Romanov women. She combined charm and grace with majesty and carried out the tradition that grand ducal courts in St. Petersburg could be brilliant and important intellectually as salons, as well as important socially for dinners and balls, and her palace served as a gathering place for the elite of the city. Across the dining table or in the drawing room she would offer her own shrewd political judgments, and she did not conceal her political ambitions for her three sons, Kyril, Boris and Andrew, all firmly under the maternal thumb. Miechen was also keen to arrange a royal marriage for her only daughter, Helen. Miechen lusted for power even though she knew that as a woman it was doubtful she could ever wield it except indirectly. Self-assured and rivalrous, Miechen would eventually see herself as an alternative tsarina; she did not hesitate to express her scorn for most of her relatives and was quick to offer her opinions. What "Aunt Miechen" said was invariably, it seemed, circulated and discussed throughout the family.

From Miechen's court came the most gossip, and she conducted a wide correspondence in Russia and abroad which she used as a means to spread her opinions. The French ambassador, Maurice Paleologue, relished the tidbits she fed him and carefully entered them into his diary. Yet Miechen was more than a provider of information; she was a true professional. She knew the job of a royal person to perfection and boasted of how well she did it. She remembered names and used them. She knew how to keep a conversation going even with the dullest partner. And her appearance and manner were quintessentially regal.

In the late 1880s, Petersburg society believed that Alexander III was almost the only husband in the capital faithful to his wife. The rest of the Romanov men seemed to love all women except their wives. This is not to suggest that promiscuity was confined to Romanov men. Gossip had it that Miechen had never loved her husband, moving from one attachment to another. Nikolasha, her husband's first cousin, was rumored to be among her lovers.

The Vladimirs became well known for throwing exuberant, even boisterous parties in restaurants as well as at home. One gathering became so drunken and disorderly that the police had to intervene. A young French actor, Germain-Lucien Guitry, kissed the Grand Duchess Maria Pavlovna, was then slapped by Grand Duke Vladimir, and in return slugged the grand duke. Enraged, Grand Duke Alexis, Vladimir's brother, threw the actor out of the dining room. The chief of police, who happened to be waiting outside, then entered to be met by Alexis, who threw a huge dish of caviar in his face. After this scandalous event, the furious emperor for a time prohibited grand dukes from visiting restaurants at all.

Alexander III made it clear that he did not like his sister-in-law because of her aggressive personality and because she had so long refused to convert from Lutheranism to the Orthodox faith. His mother, herself a German and former Lutheran, had long ago worried about this, writing to Vladimir advising him to encourage her then-prospective daughter-in-law to convert. "May she become Russian in body and in soul," she urged.

In addition, the mutual dislike between the Vladimirovichi and Alexander III's family, the Alexandrovichi, could be traced to the tense matter of the imperial succession. The Vladimirovichi were next in line to the throne after Alexander III's sons. After the trainwreck at Borki in 1888, involving Alexander III, his wife and all his children, Miechen was reported to have said that "we shall never have such a chance again."

The emperor's next oldest brother after Vladimir, Alexis Alexandrovich, was tall like almost all male Romanovs, erect and handsome until weight swelled his frame considerably and he became known as "seven puds [246 lbs.] of august flesh." When in Petersburg, Alexis Alexandrovich lived at an appropriately heavy-looking palace at 122 Moika Embankment, not far from the Winter Palace. His size gave him a certain presence, and this was enhanced by his charm.

Alexis was a lifelong bachelor, but his intimate relationship with the extraordinarily beautiful Zinaida Beauharnais, a descendant of Napoleon's Josephine, was well known in St. Petersburg and elsewhere. Zinaida was married to the Duke of Leuchtenberg, a Romanov offshoot. The story is told that one evening when Leuchtenberg returned home late from his club he found his own marital bedroom locked. He knocked and insisted that he be let in. The door therefore opened and the burly Alexis appeared, thrashed the duke and threw him downstairs, where he was obliged to spend the rest of the night sleeping on a sofa. The next morning the duke went to the emperor himself to complain of the situation. Alexander III simply said that if the Duke of Leuchtenberg were incapable of managing his own wife he could not expect anyone else to do so for him. Furthermore the emperor said that divorce was too scandalous to be considered. Thereafter apparently the duke slept on his sofa and his wife continued to make her own arrangements upstairs.

Traveling abroad, Alexis, Vladimir and other grand dukes tended to intensify their flamboyant and sybaritic behavior. Emperors always had their own trains; grand dukes usually—but not always—had to satisfy themselves with a private car attached to a train (the Nord Express, for example, a favorite that ran twice weekly between St. Petersburg and Paris). A private railway car, rich with embossed leather on its walls, thick carpets, polished panels, inset mirrors and tulip-shaped reading lamps, usually included a bedroom with fine linen sheets and silk eiderdowns, lavatory, drawing room, kitchen, luggage storage and sleeping spaces for staff. These trains were immensely comfortable except in summer when the sun would heat up the metal roofs, causing the inner spaces to become virtually unendurable. The emperor could, and did, order his train to stop whenever he wished to have relief from the heat, to take a walk in the woods or perhaps even enjoy a picnic. Grand dukes were usually not that privileged; their private cars had generally to conform to the railroad schedules.

Paris was their favorite destination. Paris, with its restaurants and cafes, its theaters, opera and circus, suggested eating, shopping and night life: the world famous Café Americaine, Paillard, Tour d'Argent and dozens of others. The best restaurants would often keep a special chef specializing in Russian cuisine, for rich Russians frequented expensive places and sometimes craved the dishes of their homeland. The prodigal ways of the Romanovs became legendary in Paris, and the most fashionable couturiers derived much of their income from Russians. Many jewelry stores sported signs: "We Speak Russian."

Paris had introduced a new pleasure to the world, the cabaret, where the long legs of dancers moved with a machine-like precision. *Chansonniers,* dancers, actors and performers of comic monologues attracted thousands of patrons. The city of light beguiled its visitors with the soft evening glow of gas street lamps, especially along the famous grand boulevards. Thousands of electric bulbs, relatively new at that time, brightly lit the halls of Moulin Rouge and other cabarets. Life was at a boil, the music of the cakewalk expressing its exuberance. The Parisian crowd was merry and mixed, with young dandies in top hats, tail-coats, white scarfs and black cloaks, walking arm in arm, joking on their way to visit prostitutes. Courtesans of all grades were in abundance; many of them would have their mansions in the center of the city and would compete for attention dining at Maxim's or strolling in the Bois de Boulogne, and even mixing with ladies of high society at official receptions.

Despite the fact that France was conspicuous for its aggressive republicanism, the Romanovs felt very much at home there, and sometimes more grand dukes were to be found in Paris than in Petersburg. Paris returned the admiration. Grand Duke Alexis was so imposing that Parisians would stop on the sidewalk as he passed and exclaim, "What a handsome man!"

Alexander III appointed Alexis head of the Imperial Navy, but Alexis never allowed his naval duties to interfere with his travel schedule. He was known as a "good-humored sailor who prefers to conduct his nautical manoeuvres at Monte Carlo or Paris . . . [and] the hero of more stories than would fill a library of modern Decamerons." La Goulue, one of the great Parisian courtesans of the nineties, a cancan dancer and model for Toulouse-Lautrec, danced especially for the grand duke, who afterwards expressed his appreciation by literally covering her with banknotes of large denomination.

Alexis Alexandrovich was not really interested "in anything that did not pertain to love-making, food and liquor." His profound knowledge of these matters was unquestionable, but his understanding of naval affairs remained severely limited, and his idea of a conference with his admirals was to summon them for a sumptuous dinner and then regale them with sea stories of which his supply was rather limited. His young cousin Sandro later claimed to be able to recite them all by heart since he had heard them so many times.

Alexander III had confidence in the dependability of another brother, Sergei Alexandrovich. Sergei, the fourth of Alexander II's surviving sons, an ardent church-attender and conscientious regimental commander, wholeheartedly supported Alexander III's conservative political course and consistently advised him to continue his campaign against revolutionary radicals. Sergei was almost a model younger brother to the emperor. And yet his behavior could be unconventional.

When Sergei commanded the elite Preobrazhensky Regiment, he would often dine at the officer's mess and perform a special ritual there. Each of the officers would send a glass of champagne to Sergei Alexandrovich through a servant who would report: "Lieutenant So-and-So drinks the health of your Imperial Highness." Sergei would sip from the new glass and put it on the table, so by the end of the dinner, sitting like "a pagan god with the wine sacrificed to him," he would have as many as seventy glasses of champagne in front of him.

The one side of Sergei that did not meet Alexander's standard of conservatism and morality was his homosexual promiscuity. Sergei was as close to overt in his sexual behavior as a man of his position could be in Russia in the 1880s. He was far from being the only homosexual or bisexual among the Romanovs, but his cousin Nicholas Mikhailovich (Bimbo) remained discreet about his preferences; and, insofar as the world knew, Grand Duke Dmitri Constantinovich and Prince Peter of Oldenburg just "had no interest in women." Grand Duke Constantine Constantinovich, the poet K.R., remained highly discreet, confiding his unorthodox sexual escapades to his diary, recounting there his visits to bathhouses and his later remorse.

Most of the family had little use for Sergei, not so much because of his sexual orientation as because they found him enigmatic, cold and inaccessible. Outsiders shared this distaste. Consuelo Vanderbilt, dining with the grand duke, wrote that the tall and lean Sergei, strikingly handsome, had nonetheless an air of cruelty about him, a suggestion of evil. "I thought what a magnificent Mephistopheles he would make and the self-satisfied gleam I caught in his eye made me realize that he sensed my thought."

Nonetheless in 1884 Sergei Alexandrovich persuaded a beautiful German princess, Elizabeth of Hesse, to marry him. She was the older sister of Alix, or Alexandra, who would later marry Nicholas II. The family called her Ella. She was yet another of Queen Victoria's many grandchildren. Because Ella's mother, Princess Alice, had died young, Victoria thought of herself as a second mother to Alice's children. The old queen had fought vigorously against Ella's marriage to Sergei. Perhaps because she herself had married her first cousin, Victoria liked best to see marriages between her own grandchildren. Not that she favored the suit of another of Ella's admirers, her grandson the future Kaiser Wilhelm II; Victoria liked the Prussians as little as she liked the Russians. Victoria wrote to her eldest daughter, Vicky, Wilhelm's mother, of her apprehensions about a Russian match for the beautiful Ella. She feared "the *very bad state* of Society & its total *want of principle*, from the *Grand Dukes downwards*" and worried that Ella would be spending a great deal of time outside Russia and thereby likely to visit her. "I cld. *not* have a Russian Gd. Duke staying with me often or for long—That wld be *utterly impossible* . . . "

Ella, her sisters and brother had not enjoyed a very easy life as children. Their mother died young; their father, Louis of Hesse, was not rich, and their visits to their grandmother were their only experience of great luxury. Ella never felt as close to Victoria as did her younger sister Alix or some of the other granddaughters. For Ella, Sergei had the attraction of being fabulously rich as well as being a protective eight years older than she. And because Sergei's mother, Marie, had been a princess of Hesse-Darmstadt before her marriage to Alexander II, he had known Ella for years from various family gatherings.

So the old queen's will did not prevail. Ella married Sergei and she was duly prepared for her wedding according to the family ritual, wearing the crown worn by every Romanov bride since Catherine the Great. Her earrings were so heavy that they had to be looped to the top of the ears by a golden wire. Ella's beauty was such that her ladies-in-waiting whispered that she was the most beautiful bride ever to be married in the palace church.

However, the couple's life was shaped by Sergei's generally well-known although never discussed sexual orientation. The couple slept in the same bed but remained childless. Sergei Alexandrovich allegedly proposed to his wife more than once that she should chose a "husband" among her entourage. For him she seems to have remained more an object of possession than affection, a beautiful object whom he loved to adorn with jewels and to parade before society. Both Sergei and Ella were cold personalities, and perhaps this commonality drew them together.

Paul, the youngest grand ducal son of Alexander II, was emotionally fragile, a spoiled youngest son, and unfortunate in his love life. He was at least half in love with his beautiful neglected sister-in-law, Ella. He married first the Greek princess Alexandra, daughter of King George, Minnie's Danish favorite brother, and George's Romanov wife, Olga Constantinovna. For a while the two couples, Sergei with Ella, and Paul with Alexandra, shared an idyllic life, taking trips abroad together and enjoying Sergei's country estate at Ilinskoye. Alexandra and Paul happily had their first daughter, Grand Duchess Maria Pavlovna (Junior, to distinguish her from Miechen, her older namesake). But when Alexandra was pregnant for the second time, their idyll collapsed. Alexandra was careless on a boating trip at Ilinskoye and gave birth prematurely to a boy. She died. The boy survived, Grand Duke Dmitri Pavlovich. Paul, restless and desperately unhappy, virtually abandoned the two children and left Russia.

When he did so, Sergei, with the emperor's blessing, happily assumed custody of Paul's two motherless children, Maria and Dmitri. Often Sergei would bathe Dmitri himself and put both children to bed. He would happily admit in his diary: "I am enjoying raising Dmitri." Little Maria was a source of joy too. Sergei would mark the tiny pleasures the children gave him, for instance Maria slapping him on the shoulder and repeating "pretty uncle" in English. "She is so cute," he wrote.

Alexander III not only successfully stopped some of the worst excesses of Romanov family behavior but his corrections of his father's other "errors" seemed also to be working well. He kept the nation at peace. He repressed liberalism. But his successes did not bring him joy. In April 1892, he wrote a letter to his wife mourning the death of a favorite dog, Kamchatka. "Can I have at least one selfless friend among people? No, I cannot; but a dog can be one and Kamchatka was such." Deceived by his phlegmatic and resolute manner, outsiders did not see the tsar's quiet sadness, the terrible loneliness of his exalted position.

In his day, many Russians believed that Alexander III had the "noblest heart, more than that, a royal heart," a heart the "purity of which had remained intact." He had a *muzhik* or peasant air about him, almost a cultivated coarseness, that endeared him to many of his subjects. Although he was not a cultured man, his associates agreed that the tsar was a "model" family man and master, governed by a strong sense of duty. His minister of finance said that no other Romanov of his time respected a "ruble belonging to the state" as much as the tsar did.

The emperor's tastes were ruthlessly simple, perhaps in protest to what he had perceived as the degenerate extravagance of his father's court. His servant would endlessly darn his trousers, for the emperor hated to buy new clothes and his temper would flare if anyone suggested such an expenditure. It was bad enough, he thought, to keep the many military uniforms that he was obliged to have. At the time of his death, Alexander's wardrobe held thirteen uniforms of different Russian regiments plus four foreign ones: Danish, Austrian, Bavarian and British. Adding to the ceremonial clothing, the tsar had in all more than fifty orders, among them the Cross of Malta and decorations from Bukhara, Montenegro, Monaco and even the Kingdom of Hawai'i.

Alexander relished plain and ample Russian dishes, and even when mortally ill, before he lost all appetite, he would ask from time to time to be served a meal taken from the soldiers' barracks or from his company of hunters. The tsar's appetite was apparent from his size. He never worried that the food served at his court was notoriously bad; his sole concern was his own tendency toward obesity. But his attempts to diet were never successful. He also had a fondness for hard liquor. The empress tried to curb his drinking when his health began to decline, but Alexander had special boots made with a secret pocket large enough to hold a flask, and the chief of his bodyguard remembered drinking with the emperor when the empress was not around.

Although the emperor's size and strength seemed almost threatening, his eyes normally shone with kindness, and the power of his presence was somewhat offset by the clumsiness of his movements. Otherwise courageous, he had a peculiar idiosyncrasy: He was a bad rider and afraid of horses. The emperor always demanded a reliable mount; he was not easily persuaded to try a new one. Fortunately, unlike his son Nicky, he was so tall and regal that he did not require a horse to establish his overwhelming presence.

Alexander spent as much time as possible in his beloved Gatchina, relatively remote from Petersburg society, a world he thoroughly disliked. He felt secure and comfortable in the country and relished the simplicity of the life he could create there. He and his family occupied several modest rooms on the first floor of the palace, rooms that had been intended as quarters for servants. In these tiny apartments he would discuss state matters, ignoring the sumptuous halls in the center of the building used by his predecessors. At midnight Alexander would withdraw to his study where he would spend several more hours working. The next morning at nine o'clock he would start receiving reports.

Gatchina provided simple pleasures, like fishing in the autumn after midnight. The emperor would share a boat with a court fisherman and sailors would row. Another boat with sailors would follow behind. The fisherman would light up the surface of the water with a torch; fish would be attracted by the bright light and approach the surface. The emperor would then spear them. Along the shores of the narrow lake, twenty soldiers would follow the imperial progress. The emperor would spend much time doing this, sometimes returning home only as the late gray autumn dawn broke, having spent five hours on the water. Sometimes he would even go ice fishing in February and once complained to the empress that he had been fishing three times at the lake, but there were few fish and the nights were "a bit cool." He grudgingly returned home "as early as 1:15 a.m. and went to work."

Usually the tsar would go to Gatchina in autumn after spending the summer at the palace of Peterhof. Peterhof, a Russian Versailles, with its geometrical plantings, flower beds and elaborate fountains and statuary, was too formal and too French for his taste. But Alexander would go to Peterhof in order to sail from there to the small rocky islands off the southern coast of Finland, which his wife, Minnie, perhaps due to her Scandinavian childhood, liked immensely. Finland was known as a place where the sea was full of islands and the land was full of lakes. Some of the islets, when seen through the shimmering haze of a summer day, resembled ships. Everywhere, on land and in the water, bare igneous rock sprang up, but the thin soil nurtured a profusion of summer flowers, their colors offset by the immaculately white birch trees.

Petersburg and the Winter Palace was obligatory only for the high season, from New Year's Day until Lent. Alexander would write to his

wife on April 12, 1892: "It is boring here in Petersburg, I feel home-
sick for dear Gatchina, it is so weird to live in the Winter Palace; I
have the feeling that I am on a trip and I have absolutely no feeling
that I am at home, though I like these rooms and they are really wonderful, but yet my small room at the Anichkov is by far better for me."

Another place the emperor enjoyed and visited regularly was Spala,
the hunting camp in the immense Polish forest preserve called
Belovezh Pushcha (White Forest), at that time the only place where the
huge European bison could still be found. By Alexander III's reign,
only about eight hundred of these survivors of the Ice Age survived to
roam in the depths of the forest, one of Europe's biggest, but other
wildlife could be found there in profusion. The tsar's lodge was ample
but simple, built in a dark rustic style very much to Alexander's own
taste.

Many of the Romanovs loved the Crimea, a Russian Riviera, albeit
one wilder, more dramatic, more naturally beautiful. The Greeks, the
Romans, the Genoese and the Tatars had all left their imprint upon
this large peninsula jutting out into the Black Sea. Catherine the Great
had wrested the territory from the hands of the Turks in 1783 and so
it had not been long a part of Russia and was still largely undeveloped.
The mild, almost Mediterranean, climate attracted rich Russians,
among them the Romanovs, anxious to escape at least part of the long
dark winters of the north and eager for a life simpler than the formality of the capital city.

After getting off the train at the Sevastopol terminus, visitors from
the north would ride by carriage to the southeast over pleasant but unremarkable countryside. Then, they would pass through the Baidar
Gate, a mountain pass opening the way to Yalta and the southern
shore of the Crimean Peninsula, a site commanding the sea and offering a stunning vista of water and mountain.

On the shore, broken columns and pieces of stone through which
roses and oleanders pushed their way stood as evidence of ancient civilizations, adding a romantic and picturesquely antique flavor to the
gardens of contemporary villas.

The palace that Alexander III had at Livadia outside Yalta was
modest, resembling nothing in St. Petersburg, looking instead like the
villa of a provincial bureaucrat of the Ottoman Empire, with elaborate wooden galleries and balconies giving as much shade and fresh air
as possible. The apparent model for it was a palace of the Crimean

khans in Bakhchisarai on the other side of the mountains. The park around the palace burgeoned with growth, plantings coming to the very windows. The subtropical Crimean climate fascinated Alexander III, who bought land there to plant grape vines. By the time of his death, the Massandra vineyard would produce more than two million bottles yearly. The rich amber Madeira of that winery was probably the only Russian wine that could compete in the international market.

Yalta was often called the "Russian Cannes." But its sounds were not Russian, its smells were not Russian. The braying of donkeys, the chants of the muezzin summoning the faithful to prayer, the pungent odors of the market all conveyed the atmosphere of the Middle East. Nor was Yalta like Cannes. Despite the attractively exotic atmosphere, the Crimea did not draw large numbers of tourists. Foreigners rarely came. The area lacked the hotels, restaurants, theaters, clubs, the flow of people, the conversation, the parade of fashion—and above all else, the gambling—that the south of France featured so handsomely. For fun, most Romanovs chose France over Russia, and came to their own southland only if they happened to own houses there and wanted a restful and quiet time.

At Massandra, Alexander III chose to build a second imperial residence, a "hunting lodge," in the French Renaissance style situated on a foothill and providing a marvelous vista of the Yalta bay. The elaborate architecture was more to his wife's taste than to his own, and ultimately it was she, not he, who would live there. Remote from the water as it was (and still is), nonetheless in front of the palace one could hear the sound of the waves crashing far below. Pine groves covered the estate with an everlasting fresh scent especially strong on a hot summer day. The smallish park eased into forest with abundant game birds. Wolves, deer and foxes prowled beyond rocky glades to which the Romanovs playfully gave names like "Hurrah!" and "Bravo."

Minnie enjoyed a relatively free life there. Her favorite sport was riding one of her horses on the numerous steep mountain paths through the pine forests, crossing streams and waterfalls, turbulent in late winter and early spring, and even mounting to the peak of Ai Petri. Vineyards crawled up the cypress-studded hillsides, and exuberant flowers of every hue grew everywhere: on the ground, on shrubs, on trees. From the pink and white almond blossoms of early spring to the red and golden fruits of late summer and autumn, the eye, the nose and the tongue could find pleasure. The plateau above Yalta was covered by sharp, finger-size tridents of limestone, known locally as "dragon's teeth," providing a spectacular but dangerous ride for the horseman. Much of the peninsula remained unbroken forest and steppe, a great plateau interrupted by craggy mountains and deep valleys.

Alexander III would describe one departure from Sevastopol, the naval base made famous in the Crimean War, in what was for him almost poetic terms: "The evening was wonderful. . . . Sevastopol with its wonderful bays and the squadron at the harbor, lighted by the rays of the setting sun and the smoke of the salute also pink because of the sunset, presented a marvelous picture."

Not all these trips were so wonderful. The family always remembered a crash of the imperial railway train at Borki, a tiny village in Ukraine, near Kharkov, on October 17, 1888, killing twenty-one people, and Alexander would tell his wife, who felt deeply emotional about the site of the crash, that they should return there with all the children and thank God for the miraculous rescue. The train had been speeding—the emperor liked to go fast—but the condition of the track could not sustain high speeds. At the moment of the catastrophe the emperor and his whole family were sitting in the dining car. The roof of the carriage collapsed, and the emperor, demonstrating his almost superhuman physical strength, according to legend at any rate, held it on his back until the others could get out of the car. The first thing people heard after the crash was the voice of the empress: "The children!" Alexander described the Borki accident to his brother Sergei as a series of "trials: fear, anguish, profound sadness and finally joy and thanks to the Creator."

In between stays in their various palaces, Sasha and Minnie would tour Russia, showing their faces to the public, the tsar giving speeches and presiding over civic ceremonies, the couple making their subjects happy by distributing lavish gifts: gold cigarette cases, tie pins, and cufflinks studded with diamonds, rubies or sapphires to members of the privileged classes, lesser objects to the masses.

In the summer, the emperor, his wife and children would travel aboard their yacht across the Baltic Sea to Copenhagen. Here lay the opportunity for the Romanovs to enjoy the extended family. King Christian IX of Denmark, Minnie's father, himself of German origin, was known as the "grandfather of Europe" because so many of his descendants either married monarchs or became monarchs themselves.

Everyone congregated there, some liking the experience better than others. Sasha and Minnie delighted in the opportunity to behave in a "bourgeois" manner. They would send away the servants, and the tsar, with some other royal persons, would serve meals to the others. Alexander was also reported to visit little shops in Copenhagen incognito, buying trinkets, something he could never do in Russia. The atmosphere was relaxed; royal relatives had a tacit understanding that they would simply enjoy one another's company and never talk politics.

Once King Oscar of Sweden was paying a state visit to the King of Denmark. The tsar, also there, went to the top floor of the house where some of the children were staying, attached a hose to a bathroom faucet, and began to squirt it out the window. Seeing King Oscar below, he deliberately turned the hose on him. The king, his dignity offended, bitterly complained to his Danish host, King Christian, who upbraided his grandchildren for the offense. Then to his embarrassment, he learned from them the identity of the culprit. The drenched Swedish monarch departed not at all amused, but the children of the extended family all adored "Uncle Sasha" because of his playfulness. They had in fact given him the garden hose.

On the other hand, the epicurean Edward, Prince of Wales, future King Edward VII, had little interest in practical jokes and no fondness for the simple life. He cordially disliked visiting these Danish relatives who might serve him stewed rhubarb and expected everyone to be in bed by ten.

The Danes formed a link between the Romanovs and the British royal family: Minnie was a sister of Queen Alexandra, Edward VII's wife. Throughout their lives, the two sisters remained unusually close, and met regularly every summer in Denmark.

Queen Alexandra's mother-in-law, Queen Victoria, was like King Christian commonly known as a grandparent of Europe. Married to her first cousin, Albert of the House of Coburg, she bore nine children in twenty years even though she was frank to say that she did not like bearing or raising children. Writing to her oldest daughter, Vicky, in 1870 she would say, "Children are a terrible anxiety and the sorrow they cause is far greater than the pleasure they give." And when Victoria's grandchildren began to arrive, as they did in great number, she remarked that "it seems to me to go on like the rabbits in Windsor Park!"

Eight of Victoria's grandchildren would wear crowns either as reigning monarchs, like her eldest daughter Vicky's son, the future

Kaiser Wilhelm II, or as royal consorts like Alexandra of Hesse who would be wife of the future tsar Nicholas II. But Victoria herself seldom came to Copenhagen, and spoke of this extended European family with some distaste as "the royal mob." She liked them in gatherings, it seems, only if she were at the center, her accustomed place, and could exercise control over the whole. At home, Victoria's great grandson, Edward, Duke of Windsor, said that "such was the majesty that surrounded Queen Victoria that she was almost regarded as a divinity, of whom even her own family stood in awe." The longevity of her rule increased her authority as a figure in international affairs, and at home her virtues seemed to personify those most admired at the time. Even the great Bismarck was somewhat daunted at the prospect of meeting the old queen. After a one hour session with her, discussing only noncontroversial matters, Bismarck emerged "mopping his brow in relief, exclaiming with admiration that 'one could do business with her.'"

Victoria was short—four feet eleven inches—and, even as a young woman, fat—181 pounds. Her features were not beautiful and she was physically unimposing. Her immense authority derived not from her appearance, not simply from her position, and certainly not from her charm. "Callous, obstinate, outspoken, capricious, and inordinately selfish," are words biographers now use to describe her. Victoria thought first of her own convenience, rarely of the feelings of others. Court life dictated that, above all, the Queen must be obeyed. She heard only what people thought she would like to hear; she talked only of what she wished to discuss. The result was tyrannous tedium for all around her, including her hapless relatives. Yet Victoria is not to be compared to the Emperor of Russia. Her powers were not those of an autocrat. She might dominate the table; she could not dominate the state. "The doyenne of monarchs" she thought herself, and others were inclined to accept her judgment, although she was only a queen until she became Empress of India in 1876, a title that she relished but promised not to use in England since many of her subjects thought it so "un-English."

Victoria as a young unmarried woman met Alexander Nikolaevich, the future Alexander II, who was then on a visit to England. It was May 1839 and the new queen had just turned twenty. She confided to her journal that "I am really quite in love with the Grand-Duke; he is a dear, delightful young man. . . . I danced with [him] and we had such fun and laughter. . . . I never enjoyed myself more. We were all so merry; I got to bed by a 1/4 to 3, but could not sleep till 5." Alexander was certainly handsome. Yet one of Victoria's court ladies wrote another to say, "How dreadful it would be if the Queen were to fall in love with him! For actually he is the only man whom she could not possibly marry."

Alexander left England and that was the end of the relationship. The occasion proved the high point in Victoria's relationship with the Romanovs. When Alexander's father, Tsar Nicholas I, visited England five years later in 1844, the queen disliked him. Ten years later her country and his would be at war. Thirty years later, Victoria's second son, Prince Alfred of Edinburgh, a well-traveled hard-drinking naval officer, married Maria Alexandrovna, the only surviving daughter of Alexander II. The courtship was protracted, making both sides apprehensive. Alfred was eleven years older than "Marie," as the British would call her, and rumors of her affairs had reached British ears, prejudicing many there against the match. Furthermore, whereas Marie was stout and pudding faced, Alfred was certainly the best looking of Victoria's sons, blue-eyed with skin tanned by his extended stays at sea.

When Marie came to England she aroused the intense jealousy of her new in-laws, first by attempting to assert precedence over them because she was the daughter of an emperor and then by flaunting her magnificent collection of jewels. Marie's sapphires and rubies, not to mention her pearls and diamonds, outshone anything the British royals had, although Victoria and her successors would increase that collection enormously. When the queen first saw Marie bedecked, Victoria shrugged her shoulders "like a bird whose plummage has been ruffled, drawing down the corners of her mouth in an expression those around her had grown to dread."

Alexander came to England to visit his daughter, but the spark between Victoria and him was dead. This time she found him "kind but . . . terribly altered, so thin, and his face looks so old, sad, and careworn." When she learned of Alexander's murder, Victoria, having herself survived many assassination attempts, wrote in her journal that she felt "quite shaken and stunned. . . . May God protect all dear ones! Poor, poor Emperor, in spite of his failings, he was a good and amiable man, and had been a good ruler, wishing to do the best for his country."

For Victoria, Alexander II was the exception not only among Romanovs but also among Russians. In her correspondence, she spoke frankly of her dislike of Russian autocracy, of Russia as "that horrid, corrupt Country," and of Alexander III. "I have *such* a dislike to the fat Czar. I think him a violent . . . Asiatic full of hate, passion & tyranny."

Those who knew Alexander III intimately, as his wife Minnie did, would have disagreed with Queen Victoria profoundly. Matched at the deathbed of Alexander's elder brother Nicholas, married for duty, not for love, Sasha and Minnie nonetheless looked and acted the perfect couple. They lived in a peculiar symbiosis of Sasha's plainness and Minnie's refinement. He relied always upon her approval and in public she in turn was careful always to defer to him, her intense femininity softening his heavy masculinity, though in private she could make her will known. Minnie had been brought up to believe in the superiority of the male sex; she was not prepared to challenge Sasha in any way, at least in public. And Sasha, while scrupulously faithful to his marriage vows, was not one to be subdued by a wife. In each case this was unusual for a Romanov.

With her two daughters Minnie was strict and demanding, always reminding them of their royal duties. With her three growing sons she was far more permissive than with the girls, more like an older sister or intimate friend than mother, conspiring with the boys to deflect the temper of their father. Minnie would wheedle, charm and deceive Sasha. Nicky was especially close to his mother, ready to accept her advice, and unfortunately she encouraged his dependence on her rather than helping him to develop a style of leadership suitable for his future responsibilities.

Minnie had grown up poor—at least by royal standards. Life at the Danish court was exceptionally modest. The young princess received little education and never developed any real interest in books or ideas. A strong and simple religious faith, which she would carry over into Orthodoxy, filled some of that void. Minnie could believe in miracles but, unlike many of the Romanovs, she was not attracted to mysticism and the occult and would come to abhor these practices in her later years.

Stubborn, willful and short-tempered, Minnie would at times stamp her feet and cry like a spoiled child, but she was usually cheerful. She laughed easily and had a quick sense of the ridiculous. She knew what the public wanted of her and relished her role as empress, playing it extremely well, taking an almost childish delight in brilliant jewels, stylish clothing and grand parties. People responded readily to her pleasure. Physically small, she stood with royal carriage and a vital presence, commanding any room she entered. Her public both admired and liked her.

Within the extended family, Minnie made it clear to everyone that she was doyenne of the Romanov women. With her gregarious nature and continuing close links to her own Danish kin and with the greater European royal family, she diluted the provincial German influence among Romanovs. Physically Minnie could not compete with her sister Alexandra, Queen of England, generally hailed as the greatest royal beauty in Europe, and yet the difference cast no shadow on their friendship.

Minnie's was a beauty of manner more than a beauty of feature. Yet when her teeth started to deteriorate in the late 1880s and her smile became awkward, even people who did not like her had to admit that she still gave the impression of a "graceful and elegant young person," always young for her years. When she was dancing in the Winter Palace with diadem and necklace made of diamonds and turquoise, the only thing the critics could find to say against her was that she did not dance the mazurka very well.

As empress Minnie gave her husband no problems. She had no political ambitions. She remained a close and loving companion to her husband and the tsar was glad to satisfy her whims. In their first years of marriage they spent very little time apart; their longest separation was in 1877–78 when Alexander served with the Russian troops in the Balkans. Later Minnie would be absent frequently, visiting their third son, George, who lived in Abas-Tuman in the Caucasus hoping desperately that the mountain air would cure his tuberculosis. Alexander III was not particularly keen on writing letters, but there remain several hundred of them to his bride and later wife. He would address her as "my sweet darling Minnie." To him, her rooms when she was away would look "empty and everything is different."

Sasha and Minnie had six children: Nicholas (1868), Alexander (1869), George (1871), Xenia (1875), Michael (1878) and Olga (1882). "Of course," Sasha wrote in 1892, "the children are a great consolation, only with them one can have moral repose, enjoying them and being happy looking at them. Poor Sergei and Ella," the emperor would sigh, referring to his childless brother and sister-in-law, "I often think about them; for their whole life they are deprived of this great consolation and the blessing of God." Sasha and Minnie's youngest child, Olga, was born on June 1, 1882 in Peterhof, and nine years later the emperor would tell his wife in a letter that it had been the first happy event since that Sunday afternoon of horror, March 1, 1881, the assassination of his father.

But he would also separately mention the sorrows children brought.

Their second child, Alexander, died in infancy on May 26, 1870. Twenty-one years later, the emperor and the empress would exchange messages on the sad anniversary of that day. Sasha would write: "This date has been merry and happy only once. Yes, it is a wound which cannot be healed through our whole lives and which becomes more open and sore with each year! Yes, when I think that our angel Alexander would be twenty-two now, when I think that all the three older boys could be together and almost the same age, and we will never have him with us in this life, my soul is torn apart by despair and sadness."

Yet while the children were small family life seemed idyllic, especially when Michael and Olga were still very young. Loving horseplay himself, the emperor was lenient with his children, looking the other way when they threw bread pellets at each other across the dining table. Relishing their high spirits, he instructed their tutors: "I do not need porcelain, I want normal healthy Russian children."

Michael tried to imitate his adored father: "Dear Papa, I hope your hunting was a success and you killed many deer etc., while my crow-hunting is not too good." When his father was away, Michael missed him: "Everything is the same in your rooms. I sometimes go there and I have a feeling that you are here."

Olga was a tender and loving girl, especially close to her father. She reported to him that she had found a bird without a beak. "I took it and gave it some water and bread and milk." When the bird died, Olga decided she would bury it at a special bird cemetery she and Michael had made.

Nicky, the heir, had grown up a withdrawn and shy young man, handsome, and for a Romanov male, short of stature. Nicky's chief interest in life seemed to be having fun. To his father's disapproval, he would sometimes "disappear" in Petersburg for several days. The tsar felt that Nicky, although in his early twenties, was still a child, enjoying popularity in the world of adults because of his privileged status. The exasperated emperor would report to the empress that after a performance of *Faust,* Nicky and a cousin "must have gone somewhere else, for now it is 1.30 A.M. and he's not in yet!" Later he snarled, "Nicky is out to have a good time."

Nicky would especially relish the company of two of his father's first cousins who were the *tsesarevich's* age, the "Caucasians," debonair and darkly handsome Grand Duke Alexander Mikhailovich (Sandro) and the latter's brother, Sergei Mikhailovich. Another cousin close to him was Prince George of Greece, of whom the emperor's advisor, Sergei Witte, wrote disapprovingly that he was very likely to act in a manner "which is far from being a model for grand dukes and princes."

April 10, 1892, was a typical day for the heir. Nicky, Sandro and Sergei had five o'clock tea with the emperor in the Winter Palace, then they inspected the military portrait gallery there. Afterwards Nicky and Sandro went to the opera and subsequently disappeared, irritating the emperor, who felt unable to control his grown-up son. On April 16th, the emperor informed his wife with utmost displeasure that Nicky was in St. Petersburg, "doing I don't know what."

Actually, "I don't know what" was a euphemism for womanizing. Court slang had a special term for sex without consequences, "potato," and young Nicholas would often refer in his diary to "potato parties." And yet despite the paternal grumblings, it was likely that it was Alexander III himself who helped Nicky lose his virginity by finding a girl for him. In 1889 the rumor spread in St. Petersburg that a ballet starlet, Labunskaya, had been chosen as mistress for the *tsesarevich* at a salary of eighteen thousand rubles a year, with her only obligation being "to visit the palace *when necessary.*" Nicholas's subsequent romance with another ballet dancer Mathilde Kshesinskaya is again reported to have been arranged by his considerate father.

Mathilde was a Polish-born woman whose father was a distinguished character dancer, famous for his mazurka. Theirs was a family of dancers; Mathilde, her brother and sister all graduated from the Imperial Ballet School. Tiny (five feet tall), vain and hardworking, Mathilde developed an extraordinary and demanding technique; when practicing she would put four chairs in a square and swing her legs within the tight space of the square. If she had touched the back of a chair, the force of her swing would immediately have broken a leg. Kshesinskaya was unquestionably a brilliant dancer, one of the best of her generation, but her great success was as much derived from the attractiveness of her face and the effervescence of her personality as it was from her artistry on stage. People always noticed her.

The ballet had become a notable feature of Russian life at the end of the imperial era, a national institution financially supported by the government and one in which the emperor and the Romanov family took a keen personal interest. The Romanovs appreciated music in general and loved opera, but ballet infatuated them. The Imperial Ballet was French in inspiration; its longtime choreographer, Marius Petipa, had been born in France. Petipa, himself originally a dancer, brought to St. Petersburg his profound knowledge and direct experience of the French tradition of dance. Under his inspired direction the form would take on a distinctly Russian coloration and character, and the Russian ballet developed a highly sophisticated following. The Russian audience appreciated and relished the finer points of a dancer's technique just as an Italian audience would appreciate and relish the lustrous high C of a tenor singing an aria. In both cases the artistry of course lay in making it all seem easy. When a tenor cracked, the Italian response was catcalls and rotten vegetables. When a dancer made a mistake, a Russian audience responded with an icy silence.

Twice weekly, during the season, the ballet performed at the Mariinsky Theater, and these performances became social as well as artistic events. At the intermissions, those sitting in boxes would adjourn to anterooms behind the boxes to smoke, nibble, sip and chat. The patrons were for the most part regular subscribers who all knew each other and relished exchanging the latest gossip.

Nicky began to visit Kshesinskaya's house, often with his Mikhailovich cousins. Her family would hide themselves away while she served champagne to her guests. Kshesinskaya remembered an evening when the future emperor danced for *her*. Holding a basket in his hand, with a handkerchief tied to his forehead, he danced Little Red Riding Hood, from *The Sleeping Beauty*, one of Kshesinskaya's famous roles. She says that he also danced the wolf but offers us no details of that performance. The affair between the prince and the dancer, a two year idyll, would end with Nicky's engagement and marriage.

Despite his father's emphasis on respectability, the milieu in which the heir lived was as far from puritanism as one can possibly imagine. He would spend hours fascinated by the bawdy talk of young officers of the Guard, sometimes until 3 A.M., while the old generals were drowsing in the corner. Sometimes the party would become a drinking orgy. Nicky and his friends would start imitating wolves. They would undress, go outdoors stark naked, sit on the ground and howl to the sky. Servants would bring out a large basin of vodka or champagne, and the young aristocrats would rush to it on all fours, licking the alcohol, biting one another and yelping. If this experience influenced Nicky's dance for Kschesinskaya, her discretion in recalling it seems appropriate.

Nicky's romance with the dancer ousted these bachelor revels and the "potato parties" from his life. After December 1891, when the Italian Carlotta Brianza retired, Kshesinskaya reigned supreme in Russian ballet, her position not at all damaged by her imperial liaison. Then Alexander III, perhaps fearful of the intensity of Nicky's feelings, sent him on a trip around the world.

During his travels, Nicky would send letters to his parents describing all the wonderful things he saw, but the parents were not to know about the real sightseeing the heir did. While describing with casual piety his meeting with an Orthodox Patriarch in Egypt, Nicky would secretly savor a visit to Egyptian prostitutes. At first he had not liked them, but when they took their clothes off and a companion of his, Prince Oukhtomsky, started "doing things" with the girls, Nicky liked that very much. Nicky's brother George was along on the trip but returned before schedule because of his failing struggle with tuberculosis. "Greek Georgie," the cousin of whom Witte so disapproved, continued with the group.

In Japan, a lunatic Japanese policeman attacked Nicky with a sword; the *tsesarevich* got much sympathy, a permanent scar and periodic headaches, and a life-long dislike for the Japanese. Describing this incident, which happened on the shores of Lake Biwa at Otsu, near Kyoto, Nicky spoke of his fear that he would collapse, for the blood from his wound had "spouted like a fountain." Traveling home from Japan via the Russian Far East, in newly founded Vladivostok, Nicky was struck with the city's resemblance to Sevastopol and its bays; he was also impressed by its size. He wrote to his apprehensive parents that he was upset that his wound obliged him to keep his bandage on and to totter around "like an old general."

When Nicholas returned from his year-long journey, he took a house for Kshesinskaya at 18 English Prospect, and he started a serious quasi–family life with her which would last for two years. The house itself was loaded with ballet associations: Grand Duke Constantine Nikolaevich had built it for the dancer Kuznetsova; Grand Duke Nicholas Nikolaevich Senior had lived there with his dancer, Chislova, who had borne him two sons and two daughters.

But the *tsesarevich*'s romance was too public to be tolerated by the family and by the court. When on December 6, 1892, the emperor and the entire court were present at the first performance of Tchaikovsky's opera *Yolanta*, and the baritone sang, "Who can compare with my Mathilda?" the audience giggled, to the embarrassment of the imperial party.

St. Petersburg high society was wondering who would become the *tsesarevich*'s wife. The guesses varied from a Montenegrin to a German princess. The grande dames of gossip excluded Nicky's ultimate choice, Alix of Hesse, because she was too tall.

Aside from Nicky's escapades, the imperial couple had their other children to worry about. In February 1891, doctors detected the dreaded Koch bacillus in their son Grand Duke George; in the spring of 1892, he began to cough up blood. When George had to interrupt his world tour with Nicky, he fell into a depression, withdrawing to his Caucasus mountain villa, Abas-Tuman, where, everyone hoped, the climate would cure him. His guardians telegraphed medical reports periodically to the emperor. On January 3, 1894: "Condition of the grand duke satisfactory, no lesions discovered during examination. Weight 162 3/4. His Highness walks a lot. Hunting scheduled for today, a trip to a mountain pass also scheduled." In May, however, George began to cough and to run a fever. "What a misfortune and trial the Lord has sent us, to be away from our dear son for so long and right now, in the best years of his life, youth, merriment, freedom!" the tsar would exclaim.

George's health was not the tsar's only concern. All was not well in Alexander's relationships with his children and he felt bewildered by their cold behavior toward him. In 1892 George would not congratulate his father on his birthday (February 26th). This relationship with George, and the one with his older daughter, Xenia, would "torture me throughout this winter" of 1891–92, the emperor wrote. On April 16, 1892, Alexander said plaintively to the empress then visiting in Abas-Tuman, "Kiss Georgy and Xenia for me, if they still remember me and love me!"

Xenia was clearly her mother's favorite daughter. Among the Alexandrovichi she had the least colorful personality; she was rather plain in appearance—her gray-green eyes her most pleasing feature—shallow in her interests, conventional in her tastes, but tractable. The stronger personalities around her tended to submerge the unobtrusive Xenia. Olga, her younger sister, with the rough hewn face of a peasant woman, was much like her father: stubborn, resolute and attracted to simplicity. Unlike Olga, Xenia had given food for her father's sad thoughts: "Xenia ignores me, I am an absolute stranger to her; she will not talk to me, she never asks questions, never asks for something and I would be so glad to please her in any possible way."

Xenia's neglect of her father could have been explained by her new romance. In May 1890, her dashing and glamourous cousin Sandro, Grand Duke Alexander Mikhailovich, fell in love with her and immediately confessed his feelings to his brother, George Mikhailovich, anxiously asking whom did he think Xenia preferred, Sandro or their brother Sergei, and did George think the imperial parents would agree to Xenia marrying either of the two? Sandro was ambitious although he tried to conceal it, unusually good looking and a far more complex character than Xenia.

He was like quicksilver, the most restless male Romanov of his generation: amorous, adventurous, incapable of sticking to anybody or any project for any length of time. His active mind swarmed with schemes to gain glory, power and more wealth, but he lacked both clarity of vision and a sense of responsibility. As an entrepreneur he would have gone bankrupt; as a politician he would have ended in jail; as an admiral he would have lost all of his ships. But being a grand duke he was protected from all these calamities.

Sandro believed himself a profound thinker. He was not. However, he was a keen observer of family foibles and wielded a clever pen. For most of the family he had little respect, regarding them as unimaginative, hyperconservative and paralyzed by inertia. The family heartily reciprocated, refusing to take Sandro seriously. With Minnie, however, after an uncertain beginning, he developed and sustained a warm friendship.

As a youth, when he played with his cousin Nicky, the *tsesarevich*, the Greek prince Georgie, and his own younger brother, Sergei, Sandro always wanted to lead. The four together cruised St. Petersburg chasing adventure, making fun of everybody and raising eyebrows.

Sandro was the unchallenged leader of that group: mischievous, bold, imaginative and fast.

When Sandro forsook his old companions for Xenia, Greek Georgie wrote Nicky of his disgust at the "gymnastic, sucking, sniffing and similar activities which these two persons indulged in all day. They almost broke the ottoman and generally behaved in the most inappropriate way; for instance they would lie down on top of each other, even in my presence, in what you might call an attempt to play Papa and Mama."

Blithely unaware of the heavy romance, Alexander III invited Sandro to accompany the family on a cruise to the Finnish islands on board the imperial yacht *Tsarevna*. The trip proved to be great fun. When the family went ashore everyone would gather flowers and strawberries and set out a picnic. Sandro cooked the mushrooms they found, Minnie was entrusted with potatoes, Xenia cooked shashlik and peeled potatoes for her mother (the empress had very limited cooking skills), the emperor set the table. Alexander III liked to encourage everyone to try cooking whether experienced or not and, never without appetite, he promised always to eat the result. Prince Nicholas of Greece, a nephew of the tsar, on one occasion filled his cooking pan with butter and put in some pieces of meat, nuts, grapes, mushrooms, cream, pepper and anything else he could find. When the concoction had browned, he served it up to the tsar, who ate it all and stoutly pronounced it excellent.

Aboard ship, Sandro and Xenia spent much time together on the deck. Minnie, reluctant to lose her companionship, did not want Xenia to marry yet. Although she would grow to be fond of Sandro, she did not like him then. Nor did the emperor, who thought Sandro too restless and unready to settle down to career or marriage. He also did not like it that Sandro's mother, Cecilia, supposedly had Jewish blood. Many Romanovs, like most of their subjects, were intensely anti-Semitic. Another obstacle to the relationship was that Sandro was already a member of the family. Imperial marriages were customarily made outside, with foreign royalty. Perhaps that was the major motivation for Alexander III finally to allow the marriage: his distrust towards all foreigners.

After a naval cruise in 1893, Sandro finally approached the emperor to ask for Xenia's hand. Nicky, as Sandro's friend, helped to prepare the way, and the tsar finally surrendered. Xenia and Sandro settled down in St. Petersburg in a palace bought for them by the emperor. Spacious but ugly, it was located downtown on the dark part of the Moika Canal.

The couple traveled to Sandro's Crimean estate, Ai Todor (St. Theodore). The Ai Todor area marks the shortest distance (170 miles) between the northern shores of the Black Sea and the Turkish coast on the south. Strabo reports that Greek navigators could see both the Crimean and Anatolian shores simultaneously while crossing the sea here. The windswept cape forms the tip of a mountainous ridge extending back into the peninsula. Only juniper can survive the bitter winter winds. But farther back, the land is more sheltered and the vegetation becomes lush, even subtropical.

Here is where the Romanovs had chosen to build their palaces, not only Sandro but also Nikolasha, Peter, Dmitri Constantinovich and George Mikhailovich. The short rocky cape of Ai Todor has a shape resembling Neptune's trident. Looming above all, not very high, just 4,044 feet, but dominating and imposing, stands the sheer wall of Mount Ai Petri (St. Peter), commanding the spaces below. The face is a sheer drop into the water and the rocky surface radiates a strange reddish color on a sunny day. The two little bays formed by the prongs are deep, with water almost always churning at the small caves and grottos piercing the walls. At the eastern side of the trident sits a vertical rock isolated in the sea, shaped like a sail and called by that name. From the highest points of the cape, a viewer can see the town of Yalta, about five miles distant, a lacy white embroidery laid out on the slopes of blue mountains.

From Ai Todor Xenia wrote that she had not yet learned to live separately from her family and was tremendously happy that she could at least stay in Russia, having married a Russian royal. In the Crimea, Xenia and Sandro would spend much time collecting stones carved by the sea. Gawkers watched the romantic royal couple through binoculars, Xenia indignantly reported to her father. Romanovs were accustomed only to formal posed photographs or the snapshots they enthusiastically took of one another, not to an intrusive public.

Meanwhile the *tsesarevich* still divided his time between Anichkov Palace where his father was temporarily staying and the boudoir of his mistress, Kshesinskaya. But Nicky had fallen in love with Alix of Hesse and she with him. His routine would soon change, and Kshesinskaya would become a thing of the past.

The emperor was anxious to get his son married and, on the night of April 8th, news that Nicholas and Alix had become engaged reached St. Petersburg. Her pictures were immediately released for sale in stores. Minnie allegedly did not like her future daughter-in-law, and some said that the shape of Alix's mouth demonstrated a strong, but difficult personality. From the very beginning, the two imperial women felt themselves to be rivals. But they had other things to worry about: The tsar was increasingly unwell. After the train accident at Borki, the tsar was believed to have contracted a kidney disease. He refused to take his ailment seriously, and the physicians, including the famous Professor Zakharyin, complained that he would not follow their recommendations.

By January 1894, Alexander's disease had become serious. His brother Vladimir wept and said that everything was finished. The doctors determined that Alexander III was suffering from Bright's Disease, for which they had no cure, and they advised him to go to Corfu or Egypt where the climate was mild. "No," Alexander said, "a Russian tsar must die in Russia," and he went to Livadia. There he was attended by Professor Zakharyin and the best physicians. Zakharyin's own precarious health allowed him to make only a few steps without having to sit down and take a rest. A whole chain of chairs was therefore set up for the doctor so that he could reach the patient's bedside. The emperor steadily declined, losing appetite even for his favorite specially cooked dishes and falling into lassitude. As one onlooker put it, "It was like seeing a magnificent building crumbling."

When it became evident that even under the tender skies of Livadia there was no terrestrial hope, the emperor summoned a famous priest, John of Kronstadt, and on October 17th, the Reverend John gave communion to the emperor. John of Kronstadt was an appropriate confessor to the emperor, for he was as much the quintessential Russian priest as Alexander was the quintessential Russian tsar. "I heal the flesh and the soul," he proclaimed, and thousands flocked to the services of this staunchly monarchist and nationalist priest. He would "sharply and nervously, as if tearing each word from his heart" pronounce the prayers before the confession, and proclaim to the multitude, "Repent!" A great swell of shouts and sobs would rise and last for ten or fifteen minutes until Reverend John would say, "Not everyone has repented!" Again the response of the congregation, uniting in a single stream of dirge-like sound. Communion would then consume several hours, with so many people wanting to receive bread and wine from John's hands.

On his deathbed Alexander III had no special words, no guidance to offer to his terrified heir. Even when Nicky was making visits abroad or performing other duties for the state, the emperor had never given him any instruction. He was not going to change now, although Nicky hovered nearby.

The last night of the tsar's life, Minnie slept only from two till four A.M. Suddenly the patient felt worse. In the early morning, fitting his swollen body into his armchair, breathing with more and more difficulty, the emperor again took communion and repeated every word of the prayers, making the sign of the cross. He stretched out his hand to be kissed by the family surrounding him, and at the very moment he was presented with a glass of wine, he fell into eternal rest.

The servants were permitted to bid farewell to the late monarch. One by one they went to his bedroom. The tsar was still sitting in the armchair where he died, Maria Fedorovna embracing him. The servants each knelt, kissed his hand and departed. Then everyone gathered downstairs to take the oath of loyalty to Nicholas II. But the self-effacing and bewildered Nicky was never the awesome presence his father was at *his* father's, Alexander II's, deathbed.

The empress, completely exhausted by her long vigil at the bed of the dying man, looked as small and thin as a child. The family feared she too would die and blessed Heaven for her adored sister Alexandra, Princess of Wales, having traveled from Britain to be with her. Minnie wrote to her son George of his father on November 4, 1894, "Throughout my whole life I have been so happy that we had such a small age difference, and I always hoped I would die sooner than he would."

The tsar's first cousin, Olga of Greece, also present at the deathbed, would write to her brother, K.R., "The sun of the Russian Land has set down! . . . He has died just exactly as He lived in simplicity and piety; that's the way my sweet sailors die and the ordinary Russians as well." Even their cousin, sardonic Nicholas Mikhailovich, also present, was touched by the pathos of the death. Alexander III was only forty-nine.

The very day the emperor died, October 26th, even before the fatal news had reached the capital, a rumor spread in St. Petersburg that the army was about to proclaim Grand Duke Vladimir the emperor. Few had confidence in the heir's ability to assume his monumental new task. Nicholas himself shrank from the crown; others in the family would have grasped it greedily, and it seemed likely that the uncles, especially Vladimir and Sergei, would try to manipulate Nicky. And the Romanov women were even stronger than their men, even the two uncles. Alexander III had been the last strong Romanov tsar. Now the women had the strength and the will to command. But they would need to seize power in order to do so.

CHAPTER THREE

Nicholas II

FAMILY AND NATION, 1894–1904

O N NOVEMBER 7, 1894, Alexander III was laid to his final rest at Sts. Peter and Paul. The embalmers failed to preserve the body adequately for the nearly two weeks between death and burial that custom decreed for a dead tsar. They could hide the growing blackness of the hands by draping the body with a pall up to the shoulders. But they could do nothing about the head. The tsar's face above its beard now looked almost black and strangely small. It was unbelievable that this giant's formidable domelike head could have shrunk so much in death.

Foreign relatives gave the corpse the required kiss but shivered inwardly in revulsion, the odor of decay was so strong. And at the last of the protracted prescribed series of requiem masses, Minnie herself had broken down and cried: "Enough! Enough! Enough!" And yet, it seemed, everyone was reluctant to let him go.

Alexander III epitomized stability at a time when to the Romanovs change seemed grimly on the march. Despite his deficiencies, Alexander had controlled the family as harshly and effectively as he controlled the nation; his unexpected death radically transformed the center of power in the dynasty. The imperial persona, the prestige and power of the imperial office, remained intact, but a pygmy had replaced a giant.

The great rite of coronation of his son Nicky held in Moscow's Kremlin on May 14, 1895, splendidly reaffirmed the wealth, power and continuity of the Romanovs. But four days later, disaster struck. At Khodynka field outside the city, a crowd of hundreds of thousands gathered for the traditional celebratory distribution of free food, drink and souvenir mugs. Rumor swept the crowd that the supply was insufficient; in the resulting crush at least one thousand were trampled to death, including many women and children.

That night the French ambassador had scheduled a great ball in honor of the coronation, for which the French government had lent magnificent antique furniture and Gobelin tapestries. Grand Duke Nicholas Mikhailovich urged the new emperor not to attend. "Do not let the enemies of the regime say that the young Tsar danced while his murdered subjects were taken to the Potter's Field." The tsar vacillated, but his fear of offending the French finally outweighed his grief for the deaths of his subjects. He attended the ball and stayed until 2 A.M., although complaining to his diary that "the heat was unbearable."

The younger members of the family blamed the catastrophe on the new emperor's uncle, Grand Duke Sergei Alexandrovich, whom they already heartily disliked. As governor of Moscow, Sergei clearly bore responsibility for all the coronation arrangements. He did offer his resignation but the emperor refused to accept it. The new tsar's sister, Grand Duchess Olga, judged that the family criticism of Sergei "actually incriminated the whole family and that at a time when family solidarity among them was so essential. When Nicky refused to dismiss Uncle Sergei, they turned on him." The Khodynka nightmare lingered in popular memory even more intensely.

Yet during the first days of his reign Nicholas beguiled everyone with his good manners, modesty and seeming candor. "I know virtually nothing," he confessed. "The last sovereign did not foresee his death and did not let me into anything," which was of course quite true but not the entire story. The King of Denmark exclaimed, "My grandson is absolutely charming, he even demonstrates qualities nobody knew he possessed."

Nicholas's own political experience was so limited when he became emperor, and his eagerness to please so great, that he became easy prey to outside influences. Sergei Witte recalls in his memoirs that Alexander III had said to him, "Don't tell me you never noticed that the Grand Duke [Nicholas] is just a boy, with childish instincts." Leo Tolstoy thought Nicholas II a kind man with a good will. Real trouble, Tolstoy said, would come from the people who surrounded the tsar.

Tolstoy was right. Nicholas selected an entourage of mixed quality. A few were conscientious and able; others were opinionated, sometimes grossly ignorant and sometimes simply bizarre. The tsar seemed to have a special talent for selecting either self-serving or incompetent advisors; his only firmness seemed to be his defense of autocracy, consistently demonstrating the desire, if not the ability, to follow his father's conservative political course. People began to joke that the young tsar was like a feather pillow: He bore the impression of the last person to sit on him. K. R. confided to his diary, July 12, 1896, that "this tendency to agree with the last opinion voiced will probably get worse over the years. How painful, how sad, and how dangerous!"

The tsar's uncles, Vladimir and Sergei, as others in the family had anticipated, tried to dominate Nicholas from the start. Sandro, never shy about advancing his own causes with the emperor, said that the uncles were always pushing "their favorite generals and admirals, their favorite ballerinas, their wonderful preachers, their miraculous physicians, their clairvoyant peasants," all deserving, if not demanding, priority attention from the emperor.

Nicholas resisted, feeling obliged to reprimand Grand Duke Vladimir for using the imperial box at the Mariinsky Theater:

> I was especially hurt that you did it without any permission. Nothing of the kind ever happened in Papa's day, and you know how strictly I adhere to everything as it was then. It is also unfair to try and take advantage of the fact that I am young and your nephew. Please bear in mind that I have become Head of the Family and I have no right to turn a blind eye to the action of any member of the Family that I find wrong or inappropriate. More than ever our family needs to remain united and firm, in accordance with your grandfather's behests. And you ought to be the first to help me in this. In future, please spare me the necessity of writing such letters which make me feel abominable.
>
> with sincere love,
> your Nicky

But Nicholas never really learned how to handle these older, larger and formidable relatives, and only their deaths, one by one, removed the problem for him.

A power struggle between the dowager and her daughter-in-law the empress posed another problem for Nicholas. An empress dowager, according to Russian custom, took precedence over her daughter-in-law. Thus at court ceremonies, it was Minnie's place to walk on the arm of the emperor, not that of his wife. Minnie was young, not yet fifty, and healthy. Her normal high spirits soon returned. When in 1899 tuberculosis finally claimed the life of Grand Duke George, Nicky's brother, Minnie weathered this family tragedy as she had the death of Sasha. She did not retreat into a passive bereavement but retained a sturdy independence and showed a new and lively interest in politics. Minnie could be far more assertive with Nicky than she had been with Sasha.

Not at all financially dependent upon her son, the new emperor, Minnie maintained several estates of her own, and she seems to have employed able managers. In 1896 she spent 43,634 rubles on the Gdov estate, but took in 55,801 in revenues. She could indulge herself. She collected pictures, especially watercolors, etchings and engravings, owning in all more than four hundred pieces. And like all the Romanov women she collected jewelry.

Nicky gave his mother Fabergé Easter eggs. In 1895, the family's first Easter without their father, Nicky gave his mother an egg called "The Palaces of Denmark," in pink enamel with a cabochon sapphire ringed by diamonds on the top. Ten miniatures of Minnie's favorite palaces and yachts were inside the egg. A subsequent Easter would bring a pink enamel egg again, decorated with pearls, in the style of Louis XV. Inside the egg there were figures of two Africans carrying a sedan chair with Catherine the Great sitting in it. A twist of a key and the figures moved. The delighted Minnie reportedly said to Fabergé, "You are an incomparable genius!"

But Nicky had less and less time for his mother. Xenia, prodded by her mother, wrote to him plaintively: "You talk to Mama so seldom I know it upsets her. It seems to her that you avoid all conversation with her." In the competition for power at court, the dowager lost, in a classic struggle described by the Russian proverb as "the night-time cuckoo will always outcuckoo the daytime one."

Nicholas was a tender and devoted husband, and the intensity of the marriage seemed to shut out the possibility of other friendships, as well as any closeness with other members of the Romanov family. Nicky lost all his intimate friends and confidants. Nicky felt he could trust only Alix. Once an official reporting to the empress heard a whistle of a bird in the next room. "What kind of bird is that?" he asked. "That is the Sovereign calling for me," the empress replied, blushed, and ran to her husband. But more and more the empress was calling the tune.

❧

Even though she had been forced to separate from the young future emperor after his engagement to Alix, Nicholas's first love, Mathilde Kshesinskaya, now had another Romanov in thrall. Since 1895 she had been living with Grand Duke Sergei Mikhailovich. Step by step Kshesinskaya was becoming extremely influential, not simply in the ballet world but in the world of arts in general. For that she cultivated Romanov connections as vigorously as she could and continued to enjoy secret protection from the tsar.

At the theater, on April 15, 1901, Kshesinskaya changed her costume before a performance without informing her superiors and appeared on the stage in a tutu. Prince Sergei Volkonsky, the Director of the Imperial Theaters, imposed a fine on her, and he was shortly thereafter summoned to the emperor. Volkonsky complained about Kshesinskaya's desire to control the ballet world, only to be met with the menacing cold silence of his sovereign. Volkonsky then proudly asked to be relieved of his duties; the emperor immediately brightened up and dismissed him.

In February 1900, Vladimir and Miechen's sons Kyril and Boris had introduced their younger brother, Grand Duke Andrew, to Mathilde. She and he soon became intimate. The youngest of the three Vladimirovichi boys, Andrew felt repressed by Kyril's gloomy ambitions, Boris's flamboyance and the grand style of his parents. But he could reach out beyond them, and he was the only Vladimirovich who was on good terms with Nicky and the other Alexandrovichi. Andrew was the only one of the three Vladimirovichi brothers who had any apparent moral principles; one could trust Andrew. Pensive and rather shy, he relished strong women, mother figures. Unlike most of his cousins, he did not enjoy the company of men only, with the boistrous debauchery and carousing of such groups. He longed for a quiet family nest, and Kshesinskaya was ready to provide it for him.

But Grand Duke Sergei Mikhailovich, brother of Sandro and Bimbo, remained her special protector, even with Andrew in the picture, and for seventeen years thereafter Sergei accepted the menage-à-trois. Kshesinskaya seems even to have been able to weather the embarrassment of becoming pregnant. Both grand dukes believed her son Vladimir to be theirs, and perhaps even his mother was unsure who the father really was. After the baby's birth, Kshesinskaya returned triumphantly to the stage, dancing in Tchaikovsky's *Swan Lake* to immense acclaim. Prince Constantine Radziwill told Kshesinskaya that she ought to be proud to have two grand dukes at her feet. To which she replied, "What's surprising about that? I have two feet."

Andrew's elder brother Boris would carry their father Vladimir's fondness for playing the Parisian boulevardier to new heights. Boris was the greatest playboy of the last generation of grand dukes. His trips abroad became legendary; his escapades in doubtful taste. He drank in the company of spongers and whores. He ran up large debts. But Miechen, his mother, protected him from the wrath of the family. Boris was her darling. Of all the Romanovs, Boris, puffy-faced, cigar in the corner of his mouth, was the least conscientious and the least regal, his behavior more resembling that of a newly rich merchant than a grand duke, determined only to have a good time.

Twelve days spent in Paris in 1901 became just a blur of ladies' faces for Boris, with "actresses" prevailing. Mornings, after a spot of cognac, he and his friends would go to the Bois de Boulogne where the women in the group would work on the schedule for the day, mainly concentrating on the serious business of where to have lunch and where to dine. Dinner would of course be accompanied by music, and late at night the real fun would begin. Here the grand ducal military education would become useful for games such as turning a restaurant into a parade ground and executing impromptu infantry maneuvers, drafting other guests to participate.

In 1902, the jovial and increasingly stout Boris had visited the United States as part of a world tour. He would long be remembered in Chicago for drinking champagne from the satin slipper of a chorus member in *The Wizard of Oz* and tipping shopgirls with twenty-dollar bills. Among those who knew him, Boris was famous for his wild and unpredictable behavior. Yet even for Boris, this excess began to lose its appeal. He remarked sadly to his brother Kyril that after a while "every woman is the same, nothing is new except the face."

The Riviera became the favorite playground of the Romanovs. George, the only son of the widow of Alexander II, the Princess Yurievskaya, made himself conspicuous by tossing coins to the crowd during festivities held to honor the Russian fleet visiting Toulon. Miechen, and also Grand Dukes Sergei Mikhailovich and Andrew (the latter two accompanying Kshesinskaya), enthusiastically patronized the casinos at Monte Carlo. Andrew even bought a villa nearby.

Watching helplessly the frivolities of the grand dukes during the first years of his reign, Nicholas, seemingly incapable of stopping debauchery and fornication, did choose to exercise his power on the matter of morganatic marriages. In the fall of 1902, the tsar's youngest uncle, Grand Duke Paul, had actually run away to Paris, taking with him suitcases holding three million rubles. Paul suffered from periodic nervous breakdowns and never seemed able to put his life together in a constructive fashion. Now he had decided to marry a new love, his mistress, a divorcee, Olga Pistolkors, whom the family considered not only an outrageously inappropriate choice for Paul, but also an unattractively ambitious, even brazen woman. A commoner and, in the judgment of many, a "fornicator," she had appeared at a Winter Palace ball wearing diamonds bequeathed to Paul by his mother, the late Empress Maria Alexandrovna. Every Romanov recognized imperial jewels. Minnie demanded that Madame Pistolkors be expelled from the party and the chamberlain thereupon asked the woman to leave, causing an immense scandal. She was said to have Paul completely under her thumb.

When Nicholas heard the news that Paul had eloped, he exploded with rage. Paul had given his word he would not do so. Paul's brothers were also fiercely indignant. Vladimir wrote to Sergei: "He [Paul] has behaved shamelessly as a member of our family and as a military man. His behavior cannot be called anything but criminal. And to *her* I said plainly that if she will become the wife of my brother, I will turn my back on her and she will never in life see my face again. What will become of him? How will he be able to live the life of an outcast? What will become of the children? My heart is heavy, my head is empty. . . . I repeat to you that I am crying for help and I embrace you with my heart filled with sadness."

Minnie wrote to Nicky of her indignation. "He [Paul] has forgotten everything, all his fundamental obligations, his children, country, service, honour, everything, he has sacrificed everything for that stupid woman, who is not worthy of it. . . . He's simply throwing dirt at our family! Awful, awful!" Nicholas stripped Paul of his army rank and grand ducal income. Despite his exile in France, the millions he took with him ensured that Paul could live comfortably. His house in Paris became a center for the local Russian colony and his wife, now using the foreign title of Countess Hohenfelzen, could play a queenly social role, freely associating with members of the imperial family who were visiting France, so little were the laws of the family and the authority of Nicholas II respected.

The tsar wrote his mother about Paul: "How painful and distressing it all is and how ashamed one feels for the sake of our family before the world! What guarantee is there now that Kyril won't start the same sort of thing tomorrow and Boris or Sergei Mikhailovich the day after? And in the end, I fear, a whole colony of members of the Russian Imperial Family will be established in Paris with their semi-legitimate and illegitimate wives! God alone knows what times we are living in, when undisguised selfishness stifles all feelings of conscience, duty or even ordinary decency!" Other older members of the family also shook their heads and worried about the younger ones, who seemed only to want the royal life of luxury without accepting the responsibilities it should entail.

By the time of their father's elopement, Paul's two children, Maria and Dmitri, had been living for some years with their uncle and aunt, Sergei and Ella. Maria Pavlovna wrote guardedly much later that her uncle, Sergei, had a "unique personality" and remained "incomprehensible" to her. "Cold, inflexible, the world called him, and not without cause, but towards Dmitri and me he displayed a tenderness almost feminine," she recalled. Yet, even in the family, Sergei was a martinet for order, discipline and punctuality. His relationship with his niece and nephew never lost its tense uneasiness. Delay of even one minute in coming to the luncheon table would prompt a reprimand, even a punishment.

Aunt Ella, as the children called her, seems in the earlier years of her marriage to have been consumed largely by vanity; certainly she showed few intellectual interests. To the designing of her own clothing Ella brought to bear her talent for sketching, her sensitivity to color, and her understanding of the importance of ceremony in grand ducal life. She spent a lot of time poring over and clipping French fashion magazines. She showed little interest in her two wards and "saw as little of us as she could," her niece remembered.

> I recall one such time when she had dressed for an outing and seemed to me particularly beautiful. It was a simple dress of white muslin but she had her hair fixed a new way—gathered, unbound, at the back of her neck by a bow of black silk—and the effect was enchanting. I exclaimed: "Oh! Auntie, you look like the picture of a little page in a fairy story." She turned to my nurse without smiling and spoke in a dry, sharp tone: "Fry, you really must teach her not to make personal remarks."

Ella spent a good deal of time selecting and putting on her clothing, dressing her hair, selecting her jewels, all with the help of maids and a mistress of the wardrobe. Sometimes she would allow Maria Pavlovna to bring her the jewels for a particular occasion. Ella loved jewelry, and when she held a ball at her house in Moscow she might disappear at midnight in order to change into a fresh dress, enabling her to put on another set of jewels. Sergei liked to adorn his wife, and as a result she possessed one of the largest and best of the grand ducal collections of precious stones.

> One evening I remember, in those early days, I saw my aunt in court dress—majestic with her sweeping train of brocade, ablaze with jewels, and resplendently beautiful. Mute before the spectacle, I raised myself to the tips of my toes and placed a kiss full of devotion on the back of her white neck, directly under a magnificent necklace heavy with sapphires. She said nothing, but I could see her eyes, and the cold, hard look in them chilled me to the heart.

In Ella's defense, life with Sergei cannot have been emotionally easy. Increasingly she would find solace in religion.

Despite the peculiarities of the household, the children did have fun. Maria and Dmitri were extraordinarily close. The long summer days at Sergei's large wooden house at Ilinskoie near Moscow imprinted themselves deeply in their memories. The Moscow River, where the children could swim, flowed nearby the house, and from its banks, Maria Pavlovna recalled,

> came the lowing of cows, the bleating of sheep, and the cries of the village children who went in bathing with their beasts. In these cries heard afar, I find again all the atmosphere of Ilinskoie in summer. When I close my eyes on a hot day in July it seems to me that I can still hear them.

Everyone enjoyed exploring the woods in the search for berries and, after a rainfall, mushrooms. Ella would take her sketchbook and Sergei a book. He would read aloud while she drew. Great thunderstorms punctuated the heat of summer, shaking the house with the violence of their winds but bringing a welcome coolness in their wake.

Sometimes in the late afternoon the servants would harness horses to one of the carriages and the family would go to call on the neighbors for tea, perhaps at the Yusupovs, who had two sons, both older than Maria and Dmitri, but fun to play with; one of the Yusupovs, Felix, would become a great friend of Dmitri. Maria Pavlovna would enjoy irritating the grown-ups with wild rides in a pony cart and loud belches. Excursions were easy when the weather was fair and the condition of the roads good.

The children, told immediately of their father's elopement and consequent marriage, were devastated. The eleven-year-old Dmitri wrote to his father, "When we got your letter, we started crying awfully." The children, living with Uncle Sergei and Aunt Ella, felt abandoned and used their childish charms to try to get the empress dowager to persuade Nicky to allow their father to return, writing to her to say that "we are so sad and so grieved that our dear Papa cannot come back."

❧

But morganatic marriages were far from the most serious disruption that faced the world in which Maria Pavlovna was growing up. In her memory, "The landscape was everywhere the same, plain but smiling; vast fields of wheat, meadows covered with a sweet, tufted grass, with bell-flowers and daisies; forests of pine, oak, birch; and a few villages always looking alike, with their wooden hovels." But the Romanovs fled from reality. The grimness of Russian village life remained remote from the consciousness of these lords of the manor.

Russian aristocracy went to the country in the summer to enjoy cool weather on estates with swept gravel paths, ancient towering oaks, carefully tended flower beds. For these people of privilege this was the world of Turgenev's idyllic stories brought to life: clear streams, lush meadows, strands of greenish golden wheat springing out of the rich chocolate-colored earth. Their children could play in the orchards, swim, ride bicycles, ride horseback and join their elders in lavish picnics. But for the peasantry, summer was a time not for leisure but of hard work. The harvest had to be got in fast because the Russian summer is so short.

Peasant menfolk were less often around the great manor houses than were peasant women. The women might be hired by the day to work in the gardens or perhaps for the most menial tasks within the house. They sometimes sang as they worked and would banter with their employer's children, who were more able to communicate with them than were their elders. But peasant children seldom played with the children of the elite. The great houses formed their own isolated worlds.

The gentry lived their own lives, hardly noticing the peasantry. So detached were they from harsher realities that they could cultivate a sentimental myth of the happy farmer, working away in a pastoral scene, enjoying the rhythm of the seasons, marking the religious holidays with feast and celebration, and adoring his tsar in inarticulate awe.

But rich and poor spoke differently, dressed differently, thought differently. It was as if the poor were centuries behind the rich. In effect two nations, two cultures, existed in Russia: a tiny one of the rich and a vast one of the poor. An English member of Parliament visiting Russia in the 1890s remarked that "in no other great country in the world is poverty to so great an extent the national characteristic of the people." Russian peasant life compared badly with that of Western Europe, and most Russians were peasants. In good times the average Russian ate only one fourth what his American counterpart did. When crops were bad, he starved. Misery was profound and life, even at the best of times, marginal. The peasant had no stake in the system, no loyalty to it. He was doomed to a life he could not escape except by death.

One Russian traveler reports an autumn visit to a village in the province of Tula, not far from Moscow. The houses were crudely built log huts, patched together with dung, straw and clay.

We went in and could not stay more than a few minutes: soot and smoke hurt the eyes too much. None the less, we were able to observe enough. To the left of the door, on a wooden bunk thinly covered with dirty straw lay our driver's sick brother. . . . badly injured after a fall off a tree. . . . His young wife was looking after him. Some tattered children were lying on top of the stove. . . . To the right of the door two soldiers were having their supper of cabbage soup and water. . . . Our driver did not inquire after his brother . . . People just stared at u.s. . . . The stench and dirt were appalling.

Barefoot children with pinched faces and bellies distended from malnutrition gawked at visitors. Peasants rarely ate meat. Cabbage, onions, turnips and rye bread furnished the staples, but often there was not enough of these. Some houses were too poor even to have cockroaches.

Cattle and poultry often shared indoor space with humans and outside wandered freely through the streets, contributing to the filth and stench of the village. Overcrowding promoted rapid spread of common diseases such as diphtheria, typhus, dysentery, cholera and, of course, tuberculosis. Drinking water was often impure; intestinal parasites were legion. Syphilis raged and so did any ailment due to excessive drinking. Vodka, a state monopoly, provided common solace. The government enriched itself by making peasants—and workers—drunk. In the villages, along with squalor and drunkenness went ignorance and superstition, disgruntlement and a deep suspicion toward anyone in authority. Railroads were few and roads primitive, making the outside world so remote as to seem beyond any village understanding. In 1897 fewer than one Russian in five could read. Such was the bitter fruit of serfdom.

Interaction between the two classes was so limited that the rich were blithely ignorant of how the poor resented them, and the alienation of the elite class from the rest of Russia was increased by their foreign tastes and frequent travels and sojourns in Germany and France. Maria Pavlovna puzzled over why her family and the people around her showed so little concern for Russia's agrarian problem. Their travels abroad should have showed them that farmers in western Europe "lived in clean houses behind muslin curtains and their children were college graduates." But the Romanovs and most other aristocrats did not think about such things.

Russia had not only an agrarian problem but an urban problem too. The reforms of Alexander II and the stability provided by his son, Alexander III, had supported fast industrialization in Russia. Sergei Witte as finance minister had successfully promoted it. The chimneys of the new factories smudging city skies meant the presence of a new class of Russians, those who toiled in the factories. Hundreds of thousands of peasants moved to cities to become workers there.

Young Russian capitalism was greedy, and factories rose more quickly than safety codes, child labor laws or any regulations to protect the workers in them. World War II hero Marshal Georgy Zhukov grew up at the turn of the century, being sent from the countryside at age ten to work for a Moscow furrier. "Beggars got more money than we did," he remembered. The working day sometimes lasted for fifteen hours, never less than eleven. Workers slept on the shop floor and got thin soup to eat. Like the other boys, Georgy was mercilessly beaten by the furrier, his wife and the older workers. The boys did not complain; all workshop owners abused their apprentices. "That was the way things were supposed to be."

The result of the new factories was a growing group of ill housed, underfed, underpaid and angry people. The urban mortality rate, especially among infants, was so high that the Russian working class would have disappeared without the constant human influx from the countryside. The rage of the cities therefore came to match the rage of the countryside. War and defeat would set a match to that rage. It began in the Far East.

The future Nicholas II first became interested in "the Orient" in May 1881, soon after his grandfather's assassination. The Empress Maria Fedorovna had invited the famous Russian explorer, Nicholas Przhevalsky, to Gatchina Palace to give several lessons to the thirteen-year-old Nicky. Przhevalsky had spent years traveling in the remote steppes, deserts and mountains of the Asian heartland where Mongolia, Tibet and Central Asia meet. He was a scientist who named animal species after himself and, so rumor had it, he was also a Russian intelligence agent used as a player in "the great game" fought with the British across Eurasia. Przhevalsky had ignited in Nicholas's heart some interest in vast and wonderful Asia, dangling the possibility of

Russia stretching out to rule all the non-Chinese people of northern Eurasia.

Przhevalsky's vision of empire in the east seized many Russians at the turn of the century. Nicholas II inherited from his father an unusual character who for years showered both of them with memoranda on Russian expansion in Asia. His name was Peter Badmaev. He called himself a Tibetan healer, and his popularity in high society may have been related to the fact that he was a distributor of exotic drugs. Some suspected that he was able to manipulate people by feeding them with these special medicines. Badmaev perceived himself as an apostle of Russian expansion in Asia, and both Nicholas II and his father regarded him with a mixture of suspicion and fascination.

In February 1893, Badmaev sent a long memorandum to the emperor pointing out that if, in the past, alien peoples had frequently ruled over China, why could the Russians not do so? Alexander III had responded sceptically, "This is all so new and fantastic that one can hardly believe in the possibility of success."

After the father's death, Badmaev shifted to the far more susceptible son, perceiving that Nicholas was a romantic, a daydreamer, with a special attachment to Asia. Badmaev tempted the young tsar with the idea that it would be possible for Russia to secure influence in Mongolia, Tibet and parts of China without a military occupation, merely by supplying the Mongols with modern weapons, and Badmaev asked the tsar for a grant of two million rubles to finance his scheme.

By this time Nicholas had experienced his own Orient. Driven by his personal interest in the Far East, Alexander III had chosen it as the destination of his son's "coming of age" tour. Sending the heir to the throne on a trip abroad after completing his education was a Russian royal tradition, but Nicholas was the first Russian prince of the blood to be sent to East Asia.

On his sea journey eastward he passed along the edge of the continent, the land core of which was entirely dominated by his father's tsardom. His westward journey home across Siberia gave him a sense of the huge potential of that land. Such a journey inevitably left a strong imprint upon a young man, especially because it had been his first such trip.

Nicholas seems to have learned little of substance from this great experience. His diary shows scant intellectual curiosity about the peoples and cultures to which he was exposed, and this was a major opportunity lost. But perhaps it was then that Nicholas had got the first vague idea that his future glory, his mission, was to be connected with the Far East. Witte would later remark, "The emperor wanted to spread the influence of Russia towards the Far East, he got carried away by the idea because he had become free for the first time in his life during his trip to the Far East. But of course at that time he did not have any definitive program, only a spontaneous desire to move toward the Far East and to seize its territories."

The ugly episode in which Nicholas had been attacked and wounded by a Japanese fanatic remained in his memory and colored his attitude toward the Japanese. This is what he remembered, not the extraordinary strides the Japanese had made toward building a modern state. His diary entries show that every year thereafter Nicholas quietly celebrated the anniversary of the assault as a day when he had been saved by God. Nicholas was not simply a deeply religious, even mystical, person. Perhaps he then associated that brush with death in Japan with God's plan for him, connecting his life in an esoteric way with the eastern boundaries of his empire.

Reality gave some substance to the dreams of Badmaev and Nicholas. In the late nineteenth century, Russia as a nation rediscovered its Far East because economic development was demanding new space and new resources. More and more Russians were moving eastward across Siberia.

In 1884 Nicky had met for the first time his German cousin, Willy, the future Kaiser Wilhelm II, who did all he could to encourage Nicholas's interest in East Asia. Germany wanted Russia fully occupied there, not in Europe. Four years before his ascension to the German throne in 1888, the young Willy had visited St. Petersburg to celebrate Nicky's coming of age party. Willy found the giant tsar, Alexander III, his towering brothers and the opulence of the Winter Palace to be almost overwhelming. The Prussian court had always been a humble one, and Willy's grandfather had amazed Emperor Alexander I by admitting that neither he nor his family had ever seen a lobster. Willy found even the food served at Alexander's court "excellent," a judgment few would share considering that monarch's frugality. But despite the awe Willy had for his Russian experience, he would attempt to manipulate his younger cousin, the future tsar, throughout their relationship. Willy was particularly anxious for the tsar to focus his attention on East Asia and away from Europe.

In September 1895, Willy sent an engraving to Nicky (made by a German artist using the kaiser's own sketch) depicting a sinister Buddha looming darkly on the horizon, with Germany and Russia standing watchfully as the Christian guardians of peace. The engraving was accompanied by a letter in which Willy suggested they unite to crush "Buddhism, paganism and barbarism." Later, after a meeting with the tsar, in June 1897, when the royal yachts parted, Willy ran up the signal: "The Admiral of the Atlantic welcomes the Admiral of the Pacific." The enraged Nicholas, who hated being treated as a little brother, replied curtly, "Bon voyage," and whispered, "He should be locked up in a madhouse."

Nicky's brother-in-law and childhood friend Sandro was also a strong proponent of expansion in the Far East. In May 1895, he raised a toast at the Naval Club to the attainment for Russia of an ice-free port there. Sandro promoted what he perceived to be Russia's East Asian commercial as well as strategic interests. Influenced both by an army officer, Alexander Bezobrazov, who was dismissed by his own wife as "insane," and also by monetary and political ambitions, Sandro suggested to the tsar in the spring of 1898 that he buy forestry concessions abroad in Korea, along the valley of the Yalu River, where timber could easily be floated out and sold. The tsar thereupon ordered Witte in January 1903 to finance the project with a credit of two million rubles.

This would be the first step toward disaster, a war with Japan in 1904–05. In China's northeast, Russia had already occupied the Liaotung peninsula. There lay Port Arthur, a major naval base, built by the Chinese with foreign capital and briefly occupied by Japan after its triumph over China in 1894–95. Vladivostok, Russia's largest Far Eastern seaport, did not provide year-round free access to blue water.

Nicholas waffled. On the one hand he was saying that he did not want war. On the other, he was backing Russian investment in Korea and the absorption of Manchuria, China's northeast. Japan was ready to fight Russian expansion. The diplomatic clash between the two nations in Manchuria and Korea finally came to the boiling point on January 25, 1904, when the St. Petersburg public was informed that Russia and Japan had recalled their envoys from each other's capital. Grand Duke Andrew wrote in his diary: "What will happen tomorrow, only God knows—blood or peace."

❧

In the early hours of January 27th, Nicholas at the Winter Palace received a telegram sent by his Viceroy of the Far East, Admiral Alexeev, at 4:30 A.M., Port Arthur time. "Around midnight of January 26th–27th, Japanese destroyers undertook a sudden torpedo attack on our squadron stationed at the outer roadstead of Port Arthur base. The battleships *Retvizan* and *Tsesarevich* and the cruiser *Pallada* have been holed, the degree of the damage is being examined."

About 1 A.M., the Foreign Minister, Count Vladimir Lamsdorf, was awakened in his apartment. Holding the telegram from Port Arthur, still in his dressing-gown, Lamsdorf said in disgust, "Now they've done it!" Lamsdorf had in mind not the Japanese but the tsar and his advisors.

Later in the day, at 3:30 P.M., the whole imperial family gathered in the Golden Hall of the Winter Palace, and at 4 o'clock they proceeded to the palace chapel. Grand Duke Andrew was struck by the idea that most of the Romanovs present, including himself, had never heard the special mass then sung, a prayer to God for victory. A new generation had grown up who had never experienced war—Alexander III's reign had secured peace for a quarter of a century. Yet the young Romanovs were confident that "God will not let a pagan trample upon an Orthodox country."

On January 28th, churches all over the country offered masses for victory in the new war. In Moscow, Grand Duke Sergei took Maria and Dmitri to the Uspenskii Cathedral in the Kremlin, where the manifesto declaring war was proclaimed. The cathedral was packed and the children were thrilled. However, Sergei was enraged that some Moscow students, ever hostile to government suppression of political liberties, were demonstrating. Instead of showing their patriotism, these "rascals" were "supporting the Japanese!" he fumed.

When the nation went to war, Grand Duke Kyril set what people said was a noble example for the rest of the men in the Romanov family by volunteering for action as a junior officer in the navy. But Kyril, lean, haughty, with melancholic eyes, had more than patriotism in mind. He wanted to become a hero. Should anything happen to Nicky, his closest male relative would become tsar. Kyril was third in the line of succession.

First, of course, stood an Alexandrovich. With the death of the tubercular Grand Duke George, Grand Duke Michael, youngest brother of the emperor, had become the heir. After Michael stood the tsar's uncle Vladimir, Kyril's father. The empress had thus far given birth only to girls—four of them.

Alix had always been strongly religious. Having abandoned her German Lutheranism to marry Nicky, she became Orthodox with the overwhelming zeal of the convert. She learned not the faith of modern Russian religious philosophers or learned prelates but that of the superstitious peasantry, fervently embracing self-proclaimed prophets, village saints and miracle-working icons. She became peculiarly vulnerable to religious charlatans.

Desperately wanting a son and heir, before 1904 Alix had unsuccessfully resorted to the services of various mystics. She then decided to create her very own saint to whom she would appeal for help. She insisted on the canonizing of Seraphim of Sarov, a visionary and healer of the earlier nineteenth century who had talked with the Virgin Mary. In July 1903, Alix went to Sarov and bathed at night in the saint's holy spring. She became pregnant again three months later.

Kyril could hope at best that the fifth child would also be a girl, keeping him as third in the line of succession. The vision of a crown lying just beyond his grasp tormented him. Consumed by malice and envy, Kyril was isolated in his rage. Other branches of the family did not like him; he never made friends with his cousins. Miechen had chosen a sailor's career for Kyril but, unlike his cousin Sandro, also a navy man, he disliked the navy and its routine intensely and put out to sea from St. Petersburg only grudgingly.

During Kyril's naval career, Nicholas was wary of the grand duke's pretensions. Therefore he secretly issued orders to the naval authorities designed to reduce Kyril's prestige: the grand ducal flag was to be flown only with the special permission of the emperor, the officers were to salute Kyril only when ashore, and the captain of the ship, not Kyril, would rank first. The ship's captain was to inform the local authorities of places visited that Kyril was traveling only as a naval lieutenant, and that he had no right to make official visits or to give or attend official receptions. While aboard ship, Kyril was to be considered equal to other officers of his rank, performing the same duties as such officers, with the exceptions of taking the crew ashore and the physical labor of loading coal and food.

Nonetheless in 1904, not only politics but also romance made Kyril long for military distinction. He had fallen in love with Princess Victoria Melita of Great Britain, known in a family of many Victorias as "Ducky." Ducky was a granddaughter of Queen Victoria, and her father was Prince Alfred of Edinburgh, Queen Victoria's second son. Her mother, Marie of Coburg, was a sister of Emperor Alexander III and of Kyril's father Vladimir. Ducky was tall, statuesque, but with too little chin to be conventionally beautiful. At the same time she had a good figure, deep blue eyes and dark complexion.

Kyril and Ducky were first cousins, and the Orthodox Church forbids marriage between first cousins. Another strike against their marriage was that Ducky had recently divorced her first husband, Ernst Ludwig of Hesse-Darmstadt, who was the brother of Alix, the empress. Ducky's marriage with Ernie seems to have been doomed from the start, as the couple were incompatible. Ducky loved horses; Ernie feared them. The only thing he seemed to have liked about the stables was the handsome young boys who worked there. Ernie was artistic. Although Ducky was an enthusiastic painter, she never took art seriously. Instead Ducky was attracted to politics and found the routines of court life in Darmstadt to be increasingly boring and intolerably confining.

But for a royal princess at that time to leave her husband for another man, regardless of cause, was scandalous. Much as Ducky chafed, divorce was unthinkable, at least while Queen Victoria was still alive. After the old queen's death, however, Ducky left her husband and sued for divorce. When it became apparent soon afterwards that Kyril and she wished to marry, both Nicholas II and especially his wife were appalled. Alexandra had never liked her cousin Ducky; the divorce, for which she blamed Ducky totally, simply made matters worse.

Kyril therefore would have two strikes against him when he went to the emperor, as he eventually must, for imperial permission to wed. In the meantime he returned from Germany to St. Petersburg where he assumed, in Grand Duchess Xenia's words, "a languid expression of persecuted innocence." Nicky's sister believed that "the only honorable thing for him to do—is to marry her and take the corresponding punishment, but he doesn't want to do that!" Now Kyril hoped that his going to the front would improve his standing with the tsar.

Kyril's departure ceremony at the Nikolaevsky railway station hardly pleased Nicholas: The Preobrazhensky regiment, Russia's most prestigious, was there in all its magnificence; other elite units and crowds of people had also come to say farewell to the young "hero." Amidst the enthusiastic shouts, many thrust small icons into Kyril's hands. His brother Boris would later depart for the front, with a similarly grand ceremony. The commander of the Pacific fleet, Admiral Stepan Makarov, had appointed Kyril to be a staff officer of the fleet, to report aboard the flagship *Petropavlovsk*. The officers at Port Arthur grumbled about such an important assignment being given to someone of such limited professional experience.

Nicholas too wanted to go to the front but could not. He believed that a tsar's rightful place was with his troops, but his generals and advisors disagreed. Reluctantly he acceded to their wishes.

At eleven o'clock in the morning of March 31, 1904, Grand Duke Boris hastily galloped up to the heights of Dacha Hill, on the rim of Port Arthur town. He abruptly stopped his horse and stared at the sea far below. Then he sobbed, rocking in the saddle, took out a handkerchief and buried his face in it. The battleship *Petropavlovsk*, his older brother Kyril aboard, had exploded and sunk.

The Russians had received the news that a Japanese fleet was approaching Port Arthur. Eagerly Admiral Makarov had put to sea in order to give support both to a Russian cruiser previously sent out to reconnoiter and to a flotilla of torpedo boats returning to harbor from a night patrol. When the admiral saw that the Japanese ships would far outgun and outnumber the Russians, he decided that the best tactic would be to withdraw his ships to the shelter of their base and the protective fire of the guns of its shore batteries. Flying Makarov's flag, at 9:53, *Petropavlovsk* suddenly experienced an explosion on her starboard side.

Kyril was standing on the bridge of the battleship when a second and more violent explosion burst under his feet. A huge column of black, brown and greenish smoke and flame soared to a height of two hundred feet, engulfing the ship and sending bits of guns, engines and crew whirling in the air like a monstrous tornado. When the smoke partially cleared, observers on shore could see the hull of the ship already stern high and half under water, her bow nosing into the sea.

The force of the explosions had blown off the bridge, the foremast, the funnels and the bow turret. The hot boilers, hit by a flood of cold sea water, had then burst, sending forth a dense cloud of steam; the ship's propeller was still revolving, with its naked, murderously sharp blades menacing those few crew members who had managed to jump overboard or had been blown there. *Petropavlovsk* was surrounded by leaping flames, and in less than two minutes the sea seemed to open and it sank bow downwards. The water was coated with coal dust. Human howling filled the air; the sea itself seemed to be moaning, as scores of dazed survivors struggled to grab bits of floating woodwork in order to stay afloat in the cold water. *Petropavlovsk* carried no lifeboats.

Almost miraculously Kyril survived by clutching a drifting piece of one of the ship's boats. He later wrote that what had saved him was his clothing:

> . . . it was bitterly cold, and the water, incidentally, was just a few degrees above zero. I was dressed in a padded coat, underneath which I had a fur-lined jacket and an English woolen sweater. This very likely gave me some buoyancy, otherwise I would have gone to join the rest of the six hundred and thirty-one who perished.

Ultimately only fifty-three people survived the catastrophe. The mortality rate from the sinking of *Petropavlovsk* was heavy because most men were at their battle stations at the time the ship was hit. They were stunned, badly wounded or killed by the explosions, or they drowned immediately thereafter in the rapid sinking of the ship. Worse yet was the loss of Russia's most respected admiral, Makarov, a gifted leader, who inspired great admiration and devotion from his men. All that would ever be found of Makarov was his greatcoat, recognizable by its shoulder tabs, floating on the surface of the water.

Boris, standing on the hilltop, was convinced from the horror of the scene that Kyril could not possibly have survived. Then he received the deliriously happy news that his brother had been plucked alive from the water by the destroyer *Besshumny*. On board Kyril was brought to the captain's cabin, dressed in dry clothing and put to bed, still unconscious. Once ashore, regaining consciousness, Kyril fell into hysteria and was taken to Boris's train, where physicians applied ice to his head. The doctors feared Kyril would have a nervous breakdown; the train pulled out of Port Arthur, heading north and west to Moscow.

Boris sent a telegram home. The message reached the Vladimirovichi the same day, March 31st, around 9 o'clock in the morning. The family did not know what to do, whether to rejoice or to mourn. Kyril was miraculously saved; almost everyone else had perished. The Vladimirovichi went to church for a thanksgiving mass, and at a lunch afterwards, Aunt Minnie herself offered her sympathies.

But when Kyril returned to St. Petersburg shortly thereafter, he failed to make a courtesy call upon the tsar, and the Minister of Court had to remind him that it was his duty both as an aide-de-camp and a grand duke to do so. Earlier Kyril's father Vladimir had asked Nicky to let Kyril go abroad to recover after the *Petropavlovsk* disaster. The tsar was appalled: "To go abroad at such a time!"

The war continued to go badly for Russia, but the entire nation could celebrate when the guns of Sts. Peter and Paul fired a twenty-one gun salute on July 30, 1904, signifying the birth of a long-awaited son to the imperial couple. Baby Alexis would now be the *tsesarevich*. Nicky's younger brother, Misha, the Grand Duke Michael Alexandrovich, was "radiant with happiness at no longer being heir." Misha had no more appetite for power than had Nicky but Misha, it seemed, would be spared the awful responsibility of tsardom.

❧

Neither the war nor the growing social tensions provoked by it prevented the Romanovs from happily indulging themselves in an important royal function, patronizing the arts. The reign of Nicholas II became an age of bold experimentation for Russians in all of the arts. Although the emperor remained rigidly conventional, a new sense of liberation grasped the grand dukes as it did so many others. The *fin de siècle* decadent lifestyle, spearheaded by artists revolutionizing traditional forms, seemed appealing and exciting, with the sternly disapproving father-figure of Alexander III now gone. Suddenly authority could be successfully challenged—artistic and moral authority first, but political authority would come next.

For most of the Romanovs, knowledge of the arts began and ended with ballet, but the family prized Vladimir Serov, the best Russian impressionist, whose work demonstrated the influence of Corot and Cezanne. Serov's break with the Russian realists did not dismay the Romanovs; Serov would paint a number of Romanov portraits. In 1893 he painted Xenia, Michael and Olga; Olga was then just a child in a pink dress, her golden hair flowing loosely, like the Velasquez portraits of Spanish infantas. In 1895 Serov painted a picture commissioned by the nobility of the city of Kharkov to commemorate the Borki train crash of 1888. When Nicholas II saw the picture, the tsar, whose view of impressionism was conventional, said to Serov, "But the painting is not yet finished." Nonetheless Serov would later execute Nicholas's portrait as well.

Sergei Diaghilev, most famous for his brilliant work as a shaper of the ballet theater, promoted the arts in general enthusiastically. He organized an exhibition of historical Russian portraits at the Tauride Palace in St. Petersburg, opening in February 1905 but reflecting years of extremely thorough preparation.

Grand Duke Nicholas Mikhailovich was instrumental in putting on the exhibition at the Tauride. The grand duke was known to the family humorously and affectionately as "Uncle Bimbo," a word not at all carrying its current English meaning. He was the only older person in the family whom the younger generation sincerely liked as a friend. His purse as well as his advice were always at their disposal. Uncle Bimbo in turn cherished these family friendships; his was a lonely life. He never married but had many liaisons—with men as well as with women, although unlike his cousin, Sergei Alexandrovich, he did not allow these tastes to become public knowledge.

Uncle Bimbo was one of the few Romanovs to have any serious intellectual interests and the only one to pursue the study of history. Professional historians acknowledged that his work on the reign of Alexander I, his great uncle, was excellent. But his chief desire was to shock the family and the social elite. "Dry and sardonic," his cousin K.R. called him. Too cynical to be attracted to religion, Bimbo became a freemason and declared he was a socialist.

The grand duke delighted in unconventional dress as well as unorthodox behavior. He would drive around town in a shabby hired *drozhky* (horse cab), cigar planted in his mouth, slouch hat pulled down low on his head. He relished gossip and wit. His relentless carping about Nicholas and Alexandra was widely repeated and damaged not only the imperial couple but also the dynasty itself. Alexandra would write her husband that Bimbo was one of "my greatest enemies in the family."

Bimbo denounced monarchy but relished all the perquisites of being a grand duke, conspicuously losing enormous sums at the gambling tables of Monte Carlo or flourishing his diamond-encrusted gold cigarette case in the company of dazzled, poverty-stricken writers, composers and artists. Within the family, Bimbo's self-chosen role was that of the wit, even the buffoon, an aging *enfant terrible*. Bimbo could not be a statesman; he could not be a truly important person. But he could be notorious. Like all grand dukes, he was nominally at least a military officer, in his case a general in the army; a Romanov was still obliged to conform to conventional expectations of leadership. But Bimbo always chose the unconventional when he could; the arts formed a realm in which he could lead.

The Tauride Palace was the place he chose for Diaghilev's show, in which St. Petersburg was presented with a stunning visual document of Russia's historical past. Diaghilev was not satisfied to show well-known works hanging in St. Petersburg or Moscow palaces; he combed the countryside and cultivated an encyclopedic knowledge of his subject, working in libraries and government archives, advertising for information, and finding pictures from abroad and from obscure country houses. Diaghilev would assemble nearly three thousand paintings for the great exhibition.

The celebrated artist Leon Bakst, who also did ballet scenery, created the gallery backgrounds, each dedicated to one of the reigning monarchs of the Romanov house. Every ruler was honored by a full length portrait, hung beneath a canopy and surrounded by pictures of his (or her) advisors and ministers. Much later Diaghilev would vividly describe to the English writer Osbert Sitwell the sinister atmosphere of the room dedicated to the mad Emperor Paul, murdered by his own courtiers in 1801. Nicholas II and other Romanovs came to the Tauride, and we have a report from Diaghilev of their reaction to it. The tsar was interested in history, and yet on this occasion he said nothing. Perhaps, Diaghilev mused, "He might have seen in the faces of his ancestors bitter reproaches and terrible warnings of approaching disaster."

The exhibition proved to be far more of a historical punctuation mark than the pompous celebration of the three hundredth anniversary of the founding of the Romanov dynasty, which would take place with much fanfare in 1913. Diaghilev later spoke at a Moscow banquet held in his honor and startled his audience by boldly asking, "Don't you feel that this long gallery of portraits of big and small people that I brought to live in the beautiful halls of the Palais Tauride is only a grandiose summing-up of a brilliant, but, alas! dead period in our history? . . . The end of an era is revealed here, in those gloomy dark palaces. . . . Here are ending their lives not only people, but pages of history."

CHAPTER FOUR

✥

A Faltering Monarchy

1905–1914

ON JANUARY 6, 1905, the Romanovs were standing on the granite embankment outside of the Winter Palace, celebrating the annual ritual of consecrating the waters of the Neva. During the customary artillery salute, one of the large guns across the river mistakenly fired caseshot instead of blanks. Bullets hit the ice on the river, the embankment and the facade of the Winter Palace itself, breaking four windows and wounding one policeman. Workers were striking; the public mood had been stormy; and the Romanovs for a while suspected an assassination attempt.

The next day, Grand Duke Andrew, watching mobs in the street from his palace on the English Embankment, wrote peevishly in his diary, "The workers' strike deprived me of electricity. A loud crowd passed through Gallernaya Street." Three days following, on Sunday, servants awoke the grand duke at 9 A.M. to inform him that soldiers of the guard had arrived to protect his house. The grand duke greeted the troops himself, then he went out to attend mass and was shocked to see the entire city full of soldiers. Patrols stood at the bridges and street corners, and completely surrounded the Winter Palace.

At 2 P.M., a large number of workers, carrying portraits of Nicholas II, had gathered at the square in front of the Winter Palace asking the sovereign to talk to them. When they refused to disperse, the troops opened fire. That day, "Bloody Sunday," January 9, 1905, St. Petersburg saw hundreds killed and thousands wounded.

Bloody Sunday destroyed the ancient myth of the Good Tsar as protector of the common people against the evils of the state and ushered in what Minnie would call a year of nightmares. Nicholas II, failing to grasp that a profound shift in public opinion had happened, moved himself and the Romanovs one more step toward political extinction. The first Romanov to pay the price was the Grand Duke Sergei Alexandrovich.

The outbreak of war with Japan had found Sergei, Ella and their two wards in Moscow. Ella and her ladies began to work intensively, rolling bandages and organizing nursing for the wounded. Sergei, whom everyone knew to be highly unsympathetic to political reform, had for this reason become a target for terrorists and he knew it. One of them, Boris Savinkov, wrote, "He was running scared, changing palaces, trying to avoid a death that was already inescapable, already creeping up on him." Even though Sergei had now retreated to a palace within the fastness of the Kremlin itself, he was not safe. He could not simply stay there unless he were to forego a normal life.

On February 4, 1905, shortly after Sergei had left the palace, Ella heard a sharp explosion outside near the Spassky Gate. Fearing the worst, she rushed out to find that a bomb, thrown from a distance of four feet, had blown her husband to pieces. This event had been planned to take place earlier but the terrorist, seeing the two children, Dmitri and Maria, riding in Sergei's carriage, found it impossible to throw the bomb.

Now the assassin was struggling with the police, crying, "Down with the tsar! Long live revolution!" As a crowd gathered, Ella herself attempted to gather the pieces of clothing and bits of flesh flecking the snow with crimson. She later recalled that at the time she had but one thought: "To collect all that as quickly as possible. Sergei hated blood and mess so much!"

One of the persons who heard the explosion was a young boy, Boris Pasternak, who would later write a poem about it:

> It is snowing hard.
> Snowfall in the night.
> By the morning

it clears.
A peal of thunder
Arrives from the Kremlin and rolls.
The trustee of my school . . .
Sergei Alexandrovich . . .
He is going . . .
On that day
I started to love thunderstorms.

The bell of Chudov Monastery began to toll as Ella followed a stretcher carrying all that could be found of her husband's body back to the palace. That night, her stunned wards, Maria and Dmitri, whispered together. "What do you think," Dmitri asked. "Will we be . . . happier?"

About two hours before dinner, the news reached Peterhof, the palace on the Baltic shore where the emperor was staying. Nicholas had invited a visiting Prussian prince to dine; he came and the news did not alter the mood. No one mentioned the murder. After dinner, to the amazement of the royal guest, Nicky and his brother-in-law Sandro "amused themselves by trying to push each other off the long narrow sofa."

The next day, February 5th, in St. Petersburg the weather was at its worst. Daytime snowfall had changed into icy rain and fog. At 7:30 the whole Romanov family except Nicky, Alix and Minnie went to church for a requiem mass. The emperor was advised that it would be safer for him not to leave Peterhof.

Despite Nicky's behavior at the dinner party, all the family were shocked at Sergei's violent death. No Romanov had been killed since March 1, 1881. Members of the dynasty who could not even remember that terrible event were now in their mid-twenties. Most alarming was that now it seemed grand dukes as well as emperors were potential targets for bombs.

But Sergei's death was merely one episode in what had become a spontaneous and random revolutionary upheaval. Strikes, arson and killings erupted out of anger at the Romanov monarchy. Many groups saw 1905 as a golden opportunity to grab power and attempted to exploit revolutionary elements to build their own political prominence.

The radicals were divided into two core groups: the Socialist Revolutionaries (SRs) and the Bolsheviks, the latter in 1905 already led by

Vladimir I. Lenin. Terror and the violent liberation of the peasantry formed the major pillars of the SR program. The Bolsheviks tried to influence the urban workers, the "proletariat." Being good Marxists, the Bolsheviks believed that the proletariat was the engine of history but that it required the enlightened guidance of professional revolutionaries. Bolshevik success was only partial; the workers in most cases acted on their own. The most dramatic episodes of the revolution happened unstaged by any political party, and Russia seemed to fall under the law of the mob, slipping into social as well as political chaos, the public increasingly indifferent to crime and even murder.

But the Black Sea fleet shocked the nation. In June 1905, the crew of the battleship *Potemkin* mutinied. Excited by revolution in the city, sailors had begun to seethe with wrath toward their officers. On a day when they were given rotten meat, crawling with maggots, they began to riot. Raising the red flag, the crew tossed some of their officers overboard to drown, killing others on board. Sailing to Odessa, the sailors tried to coordinate their revolt with the revolutionaries there, to set the southern steppes of Russia ablaze with revolutionary fire. The upheaval resulted in a massacre on the Odessa waterfront, carried out by troops loyal to the government.

Potemkin put to sea, trying to land her crew in a Crimean port, either Feodosia or Yalta, and finally fleeing to Constanza in Romania and surrendering there. But *Potemkin* would become a powerful icon of revolution, and naval mutiny seemed to be infectious. Nicholas II angrily wrote in his diary, "Only the devil knows what is happening to the Black Sea fleet." A few months later, in November, a revolt broke out in the Sevastopol squadron. Again, sailors themselves initiated the uprising, and one officer even participated.

The treason of a naval officer, the navy being the special pride of the dynasty, seemed especially outrageous to the Romanovs. The empress dowager, normally not a bloodthirsty person, begged Nicky from her Danish retreat not to spare the life of "this scoundrel."

The struggle shifted to the smaller provincial cities and the countryside. Strikes paralyzed urban life and peasants went on a rampage of looting and burning. Thousands of rich landowners in the heart of Russia lost their manor houses to the mob. Rumor had it that the tsar's yacht was ready to take him and his family to safety in Denmark.

War continued to rage in the Far East, with no news of Russian victories. On May 27, 1905, in the straits of Tsushima separating Japan from Korea, in one of the most decisive battles in world history, the Japanese virtually annihilated the Russian Baltic fleet. Survivors described with horror giant battleships capsizing, looking like bleeding whales in the rays of sunset, with hundreds of seamen, trapped inside the narrow pitch-dark passageways and compartments slowly filling with water, dying in unimaginable agony.

Tsushima meant that the war with Japan was over for Russia. Incredibly, it seemed that the Japanese had triumphed over the Russians; a parvenu—from the European perspective—Asian nation for the first time in modern history defeating a major European power. Russia sank into profound humiliation, and the Russian people blamed the emperor for that humiliation. Street fights convulsed Moscow.

Theodore Roosevelt brokered a peace conference, held in Portsmouth, New Hampshire, in the late summer of 1905. Sergei Witte, now the nation's leading statesman, arrived home from negotiating there a brilliant settlement for Russia; despite the defeat, Russia paid no indemnity and lost only a small amount of territory.

The energetic and competent Witte was the obvious choice to lead the nation out of chaos. He presented two recommendations to the emperor concerning the growing domestic crisis: either set up a military dictatorship and crush all opposition, or grant the people a parliament with legislative powers. Witte himself, although reluctantly, greatly favored the latter. A constitution, he said, or "rivers of blood." The British historian Sir Bernard Pares relates that Witte told him, "'I have a constitution in my head; but as to my heart'—and he spat on the floor."

Not liking either choice—even less hearing them presented by Witte, whom he had long disliked—the emperor consulted other advisors, including his older cousin, the energetic and excitable Grand Duke Nicholas Nikolaevich (Nikolasha), with whom he would soon replace Grand Duke Vladimir as commander of the St. Petersburg military district on October 26, 1905. The immensely imposing and intensely loyal Nikolasha, an obvious choice for military dictator, had no wish for such an assignment. Indeed he told the Court Minister Count Vladimir Frederix that "if the Emperor does not accept the Witte programme, if he wants to force me to become Dictator, I shall take this revolver and kill myself in his presence." Nikolasha's vehemence annoyed both the emperor and his wife, and they would later unfairly blame the grand duke for the fact that Russia had a constitution.

Although Nicholas II hated constitutions, he now understood that he had no choice. Nevertheless he seems not to have grasped fully that his power was no longer absolute. To Nicholas, a tsar's power remained sacred, held in divine trust given him by his predecessors, sworn in his coronation oath, and to be passed on without any compromise to his heir. Many Russians felt as Nicholas did, facing the inevitability of change only with great reluctance.

The constitution the tsar granted to the nation on October 17, 1905, pacified the forces of revolution, although unrest persisted for two more years. The document gave civil rights such as freedom of speech, assembly and association to all Russians, and it established a national legislature, the duma. Members of the duma were elected by a wide, though not universal male suffrage. The duma had to approve all laws but had no say in foreign affairs or military matters. Only the emperor could appoint or dismiss ministers.

By the beginning of 1906, Nicky believed that the worst now lay behind. Several political parties of the opposition appeared tamed and ready to operate within the new parliamentary framework. The Constitutional Democrats, or "Cadets" as they were known, a liberal party that had emerged from the unrest, dominated the duma. The Cadets were led by several outstanding intellectuals, among them history professor Paul Miliukov and a prominent lawyer, Vladimir Nabokov, the father of the future author of *Lolita* (who in 1906 was only seven). Russia embarked upon its first experiment with democracy.

Lenin saw the 1905 revolution as a "dress rehearsal" for Bolshevism, demonstrating that the bourgeoisie was politically "bankrupt" and that the peasantry possessed huge revolutionary potential. For political focus, all these emotions awaited the hand of a gifted leader. Lenin exulted, seeing opportunity; moderates worried, seeing danger.

Most Russian intellectuals, appalled by the violence of the mob, no longer idealized the factory worker or the peasant as many had before. A sense of depression, even doom, gripped the elite, even many of the Romanovs. "All Russia is a madhouse," Witte wrote to a friend, after an ungrateful Nicholas II had dismissed him. Witte, wanting both modernization and autocracy, had tried but failed to reconcile the two.

The dynasty enjoyed a reprieve, thanks to the loyalty of the army, but Nicholas was now sitting on a throne of bayonets. The workers were singing:

Nicholas, tsar, praise be to you!
Our sovereign, devil's son too.
Merciless butcher, be drowned in blood.
Let all the Romanovs meet death in the flood.
Like maggots will perish all of your kin.
You will also die because you have sinned,
kept people in jails, many are dead,
millions of others have no bread.

Nicholas II opened the first duma on April 27, 1906, in the St. George Hall of the Winter Palace. Some of the new deputies wore tailcoats, some suits, some were in traditional Russian dress. Nothing like this had ever been seen before in the palace. Nicholas was wearing a Preobrazhensky regimental uniform. The dowager wore a white Russian dress trimmed with sable, Alix, a gold and white dress and a diadem made of the huge pearls of Catherine the Great. The royal crown and other regalia were also taken to the St. George Hall. All the Romanov family was present, and the dynasty in all its splendor faced the parliament. A solemn *Te Deum* opened the session. Then Nicholas sat on a throne and read his speech, finishing it with the words, "May God help me and all of you!"

His sister Olga remembered "the large group of deputies from among the peasants and factory people. The peasants looked sullen. But the workmen were worse: They looked as though they hated us." Minnie, shocked to see all the commoners in the Winter Palace, also noted "their strange hatred for us all."

Controversy raged within the Romanov family, but Russia seemed in 1907 to be recovering from its trauma. The new duma had become a public forum for the opposition, a symbol of pluralistic opinion, although one without any real say in state matters. Despite its lack of power, Nicky and the other Romanovs continued to hate it. The tsar had the duma dissolved in 1907, hoping to get a less radical body elected, and the elections went as he hoped. Four elections took place between 1906 and 1912, and after 1907 the number of monarchist seats began to grow. The country's increasing conservatism seemed to promise more stability. In practical terms this meant that the tsar could cooperate with the duma, although he still intensely disliked the idea of sharing power with any elected body.

Nicholas was still in his own mind an autocrat, stubbornly convinced that all of Russia was his personal property and private fiefdom. In the twentieth century Nicholas II temperamentally remained a seventeenth-century monarch.

Nicholas appointed Peter Stolypin as his prime minister in 1907. Large, balding, with an imposing black beard, Stolypin was immensely competent. He restored order in the country with an imaginative yet iron hand, starting land reform and promoting private farming. At the same time the prime minister showed no mercy for revolutionaries. Execution by hanging came to be known as wearing a "Stolypin necktie."

An assassin's bullet cut Stolypin's career short in 1911, and his last public words were "I am happy to die for the tsar." There is little doubt that the killing had been arranged by the Okhrana, the tsarist secret police, ordered by intensely conservative officials who feared the implications of Stolypin's encouragement of moderate reform.

Nicholas, having found himself from the beginning of his reign successively under the pressure of two powerful personalities, first Witte and then Stolypin, now decided that he would put only pliable people in the top position of the state. Alix, his wife, enthusiastically supported this attempt at renewed autocracy.

Increasingly both the family and the public believed Empress Alexandra Fedorovna to be the evil genius controlling the tsar, thinking Nicholas too weak to assert his will. Indeed Nicky came to depend upon her advice excessively. Alix's *idée fixe* was unchangeable autocracy. She hated the idea of a constitutional monarchy and everything associated with it: a free press, political pluralism, the duma and association with liberals in power in the Western European capitals. The empress saw the 1905 liberal innovations as a great tragedy for the family and longed for a Russia without taint of liberalism, in effect a huge estate for her and Nicky to pass on to their son Alexis.

The birth of the heir did not cause the imperial couple to reemerge into society or to rekindle links with the rest of the family. Nicholas was invariably courteous, but his behavior toward other Romanovs was merely polite, never warm. He avoided argument or confrontation at all costs. He performed his duties but did little beyond them. With a handful of exceptions, including his mother, his cousins Nikolasha, Sandro and Dmitri Pavlovich, sister Olga, and brother Michael, the tsar saw family members only five or six times a year and then only at formal ceremonial occasions. Because his contacts with the family became so limited, and his respect for public opinion as expressed through the newspapers was so slight, Nicholas became isolated from the nation, a captive of his own and his wife's faulty perceptions and illusions.

Romanov belief in tsardom and the Romanov sense of dynastic tradition remained so strong that no one anticipated a deluge. No one seems to have transferred money outside of Russia. Some owned apartments in Paris or villas on the Riviera, but these were intended only for brief private holidays away from the eye of the court, not for a rainy day. But the grand dukes did express apprehension about their future status in this new constitutional world. On April 13th, they held a conference at Vladimir's palace with K.R., Nikolasha, Sandro and Andrew present along with two high court dignitaries. It was beginning to dawn on the Romanovs that political changes might threaten their wealth. They were worried that the parliament would attempt to regulate and even curtail their status as an imperial family. They were most concerned about allowances and property rights.

Should lands providing income for the family be regarded as the property of the emperor or of the family? The Romanovs complained that, during the war with Japan, by Nicky's order two million rubles had been arbitrarily taken from these funds and given to the wounded "in the name of the imperial house." The conference agreed that the appanages were the property of the imperial house as a whole with the sovereign acting as guardian.

On July 30th, concerned about continuing unrest in the countryside, Nicholas summoned his cousins K.R. and Dmitri Constantinovich, along with Uncle Vladimir, Nikolasha and brother Peter, to Peterhof. Nicholas suggested that to quell peasant anger, the family should sell to the peasants 1,800,000 acres of crown lands. Nikolasha and Peter agreed with the emperor. Vladimir, however, vehemently objected. "If you make concessions in Russia, it is counter-productive; you give your hand and they are out for your head." Vladimir also complained that only a few of the Romanovs were present at the meeting and many of those absent were of age, alluding to the fact that none of his three sons had been invited. On hearing this, Nicholas backed down and agreed to postpone his decision.

On August 9th, at Peterhof, the emperor again summoned a family circle, this time a larger one, including K.R. and Dmitri, Nikolasha and Peter again, the Mikhailovichi (Nicholas, George and Sergei), and Vladimir with his sons Boris and Andrew. Now, apparently wanting to take a tougher line than he had ten days earlier, the emperor suggested transfering land to the peasants as a "sacrifice." The grand dukes groaned at the idea of such a material loss which would result in radical cuts to their allowances. The family conference therefore decided to sell the land to the peasants rather than to give it to them.

These arguments over money further diminished the Romanov sense of duty to the state and dynasty. Nicholas II not only found it difficult to govern his people but also to discipline his family. Though in the matter of marriages, he had the power and authority of the law, the church and custom on his side, he faltered when his authority was challenged. Nicholas II lacked his father's strength of will.

In the midst of the national disaster, on September 25, 1905, Kyril defied the emperor and persuaded a compliant priest to marry him to Ducky in Germany. Alexis's birth had put Kyril one step further from the throne, removing his imperial aims as an obstacle to the marriage. Kyril wrote in his memoirs, "I considered it would be easier for the Emperor to make a decision if he were to be confronted with a *fait accompli*." Other than Ducky's mother, Marie of Coburg, the only other Romanov to join the wedding celebration was Uncle Alexis Alexandrovich, who happened to be nearby at the time. The grand duke was certainly never a slave to convention and he always enjoyed a party. "He added gaiety to this occasion with his open breezy personality and huge voice," Kyril fondly remembered.

Soon after the wedding Kyril went back to St. Petersburg to inform his family of the event. The evening of his arrival, while playing bridge with his father and others, the Minister of the Court arrived at the Vladimir Palace to inform Kyril that he was to leave Russia within forty-eight hours, that he was deprived of all allowances and honors including the title of grand duke, and that his name was removed from the Navy list.

What Kyril had done violated both the Romanov family statute and Church law. Yet he professed to be astonished by the severity of this punishment and his parents exploded in fury. Miechen, his mother, never forgave Nicholas, although she blamed the empress more than she did the emperor for the harshness of Kyril's punishment. Nicholas wrote to his mother, the dowager, about Miechen with malicious satisfaction, "How she must hate us just now!"

Grand Duke Vladimir then staged a terrific scene in the emperor's office, shouting indignantly at his nephew, tearing off his medals and threatening to resign all his posts. The emperor remained adamant in the face of this criticism. Ducky's mother, Marie of Coburg, had interceded with Minnie, her sister-in-law, begging that Kyril be allowed to keep his title because "he has married not just somebody, but my daughter." Nicky did relent and let Kyril keep his title, but this was his only concession. Kyril was obliged to go into exile.

On July 15, 1907, Nicky, unable to stay angry for long, finally recognized Kyril's wedding and allowed his wife to assume the title of grand duchess. Hereafter she would be known as the Grand Duchess Victoria. Miechen, who was first with the news, sent Kyril a telegram exulting, "Ta Femme est Grande Duchesse!" Though these five words meant an imperial pardon for Kyril, a restoration of all his lost honors, privileges—and income—would not come until his father's death, two years later.

In the matter of another grand ducal marriage, the emperor continued to stand fast in his disapproval. Rumors were swirling about the romantic life of the tsar's younger brother Misha, not yet married. His name had earlier been attached to that of a young lady-in-waiting to his sister, a highly inappropriate match for a grand duke. Even less appropriate was his current interest in a twice-divorced commoner, Natalia (Natasha) Wulfert, and the public did not know that Michael had asked Nicky for permission to marry her. Marriage with a divorcee required permission of the emperor. Natasha, a strikingly beautiful and elegant woman with slightly Levantine features, could have stepped from an Ottoman miniature. Since early youth she had set her heart on becoming a social success. For a woman of her generation and background, that meant making a brilliant marriage. Restlessly moving from one infatuation to another, she finally met the man who satisfied her highest ambitions, Grand Duke Michael Alexandrovich. However, she had to wage a real battle to gain her objective.

The family generally dismissed Misha as charming but weak. His younger sister Olga always called him affectionately "Floppy," and most would find that nickname appropriate. Sergei Witte saw Michael differently and felt he was misunderstood. To Witte, the young grand duke had "a clear mind, an unshakeable conviction in his opinions and a crystalline moral purity. Misha keeps away from affairs of state, does not offer his opinions and, perhaps, hides behind the perception of him as a good-natured, unremarkable boy."

Conspicuous in his childhood as the favorite son of Alexander III, in his adulthood Michael sought privacy above all else, fleeing all administrative and social responsibility. His worst years, he thought, were those when he had been *tsesarevich*, heir to the throne after his older brother Georgie had died and before Nicky and Alix had Alexis. The last thing in the world Michael wanted was to be a tsar. He liked fast cars, beautiful women and military camaraderie. Tall and well built, Michael was the only son of Alexander III to inherit the emperor's extraordinarily strong hands. Like his father, Michael could amuse children by feats like bending a coin in two.

Michael had previously acceded to Nicholas's order forbidding him to marry Natasha, but now, in 1912, Michael mustered the courage to defy the tsar and family law and eloped with the lady abroad. Nicholas had gotten wind of the planned elopement and dispatched agents to follow the grand duke and report his every movement. But in the autumn of that year, Michael was able to give his pursuers the slip by choosing an obscure Serbian Orthodox church in Vienna for his wedding. No one would expect a Romanov to wed in anything but a Russian Orthodox church. Thus even the feckless Michael had successfully defied his older brother.

Nicholas's behavior toward both Kyril and Misha set a disastrous pattern of imperial leadership of the family. He might react strongly at first when a family member broke the rules, but under pressure ultimately he would bend. In the long run, the rules seemed not to matter.

"What harm our family does to itself, how it undermines the Emperor and the ruling house. The further we go, the worse it gets," K.R. lamented. "Where do we have a strong authority, acting with reflection and continuity? One becomes more and more fearful for the future. Everywhere is arbitrary rule, indulgence, weakness."

In 1905, the same year that Sergei had been assassinated, Alexis had resigned as the royal patron of the Navy in order to assume responsibility for the Tsushima debacle. His mistress, Eliza Baletta, an actress at the Mikhailovsky Theater in St. Petersburg, was reported to have cost Russia more than the whole Tsushima catastrophe, and a contemporary wrote that the pockets of Grand Duke Alexis contained the equivalent of a couple of battleships and two million rubles of embezzled Red Cross money. Indeed Alexis allegedly gave Baletta a wonderful ruby cross, which she proudly showed off when the rumor about embezzlement spread. In 1908, the grand duke died in France of pneumonia.

Meanwhile, two thousand miles east of St. Petersburg, living in Tashkent like an Oriental potentate, was Alexis's first cousin, Grand Duke Nicholas Constantinovich, who had many years earlier been permanently exiled at the age of twenty-four for stealing his mother's diamonds. His downtown palace challenged the cathedral for architectural prominence. Reflecting Asian attitudes toward separating the sexes, men occupied its left wing, women the right. Within a large walled courtyard, roses flowered in a huge spiral, from snow-white in the beginning to blood-red at the heart, and the palace also boasted a Japanese garden with streams, bridges and dwarf fruit trees. The grand duke maintained a zoo with monkeys, flamingos and pelicans, and other creatures exotic to Central Asia.

Nicholas Constantinovich was an avid year-round hunter, not only for duck, pheasant and boar, but also for leopard and tiger. At the nearby mouths of two great Central Asian rivers, Amu Darya and Syr Darya, tigers lived in the reedy thickets, feeding on boar. Leopards prowled the great mountains farther south. Nomadic Turkmenians organized a most exotic hunt for the exiled Romanov. The grand duke would mount a black stallion with a white star on its forehead. To the left of the stallion ran a hound, a trained leopard ran to the right. The large and graceful cat could catch and pin down a steppe antelope by a single strike of its paws, never using its teeth. The grand duke would then gallop up and cut the antelope's throat, using a dagger with an ivory shaft.

Nicholas Constantinovich's theft had deeply embarrassed the family, and in St. Petersburg he became a forgotten man. Not so some of his Romanov kinsmen. Paul Alexandrovich remained in disgrace, still in Paris, exiled because of his morganatic marriage. He had thought that his close relationship with his imperial nephew, only eight years younger than he, would reconcile the emperor to this marriage, but that was not the case. Only when Paul's daughter, the younger Maria Pavlovna ("Marie" as the Swedes would call her) married Swedish Prince William in 1907, was her father allowed to come to Russia and meet her bridegroom. This made her "deliriously happy," and presumably pleased Paul as well.

Marie's foster mother Ella, the Grand Duchess Elizabeth, became the most devout of the Romanovs. A fervent member of the Orthodox Church, she founded a new order of nuns who would devote themselves under her leadership, not to the cloister and to prayer, but to nursing, charity and active good works. In order to do this, Ella had to fight the extreme conservatism of the Church authorities, who were reluctant to contemplate anything as radical as she proposed. She sorted through her jewelry and gave it away or sold it, not even keeping her wedding ring. She bought land in Moscow on which to build a church, a hospital, a home for the elderly, an orphanage and modest living quarters for herself. Thereafter, Ella, in her religious garb, elegantly simple and designed by herself, appeared only at the margins of the family. She occasionally visited her sister, the empress; she attended family weddings and funerals, but never the parties afterward. She saw those closest to her, but always privately.

Meanwhile, for Marie, marriage to Prince William of Sweden was proving a total failure. The marriage had been arranged by Ella, with the tsar's approval, without even consulting Marie. She was only sixteen, and she first learned of her wedding from a telegram that her aunt left inadvertently on a table. Once married, she found her husband cold, shy and neglectful. When she tried to approach him, he would retreat into tears.

Marie brought to her marriage, and kept, her title of Imperial Highness (her husband was only a Royal Highness), a quantity of jewels and a large amount of money. She was far richer than he, and this fact did not strengthen their relationship. It was she who built a palace, Oak Hill, for the two of them. She was quick to add Swedish to her other five languages and became more popular with the Swedes than her husband was. Swedish courtiers praised her for working hard, not only on the language but also in mastering Swedish customs, whereas her husband was seen as lazy, inattentive and rude. Marie developed a good rapport with her father-in-law, King Gustav VI. He seemed to appreciate her effervescence, charm and unconventionality. Marie enjoyed riding with young Swedish officers and in general exercising her high spirits. Her son Lennart, then tiny, remembers sitting in her lap when they slid down a flight of stairs at the palace on a large silver tray.

Marie studied at the Arts & Crafts Academy in Stockholm and made an illustrated ABC book about Lennart for Lennart. It was later published. This was the first of several books she would write. Like her cousin Sandro, she had literary talent.

Marie was the only modern Romanov woman of her generation. The traditional set of female values prescribed by the family—marriage, children, church and royal entertainment—did not suit her. She felt confined by her status, although she certainly enjoyed the wealth and prestige of it. She longed for the freedom her European contemporaries enjoyed, a freedom that allowed driving an automobile herself, wearing unconventional clothing, smoking or visiting nightclubs. Marie would have done nicely had she been born to an ex-pat American millionaire family living in Paris. But unfortunately for her she was a grand duchess of Russia, now a Swedish princess.

King Gustav, sensing Marie's marital unhappiness, sent her and William as official representatives to the coronation of the King of Siam in 1912. This was a five-month trip and an opportunity for Marie at least to flirt with other men, which she found thoroughly enjoyable. In 1913, Marie and William left Sweden again on a representational visit, this time to Leipzig to celebrate the centenary of Napoleon's defeat at the Battle of the Nations. On the trip, in Berlin, Marie found the courage to tell her husband the shocking news that she wanted a divorce.

Abandoning her little Lennart in Stockholm, Marie, energetic and independent, returned to Russia to try to build a new life there. She would forever after look unsuccessfully for love. Of her childhood, she was later to write, nothing now remained except "painful memories." Her Aunt Ella was now totally occupied with her religious order; their relationship improved a bit but would never be close. Her father and stepmother were still in France but about to begin a life for themselves at Tsarskoye Selo in the suburbs of St. Petersburg. But Marie's beloved brother Dmitri was still nearby, and at a dance in Moscow in the presence of the court, the two danced seven dances consecutively. The tsar laughed but sent his equerry to split the couple. Psychologically, if not physically, the relationship was incestuous. Emotionally troubled, Marie suffered terribly from what she thought was Dmitri's neglect of her. He, apparently dismayed at the intensity of her feeling, instinctively distanced himself.

Dmitri spent a lot of time with the tsar's family, with whom he became a great favorite, almost an adopted son. Because Nicholas and Alexandra had watched Dmitri grow up, they felt an almost parental interest in him. In September 1909, Dmitri enjoyed the beach in the Crimea with the imperial family. They visited Sandro and Xenia at nearby Ai Todor to join in archaeological excavations on a cape that in ancient times had been the site of a Roman fortress.

Sandro complained to his mother-in-law, the dowager, that he had enjoyed no personal relationship with Nicky since 1902, that Nicky and Alix had repeatedly shown lack of interest in Xenia and him, and that, if "God forbid, we have to spend the winter in St. Petersburg, we would meet them perhaps only five times and that solely at some official ceremonies." This is not altogether true; occasionally he and Nicky would have time together. But Sandro's real frustration was professional. He had little to do. He believed he was qualified to handle naval affairs, "but having lost any faith in the Navy, I cannot do that in the chaos we have now." The navy was still reeling from the double humiliations of defeat by the Japanese and mutiny during the revolution of 1905.

Moreover, by 1909, everybody knew that Sandro had started living a separate life from Xenia, who looked thin and very sad. Sandro was reported to have moved out of the marital bedroom entirely. Minnie was unhappy about the estrangement; she had come to like Sandro and to depend on him, and Xenia was her favorite daughter. Their children, six boys and one girl, were Minnie's favorite grandchildren. She especially doted on the girl, beautiful Irina.

Back in St. Petersburg, Nicholas and Alexandra devoted themselves more and more to the quiet pleasures of their private life and appeared in public only when formal ceremonies made it necessary. Miechen, disliking Alix more and more, carried on a tradition of lavish hospitality even after the death of her husband, Vladimir, in 1909, in part because of Alix's reclusiveness.

Around this time the Montenegrin wives of two grand dukes further from the imperial succession emerged into prominence in St. Petersburg society. Nikolasha and Peter, the two sons of Alexander II's brother Nicholas, had married two of the daughters of King Nicholas of Montenegro, that tiny and impoverished country's one and only king.

Montenegro, like its larger neighbor Serbia, was unusual among Balkan states for having a native, not German, ruling house, and Nicholas I was surely one of Europe's more colorful monarchs. Tall and ample, a formidable figure, with generous drooping moustache and piercing eyes set rather closely together, Nicholas was always photographed in native dress, with his chest heavily bedecked with an assortment of large medals. He was able to magnify the importance of his country by his adept diplomacy, allowing himself to be courted by the great powers and craftily playing off one against another, collecting subsidies wherever he could. The king spoke half a dozen languages, wrote poetry and plays, yet knew many of his subjects by name and liked to dispense justice to petitioners, sitting under a large tree outside his palace in Cetinje, the modest national capital.

Militsa and Anastasia, called Stana by the family, were but two of Nicholas's twelve exuberant children. A third, Elena, married King Victor Emanuel of Italy, who was as conspicuous for his shortness as Elena was for her height. Because they were Slavic and Orthodox, the two princesses enjoyed the benevolence of Alexander III and were invited to Russia to be educated at the Smolny Institute, a school for "noble maidens" in St. Petersburg. Witte commented that, by the end of Alexander III's reign, Russia had a "real flock of all sorts of grand dukes," and the emperor, demonstrating his friendship to Montenegro, allowed two "second-rate grand dukes" to marry the daughters of the king.

Because of the remoteness of the Nikolaevichi from the imperial succession it was considered unimportant politically whom they married. Peter's marriage to Militsa was arranged; the family was chiefly concerned with his health. His lungs were weak and tuberculosis ran in the family. A "big healthy girl from the mountains" was judged an appropriate mate for this quiet Romanov, whose only true interest in life was Middle Eastern architecture. With Militsa taking care of everything else, Peter kept himself happily busy designing two palaces in the Crimea—for himself and for his cousin Dmitri Constantinovich.

Nikolasha, Peter's older brother, had a heated romance with Stana, Militsa's sister, who had been divorced from Romanov cousin Duke George of Leuchtenberg. Two close sisters thus married two close brothers. The Montenegrin girls held their husbands by iron hands. Nikolasha, violently anti-foreign, would nonetheless talk to Stana in French and would admit that it felt "weird" to write to her in Russian. The two sisters, in correspondence between the two of them, exchanged bottomless cocktails of family news, politics, European and St. Petersburg gossip, written in a mixture of French, Russian and Serbo-Croatian. In society the two aggressive women acquired the nickname of the "black plague," the "black" deriving both from their homeland and their complexions.

The real career of the two women had started when Nicholas married Alix. The new empress was not liked in St. Petersburg, and the Montenegrin girls were the only grand duchesses who kowtowed to her. As Minnie began to lose influence over Nicky, Alix's influence, and ultimately that of her friends, grew. Taking advantage of their connections at court, the "black plague" started to draw money from the state treasury for themselves and for their homeland, for which they constantly acted as energetic lobbyists. Theirs was not so much a matter of social ambition as of political scheming; they wanted to advance the interests of their homeland. But the sisters became so notorious that Sergei Witte, usually not at a loss for the appropriately cutting phrase, simply sighed in his memoirs, "Oh, these two . . . from Montenegro . . . haven't they created troubles for Russia, indeed."

Like so many in St. Petersburg at the time, the Montenegrin sisters were curious about the supernatural, experimenting with ouija boards and seances. "We should search for truth in simple folk," they said, and claimed to find it in a peasant from Siberia with piercing eyes, uncombed beard, and rancid odor, a man of an imposing physical presence, radiating a powerful aura of sexuality. He combined the mystic with the erotic. Nicholas II wrote in his diary, November 1, 1905, "We have got to know a man of God, Grigory, from Tobolsk Province." The "black plague" had brought this new miracle-worker to the empress. When eventually they were to become disenchanted with him, they would find their relationship with Alix cooling as well.

Rasputin had made his debut. He would do more damage to the Romanov monarchy than any other person in Russia, even any of the Romanovs.

CHAPTER FIVE

❧

The Great War

1914–1917

ON SUNDAY, JULY 20, 1914, a hot and sunny day, Nicholas II
went to the Winter Palace. Crown ministers, the great officials
of the court and the Romanov family were standing in the palace's
large Nicholas Hall. The emperor entered, flanked by the towering figure of Nikolasha, commander-in-chief of the Russian armies, walking
at his side. One observer thought Nicky that day looked "younger and
more handsome" than he had a few months earlier when, under the
pressure of family problems, his face was "flaccid and uncertain." On
this occasion his voice rang out strongly and agreeably to the ear; his
words seemed well and carefully chosen, his audience especially attentive. If there was one imperial duty Nicholas II could do well, if
emotionally moved, it was to speak to the public, either from a prepared text or extemporaneously.

I welcome you in these solemn and anxious days through which
all Russia is passing. Germany, followed by Austria, has declared
war on Russia. The great wave of patriotism and loyalty to the
Throne which has swept our native land is to me, and presumably also to you, a token that our great Mother Russia will carry
on that war, sent us as a visitation by God, to its desired con-

summation. This unanimous impulse of love on the part of my people and their readiness to sacrifice everything, even life itself, gives me the necessary strength, calmly and steadfastly to anticipate the future. . . . I am certain that each of you, at your respective posts, will help me to bear the trials which are sent to us, and that we all, beginning with myself, will do our duty to the end. Great is the God of the Russian land.

Cheers rang throughout the hall; the emperor's eyes welled with tears; he made the sign of the Cross, as did everyone, and they all sang, "Lord, save thy people." Within five years, most of those standing there would be dead.

The enthusiasm of the Russian educated classes for the war was genuine and profound. Intellectuals saw opportunity for a spiritual renewal of the nation; the press rejoiced in a new sense of national unity. The emperor's popularity soared. Despite his pathetic past, he would now be remembered, some said, as "Nicholas the Great." Spontaneous demonstrations of support broke out in front of the Winter Palace. In the public view this war was not to be compared to that with Japan ten years earlier. Workers in St. Petersburg stopped striking and doubled their productivity on their own initiative.

Yet worker enthusiasm rapidly eroded, patriotism was not universal, and the masses remained indifferent. Peasants, and most Russians still were peasants, did not understand why they should leave their fields and their families for the battlefield. What did they care about large issues such as the Black Sea Straits question? Bread meant a lot more than the Bosporus.

The emperor proposed to assume the supreme command himself, to the dismay, even alarm, of his ministers, who did not have a high opinion of his military competence and who did not want to see the prestige of the emperor exposed to the possibility of damage from any defeats on the battlefield. With deep regret Nicholas thereupon followed the advice of his ministers and instead appointed his older cousin, Nikolasha, to the post. Nikolasha was not only a professional military officer, he was also the most respected of all the Romanovs.

In personality and in professional interests Nikolasha resembled his grandfather, the Iron Tsar, Nicholas I. He had long taken a prominent place in public affairs. After the war with Japan, he served as head of the Council of State Defense; at the time of the 1905 revolution, Nikolasha was instrumental in persuading the emperor to sign the constitutional manifesto. Nikolasha was always an ardent monarchist, but he was also ready to accept compromise when he perceived it to be necessary. When the story of ineptitude and corruption during the war with Japan became better known, Nikolasha came in for his share of criticism but nonetheless preserved his popularity.

He had always been a tough commander. Appointed to head the St. Petersburg military district in 1905, he was at first disliked by the officers who were accustomed to the relaxed style of the Grand Duke Vladimir. But by 1914 Nikolasha had become the most popular general with the officer corps. Even the most professional judged Nikolasha exceptional. Soldiers, too, liked the plain grand duke, calling him "the all-seeing eye." When Nikolasha was named commander-in-chief, the congress of the provincial assemblies referred to him as a "bogatyr," a folk warrior of early Russia, heroic in stature and strength, with the special mission of guarding Russia, a virtual demigod close to the Greek notion of hero.

Called by the young Romanovs "Uncle the Terrible," he was a formidable character, in part because of his height—he was the tallest of all the Romanovs—but also because of his forbidding manner, especially toward his younger relatives whom he was quick to dismiss as pleasure-loving and irresponsible. Nikolasha's major interest was nature; he was happiest to be out of doors, whether caring for his estates, hunting with his hounds or breeding his livestock. Nikolasha treated his servants as he treated his soldiers, in a paternal manner combining attention with severity.

He was known to be profoundly religious, praying in the morning, at night and before and after meals. He was a mystic, believing in miracles and divine revelation, and he became a victim of an age in which people trusted prophets more than priests. As his friend and chaplain, Georgy Shavelsky, put it, the moral side of his religion yielded to the idea of divine intervention. Nikolasha's religious ardor limited his capacity as a leader. If things went wrong, Nikolasha said it was God's will and that was that. Nikolasha's propensity for mysticism was strengthened by his wife, Stana of Montenegro, who had the same proclivities, and Nikolasha, like so many Romanov males, leaned heavily on his wife.

Despite his awesome reputation, he was neither strategist nor statesman. His harshness of manner was offset by his sentimentality.

When emotionally moved or distressed he would cry like a child, not ashamed of his tears. The grand duke did not seek the post of supreme commander and admitted that when he received the emperor's order, he "spent much of his time crying because he did not know how to approach his new duties." Nikolasha established and maintained his extraordinarily good reputation on the basis of public perception of his character rather than on genuine professional competence.

Nikolasha took command with a big handicap. The grand strategy that he was obliged to execute had already been formed; he had had no voice in conceiving it. Russia had committed herself to France, and Russia was so anxious to honor that commitment that Nikolasha felt obliged to order his troops into action against the Germans before they could be fully mobilized or fully equipped and with only sketchy planning of the details of the advance. Nikolasha left for the front on July 31st, departing St. Petersburg at midnight from a darkened and deserted station. Most of the members of his staff knew only the name of their destination, Baranovichi, on the western frontier. Those who were briefed on Russia's plan of war knew that an attack was imminent.

The result of that first Russian lunge into East Prussia was, on its face, disaster. The two Russian armies were commanded by two men who had made their reputations leading cavalry divisions in the war against Japan, cordially disliked each other, and now failed to coordinate their movements against the Germans. One army was crushed at Tannenberg while the other stood by and did nothing to help. Alexander Samsonov, the dazed commander of the first army, wandered in the woods and shot himself in despair. A German eyewitness returned to Berlin and reported that he would never forget the ghastly sight of thousands of screaming men and horses driven into two huge swampy lakes to drown. To shorten their agony the Germans fired machine guns on them. Nonetheless "there was movement seen among them for a week after."

Within weeks of the outbreak of hostilities, Russia had lost a quarter of a million men, a large chunk of territory, and much equipment, which was harder to replace than the men. When a French officer tried to express his sympathy to the grand duke, Nikolasha said simply, "We are happy to have made such sacrifices for our allies." And indeed, despite the debacle, the Russian sacrifice had been of very great aid to the French. The Russian attack on the eastern front, coming sooner than the Germans expected, had caused them to redeploy two army corps and a cavalry division from the western front at a crucial time in the struggle there. These German troops arrived too late to fight at Tannenberg, but the French won the battle of the Marne and Paris was saved. "Lunch in Paris, dinner in St. Petersburg" had been the kaiser's terse summation of German grand strategy. The German plan failed. The Russian sacrifice may have decided the whole course of the war; certainly it denied the Germans a quick victory.

And for the Russians, the war soon began to go much better. Because much of Poland was then part of Russia, the Russian empire extended in a long western salient, with German East Prussia lying to the north and Austrian Galicia to the south. That southern frontier would prove to be soft, and there Russian arms achieved a string of victories. Austria-Hungary, the Dual Monarchy, proved to be ludicrously ineffective in the war. Its troops seemed more eager to flee than to fight; many of them were Slavs and felt more sympathetic with their Russian enemies than with their Austrian masters. Unlike the Germans, the Austrians never seriously threatened the Russians.

Russia seized most of Austrian Poland, threatened to roll over the Carpathian Mountains into the wide plains of Hungary, and even seemed to menace the security of Berlin, lying close as it did to Germany's eastern frontier. Nikolasha issued an appeal to the Polish people to support the Allied cause. In return for this support he promised to unite all of Poland, although under the sceptre of the Russian tsar. He promised the Poles a Poland free in language, religion and self-government, although the word "autonomy" was not mentioned. After the capture of the great Austrian fortress of Przemysl in March 1915 with the taking of more than one hundred thousand prisoners including nine generals, the emperor showed his pleasure by bestowing upon Nikolasha a diamond-studded sword.

The Russian army had achieved much, and its rough handling of Austria-Hungary scored the first great victory for the Allies. Contemporary foreign military observers exaggerated the quality and potential of the Russian soldier, his simple faith and his capacity for stoic endurance. But the German commanders, Hindenburg and Ludendorff, used railways with consummate skill to shuttle their armies around to maximum advantage; they rallied their forces, summoned their superior weapons and put the Russians on the defensive.

The Russians lacked guns, ammunition or even boots and warm underwear for their soldiers. Men fought barefoot in the snows of the

Carpathians. Like everyone else Russia anticipated a short war and planned accordingly. What Russians would suffer others would also, although not to the same degree.

Nor were rifles and boots all that was needed. The men required training from able and energetic officers, of whom there were few. Within several months of the war's beginning, the losses in killed and wounded were so heavy that according to General Alexei Brusilov, one of Russia's ablest commanders, "the professional character of our forces disappeared and the army became more and more like a badly trained militia."

The incompetence of authority was glaringly obvious. In Pinsk, fifty-eight wounded soldiers lay for two days under an open sky, without food and without medical attention, while a few feet away one military hospital stood half empty and a second was not yet officially opened. One Hussar regiment did not have a single surgeon; its two "doctors" were a dentist and a psychiatrist. Wounded men sometimes reported that they had to resort to bribes to get any attention, and that they were robbed by the very people who should have cared for them.

Thus despite the successes against Austria-Hungary, within the first year of war the army had begun its disintegration into a disease-ridden, hungry, dispirited mob over whom their officers exercised less and less control. The men lost all confidence in their officers and felt increasingly hostile toward them. Officers feared leading their troops into battle lest they be shot in the back by their own men.

Not only did Russian planners have no notion of quantities needed to wage modern war, they were also unready for innovation in modes of warfare. In June 1915, the Germans introduced poison gas on a large scale. The Russians had some gas masks but they were in storage, not in the hands of the troops. Newspapers reported reassuringly that soldiers nonetheless had time to take "the necessary measures." These measures turned out to be "urinating on handkerchiefs and tying them round the face." More than a thousand men then died of gas poisoning.

The Russians used few telephones because of a shortage of wire, and the Germans knew exactly what their enemies were up to because they were intercepting Russian army radio broadcasts, carelessly made in the clear instead of in code. It seemed that Russia simply did not know how to make modern war and Germany did. Germany possessed the world's best war machine. German prowess on the battlefield reflected tremendous powers of organization, of disciplined effort and of industrial and agricultural accomplishment, all of which were not part of the Russian experience.

The high command, wringing its hands as the German juggernaut plunged deeply into Russia in the autumn of 1915, increasingly seemed to put its faith in the tactic that had worked in 1812 against Napoleon, trading space for time. Perhaps the Germans could be conquered by the huge distances and the impenetrable swamp and forest of Russia, by the impassable roads, and the grace of St. George, patron saint of the Russian army.

The Russian retreat assumed awesome proportions, and headquarters seemed determined to lay waste all territory that the Germans might try to occupy. This was a "scorched earth" policy before that phrase had been coined. Not only troops but also civilians choked all roads leading to the east. The authorities did not insist that all civilians leave, only those whose villages might be in the line of fire, but civilians left in fear, fear of German atrocities and fear of loss of their cattle, horses and other animals. Peasant farmers felt they had no choice but to take their transportable wealth and flee. To where they did not know. They traveled in wooden horse-drawn carts, father with reins in his hand, mother sitting on top of a load of the most precious household goods, children trudging alongside, driving ahead the animals: cattle, geese, pigs. Many sickened and died along the way, from hunger, exposure and disease. Dead animals and human corpses littered the roadside along with a pathetic array of abandoned goods. Refugees fanned out over western Russia, adding to the problems of the homefront: food shortages, soaring costs of living, growing chaos and profound pessimism.

The war isolated cosmopolitan St. Petersburg and caused it to become inward and xenophobic. The government gave the city a new, Russian name, Petrograd, to replace its old German-sounding one. Anti-German feelings broke out everywhere. Musicians no longer played Beethoven or Bach. Even Christmas trees, because they were originally a German custom, were now banned. In the United States, similar changes took place: sauerkraut became "liberty cabbage"; hamburger, "salisbury steak"; and frankfurters, "hot dogs." In England it became "unpatriotic" even to keep a dachshund. All Germans were suspected of being spies and many were rounded up for detention. In all the Allied countries, culture identified as German went into hiding, just as in Germany it had become a crime to speak English over the telephone or in any public place.

In Russia animosity smoldered against anyone with a German surname, and suspicions of subversive German influences at court, centering around the Empress Alexandra, were rife. The empress could rightly be accused of many things, but lack of patriotism for her adopted country was certainly not one of them. Emotionally she had become intensely Russian, and she identified Germany with Prussia and with the Hohenzollerns, whom she thoroughly detested. Her tastes were resolutely English, never German. Nonetheless the wildest stories of chicanery and espionage circulated, even in the highest circles. Even the family, it seems, because most of them so disliked Alexandra, were prepared to think the worst.

Wartime society became more provincial. Before the war, many rich Russians, not simply grand dukes, traveled often to western Europe and were commonly seen on the smartest streets, shopping in the most expensive stores, eating in the most epicurean restaurants of cities like Paris, London, Rome, Cannes, Biarritz or Saint-Moritz. Even those who were only moderately prosperous frequently spent their vacations in Germany or Switzerland. As a result, a large number of Russian tastemakers and opinion shapers had long been influenced by cultural currents in western Europe. There many Russians acquired their clothing, books, jewelry, objects of art, furniture and automobiles—as well as their attitudes and judgments.

Now combat virtually closed off the outside world. Enemy blockades barred Russian ships from sailing out of the Baltic or Black Seas. Vladivostok on the Pacific and Arkhangel on the White Sea were Russia's only open seaports; the former was vastly remote and the latter icebound half the year. To this new separation from the outside world and lack of stimulation resulting from it, French Ambassador Maurice Paleologue attributed the widespread fatigue and pessimism he was beginning to encounter in Petrograd. Society became more hedonistic, war seeming to intensify the spirit of reckless abandon.

All over Russia self-indulgence shaped changing attitudes toward sex, narcotics and the spending of money. Petrograd became prostitute-infested, ladies of the evening cruising the sidewalks adjoining restaurants, hotels and parks. Bohemian types assembled in private apartments where they held "Athenian nights," the details of which were discussed in town in shocked but avid whispers. Several hotels were actually brothels; syphilis and other venereal diseases were on the rise. Some of the members of the demimonde were unsuccessful actresses; others were singers and dancers from nightspots like "Buff," for whom selling their bodies was almost part of their employment contracts. Others, to be met in more refined cabarets, adopted the airs of goddesses, obliging their patrons to content themselves with simply kissing their long slender hands armored with bejewelled rings and heavy gold bracelets.

The generation of Alexander III had been religious, Alexander himself calmly and rationally, Nikolasha with exaltation and deep mysticism. Ella had made herself a Bride of Christ. Even the sexually promiscuous Sergei Alexandrovich had filled the pages of his diary with appeals to the Lord and would inevitably open each new year with the entry, "Bless me, oh Lord!" In the next generation, the religiosity of Nicholas and Alexandra appeared the exception rather than the rule. And the generation that followed Nicholas, that of Dmitri, Marie, the sons of Sandro and Xenia, and the young Constantinovichi, was determinedly secular. Grand Duchess Xenia was in despair that her son Fedor, though close to his grandmother the dowager, was cynical about his religious duties and became, in his mother's words, "unkind and corrupted." The behavior of the Romanovs reflected, and perhaps encouraged, a national trend.

The increasing notoriety of Rasputin, the "holy man" whom the "black plague" had first introduced to Alix, epitomized to many people the worst of the new era. Rasputin was a gifted healer and drew many admirers as a result of his successes. No one was more vulnerable to his appeal on that score than the empress.

Alix's only son, the heir, was a hemophiliac; a bruise could lead to a hemorrhage and death. Alexis inherited this gene from Alix, who had inherited it from Queen Victoria. Thus Alix bore a sense of guilt as well as profound anxiety about her son's illness. Again and again the boy would spend time in bed, moaning and crying, and the empress had to shuttle between her public duties and her private anxieties, putting on the mask of a hostess one minute and becoming a nurse the next. Nicky and Alix sought to keep their son's illness as private as possible, even within the family. The Vladimirovichi were all too eager to secure the throne for themselves. The empress was consumed by her son's illness, the doctors then could do virtually nothing, and at official ceremonies she was preoccupied and showed extreme fatigue. She began to age rapidly.

The only person who seemed to be able to help Alexis was Rasputin, and this gave him unparalleled intimacy with the tsar's family. Rasputin hinted that the empress was his mistress and that the tsar had to kiss his hand. These stories, widely believed, severely damaged the prestige of the imperial couple.

Rasputin himself seems simply to have wanted the good life, especially influence and command over people. Increasingly he was engaged both in politics and debauchery. He had seduced many court ladies who were tired of lovers from the same social circle, many of them perfumed dandies no different from their husbands. They responded eagerly to the earthy Rasputin. He never commanded the respect of the nation or its capital. No institution of the Romanov monarchy, be it the church, the army or the civil bureaucracy had any sympathy towards the "elder." His following was substantial only in terms of its social prominence. All in all, only several hundred people visited Rasputin's dingy apartment, but many of them were wives and daughters of important bureaucrats.

Mentally shallow, grossly ignorant, Rasputin had no grand plan for Russia and was incapable even of persisting intrigues. He would praise and promote with the empress those politicians, industrialists and bankers who embraced him, brought him cases of champagne and his favorite Madeira, took him to the palaces of the elite, and discussed state matters with him as if he were an authority in such matters. The credulous, the greedy, the unscrupulous and those burdened with the fewest principles consorted with this dirty, barely literate man and cajoled him for favors. In most cases Rasputin pushed the cause of his favorites out of sheer vanity, to prove his own importance. He could move his people into the void created by the absence of first class leaders in Russia.

The empress called Rasputin "a man of God," but few Russians would agree. She was enraged when she learned of a short but pungent correspondence between Rasputin and Nikolasha. Rasputin had asked whether he could come to headquarters to bless the troops. Nikolasha telegraphed in response: "Come, and I will hang you." His words were repeated all over Russia and Nikolasha's popularity soared. When Duma president Rodzianko asked Nikolasha whether the story were true, the grand duke laughed and said, "Well, not exactly." But it was clear to Rodzianko that "something of the sort had actually taken place." Nikolasha was famous—and liked—for his blunt language. His actual words on this occasion may have been un-printable.

As the empress assumed more and more authority, ministers were appointed and dismissed with bewildering speed. Rapid change of office grossly handicapped bureaucratic efficiency; no one was in office long enough to begin to master his job. Within seventeen months Russia had four prime ministers. Everyone soon learned that "the patronage of Rasputin was the quickest way up the greasy pole—and criticism of him the quickest way down." No one could persuade the empress that Rasputin was anything but a holy man; she dismissed all scandal as simply vicious rumor. The emperor may have taken a more balanced view of Rasputin, but family, political leaders and anyone who, like Nikolasha, tried to persuade him of the danger of the man were met with stony silence.

✑

Russia could not boast the strategic rail network of Germany, but the Russian army high command put trains to good use both for living quarters of decent comfort, even luxury, and as a means of making command power mobile and secure. Nikolasha kept his headquarters at Baranovichi aboard two special trains, usually stopped on a siding, but ready to be moved whenever necessary. One train housed the grand duke and his suite including his brother Peter; the second housed the rest of the high command, including Grand Duke Kyril, who was there as commander of the riverine naval department. Each train had a dining car; each member of the staff had his own compartment. All told about sixty people plus guards comprised the group. The guards locked this headquarters in a protective ring and the forests around promoted a strict, almost monastic, atmosphere. Foreign observers were permitted to live and travel on board along with the grand duke and his staff. But the real decisions were being made elsewhere, on the battlefield itself where the real generals were.

Peter was inseparable from his brother Nikolasha, always there but seldom speaking. Grand Duke Peter was the first Romanov in modern times to bear the name of the greatest of all the Romanovs. But his quiet self-effacing personality bore little similarity to that of his namesake. "Petisha," as the family called him, never pretended to be anything but Nikolasha's brother. He had no friends, no independent opinions. He was "elusive by choice," in the words of his grandson, content to follow the lead of his older brother, whom he worshipped. Petisha was one of the artistic Romanovs, who, for architectural inspiration, had traveled widely, especially in the Islamic world, and in his large Crimean villa he tried to recreate the spirit of a palace or mosque of old Cairo. Being a grand duke, Peter had been thrust into a military career; his war experience illustrates this perfectly. All one can say of Peter was that he was there.

Every day Nikolasha would invite officers for lunch and dinner aboard his command train. He would greet them all, shaking hands all around in both compartments of the dining car; he was so tall that a sheet of paper hung in the doors reminding him to bend his head.

The meals were well prepared but simple. "We lunch at 12:30— three courses—and dine at 7:30: soup, joint, and sweet, a glass of vodka, claret or Madeira, and a glass of cognac with our coffee." Some generals permitted no alcohol at table, but the commander-in-chief did. Nikolasha would take one small glass of vodka and one or two glasses of wine. Meals for him were sometimes a convivial time stretched out for lengthy conversation. If the news from the battlefield were good, Nikolasha would make jokes and the atmosphere would be very relaxed. If the news from the front were bad, he would frown and the meal would pass in deep silence. When General Samsonov's army perished in Eastern Prussia, nobody was invited to the dining car at all.

Nikolasha disapproved of visits to headquarters by spouses and women in general, but tolerated them if they were infrequent and discreet. The women had to lodge at a miserable inn at the nearest town, Baranovichi, and try to stay out of sight of the commander-in-chief. When Nikolasha would spy an officer taking his wife for a walk in the woods, he would ignore him, but later, at dinner, give him a meaningful look. Nikolasha himself lived a monkish existence. During the whole year of his supreme command he saw his wife only once, at the railway station, when she was on her way to Kiev. His only diversions were to ride his horse or to go out for an excursion in his automobile.

When the emperor would visit headquarters, the atmosphere would become tense. Some suggested that Nikolasha was privately demanding that the empress be sent to a convent. Whether or not he said it to the emperor, he certainly said it to many others, and so did his wife Stana. Nikolasha warned the emperor that the Rasputin clique, which enjoyed the favor of the empress, was ruining the country, and to some of his associates he confided, "Just imagine my horror that Rasputin got to the tsar through my house!"

Because the "black plague" had long ago fallen out with Rasputin, their relationship with the empress had cooled greatly, affecting their husbands also.

Rasputin, well aware of Nikolasha's opinion of him, now attempted to alienate the empress further from the grand duke by saying that Nikolasha was aspiring to the throne. Some courtiers in Petrograd picked up that theme and began to circulate a portrait of Nikolasha bearing the caption, "Nicholas III." Recalling his insistence to the tsar that a constitution would be preferable to a dictatorship, the liberal opposition tended to form around Nikolasha even though he made no effort to cultivate a political following. The grand duke's aura as a military hero enhanced his political attractiveness, and he seemed a powerful personality fit to unify and lead the nation in a way that Nicholas II could not. The harsh, even brutal, way in which Nikolasha disciplined his top generals forged a legend of steely perfection about him that remained intact despite the calamities that the army was enduring. As the war progressed, the grand duke lost some of his vital energies and those officers immediately subordinate to him did not fill the gap. Duma president Rodzianko said after visting them that "they left an impression of mournful helplessness." Yet with the troops Nikolasha remained wildly popular. With his enormous height and impressive bearing he looked like a hero, and he carried himself like one. No one could ever accuse Nikolasha of being dishonest or of intriguing at court. He remained intensely loyal to those who gained his confidence; this became a fault when ties of friendship took precedence over judgments of professional competence.

Once at headquarters the tsar said rather maliciously, "You know, Nikolasha, I used to be very much afraid of you, when you commanded the Life Guard Hussar regiment and I was an officer there." The grand duke, embarrassed, smiled. "I hope, Majesty, that the fear is now gone."

The fear had not gone, and this was a problem.

The tsar and his circle began to discuss the removing of Nikolasha from his command and having the emperor replace him. The cabinet ministers begged Nicholas II to keep Nikolasha at his post, arguing that to do otherwise would be disastrous for Russia. They particularly feared the consequences of the tsar's taking command. The family, including the dowager, joined in the outcry, and in a political campaign to discredit Alexandra and the government she was shaping. Ironically, by doing this the Romanovs became agents for their own destruction. The success of the campaign against the empress shattered the credibility of the government and affected not only the prestige of the tsar but also that of the dynasty.

Grand Duke Dmitri, now a twenty-four-year-old lieutenant, asked for permission to go to the capital to intercede with the tsar, even though he had never been very close to Nikolasha. Nikolasha banned the trip; an officer should not interfere in such matters, he said. But Dmitri got what he wanted because the dowager intervened with Nikolasha on his behalf. Dmitri returned after his interview with the emperor and reported that Nicholas had told him, "Don't worry! I will do what my conscience says."

His conscience, it seems, told the tsar to fire Nikolasha and send him off to the Caucasus to oversee the war against the Turks, not unimportant but a secondary front. Nikolasha accepted the order, saying that he had been brought up to be loyal to his sovereign. He was removed not because he was a bad general, but because the Empress Alexandra wanted him out, and the tsar could not say no to his wife. The emperor wrote in his diary with great relief, "Everything has passed well!" When Nikolasha asked the emperor if he should leave immediately, Nicholas said in friendly fashion, "Why should you? Stay for two or three more days if you wish."

The emperor's decision to assume the command himself meant two things. First, the real direction of the army would come from the chief of staff, even more than it had under Nikolasha; everyone knew that the emperor had absolutely no competence in military matters. And second, the emperor would be absent from home for long periods of time, leaving a power vacuum in his absence. Here lay opportunity for Alix.

The empress was delighted to see Nikolasha leave his command; she had been pushing the emperor to relieve him for some time, not simply because of the grand duke's attitude toward Rasputin but also because she really had come to believe that Nikolasha's loyalty to the emperor was questionable and that he was using the prestige and power of his post to deflect popular allegiance from the emperor to himself. Alexandra did not want to lose her husband's companionship at home in Tsarskoye Selo, but she believed firmly in the notion of a mystical link between tsar and people and thought, as did the emperor, that his presence at army headquarters would enhance the strength of that bond. That, to her, seemed most important.

When she heard that Nicky had fired Nikolasha, Minnie was thrown into despair: "My dear boy couldn't have done that. It is *she*!" Full of gloom, Minnie said that the situation reminded her of the last year of the reign of the unfortunate Paul I when he dismissed all the loyal people around him—and conspirators killed him.

The troops also took the news hard. The grand duke was not guilty of the biggest problem at the front, which was the shortage of ammunition. This was the responsibility of those who had been preparing the country for a European war long before 1914. Nikolasha's army reacted almost unanimously: "He was loved by his men and his officers. He was feared only by the higher chiefs," the soldiers said.

Nikolasha arrived at Tiflis (Tbilisi) in September 1915. The Caucasian front he was now to command lay on the periphery of the war. Perhaps to deprive the grand duke of any chance for success there, the tsar had removed several units from his army. Nonetheless Nikolasha would enjoy a triumph, although the laurels were due as much to his subordinate commanders, especially General Nicholas Yudenich, as they were to him. In the beginning of 1916, Yudenich captured the Turkish fortress city of Erzerum, seeking merely approval of his plans from the grand duke.

But it was Nikolasha himself who decided to send a Russian force under the command of General Nicholas Baratov into Persia. Baratov's troops landed on the Caspian coast and successfully occupied the northern part of Persia. The British had moved into the south, and so the Germans were prevented from establishing a sphere of influence there. The Russian presence in Persia would become unexpectedly important to the Romanov family.

All of the grand dukes were trained for military service; in Russia they were not even allowed to wear civilian dress except when participating in sports. Then they wore special clothing with a double-headed eagle on the shirt. The war provided opportunity for all of them to serve. But most of the grand dukes simply had staff assignments or merely nominal commands. Kyril commanded a mock navy, the riverine fleet; Boris was named "Ataman," or chief, of all the Cossacks; the tsar assigned Sandro, former navy man, to the air force.

None except Nikolasha seems to have gained any reputation for leadership, with the exception of Michael, younger brother of the tsar.

With the national emergency of war, Nicholas felt he should pardon Michael and allow him to return to Russia, bringing his bride along. Nicholas gave his brother command in Galicia of a Caucasian cavalry division consisting of volunteers from Moslem nationalities. In testimony to its ferocity, it was given the nickname "Wild." Michael proved to be a good officer, much liked by his men.

The sons of Grand Duke Constantine Constantinovich, K.R., had joined the regular army. Prince Oleg was mortally wounded on September 27, 1914. When his division went on the attack, Oleg, commanding a cavalry platoon, volunteered to chase a group of German horsemen. One of them, already wounded, fired and hit the young prince. His wound festered and gangrene set in; the doctors could do nothing. The emperor sent a telegram to Oleg, granting him the St. George Cross, a top military honor. Oleg said that it would be "good for the troops to know that the blood of the Imperial House had been spilled." Oleg was the only Romanov to die in action during World War I.

Grand Duke Sergei Mikhailovich, Sandro's younger brother, in chronic bad health like so many other Romanov men, nonetheless served first as inspector of artillery and later undertook to rationalize the procurement of guns and shell. His own competence cannot be judged, but clearly he was ill served. The artillery department, British observer General Alfred Knox judged, was staffed by experts whose knowledge was completely outdated and whose work patterns were maddeningly slow and bureaucratic. No one had anticipated the awesome quantities of ammunition, weaponry and all other materiel that modern warfare devoured. But even worse than the shortages, which could perhaps be attributed to honest mistakes, was the corruption, the thieves who operated under the shelter of Sergei Mikhailovich's name and reputation. Kshesinskaya, his mistress, was rumored to be lining her pockets with kickbacks from arms contractors, and indeed she sent her own emissary to France to negotiate with Creuzot, the armorer. Headquarters tried to cut its own deals with suppliers. Imports of guns and shells were both inadequate in quantity and exorbitant in price. Corruption was not confined to the artillery department; it became endemic in the whole process of military procurement, and everyone was aware of it.

Sergei's older brother, Bimbo, Grand Duke Nicholas Mikhailovich, had no ambitions for a military career and his personality was ill suited to it, but he did nourish political aspirations. In April 1916, he tried to persuade the tsar to send him as a representative to a future peace conference, an Allied victory now seeming increasingly likely. Nicholas found it "weird" that Uncle Bimbo should think himself suitable for such a state task and refused even to consider it. To prove his loyalty to the emperor, the Romanov "Philippe Egalité" (as he was called by the younger grand dukes) tried to play on the tsar's jealousy of Nikolasha's appeal to the public. He wrote Nicholas that Nikolasha's reputation was a product of Stana's efforts. She was widely distributing numerous portraits, postcards and calendars with Nikolasha on them. Bimbo hinted darkly that Nikolasha's popularity, in view of the nervous mood of the Russian public, threatened the legitimate line of succession, inflating the potential importance of Nikolasha's brother Peter and nephew Roman, suggesting that, through them, the childless Nikolasha could found an alternative branch of the dynasty.

Despite wartime alliance, the ancient Russian sense of rivalry, even enmity, toward Great Britain smouldered, and one June evening in 1916 the Grand Duke Boris got into real trouble because of it. Boris was having supper at military headquarters with some of his friends, joined by a British officer, Major Thornhill. After a glass or two of champagne, and probably more, Boris burst out in anger, exclaiming to the Englishman that

> England doesn't care a straw about this war; she is letting her allies be killed. The French have been suffering massacre at Verdun for four months, and you haven't even left your trenches. We Russians would have been in Baghdad long ago if you hadn't begged us not to enter the place, to save you from admitting your inability to get there yourselves . . . you can be certain that the moment peace is signed with Germany we shall go to war with you!

Furious, Major Thornhill reported the incident to Ambassador Buchanan, who lodged an official protest at court. The empress urged her husband "to send for Boris and wash his head—how dare he say such things—[he] can think what he likes, but to have the impertinence of speaking to an Englishman before others, is rather strong—you must have him reprimanded, he dare not behave so, *the insolent fellow.*" But the damage was done and the British thought that many Russians privately would echo Boris's sentiments. They were right. Boris's father, Grand Duke Vladimir, had remarked in 1898 that he hoped "to live long enough to hear England's death rattle."

But few took anything Boris said seriously; he had a reputation as a man primarily interested in pursuing his own pleasure. Certainly he did little now to contribute to the war effort. His military responsibilities were only vaguely defined and allowed him to travel to attractive places such as the Crimea. He was in excellent health, in his late thirties, rich and privileged. Yet he seemed to have trouble living within his income and ran up a huge debt of nearly half a million rubles with his mother. In one year he spent more than twenty-five thousand rubles for meals, sixteen thousand for servants, and eight thousand for automobiles, and he gave forty-six rubles to the church. Boris's mother wanted to marry him to Olga, Nicholas and Alexandra's oldest daughter. Olga was still a teenager, but she was reaching an age suitable for marriage. The empress was appalled at the idea and wrote to her husband:

> The oftener I think about Boris, the more I realise what an awful set his wife wld. be dragged into. His & Miechen's friends, rich french people, russian bankers, 'the society' . . . intrigues without end—fast manners & conversations & Ducky not a suitable sister-in-law at all—& then Boris' mad past. . . . So give over a well used half worn out, blase young man, to a pure, fresh young girl 18 years his junior & to live in a house in wh. many a woman has 'shared' his life . . . an inexperienced young girl would suffer terribly, to have her husband 4, 5th hand or more.

Miechen of course did not see it this way, and she never forgave the empress for her refusal to consider the match.

Grand Duke Dmitri Pavlovich served at the front in the late summer and autumn of 1914, but the army thereafter relegated him to a ceremonial role at headquarters. The emperor enjoyed Dmitri's conversation and his jokes, and he was a favorite companion of Nicholas for walks and rides. Dmitri skillfully played upon the imperial couple's detestation for Miechen and her Vladimirovichi family, reporting that she said that she enjoyed living at Tsarskoye Selo with the emperor away.

Emperor Alexander II and his daughter Marie, who married Queen Victoria's second son, Alfred. When Marie came to England as a royal daughter-in-law, Victoria openly envied her splendid collection of jewelry. [Royal Danish Library]

Alexander III, the muzhik *tsar, and his wife, Minnie, in Spala. [Krasnogorsk]*

European royals on holiday in Denmark, celebrating Minnie's birthday by spelling out the first initial of her name. Her daughter, Olga, is at center, with the empress seated in the rear. [Royal Danish Library]

Three royal consorts. Olga of Greece (middle), herself a Romanov, is married to William of Denmark (King George I of Greece), brother of the other two ladies in the picture. Left is Queen Alexandra, wife of Edward VII of Great Britain; right is her sister Minnie, Empress Maria Fedorovna of Russia. [Royal Danish Library]

Grand Duke Vladimir Alexandrovich, brother of Alexander III, a patron of the arts who enjoyed a party as much as anyone. [Krasnogorsk]

Е. И. В. Вел. Кн. Марія Павловна.

Grand Duchess Maria Pavlovna Sr., wife of Grand Duke Vladimir, known in the family as Miechen. She was among the most politically ambitious of the Romanov women. In 1920, Queen Mary bought the tiara she is wearing; Queen Elizabeth II now wears it. [Royal Danish Library]

Grand Duke Boris Vladimirovich called this picture "Les Apaches." The person at his back is Princess Radziwill, 1910. [Krasnogorsk]

The celebrated ballet star Kshesinskaya with her son, Vladimir (Vova). No one knew for sure which Romanov grand duke was his father: Andrew Vladimirovich or Sergei Mikhailovich. [Pleshakov]

Olga, Michael, George and their mother, Minnie, now a widow and dowager empress. Her oldest son, Nicky, is Emperor Nicholas II. George the tsesarevich (heir apparent) is dying of tuberculosis. [Royal Danish Library]

Nicky and Ella, Grand Duchess Elizabeth. Sister of his future wife Alexandra of Hesse and wife of Grand Duke Sergei Alexandrovich, Ella was both sister-in-law and aunt to Nicky. The photograph is of a family performance of Eugene Onegin *in which Nicky played Onegin and Ella was Tatiana. The performance was meant to be a "final examination" in Russian for Ella. She demonstrated her linguistic skills and also showed off some of her spectacular jewelry. A statue of Ella, now a saint in the Orthodox Church, stands in Westminster Abbey*

alongside nine other statues representing Christian martyrs who have died in the twentieth century. Queen Elizabeth II and Philip, Duke of Edinburgh, attended the unveiling on July 8, 1998. [Krasnogorsk]

Nicholas and Alexandra, the new rulers of Russia, inspecting Moscow from the roof of the Kremlin. Alexandra was never liked in Russia; people kept saying that there was something vicious in the shape of her lips. Certainly she never smiled in public. [Krasnogorsk]

Grand Duke Alexander Mikhailovich (Sandro), Grand Duchess Xenia Alexandrovna, and children at Sandro's estate, Ai Todor, in the Crimea. They would have two more children but what looked like a happy marriage was not. They spent most of their lives separated, but she would not grant him a divorce. [Krasnogorsk]

Grand Duke Nicholas Mikhailovich (Bimbo), who liked to cultivate the image of cynical man-about-town. [Pleshakov]

Grand Duke Sergei Alexandrovich; his sister-in-law, Minnie; his niece, Grand Duchess Xenia Alexandrovna; and his younger brother, Grand Duke Paul Alexandrovich, c. 1880. [Krasnogorsk]

Grand Duke Dmitri Pavlovich and his older sister, Grand Duchess Maria Pavlovna Jr. These two children were adopted by their uncle and aunt, Sergei and Ella, after their mother died and their father subsequently eloped to Paris with Olga Pistolkors. [Krasnogorsk]

[left] Princess Olga Paley (Pistolkors), married Grand Duke Paul Alexandrovich to the general dismay of the family. They intensely disliked her pleasure at being the wife of a grand duke. [Cartier]

[right] Aboard the imperial yacht, Standart. Alix (Empress Alexandra Fedorovna), Misha (Grand Duke Michael Alexandrovich), an unidentified woman, and Nicholas II. Nicky was always fit; Michael inherited their father's strength and could tear a pack of cards in two. Such informal photographs of the imperial family are rare since it was considered improper for the public to see these godlike figures at play. [Krasnogorsk]

Grand Duke Nicholas
Nikolaevich (Nikolasha)
conferring with the tsar.
Nicholas II never felt
comfortable with his older—
and taller—cousin.
[Royal Danish Library]

[above] Grand Duchess Anastasia
Nikolaevna (Stana), daughter of
the king of Montenegro and wife
of Nikolasha. She and her sister
Militsa lobbied at the Russian
imperial court for the interests of
Montenegro and were known as
"the black plague." [Krasnogorsk]

[left] Grand Duchess Militsa Nikolaevna
married Grand Duke Peter Nikolaevich,
Nikolasha's taciturn brother.
[Krasnogorsk]

Alexandra worried about the stories she heard about Dmitri's wild behavior in Petrograd, his friendships and his frivolities. He seemed to be going astray. "Do, if only possible, find an occasion of speaking to Dmitri about his goings on in town and at such a time," she wrote to her husband. Outwardly Dmitri seemed unchanged, not dissipated by the fast life he was leading. He was a wit; he was charming; he was *the* person everybody in Petrograd wanted to see—a darling of all. He could telegraph the dowager, "Would be very glad if you reserve an appointment for me. Kissing your sweet little hands. Your Dmitri."

Dmitri had grown up to be a handsome, indeed dashing, young man but a Romanov Hamlet, tormented by many things simultaneously: his childhood as a virtual orphan, with his mother dead and his father banned from Russia; the terrible death of his guardian Grand Duke Sergei; his sister, closer to him than any other person, taken to Sweden in the duty of a royal marriage; and his ironic intimacy with the emperor and empress who had made him almost a member of their family but actually had deprived him in childhood of a father and in adolescence a sister. Dmitri remained always an outsider.

Dmitri's major peacetime regimental duty had been training horses for jumping and he himself became very good at it. Indeed, he was the best rider in the whole Guards cavalry, and in 1912, he rode for Russia in the Stockholm Olympics. Riding an Irish horse, he came in seventh in the jumping competition, sharing this place with three other riders. His equestrian success sparked the jealousy of Kyril, who already envied Dmitri's closeness to the imperial family and his dazzling social reputation. In 1912, at the centennial celebration of Napoleon's defeat at Borodino, when the Romanovs visited the battlefield, Kyril noticed a high fence and said to Dmitri, "Well, Olympian, show us how to jump!" Dmitri took the hurdle without fault, leaving Kyril with a festering sense of chagrin.

The emperor had pardoned Dmitri's father, Paul, his last surviving uncle, and permitted him to return to Russia when the war had broken out. Paul's second wife, Olga, had shrewdly asked Rasputin to intercede on her husband's behalf. She had been eager to drop her German title for a Russian one, and Paul secured permission from the emperor for his wife to be promoted from Countess Hohenfelsen to Princess Paley, taking the name of a Cossack chief to whom she was related.

There was no love lost between Dmitri and his stepmother. Olga, Princess Paley, had her own son by Paul, Vladimir, upon whom she doted. The fact that her own morganatic marriage meant that Vladimir could never be a grand duke like Dmitri irritated her tremendously. Dmitri, on his part, wrote to the emperor saying that he saw the "honorable family of Countess Hohenfelsen" as little as possible, thus making life in St. Petersburg, he said, much more peaceful.

Dmitri could only pity his father, so dominated by his aggressive second wife. In October 1916, Princess Paley was outraged to find that Grand Duke Paul had been choosing wines from their cellar and taking them to army headquarters, where he was then stationed. "I would somehow understand if you treated the Sovereign to it," the princess complained, "but to waste it on Dmitri or Grand Duke George Mikhailovich was totally unnecessary."

Princess Paley believed that Dmitri was scheming not only against her son but also against his own father. She wrote to her husband, "I have been telling you in every letter; 'don't trust Dmitri,' and I myself was deceived by his damned tricks! I have rarely *hated* people, *as I hate him right now!*"

Unlike Princess Paley, other Romanov women distinguished themselves during the war for their work with the wounded. They turned their palaces into hospitals and dipped into their own pockets to buy medical supplies. And they became nurses. Although they brought more commitment than skill to their ministrations, without such private efforts the Russian wounded would have had a much more bitter experience. And for the women, it meant a personal liberation, a freedom not possible in ordinary times. Dmitri's sister Marie became an army nurse early in the war. The training was rudimentary, lasting only for a few days; she received a certificate of accomplishment and left promptly for the front, August 29, 1914, reporting to the army of General Rennenkampf then in East Prussia. Dmitri was not far.

The grand duchess tried to preserve her anonymity and seems to have been successful in doing so. She began to enjoy herself thoroughly, relishing being part of the war effort. The soldiers, she believed, saw her and the other nurses as saintly figures, uniting the qualities of motherhood and wifehood, offering comfort, solace and kindness. She later wrote that "my happiness was so great that I was at times remorseful at experiencing such ecstasy in the midst of all this pain." For the first time in her life she was doing something useful.

After the disaster of Tannenberg, Marie was assigned to a new hospital established in the town of Pskov, and she would remain there for two and a half years. She who had never directed anyone except servants was now head nurse and there she worked quietly, remote from both the glittering life of the capital and the comfort of the country estate that she had always known in Russia.

The tsar's younger sister Olga especially welcomed the opportunity to escape her St. Petersburg life and become an army nurse. She had the misfortune of having been born plain in a family and society that like most prized good looks, especially for women. Only much later, in old age, would Olga's face, shaped and limned by character and experience, take on a luminous and burnished beauty. Unwilling to hurt others in any possible way, instinctively shy, stolid and patient, totally consumed by a mother whom she adored, Olga for a long time suppressed her own strong will and lived within her mother's shadow, always trying to please, mistakenly perceived by the world as simply part of Minnie's entourage.

Olga had grown up to be the most democratic of the Romanovs. She was the only member of the family to take ordinary trains and cabs. She had inherited something of her father's *muzhik* quality; she knew how to talk to cabbies and to peasants also, and delighted in nursing the peasant children at her estate in Voronezh province. Of extraordinarily simple tastes, Olga was probably the only Romanov female to have no interest in jewelry or clothing. Had she been beautiful, she would have been the Cinderella of the family.

Olga was long unhappily married and sexually frustrated; her husband, Prince Peter of Oldenburg, a minor Romanov offshoot, had no interest in women and in fact the marriage, Olga said, was never even consummated. Minnie had arranged the match and forced her daughter into it; as a result Olga could be neither wife nor mother. The traditional life patterns for a Romanov woman were therefore closed to her; her frustrations became intense.

She tried to establish herself as a professional artist. Like Bimbo, who had won the reputation of a "real historian," Olga wanted artistic acknowledgment. Her talents as a painter were only modest, but she was a grand duchess after all and the public was eager to see anything a grand duchess might offer. Once Olga sent her work to a major exhibition at St. Petersburg to which the best Russian painters, including Ilya Repin, were submitting. That year Repin had presented his *October 17th*, a painting of great power defiantly depicting how the revolutionary mobs of 1905 had reacted to Nicky's manifesto. The censor, noting the red flags in the picture, declared that the exhibition would not be opened until Repin withdrew his contribution to it. Repin smiled. He put Olga's "little sketches," as he called them, next to his own shocking work. The next day the censor reversed his judgment and allowed the exhibition to open.

Although in the years that followed, Olga's career as an artist did not develop as she would have wished, her private life improved considerably. Her husband, Peter, proved to be tolerant of his wife, allowing her in 1903 to bring into their home a tall young fair-haired army officer named Nicholas Kulikovsky whom Olga had first seen on military parade at Gatchina. She had fallen deeply in love with him, and the two lived together under Oldenburg's roof for thirteen years.

Kulikovsky was more aristocratic in appearance than Olga, but he was a commoner, totally unsuitable as husband to a grand duchess. Olga finally told her family, early in the war, that she fervently wanted to divorce Oldenburg and marry Kulikovsky. About the marriage Alix expressed her horror to Nicky: "She, an Emperor's Daughter and sister! . . . Society morals are falling to pieces . . . what would your father have said to all this?" The tsar allowed the divorce, and Olga told her mother that the local peasants said it was because Peter of Oldenburg was German.

Olga's mother was as unfeeling as Alix, although, in November 1916, she relented sufficiently to attend Olga's second wedding. Olga wrote to Minnie afterwards:

> I can't tell you how I thank you and how awfully happy and touched I am that you came to Church and to the wedding supper! Mama dear, I'll never forget how kind you were and how you put aside all your ideas and feelings for my sake. I can't imagine how you could change everything in yourself so quickly!

Minnie may have gone to the wedding, but she was too rigidly conventional ever to accept the groom as a real member of the family, and Olga's children were never as important to her as Xenia's. Olga knew this and would resent it for the rest of her life, although it was not in her character to complain about it. Her happy marriage and the satisfying work as an army nurse now gave a new joy to Olga's life.

Among the Romanov army nurses, none was more prominent or more professional than the empress, but unfortunately she received little gratitude from the public for her work. Despite her own poor health, Alexandra did not flinch from the bloodiest and most disagreeable tasks, sewing up torn genitals, assisting at amputations, performing these procedures with a cool detachment. Her skills were not those of a professional. But that was less important than the fact that her patients seemed almost disappointed to be nursed by their empress, and her hard work did little to help her unpopularity.

The emperor, on the other hand, with his charm and immense dignity—in spite of his relatively small height he always seemed taller than anyone else in the room—made a far stronger impression in the hospitals, although he did nothing but move slowly through the wards, smile and utter a few banal remarks. Nicholas had liquidated his substantial British bank account to finance military hospitals, but the public knew nothing about it.

The Great War caused European nationalism and militarism to triumph over kinship. Within the greater European royal family, cousin was obliged to fight cousin; brothers and sisters found themselves on opposing sides; wives chose their husband's countries over their own. In Russia Alix and Ella and in England their sister Victoria of Battenburg were split from their brother Ernst Ludwig and their sister Irene, who was married to the kaiser's brother. Queen Elizabeth of the Belgians, born to the Bavarian royal house, said of her German kin, "It is finished between me and them; henceforth an iron curtain has descended between us."

But in the case of Nicky and Alix, that iron curtain was descending between them and their own people, and Rasputin was responsible. Russians increasingly and universally hated the war and the moral rot it seemed to bring. To many, including Romanovs, Rasputin had come to personify that corruption, an evil that must be destroyed.

⟳

Just before the outbreak of war Grand Duke Dmitri had fallen in with Felix Yusupov, the richest man in Russia. The Yusupovs, an ancient family of Tatar origin, owned a tremendous amount of property, including roughly fifty residences throughout Russia. The Yusupov art collection rivalled that of the Romanovs and included such unique items as a mouse carved from a single sapphire, its eyes made of rubies and its tail of diamonds. Seven months before Europe's plunge into war, Felix had married the beautiful Princess Irina, only daughter of Sandro and Xenia, and Minnie's favorite granddaughter.

Felix was an extraordinarily handsome, almost beautiful young man, with large blue-gray mocking eyes, long lashes, thin nose and a mouth with a slight twist at the corners. Fond of masked balls and of theater, Felix's greatest talent would have been for the stage, an unthinkable career for a man of his social position in Russia.

Felix was well known for his overt homosexuality, and in the minds of some, the intensity of his friendship with Dmitri raised questions about the sexual tastes of the young grand duke. Older members of the family spoke with concern about Dmitri's wild social life and thought Felix a bad influence. Before his wedding Felix promised to reform. That promise made Sandro and Xenia agree to allow the marriage. Indeed the marriage proved long and successful, weathering the dramatic turn of fortune the revolution would bring to the couple.

In 1916, Felix's mother, Princess Zinaida, worried that her son seemed to be suffering from "temporary insanity." As the following events would show, the source of his anxiety and his obsession was Rasputin.

Felix had first met Grigory Rasputin, "Grishka" (the familiar diminutive his enemies sometimes condescendingly used), in 1911, driven by sheer curiosity to know this controversial holy man about whom everyone was talking. In the fall of 1916 he renewed the acquaintance.

Rasputin and Felix were fascinated with each other. Rasputin was attracted by Felix's beauty, wealth, social status, his marriage into the imperial family and the beauty of his wife. On his side, Felix felt thrilled by Rasputin's hypnotic powers but repelled by Rasputin's attempt to control his mind and body. Felix later wrote of lying on Rasputin's couch:

> His hypnotic power was tremendous. I felt the unknown force entering me and spreading all over my body. At the same time rigidity came. I felt numb. I wanted to say something, but my tongue would not move. Slowly I sank into a drowsy state, as if I had drunk a sleeping potion. The only thing I saw was Rasputin's burning stare.

Bimbo, a homosexual himself, was fairly sure that the meetings between Felix and Rasputin consisted not only of heavy drinking but also of kissing, fondling and something more. At any rate, Felix concluded that in order to break free, he must kill Rasputin.

Felix invited several people to join in a conspiracy to kill Rasputin: a right-wing politician, Vladimir Purishkevich, whom he had gotten to know only recently; his own trusted friend, Lieutenant Ivan Sukhotin; Doctor Stanislaus Lasavert (Purishkevich's choice); and Grand Duke Dmitri. Dmitri detested Rasputin, whom he thought was destroying the Romanov dynasty; and of course Dmitri was intensely loyal to Felix.

On December 16th, Rasputin told his household, "I am going to the little one," referring to Felix. Rasputin was closely watched by the tsar's secret police, whose agents were supposed to guard him from potential assailants, watching his apartment but not normally keeping him under surveillance. Felix was free to spirit Rasputin away for the killing.

From shortly after midnight until three A.M., Felix and Rasputin were alone together downstairs in the Yusupov Palace. Felix had dismissed the servants. As Grishka and Felix ate and drank, the other conspirators were gathered nervously on the floor above waiting for Grishka to get drunk. The wine he was drinking and the cakes he was eating contained potassium cyanide. To the amazement of the conspirators, the poison had no apparent effect on its victim. Earlier they had given the same poison to a large dog which had died immediately. Felix left Rasputin and ran upstairs demanding that Dmitri give him a revolver. Dmitri at first resisted but ultimately yielded. At least two other conspirators, Purishkevich and Sukhotin, had handguns too but Felix wanted to use the revolver of his intimate friend and member of the dynasty, as if to give the act special meaning.

Downstairs Felix began again talking to Grishka. Then he took out the gun and fired at his victim from a very close distance, hitting his chest and abdomen. Rasputin fell to the floor; Felix believed he was dead and went upstairs, inviting the others to come see. The doctor looked at Rasputin and declared that he was still alive but in his death agony and would stop breathing in a few minutes. Dmitri, Sukhotin and the doctor then went outside to start the car that was to take away the body.

Felix and Purishkevich remained upstairs for awhile, then Felix went downstairs again to find Grishka lying with his eyes closed. Putting his hand on the fallen man's chest, Felix saw Rasputin suddenly open first his left eye and then his right and then fix his gaze on

Felix with a wild hatred. Felix sprang back. Rasputin rose to his feet and jumped like a beast at Felix, grasping his shoulders and tearing off his epaulettes. Felix managed to tear himself away, and Grishka, with a roar and a hiss, foaming at the mouth, started to crawl up the staircase on all fours.

Felix ran for help. When he and Purishkevich returned, the room was empty and they were horrified to find Rasputin very much alive and outside, staggering around in the snowy yard. Purishkevich then fired two shots at him, one bullet hitting the leg and the other the back of Rasputin's head. Grishka fell at the gate; Felix reached him and began to beat him savagely with a rubber baton until he finally appeared to be dead.

They took the body into the house and Felix suddenly began again to hit the face of the corpse. The others tore Felix away from his prey with some difficulty, thrust him on the sofa and left him there. They then shot a dog in the yard to explain the bloodstains on the snow. A policeman came, having heard the shots, and he was told that the young gentlemen were having fun at a party and that the grand duke had killed a dog. The doctor was supposed to drive away with the corpse, but he fainted and Dmitri had to drive the car himself.

At some point on this, Rasputin's last journey, the assassins unbuttoned Rasputin's trousers to check his member, notorious in Petrograd. Rasputin's sexual prowess had provoked many conflicting rumors. Disappointingly the conspirators apparently found Rasputin's penis of ordinary size and character. They then took the corpse and tossed it into the icy Neva.

Meanwhile Felix hastily wrote a letter to the empress in which he admitted that he had held a party at his palace on December 16th, that Dmitri had killed a dog there, and that he himself had talked to Rasputin on the telephone, Rasputin inviting him to go to the gypsies with him, an invitation that he had refused.

A rumor ran through the city that Rasputin was murdered and the suspected assassins were Felix, Purishkevich and Dmitri.

On December 18th, Ella, now a mother superior, full of Christian piety, sent two telegrams, one to Dmitri and one to Felix's mother, praising the patriotic act and greedily asking for the gory details. She had for some time been convinced that Rasputin was leading the Romanovs to ruin but utterly failed to convince her sister, the empress, to that effect. On December 19th, Felix moved to Dmitri's apartment.

Bimbo visited the two and greeted them, "Gentlemen assassins, I salute you!"

People could not help wondering if Dmitri's role had been as insignificant as Felix reported. A rumor attributed to Purishkevich ran that Dmitri had actually fired the two shots that killed Rasputin. Other members of the conspiracy reportedly had concealed that fact, hoping that Dmitri would become the next Russian emperor, which could not possibly happen if he had been directly involved in such a sordid crime.

While Marie was nursing at the military hospital in Pskov, she learned of the assassination and that her brother had apparently taken a leading part with Felix Yusupov in the bloody event, without her knowing anything about it. "For the first time in my life," she wrote, "my brother appeared to me an individual being standing apart from me, and this feeling of unaccustomed estrangement made me shiver."

Because Dmitri was of imperial blood, he could not be treated like an ordinary criminal, and his personal closeness to the emperor seemed a shield against punishment. But his suspected role in the crime, his very presence at the event, shattered his friendship with the imperial couple. Dmitri swore to his father that there was no blood on his hands, but the empress could not forgive him for having been there and neither she nor the emperor ever saw him again.

Felix was elated by the sudden popularity he got from the murder; Dmitri was frightened by it, and apprehensive of the consequences. Felix wanted to talk about it and did; Dmitri kept silent.

The emperor decided that Dmitri would go into exile in Persia, to report for military duty there, on the war's most remote front. Persia was then divided between Russia and Britain, both waging war upon Turkey at its eastern flank. For Dmitri the sentence represented something of a danger. Leaving Petrograd made him more vulnerable to a possible attack by Rasputin's partisans, religious fanatics from all strata of society. In the remoteness of Central Asia a grand duke could far more easily disappear without a trace than he could at the capital. But he had no choice; the tsar's will was absolute.

At 2 A.M., December 23rd, Dmitri left Petrograd for his Persian exile. The chief of police came to announce that a special train would be ready about midnight at the Nikolaevsky Station. Two men would accompany the grand duke on the journey, but no one was supposed to come to the station to see him off. Marie defied imperial authority and drove with her brother through the deserted city streets to the station. Uncle Bimbo and Sandro also ignored the tsar's will and came to the station to see their kinsman depart.

On the silent, bitter cold, dimly lit platform the police stood watching. Dmitri was calm, but very pale. Marie and Dmitri crossed themselves and hugged each other. They did not know when or even if they would see each other again. He boarded the train and it began to edge out of the station. For a long time Marie could see through her tears Dmitri's white-gloved hand waving his cap. In the railway car Dmitri broke down and wept for the entire first day of the trip.

This was the first time in history that a member of the dynasty had been punished for any violence against a commoner.

The empress decided that Felix should be exiled too, but his punishment was a mere slap on the wrist: He was sent to the comfort of one of his many estates, although not to his largest near Kiev. Kiev had by now been turned by the dowager into an informal center for all family members who were in opposition to the empress, and Alix had no wish to strengthen that group.

On December 29th, many members of the Romanov family (Olga, Queen of Greece, Miechen, Kyril, Ducky, Boris and Andrew, Paul, Marie, Bimbo, Sergei Mikhailovich, K.R.'s widow Elizabeth Mavrikievna (Mavra) and a number of their children) assembled at the Vladimir Palace and signed a collective letter to the tsar, beseeching him to send Dmitri to one of his estates and not to Persia with its epidemics and terrible living conditions. Sandro thought the letter "silly" and did not sign it, not on moral grounds but because he thought it useless. "It almost seemed that they [the petitioners] expected the Tsar of Russia to decorate his two relatives for having committed a murder," he scoffed. None of the tsar's siblings signed. Nor did the Nikolaevichi, Nikolasha or Peter. Nor did Ella, the empress's sister, despite her hatred of Rasputin.

Many of these non-signers were not then in Petrograd. But their assent could probably have been obtained by telegraph, *if* they had been willing. Indeed some disapproved. Nicky's sister, Olga, called Rasputin's death a simple case of "a murder premeditated most vilely." That a grand duke and the husband of a grand duke's daughter should be most closely associated with it "proved how low we had fallen."

Beneath the issues of Dmitri's punishment and the murder itself lay a more profound difference of opinion. Those who signed the petition were seeking to wield the moral authority of the family as a weapon against a tsar whom they saw as weak and capricious, totally in thrall to his powerful and execrable wife. The others in the family were less sure. They may have disliked Alix and deplored her influence over Nicky, but they were not prepared to break their oath of allegiance to him.

The emperor replied to the family's petition two days later: "Nobody has the right to be involved in murder. I know that many consciences are troubled, for not only Dmitri is involved. I am surprised at your address to me." Correct though he may have been in his judgment, the tsar's reply served to cut the last ties between him and the signers of the petition. From then on, Nicky and Alix kept more and more to themselves.

The word was soon out all over the town. Dmitri's sister journeyed to Kiev to intercede with the dowager, but she refused to intervene. Minnie had never gotten along well with Alix; relations between her and her daughter-in-law were by now so strained that she knew that she could do nothing even if she were to try.

Dmitri meanwhile was well on his way to Persia. After four days of travel, he and his companions had reached Baku on the Caspian Sea, sailing the next morning to the southern, Persian shore. He was headed for the headquarters of General Nicholas Baratov, commander of the Russian army in Persia, where he was to be stationed. He felt thoroughly miserable. He had headaches and experienced difficulty in walking. He would lie down, but sleep would not come.

Dmitri had the impression that he was going to the edge of the world. At Enzeli, on the Persian Caspian coast, he was horrified to learn that the land journey would be half again as long as he had thought. General Baratov, meanwhile, was alarmed that he would now have a grand duke to serve under him. "God help me to cope with this new task!" he confided to his diary.

At the town of Kazvin, General Baratov greeted Dmitri. To Dmitri, Baratov, who was of Ossetian origins, therefore Asian, appeared cunning and only hypocritically friendly. On this score the frightened grand duke was wrong. Baratov admired him greatly: "My front has been visited by Grand Duke Dmitri Pavlovich, the hero of all Russia! for he was part of the murder of Grishka Rasputin, that horrible evil of modern Russia!" he wrote.

Dmitri, listening to the chanting priest at the New Year mass, felt he would burst into tears, so far away from the world he knew, now surrounded by complete strangers. But the atmosphere was warmly friendly, the tents were lit with hundreds of candles, a local luxury, and all the nurses and two female doctors from the nearby military hospital came by to enliven the party. Dmitri drank a lot of wine, then switched to vodka, having one shot after another in a "light and beautiful" movement of his hand. Baratov worried that "after these inevitable festivities we should revert to our routine life without vodka, otherwise the grand duke will perish here."

Dmitri impressed Baratov as a modest and unusually friendly person considering that he was a grand duke. Dmitri had in fact charmed the whole company, responding to all the toasts drunk to his health in a pleasant and clever way, as if forgetting that he was in exile and not in his own palace. Dmitri knew how to be a royal. That evening he confessed to Baratov that he was proud to have been part of the murder plot. He knew that he was very popular in Russia and the emperor thought it necessary to send him as far away as possible: "That's why I have been sent to your Persian front," he said. The grand duke reiterated that his hands had not been stained by blood, but later in the evening he pulled out a revolver by which, he said, "that mad dog" had been killed.

Any perceptive person would establish the connection: the dog in the yard that Dmitri had been saying he killed, and Rasputin, now described as "a mad dog." Was not the original version of the grand duke having shot a dog a story in code, invented by the ingenious Felix? Had not Dmitri actually performed the ritual killing as a redemption for the dynasty? Certainly Dmitri's fellow officers reasoned this way. They lauded the killing of Rasputin as a patriotic deed, without mentioning any of the circumstances of his death, simply referring to the joyful news. Dmitri himself remained publicly circumspect. Writing to his father, he said that whoever killed Rasputin was a passionate lover of the motherland. Loyalty to the monarchy meant that the assassin or assassins could not tolerate the situation in which, during the enormous strain of war, Russia was being governed by little notes written by a lecherous, dirty and almost illiterate scoundrel.

After the New Year party, Dmitri was showered with official and informal dinner invitations, and by the beginning of February, he had cheered up. A "human being is an animal which can adjust to anything," he wrote.

Although Dmitri's spirits had risen, he still felt that he could not take Holy Communion. His friends thought it was because he was not at peace with his Maker, but the matter was more complex. The Romanovs, like Nicky, Alix and Nikolasha, attracted to mysticism, had nonetheless remained faithful to Orthodoxy. Orthodoxy, after all, was firmly married to autocracy. But Dmitri had left Orthodoxy. Secretly, under the influence of the healer and political schemer Peter Badmaev, who had intrigued Nicholas II with his vision of Russian expansion into eastern Asia, Dmitri had become an adept of Asian esoteric rituals, all the rage in Petersburg high society. Now Dmitri's new faith became a major source of solace and a spiritual crutch. He fought despair and physical ailments (and hangovers) with gymnastics, breathing exercises and mantras. The teachings that gave him hope offered a potpourri of Asian philosophies, from Buddhism to Yoga.

❧

The continuing war made everybody in Russia unhappy, even angry. The "gray coats" were kept in the trenches against their will. For them, a war fought for the sake of "Serbian brethren," the Allies and the Black Sea straits was meaningless and its suffering therefore totally unjustified. Soldiers wanted to go back home to their families and blamed the government, personified by the Romanovs, for continuing the senseless massacre. Those in the comfort of the rear, still longing for victory, accused the dynasty of weak leadership, outrageous inefficiency and the absence of any military talent. Thus the Romanovs seemed to hinder both war and peace and were hated by both left and right.

Shortly after Rasputin's murder, Sandro went to see the empress at Tsarskoye Selo, talking to her for nearly two hours in her bedroom with its numerous icons and church lamps, more like a sanctuary than a place to sleep. The tsar, also present, listened mutely while the empress heatedly argued with the grand duke. Sandro tried to persuade the imperial couple to grant the nation a government that could enjoy popular trust, asserting that police power alone could no longer suppress dissent. He got nowhere and left in despair.

Sandro undoubtedly cherished his own political ambitions. As early as 1912, his older brother Bimbo, never shy about making recommendations, had proposed to Nicholas that, given Alexis's illness and Michael's disinterest in the throne, the succession rights should go to the family of Nicky's sister, Xenia, and her husband Sandro. This would mean that Sandro's offspring would start a new branch of emperors and, incidentally, cut the Vladimirovichi out of the succession.

Sandro subsequently put his own advice for political reform to the tsar in a letter that he had started to draft as early as December 25th, influenced by Rasputin's assassination. He argued that "forces inside Russia" were taking Nicholas and the nation to collapse, and that Nicholas himself was actually promoting a revolutionary mood. "We witness the unprecedented sight of a revolution carried out not from below, but from above," were the last words of his letter.

Sandro then wrote a long letter to Bimbo, expressing his enormous frustrations with Nicky's reluctance to face the growing political crisis.

> Either we sit back with folded arms and wait for the humiliation of Russia, or we take heroic measures. The situation is without issue, and such as Russia has never experienced before, and so people who love Russia find themselves at a cross roads and wonder how to act; for the first time in our lives, we have to ask how far we are bound by the oath given. In all it's a nightmare, from which I see no escape.

Rumors of a coup d'état swirled about. French ambassador Paleologue, a notorious gossip, wrote on December 23rd that grand dukes Kyril, Boris and Andrew were talking of saving the monarchy by changing the sovereign. Four guards regiments were to join in a midnight march on Tsarskoye Selo to proclaim young Alexis as emperor with Nikolasha as regent.

Prince George Lvov, influential in governmental circles because of his experience, common sense and aloofness from factional squabbles, sent an emissary to negotiate with Nikolasha. Lvov suggested that Nikolasha should become the new monarch, granting a limited constitution and appointing Lvov as prime minister. Nicholas was to be exiled, Alexandra sent to a convent, although the possibility of killing her was not excluded from the discussion. Lvov believed that Nikolasha should proclaim himself emperor, remaining in the Caucasus, surrounded by loyal troops.

If Nikolasha accepted this idea, Lvov instructed the emissary to send a telegram to St. Petersburg: "Hospital is open. Come." Nikolasha reacted evasively to Lvov's message, saying that he was not sure how the people and the army would react. Two days later he informed Lvov's emissary that he was sure that the army would not support the coup. And that was the end of Prince Lvov's conspiracy.

Michael's name as possible new emperor was mentioned, and even a date was whispered: March 1st. But a more popular candidate emerged. A group of grand dukes supported the idea of Dmitri marrying Olga, oldest daughter of the emperor, and declaring himself heir apparent. That marriage of course is what Miechen had wanted for her favorite son Boris. And so the family talked and hesitated, unable to rally around any one plan or any one person. In early January, the tsar, fearing widespread treason among the family, exiled Bimbo to his estate. The Vladimirovichi too were cut down to size. Kyril was dispatched to cold and distant Port Romanov (Murmansk) on the Arctic Ocean where he was "to thank the sailors for their service." Andrew was sent the same month for "medical treatment" in the Caucasus at Kislovodsk. Boris was ignored, dismissed as a person "interested only in getting drunk," but eventually he too would go to the Caucasus, joined by their mother, Miechen, who left St. Petersburg saying loftily that she would be back when "everything is over."

On February 23, 1917, amidst all these imperial conspiracies, bread riots broke out in Petrograd. In desperation the people took matters into their own hands. They wanted bread and they wanted peace. But they also wanted blood.

PART TWO

Descent

At the pillory we'll have a feast
For all good citizens remaining,
When with the gut of the last priest
We shall strangle the last tsar!

—Alexander Pushkin (1819)

CHAPTER SIX

"The Crown Falls from the Royal Head"

FEBRUARY 22–MARCH 3, 1917

A S THE RIOTERS, MANY OF THEM WOMEN, roamed the streets of Petrograd, shouting "give us bread" and singing the *Marseillaise,* anybody who owned property was cowering behind locked doors and shuttered windows in the third and coldest winter of the war. Arctic temperatures had slowed down the railways and stopped many factories. Fear grappled with revolutionary enthusiasm as Russia's capital slipped into increasing disorder.

On February 22nd, Nicholas left for military headquarters, the *Stavka,* which had now, after the great retreat, moved east to Mogilev. He had not been there since Rasputin's murder, spending all his time from Christmas until the eve of spring with his family at Tsarskoye Selo, chopping wood, playing dominoes and reading aloud his favorite Sherlock Holmes stories. Nicholas had been leading the quiet life he so enjoyed while attempting to direct the nation in the war effort and calm the increasingly restless and dissatisfied Romanovs. He thought he could dispel family fractiousness by dispersing its members. Scattered they could less easily plot against him.

The tsar felt more secure with all these potential troublemakers away from the capital and the center of power. And for the first time in his life he had mustered the courage to show an iron fist to the other

Romanovs. Rasputin had been a problem for him for some time, a healer for his son yet definitely a political nuisance, but on that matter he had been unable to oppose the will of his wife Alexandra. Now that conspirators had taken care of Rasputin, Nicholas could hope to control his own household.

But he was leaving Tsarskoye Selo with a heavy heart: His children were sick with what were believed to be heavy colds, and if the girls, all now in their mid teens or early twenties, seemed to be doing all right, Alexis's fragile health was always a matter of great concern. Still, the nation called. The tsar felt he had been neglecting his duty as commander-in-chief for too long. Arriving at Mogilev, Nicholas received worrisome news. The diagnosis at home was not colds but the measles. Deeply anxious, nonetheless he would not rush home. Now was the time to deal again with Russia's arch-enemy, the German kaiser. Spring seemed to promise opportunity for consolidation at home and offensive on the battlefields. But it brought about collapse instead.

The February 23rd food riots that broke out in Petrograd exploded like a natural force, a volcanic eruption. But for at least a year, many persons in authority had darkly anticipated and predicted the explosion. Two and a half years of war with Germany had enormously burdened a nation struggling to restore its fragile political and social unity, shattered in the revolution of 1905.

The riots started at the bread lines. Then they engulfed the factories. In a matter of hours, the "gray coats," the soldiers, themselves became infected. Peter's city, the core of Romanov authority for two centuries, made the revolution and carried the nation along with it. Other cities and the countryside offered neither support to the tsar nor resistance to the revolutionaries. Yet life at Mogilev headquarters remained quiet; the unrest in the capital looked isolated if chaotic, and so it was for the first three days. Only on the 25th did Nicholas send a telegram to General Sergei Khabalov at Petrograd, commanding him to stop the riots by "tomorrow," using military force.

General Khabalov was shocked by the tsar's blithe assumption that it could be easily done. Within several days, twenty-five thousand soldiers out of the one hundred sixty thousand comprising the capital's garrison were already mingling sympathetically with the crowds, and the other troops seemed unwilling to participate in a civil war. By February 27th, the number of the faithful had shrunk radically and, in a matter of hours, the position of those who had not gone over to the side of the rioters started looking desperate.

To experienced politicians at Petrograd the events looked increasingly less like a riot than a revolution. Driven by the desire to save the monarchy and to quell the violence in the streets, the Chairman of the State Duma, Michael Rodzianko, renewed his efforts to obtain the emperor's consent for a "government of popular confidence," only to meet with the infuriatingly calm stubbornness of Nicholas. The tsar's faith in his own absolute power seemed unshakeable. In the evening of the 26th, Rodzianko sent Nicholas a telegram pleading with him to "save Russia" by making constitutional concessions because he saw the situation in the capital as potentially disastrous. The tsar merely commented that "this fat man Rodzianko has again written some rubbish to which I am not even going to reply."

Terrified by the revolutionary tide, Rodzianko decided that promoting a regency for the tsar's brother Michael was the only way to save the monarchy. The feckless Misha, never involved in politics, now suddenly became a key figure. In the afternoon of the 27th, he held a prolonged conference with Rodzianko and Prime Minister Prince Nicholas Golytsin, a meeting kept secret from all the other Romanovs. The news that Michael was considering a regency apparently reached the family only a couple of days later.

Rodzianko was keeping these negotiations secret from other parliamentary leaders as well. By this time, Rodzianko was the major figure in the government, in a tempestuous and highly volatile situation. At about ten P.M. Michael telegraphed Nicholas's Chief of Staff General Michael Alexeev at Mogilev, offering himself as temporary regent. Nicholas, informed of this message by Alexeev, told the general to thank Michael for his readiness to help and to inform him that the tsar was returning to Tsarskoye Selo. The enemy at home suddenly seemed more threatening than the enemy on the front.

Michael, unable to reach his suburban residence at Gatchina because no trains were running, then went to the Winter Palace. Finding the family nest guarded by loyal soldiers, the grand duke nonetheless summarily ordered them out of the palace, telling Khabalov at 3 A.M., February 28th, that he did not want soldiers firing on the people from the "house of the Romanovs." The last thing Michael wanted to see was a repetition of the Bloody Sunday of 1905, when crowds had been slaughtered in front of the Winter Palace. Should it happen again, now, he might appear responsible for it.

In the early hours of February 28th, the troops moved back across the square from the Winter Palace to the Admiralty, many deserting on the way, and the same night the last imperial government disintegrated. The ministers simply walked out of their meeting place, the Mariinsky Palace, where Michael had conferred with them the previous evening. They would never again assemble as a government.

Revolution had become a fact. In the city, huge crowds spilled out of all the buildings, forming a dark mass of soldiers, workers and intellectuals, the revolutionary people. To the monarchists, they looked like barbarians, "Scythians." All over the city arose a "howling of the *Marseillaise*" as the surging crowds roared through the streets.

Nicholas in his Mogilev headquarters seemed to be completely out of touch with events, not realizing what was going on in the capital and that the violence even threatened the lives of his wife and children. Sergei Mikhailovich was now the only grand duke at Mogilev, in charge of artillery. Sandro, commanding the air force, was in Kiev, as was Minnie. Her daughter, Olga, was now off in the countryside on her honeymoon.

Bimbo returned to the capital on his own initiative, liberating himself from two months' confinement at his country estate. The contrary-minded Bimbo, grandson of the Iron Tsar Nicholas I, was the only truly pro-revolutionary Romanov. Other grand dukes, such as Dmitri Constantinovich in Petrograd and Sandro's brother George Mikhailovich at Gatchina, remained politically passive. The tsar's sister, Xenia, preoccupied with her large family, uninterested in politics, was also in the capital. Michael was there too, wrestling with the possibility of becoming successor to his brother. The emperor's only surviving uncle, Paul Alexandrovich, relished political intrigue and enjoyed proximity to the imperial household at Tsarskoye Selo; he was trying to introduce the idea of a constitutional monarchy, with Nicholas II remaining emperor.

Nikolasha and his faithful brother Peter were in Tiflis, at the Caucasian front, according to some reports very much aware of what was going on and even talking seriously with the local Georgian revolutionaries about Nikolasha's political prospects. Miechen, with Andrew, was still in her disguised exile at Kislovodsk in the northern Caucasus, not knowing much about what was happening but hoping that Nikolasha would "take *everything* into his hands." Although she still nourished strong hopes for her son Kyril, she was more of a realist than he and understood that, at this point, only a soldier, Nikolasha, the most popular Romanov, could curb the revolution.

Thus in this time for decision the emperor was on his own, not that he cared much any more for the opinions of the family.

On February 27th, wanting someone tougher than Khabalov seemed to be, the tsar had decided to send General Nicholas Ivanov to Petrograd with fresh troops drawn from the front. The next day, in spite of new reports of riots from the capital, the mood at headquarters was not at all alarmist, and the emperor in no haste left for Tsarskoye Selo, in Petrograd's suburbs. Nicholas was confident that his presence at the capital would restore order. The date of his departure had been duly reported to the empress. She began to count the hours before their reunion.

The imperial train left Mogilev at 5 A.M., February 28th. All the passengers were asleep, and the train headed northeast, towards the capital.

At 4 P.M., the tsar received news that the imperial train had been rerouted to Petrograd instead of Tsarskoye Selo. This had been done on the order of the Provisional Committee of the State Duma now exercising the role of a temporary government; there were those who were eager to keep Nicholas from his wife as long as possible, knowing that she would stiffen his resistance to making any concessions to political change. The tsar did not know what had caused the change in plan, but in any case Palace Commandant Vladimir Voeikov defiantly declared that the train would break through to Tsarskoye Selo via Tosno, a small railway junction less than thirty miles from the capital.

But at 2:10 A.M. March 1st, when only three hours should have separated Nicky from Alix, news came that the rebels had seized Tosno. The tsar decided to move the train southwest to Pskov, the nearest military post, in an effort to stay in touch with Mogilev, Petrograd and Tsarskoye Selo. Arriving at Pskov at 7:33 P.M., Nicholas met the commander of the northern front, General Nicholas Ruzsky, who suggested a political solution to the crisis, a compromise with the leaders of the revolution. The tsar resisted Ruzsky's suggestion; he would yield only to the formation of a new government with ministers reporting to him, not to the Duma.

Nicholas still believed he was in command, but he now learned he was cut off from headquarters at Mogilev, which was now struck by panic. The emperor, however, was less concerned about headquarters than about his wife: It must be so hard on poor Alix to go through all this by herself, he thought.

The same day, General Sir John Hanbury-Williams, head of the British military mission in Russia, sent a letter to Nicholas, calling himself an "old soldier" and not a diplomat or a politician and declaring his loyalty to Nicholas and his wife. The Englishman argued that the riots in Petrograd were due to "German intrigue," but could be crushed only if the emperor would recognize the government chosen by the rebellious people and promote freedom of speech, putting a "velvet glove on the iron hand." This letter reached the tsar in Pskov together with several others of the same tone, including one from his brother Michael, who had already offered himself as a regent.

As the evening wore on and the telegrams piled up on the tsar's desk, reporting mutiny everywhere, Nicholas finally looked into the abyss of the dynasty's misfortune and decided to grant a ministry reporting to the duma instead of to the emperor. But events were outpacing the tsar; Petrograd was now talking of abdication.

❧

It was already 4:15 P.M., March 1st, and the Committee of the State Duma, a new Russian government, was working furiously; even during a revolution there are only twenty-four hours in a day. Suddenly a secretary came in and spoke to Rodzianko.

"Allow me to report. Sailors have come and representatives of the Marine Guards. They wish to see the chairman of the State Duma."

"Tell them to go to hell!" Rodzianko exploded. "When am I to get down to business? Is there no end to this?!"

"Grand Duke Kyril Vladimirovich is with them."

Kyril, the tsar's first cousin and number three in the line of imperial succession, had just performed a flamboyant act, intended to be clever but ultimately disastrous for his reputation. He marched the Marine Guards to the Duma headquarters; his men carried the red banner of revolution instead of the imperial flag, and Kyril wore a red rosette, a revolutionary, republican symbol, on his chest. A survivor of the *Petropavlovsk* explosion, he now wanted to be a survivor of the collapse of Nicholas II.

In later years Kyril would try to explain that red parade by his desire to keep his military unit intact and his need to maintain contact with the State Duma as the last legitimate institution of Russian government. But at the time the act looked like a desperate gambit. When politics were extraordinarily fluid, and opportunities possibly unlimited, Kyril was flirting with the new authorities in an attempt to make himself the first Russian constitutional monarch.

The Committee of the State Duma was not prepared for the grand duke's visit. Someone said hesitantly to Rodzianko, "You will have to meet him."

Rodzianko went grumbling, imposing in his massive bulk.

He could not help being impressed when Kyril reported, "I am at your disposal, like the rest of the people." Rodzianko was shocked, remembering forever the red rosette gleaming on Kyril's chest. But at that hectic hour, finding some time for a glass of tea with the grand duke, Rodzianko learned that, before heading for the duma, Kyril had sent messages to the heads of units of the garrison at Tsarskoye Selo saying, "I and the Guards under my command have joined the new government. I am sure that both you and the unit under your command will want to come with us."

Revolution had won in the capital, but a formal abdication of the tsar was necessary. Who knew how different army units would react? Would they defend the tsar by launching a military expedition against the capital? Rodzianko dispatched Alexander Guchkov and Vassily Shulgin, two strong monarchists, to Mogilev with the mission of persuading an irresolute but imperturbable emperor to abdicate promptly and remove that possibility.

❧

On March 2nd, aboard the imperial train in Pskov, Nicholas arose at his ordinary time, washed, dressed, prayed and took coffee with his aides, discussing everything but the subject most on everyone's mind, the deluge. But meanwhile his Chief of Staff, General Alexeev, who had begun negotiating with the rebels in Petrograd, demanded from the commanders of the fronts their advice on the "dynastic question."

Three of these commanders, Nikolasha, Alexis Brusilov and Alexis Evert, now unambiguously advised Nicholas to abdicate. Nikolasha sent a telegram for which he would forever after be reproached: "Being a true subject, I believe that, because of the duty of my oath and its spirit, I must on my knees ask Your Imperial Majesty to save Russia and your heir. . . . Making a sign of the cross, transfer your heritage to him." General Brusilov, hero of the recent campaign, also advised abdication, with Alexis as emperor and Michael, regent.

For the tsar this was the end. Nicholas was never inclined to listen to the politicians, but to his ear the generals were far more persuasive. Alone he decided to abdicate. He would rather yield the throne than try to make himself a constitutional monarch.

At 3 P.M. on March 2nd, Nicholas sent Rodzianko a telegram in which he declared that he was abdicating in favor of his son; Alexis was to stay with his father until he came of age, and Michael was to be regent. But several hours later Nicholas summoned a trusted physician, Professor Fedorov, to ask, "Sergei Petrovich, please tell me frankly, is Alexis's disease incurable?"

"Sovereign, science tells us this disease is incurable. However, there are cases when a person suffering from it can reach considerable age. The Duke of Abruzzi has lived to be forty-two. Nobody has lasted longer than that."

Nicholas reacted, "Well, if Alexis cannot be helpful to the motherland as I wished he could be, we have every right to keep him to ourselves. We'll settle down in Livadia. The Crimean climate is very good for him."

Guchkov and Shulgin, representing the Duma, arrived at Pskov at ten P.M., on the same fateful March 2nd, lacking any sense of how the tsar would react to their attempt to persuade him to abdicate. The railway platform was lit with blue lanterns, and several tracks beyond stood a lighted train that they recognized as the emperor's. Walking over, the two took off their coats and entered the railway carriage, a large lounge car with green silk lining the walls. The emperor appeared in the doorway wearing a gray overcoat, perfectly calm; he shook hands with the representatives of the rebellious duma in Petrograd.

Guchkov spoke. He was very nervous, his sentences halting and toneless. The emperor sat, leaning slightly against the silken wall, looking straight ahead. His face was gaunt, gray and inscrutable. He was much thinner now and he had aged perceptibly. The only thing that might have been guessed from his expression was, "this is a long speech, excessively so."

Absolute power always isolates. Now Nicholas was utterly alone, making the decision to give up that power. He sought out no one in the family.

Guchkov finally finished. He and Shulgin were astonished at what the emperor said in his unaffected and precise way. "I have decided to renounce the throne. Until three o'clock this afternoon I thought I should abdicate in favor of my son Alexis. But now I have decided in favor of my brother Michael. I hope you understand the feelings of a father."

His voice dropped on this last phrase.

Guchkov and Shulgin were not prepared for this. Guchkov mumbled, "We had counted on the figure of little Alexis Nikolaevich having a softening effect on the transfer of power."

The emperor stood. Everyone now rose. Guchkov gave the emperor their draft. He took it and left, returning a short while later to hand Guchkov a sheaf of papers, and he said, "Here is the text"—two or three small sheets of notepaper used for telegrams. The text was typed. It read:

> "Not wanting to be separated from our dear son, we pass this inheritance to our brother, Grand Duke Michael Alexandrovich, and bless him on his accession to the throne of the Russian empire. . . . May God help Russia."

The draft of this manifesto had been actually prepared in headquarters that same day.

Shulgin then remarked, "Your Majesty, you deigned to say that you thought first of abdicating in favor of Grand Duke Michael Alexandrovich today at three o'clock. It would be good to indicate the time here, for it was the moment you made your decision." Shulgin did not want people to say that the manifesto had been coerced. Nicholas agreed and wrote "2 March, 15:00."

"May I know your personal plans, Your Majesty? Will Your Majesty go to Tsarskoye?" Shulgin asked.

"No. I want to go to headquarters first to say farewell. And then I would like to see my mother. Therefore I think I will either go to Kiev or ask her to come to me. And then to Tsarskoye."

Taking tea later with his aide, Count Alexander Grabbe, Nicholas said matter of factly, "Now that I am about to be freed of my responsibilities to the nation, perhaps I can fulfill my life's desire—to have a farm, somewhere in England. What do you think?"

Grabbe exclaimed, "What will become of you, of us, of Russia, now that those questionable characters are in control? Your Majesty, this is a tragic step you have taken . . . "

Nicholas said nothing and left looking somewhat hurt, Grabbe thought.

The clock stood at 11:40 P.M.

Nicholas went to his compartment and wrote in his diary, "All around me is treachery, cowardice, and deceit!"

❧

On March 3rd, at 1:15 A.M., the news spread in headquarters. "Everything is finished. It is Michael Alexandrovich." At 1:45, Nicholas sent his first telegram as an abdicated emperor, to his brother: "Petrograd: To His Majesty, hope see you soon Nicky."

The imperial train pulled out of Pskov at two A.M. The platform was brightly lit, but empty, with several men in uniform watching the train leaving. The track to Mogilev was clear and the trip without incident. Nicholas wrote in his diary that he "read a lot about Julius Caesar." He sent Michael a second telegram from his train asking forgiveness for the burden he was transferring and wishing him success. Nicholas seemed tranquil, as usual, but he looked very sad. He had been wearing a Kuban Cossack uniform, pacing the railway platform up and down in that long black coat with silver lining, despite the cold windy weather. People who watched from the train were struck by his youthful demeanor, his light and fast step, and they remembered an old court saying: "The sovereign is never in haste and never late." But Nicholas was no longer sovereign.

Now the fate of the dynasty lay in the hands of Michael. Misha was deliberately avoiding contact with other grand dukes, to their intense irritation. He had gone to the apartment of his close friend Princess Olga Putiatina at #12 Millionnaya, five hundred yards from the Winter Palace, on February 28th, where he stayed for three days, remaining in touch, however, with members of the Duma Committee. On March 2nd, he was visited by his cousin, Bimbo, who was probably trying to persuade Michael that the monarchist cause was irrevocably lost. Certainly the evidence of growing disorder Michael saw as he had passed through the streets on his way to Putiatina's apartment had not been reassuring. Looting and random acts of violence were happening in the neighborhood, a general sense of rowdiness prevailed, and a detachment of officers had been dispatched to Millionnaya to protect the grand duke.

At dawn on March 3rd, in the revolutionary fever, Alexander Kerensky called Michael to ask him whether he would receive the Provisional Government the same morning, the first official contact with the new authorities, self-proclaimed several hours before that. Kerensky, a lawyer still in his thirties, small, slender and sallow-faced, fond of posing in a Napoleonic stance, was articulate and ambitious, looking for a large place in the revolution.

The fateful meeting that then ensued took place in the same apartment, #12 Millionnaya. The grand duke joined the council at 9:15. The Provisional Government was represented by Prince Lvov, Rodzianko, Pavel Miliukov (the head of the influential Cadet party), Vladimir Nabokov, Kerensky and several others. They were joined by Guchkov and Shulgin, who had just returned from Pskov with Nicholas's abdication manifesto burning their hands.

Shulgin had undergone a remarkable experience at the railway station. He was to have briefed the "troops and the people" on the abdication of Nicholas. When he entered the room where this was to have taken place, he realized that he had never before heard a deeper silence. When he read aloud the abdication, the words fell flatly, but bayonets carried by the officers were waving like a field of grain blown by the wind. Right in front of Shulgin a young soldier was crying. Tears streamed down both his rosy cheeks.

"To Emperor Michael II, I shout 'hurrah!'" Shulgin proclaimed; and the roar of the crowd soared: ardent, sincere and deeply moving. Some Russians, it seemed, still wanted a monarchy. When Shulgin came into the corridors of the station, a railroad worker told him that Pavel Miliukov had been trying repeatedly to reach him by phone.

"Yes, it is I, Miliukov. Do not announce the manifesto. Serious changes have taken place."

"Well, what? I have already announced it."

"To whom?"

"To everybody here, a regiment of troops, the people. I proclaimed Emperor Michael."

"You shouldn't have done that. The mood here has deteriorated drastically since you left. We got the text by wire. It is completely unsatisfactory. It absolutely must mention the constituent assembly. Don't do anything further, there could be serious consequences."

Miliukov then told Shulgin to find Guchkov and take him to #12 Millionnaya Street.

The day was cold and sunny, the city gone mad. No trolleys were running, nor were there carriages or *drozhkies*. A rare truck whizzed by loaded with soldiers carrying bristling bayonets. All the stores were closed. Crowds of soldiers were everywhere, without officers and out of formation, with rifles on their shoulders, uniforms askew, walking aimlessly, with looks of dazed incomprehension on their faces.

At #12 Millionnaya, two sentries were posted inside. A great crush of people was in the entrance hall of the Putiatina apartment. In their midst, sitting in a large armchair was a young, almost boyish, officer with a thin aristocratic face, the very personification of charm, refinement and emptiness, the Grand Duke Michael Alexandrovich; he was thirty-nine. To his right and left, in a half circle of sofas and armchairs, like two wings sprouting for the new monarch, sat everyone who might comprise his entourage. No one in the family was there. Just as Nicholas had not consulted the family in his greatest political decision, neither would Michael.

At ten o'clock the session started. Guchkov and Miliukov declared that Michael did not have the right to evade the supreme responsibility of the crown, even though accepting it would put him at some considerable personal risk. Privately Miliukov thought Michael stupid. But the occasion inspired him to make the speech of his life. White as a swan, he croaked like a raven, "If you refuse, there will be anarchy! Chaos, a bloody mess." The grand duke inclined his head slightly and listened attentively.

Rodzianko and Kerensky spoke to the contrary, saying that any new tsar would incite revolutionary violence and that the future of the monarchy could be resolved only by the constituent assembly. Kerensky, with his thin, sharply defined face and stiffly brushed hair, exclaimed, "I turn to Your Highness as a Russian to a Russian! I implore you in the name of Russia to make this sacrifice!" Kerensky was convinced that for Russia monarchy was dead.

Guchkov, however, made one last effort. "If you are afraid, Your Highness, to assume the burden of the imperial crown immediately, at least declare yourself a regent or 'People's Protector,' like Cromwell." Kerensky exploded in rage, showering threats and insults. Others were appalled by his uncontrolled emotion and lack of civility.

Michael thereupon rose to his feet and said he was going to another room to think the situation over. Kerensky rushed to him. "Your Highness, promise me that you will not confer with your spouse."

Michael smiled. "Don't worry, Alexander Fedorovich, my spouse is not here right now, she is at Gatchina." Kerensky was not the only person who saw Michael as entirely under the thumb of his energetic and ambitious wife, Countess Natalya Brassova.

The grand duke then walked out, summoning Prince Lvov and Rodzianko, those whom he knew best, to accompany him. For some reason Kerensky did not protest. In half an hour Michael returned and said, "Under the circumstances I cannot assume the throne because . . ." Those present were so impressed that later they would not agree on his exact words or how the grand duke behaved, some arguing that he was crying, many others insisting that he showed great dignity and spoke firmly. This was Michael's finest hour, his chance to radiate a spirit of self-sacrifice and his opportunity to command respect for doing so.

Kerensky shouted, "Your Highness, you are the noblest person among mortals!" Then the abdication manifesto was worked out with Michael's participation. He stressed that his refusal to accept the crown was conditional and ultimately depended upon the decision of the constituent assembly. Meanwhile Princess Putiatina offered the odd group the last breakfast of the monarchy. At the table the grand duke asked Shulgin, "How did my brother conduct himself?"

"His Majesty was completely calm, surprisingly calm."

Finally the document was ready. Michael's abdication was asking the Russian people to submit to the provisional government "until such a time as a constituent assembly, which is to be convened as soon as possible on the basis of universal, direct, equal and secret suffrage, shall express the will of the people in its decision on the form of our government." The grand duke took up a pen and signed. Shulgin thought, "What a good constitutional monarch he would have been!" Kerensky raced off to the printers with the new abdication in hand. Half an hour later posters were going up all over the city: "Nicholas abdicates in favor of Michael! Michael abdicates in favor of the people!"

CHAPTER SEVEN

The First Week
of the Republic

MARCH 3–MARCH 11, 1917

Nicholas, after sending his telegrams to Michael, arrived back at Mogilev at 10:40 P.M. March 3rd. Two relatives came to meet him, Grand Dukes Boris Vladimirovich and Sergei Mikhailovich, and Nicholas heard the news about Michael's abdication. Ever faithful to the principle of autocracy, the former tsar was revolted to learn that Michael had finished his manifesto with a recommendation for universal, direct, equal and secret suffrage. "Lord knows who gave him the idea to sign his name to such a disgusting thing."

Headquarters was awaiting the new commander-in-chief, Nikolasha, who had been appointed by Nicholas on March 2nd, with the sour approval of the new government, as one of his last acts as monarch. On March 5th, the heads of the Allied missions (British, Belgian, French, Romanian and Serbian) jointly addressed the Russian frontline commanders, emphasizing their belief in ultimate joint victory and their support of Nikolasha as new commander-in-chief. Nikolasha thanked them in a telegram sent on the same day. However, already on March 8th, the British general and military observer Hanbury-Williams began to soften that support, proposing that Alexeev should publish the address of the Allies emphasizing the joint war effort and omitting any reference to Nikolasha. At that point Nikolasha was aboard a train steaming to Mogilev from the Caucasus.

For a while the Allies seemed sincerely to be concerned about the fate of the imperial couple and their children. On March 6th, when news about the violent anti-Romanov mood in the capital had reached headquarters, the heads of the Allied military missions suggested to Chief of Staff General Alexeev that they themselves should escort Nicholas to Tsarskoye Selo. Alexeev evasively replied that such an action would be "untimely."

Revolutionaries meanwhile were organizing the troops into committees and the workers into their own political action committees called soviets. On March 5th, General Alexeev was shocked to learn that in Vyborg on the Finnish Baltic coast a soldiers' committee had seized total control of the fortress and arrested its commandant. The Petrograd Soviet was demanding that "Nicholas the Bloody" and all the members of the House of Romanov be gathered "in one designated location under the dependable guard of the People's Revolutionary Army."

Several commanding officers were shot by their own troops. Discipline everywhere was collapsing. Severely disappointed by the fruits of the abdication he had been promoting, Alexeev said angrily, "The only thing left is to let our officers put on civilian dress when they are off duty. Only this can perhaps save them from the arbitrariness and the arrogance of the revolutionary soldiers."

On March 3rd, as soon as the Military General Headquarters (*Stavka*) knew that Michael too had abdicated, Sergei Mikhailovich called Sandro in Kiev and advised him to bring the Dowager Empress Maria Fedorovna to Mogilev. Nicholas had already explicitly expressed a desire to meet with his mother, with whom he was still emotionally close, even before going to his wife and children. Once armed with information, Nicholas was a realist: Probably he feared that the revolution meant that he might never be able to see his mother again. He was more confident of reunion with Alix and their children.

At that point it looked as if Nicholas and the family would soon leave the country, and on March 4th, Palace Commandant Voeikov informed his staff members at Tsarskoye Selo, "The sovereign and all of us are going to England." Nicholas asked the Provisional Government for permission to go with his family to Murmansk, Russian Arctic terminus of the wartime oceanic link with Great Britain. Meanwhile, the dowager departed Kiev to meet Nicky before he should leave Mogilev.

On March 4th, Nicholas went to the railway station by car to meet his mother. For several minutes he waited on the platform. At noon the dowager's train stopped at the place reserved for the imperial trains. Nicholas spoke to the two Cossacks guarding his mother's train, and then went into the car. He soon reappeared, escorting his mother. They went to an empty wooden barracks nearby, where they stayed for a long time, more than half an hour. It was cold and very windy outside, with snow falling heavily, coating the denuded black branches of the trees. Then the two came out, the dowager wearing her customary kind welcoming smile, Nicholas imperturbable as usual.

Only one other Romanov had come with the dowager: her son-in-law Sandro. In a letter sent from headquarters to his brother Bimbo on March 8th, Sandro showed much foresight: "I personally see that the Provisional Government has lost its balance, being completely in the power of the Soviets of workers' deputies. And if the Provisional Government does not prevail, total anarchy and the collapse of Russia will follow."

Nicholas, the dowager and Sandro drove to the governor's house for breakfast. Small talk went very badly that day. Everyone was totally preoccupied with revolution and its unknown consequences. After the meal, the dowager and Nicholas withdrew to his room, where they stayed tête-à-tête again for a long time. Then the dowager returned to her train, where she would live for the next few days, until March 9th, the day of her departure. Around seven o'clock, Nicholas told his entourage that he would dine that evening with his mother. Driving there, alone with Colonel Anatoly Mordvinov in the motorcar, Nicholas was pale and looked very thin.

"When are you going to Tsarskoye Selo, Your Majesty?" Mordvinov asked.

"I think very soon. What do people say about all that, Mordvinov?"

The loyal colonel, overcoming his natural embarrassment, said that the people were upset that Nicholas had abdicated, not in favor of his son but of his brother, a decision that could make trouble in the future.

Nicholas did not say a word in reply, but looked very pensive.

At the railway station he went to the dowager's compartment, only to return to the corridor in a few moments to say, "Mordvinov,

Mother invites you for dinner. I will tell you later when we shall leave."

Maria Fedorovna kept her radiant smile, but she was clearly feeling an enormous strain. All the members of her small suite were present. One of them, Countess Mengden, was charming as ever, though she had just received news that her older brother had been murdered by a mob of soldiers. After dinner Nicholas stayed with his mother alone again till eleven P.M. The suite was informed that the dowager would stay at headquarters as long as her son was there.

The next day, March 5th, the news about a massacre of officers of the Baltic Sea fleet reached Mogilev. The army too was beginning to lose all discipline and coherence, on its way to degenerating into an insubordinate rabble.

Nicholas went to church, where he was joined by his mother. The church was packed and the deacon hesitated but finally delivered the customary Orthodox prayer for the emperor. After the mass, mother and son kissed the holy icon of Our Lady of Vladimir recently brought to headquarters and then went to the governor's house for lunch. By that time revolutionary flags were waving everywhere above the rooftops of Mogilev; the city hall facing Nicholas's residence flew two enormous red flags. Photographs of the tsar, once seen everywhere, now had suddenly vanished.

In the morning of March 6th, the dowager summoned Sir John Hanbury-Williams to her train. In the past she had showered him with her grievances concerning Rasputin and Alix, but now she said that the major problem was how to get Nicholas safely out of the country. She emphasized that her son was refusing to go anywhere without his wife and children. Hanbury-Williams said that he had already contacted his government asking whether Nicholas could go to Britain.

But the British government, like the American and French, was showing little sympathy for the Romanovs. The foreign public was rejoicing to see Europe's most repressive autocracy swept away by the will of the people. Perhaps such a response from the Americans and French was not surprising, since these nations were republics, not monarchies, and both had experienced revolution against monarchy. But Britain was a monarchy. Only fourteen years earlier, King Edward VII had refused to restore diplomatic relations with Serbia because the Serbians had assassinated their king and queen. He remarked that "since they happened to belong to the same trade union, he was going to observe union rules, and under no circumstances would he over-look the outrage."

In 1917, George V was Britain's king. His son, David (later briefly King Edward VIII and after that, Duke of Windsor), would later claim that there was "a very real bond" between George and his first cousin Nicholas. In his letters to the tsar, George described himself as "your most devoted cousin and true friend." When they were both young the physical resemblance between them was especially striking, but Nicky's complexion was paler, his expression dreamier and his smile touched with melancholy. The Duke of Windsor related that when Nicky came to England in 1893 to attend Georgie's wedding, Georgie was mistaken for his Russian cousin by a diplomat who asked him "if he had come over especially for the Duke of York's wedding. My fa-ther [the Duke said] loved to relate the confusion of the embarrassed envoy when he replied, 'I am the Duke of York, and I suppose that I should attend my own wedding.'"

That Georgie and Nicky may have looked alike did not help Nicky now. To the British public, Nicholas was a foreign tyrant with blood on his hands, and his empress was perceived as unstable and stained by her support of "the mad monk" Rasputin. Despite ties of marriage and blood with the British royal house, despite the fact that King George V was first cousin to Nicholas and Alexandra both, the Ro-manovs had never been popular in Britain.

On March 8th, the British Government suggested that it might be appropriate for the tsar and his family to go to Denmark or Switzer-land, but the Russian Government worried that both of these nations were too close to Germany. The former tsar could be captured by the Germans and used as a counterrevolutionary pawn by them. Foreign Minister Miliukov expressed his extreme concern; he knew that pub-lic anger against the Romanovs was rising.

In the morning of March 8th, Nicholas said goodbye to his staff. He confided to his diary that he felt heartbroken. Emotions ran high all around. Many officers wept; two or three even fainted. Nicholas then received the heads of the Allied missions. The Serbian Leon-tkovich sobbed and kissed his hand. "Russia without a tsar . . . it is impossible, it can never be that way." At noon Nicholas proceeded to his mother's train, lunched with her, and remained until 4:30. Fifteen minutes later he left Mogilev. About one hundred fifty people gathered on the cold and bleak platform to bid farewell to their former sovereign, among them several members of the family: Sergei Mikhailovich, Sandro, Boris and Prince Alexander of Oldenburg. Sandro later wrote that "the absence of all other members of the imperial family causes me deep humiliation." No one else had made any attempt to come.

Nicholas, in a simple khaki blouse, wearing the decoration of which he was most proud, the Cross of St. George, tried to clear the fogged train window with his gloved hand. Those outside could see his hollow eyes and pallid face; he was smiling but sad and tense with the effort to remain calm. The train pulled out for Tsarskoye Selo and became only a wisp of smoke down the tracks to those waving farewell, and the old empress, standing on the platform, now wept without restraint.

She departed for Kiev with Sandro the next day. When she was leaving, Grand Duke Sergei Mikhailovich wondered if the old lady fully realized yet what had actually happened.

The Empress Alexandra Fedorovna, nursing her very sick offspring at Tsarskoye Selo, was isolated from events entirely. On February 27th, the Minister of War Michael Belyaev had telegraphed a warning that she should leave Tsarskoye immediately, for her safety could not be guaranteed. The empress refused to leave without her husband. He was expected to arrive at six A.M. on February 28th. On March 1st, those at Tsarskoye learned that Nicholas had been forced to direct his train to Pskov, and on that same day Grand Duke Paul came to Alix, feverish with excitement. The two then had a stormy meeting, and the following day at eleven o'clock in the morning, Alix received a letter from Paul proposing a constitution, an idea she fiercely rejected. On March 3rd, around six P.M., Paul returned and broke the "terrible news" to her: Nicky had abdicated. "I don't believe it!" she cried. "I believe in God and in the army! Neither could abandon us right now!"

Paul and his wife were very busy during this period. Paul, it seemed, now hoped to shape imperial politics, wanting, after the humiliation of imperial reprimand and exile, to be important for the first time in his life. He wanted to be not the king but the kingmaker, and his wife, the redoubtable Olga Valerianovna Paley, stood right beside him in his anger, offering him every encouragement. She wrote to Alix that Paul, "as the only living son of the Tsar-Liberator," was trying to persuade

Rodzianko that the throne should be kept by Nicholas, who could lead the nation to victory in the war under a constitutional regime.

On March 2nd, Paul wrote to Kyril that he had been in touch with the duma. He did not like the trend toward Michael for emperor and thought it due to Countess Brassova's intrigues. He was mistaken. Because Michael's entreprenerial spouse was trapped at Gatchina at the time, she was unable to join the political game. Paul thought that the Romanovs "should keep the throne for Nicky by all means. If Nicky signs a constitutional manifesto approved by us, this is exactly what the people and the Provisional Government demand." Paul also asked Kyril to talk to Rodzianko and to share his letter with him. He dispatched a messenger to travel by foot from Tsarskoye Selo to Kyril at Petrograd; the trains were not running that day. Kyril replied that he was worried that Michael, in spite of Kyril's requests, was "not working clearly and in concord with our family," but was secretly and independently negotiating with Rodzianko, which was of course true. Kyril also pompously stated that "through these difficult days I have been left alone to carry all the responsibility for Nicky and the motherland, saving the situation, recognizing the new government." Kyril probably had really hoped to become the representative of the dynasty in negotiations with the new authorities on March 1st, when he led his guardsmen to the duma. But the liberal leaders preferred to deal with Michael. Michael was softer but also more legitimate, and the ambitions of the Vladimirovichi were notorious.

Bimbo, dressed in civilian clothing, now looking like an old bureaucrat, was walking around Petrograd, openly making pro-revolutionary statements. He adored the notoriety of being called the Philippe Egalité of the Russian revolution. With his brother Sergei Mikhailovich inaccessible in Mogilev, he ordered Sergei's servants to stop all communication with the household of Sergei's mistress, Kshesinskaya; even the motorcars were prohibited to serve her. Bimbo knew that she had become extremely unpopular in Petrograd. Because "Malechka" (as Sergei had been calling her for twenty-two years) was accused of using Sergei's position as supervisor of artillery to extort bribes from industrialists supplying the guns, she was perceived as a living symbol of Romanov corruption and decadence. However, anger could have been one more reason for Bimbo's boycott. While he had been exiled to his estate, Sergei, ever loyal to Nicky, had never written to him. Bimbo thus imperiously informed his brother, still at the *Stavka,* that he should not attempt to see Malechka or their son Vova again. Relations between these two brothers, long tenuous, were thus ruptured.

Bimbo also took the initiative to disinherit the Romanovs. On March 9th, he informed the Minister of Justice (and future head) of the Provisional Government, Alexander Kerensky, that he had obtained an agreement to abandon all rights to crown lands from Grand Dukes Kyril ("easily") and Dmitri Constantinovich ("with more difficulty") and others. He was ready, he said, to proceed with disinheriting others, namely Nikolasha.

George Mikhailovich also joined the group, submitting a formal statement in which he waived his appanage income. Although transferring his lands to the state, George Mikhailovich implicitly left the question of his succession rights to the judgment of the Constituent Assembly. Grand Duke Kyril then repeated verbatim George Mikhailovich's evasive statement concerning succession rights.

Kyril was now behaving, if not as a red grand duke like Bimbo, then as a pink one. On March 9th, the French Ambassador Maurice Paleologue was shocked to see the banner of revolution waving over Kyril's palace on Glinka Street. The same day Kyril was quoted in the press as saying maliciously that "I have asked myself many times, if the former empress were not in league with Wilhelm II, but each time I have forced myself to dismiss so horrible a suspicion."

The prevailing mood among monarchists was that Nicholas had made a huge mistake abdicating, first in favor of his legal heir Alexis and then in favor of Michael. Grand Duke Sergei Mikhailovich said flatly that "after that, the end was inevitable" and Michael had been forced to give up any right to the throne years ago when he married a divorced commoner, and Nicholas had no authority to give it to him now. Furthermore, a minor could not renounce his own rights and his father could not do it for him. But Nicholas II's acts reflected his intense and persisting belief in his own absolute power.

In Petrograd, the new authorities were discussing the fate of the former emperor and his family, and Miliukov continued to confer with British ambassador Sir George Buchanan. Years later, Miliukov would say that Nicholas had wasted the several days necessary for his rescue by having returned from Pskov to Mogilev, to hesitate there whether to go to Britain or to Livadia in the Crimea. While this was happening, the Petrograd Soviet decided to arrest him as a potential leader of imperial restoration.

The Provisional Government leaders could not influence the Soviet, let alone the mob. In spite of their unwillingness to hurt the tsar, they could do nothing to help him. Kerensky declared that he himself would escort Nicholas to some seaport where he could take ship to Britain. These brave words would mean nothing. On March 10th, Buchanan told Miliukov that King George and his government were ready to give the tsar and his family asylum in Britain until the end of the war, as long as the Russian government would take care of all the expenses. Miliukov sighed, "Alas! I am afraid it is too late."

According to Miliukov, the Provisional Government could not attempt a rescue at that point because the extremist Petrograd Soviet was howling for the tsar, wanting to seize and imprison him. Abdication was not enough; they wanted punishment. In England too, opinions hardened. King George V's private secretary advised against allowing the tsar and his family to come to England, for it "would be strongly resented by the public, and would undoubtedly compromise the position of the King and Queen." The King therefore instructed Ambassador Buchanan, via the Foreign Office, that he was to tell Miliukov that "we must be allowed to withdraw from the consent previously given to the Russian government's proposal." The warship that London had promised would be waiting for Nicholas would never come. So much for blood relationship.

Meanwhile Nikolasha, newly reappointed commander-in-chief of the armed forces, was trying to get information by telegram from Prince Lvov, the head of the Provisional Government. He wanted to know about political developments throughout the empire, and particularly in the capital, so that he could efficiently lead the army. In another telegram Nikolasha insisted on keeping the title of Viceroy of the Caucasus in order to maintain stability in the area. Perhaps he was trying to keep the Caucasus as a retreat, his ultimate redoubt.

In a conversation with his younger cousin Grand Duke Andrew, Nikolasha was frank. He was sure that Alix had ruined Nicky and that abdication could have been foreseen. "The situation is becoming worse, worse, and worse!" he said emphatically, and believed that even he himself could be arrested at any time.

Nikolasha, the only truly active senior Romanov, felt obliged to assume the responsibilities of head of the family, stressing to Andrew that every member should stay where he or she was right now. The only exception was Dmitri; he should be brought back from Persia (where he might conceivably fall into German hands) to Tiflis in the Caucasus. Nikolasha told Andrew that he prohibited the latter's brothers Kyril and Boris from visiting their mother in the Caucasus, where Miechen was still staying. Nikolasha made it clear that his opinion of both of Andrew's brothers was low. "Wherever Boris goes he leaves a stench."

On March 5th, Nikolasha sent word that the army, the fleet and the military organizations of the rear should take orders only from him, and he told the press that "a return to the old regime is impossible and I would never consent to such a retrograde step." On March 6th, he left Tiflis for the *Stavka* at Mogilev, planning to be there on March 10th to meet Prince Lvov, the new Prime Minister.

Nikolasha arrived at Mogilev on March 10th, at four P.M., accompanied, among others, by his brother, Peter, and Peter's son, Prince Roman. That same day Nikolasha issued his order #1 announcing his arrival at headquarters as commander-in-chief, and the next day, in the train, he, his brother, his nephew and all the suite gave a solemn oath of allegiance to the Provisional Government. Nikolasha was very nervous and when signing the written oath, his hands shook. But his oath was no longer needed.

Nikolasha did not know it, but he had already been dismissed. The day before, March 9th, the Provisional Government had sent him a letter saying that public opinion resented the very idea of a Romanov now holding any official position, and therefore they asked him to step down, even before reaching headquarters. The letter reached Nikolasha in Mogilev only on the 11th, and that same day the grand duke reported to the Provisional Government that he was "glad to prove my love to the Motherland which has not been doubted by Russia so far" and that he had handed the supreme command over to General Alexeev. And so Nikolasha issued his order #2, in which he said that the Provisional Government thought it was "inevitable" for him as a member of the House of Romanov to leave his position, and he announced that Alexeev would be in command.

The grand dukes and prince then promptly left for the Crimea.

Two days earlier, March 9, 1917, the dethroned tsar Nicholas Romanov arrived back at Tsarskoye Selo under convoy. He had fallen unresistingly into the ruthless hands of the revolutionaries and they would never let him go. Nicholas had thus not only lost all power over others; he had also lost his own freedom, and most Romanovs would never see him, his wife or his children again.

The fall of the Romanovs caused a sensation throughout the world. In less than two years the Hapsburgs and the Hohenzollerns would also topple, joined in the dustheap of history by the Ottoman sultanate.

In Rome with his ballet company, Diaghilev had to find a melody representing Russia at the opening night of their season. Rather than the customary anthem, "God Save the Tsar," he chose the song of the Volga boatmen, and Stravinsky sat up all night to orchestrate it.

In Paris, Miechen's close friend, Madame de Chevigne, held a dinner party at which her son-in-law François de Croiset teased her by saying that the grand duchess was now likely to arrive in Paris penniless and would need to be provided for throughout the rest of her life. A few moments after Croiset had said goodnight, pretending to be leaving, the butler entered to announce, "Her Imperial Highness, the Grand Duchess Vladimir!"

In fact, however, that lady was fiercely struggling for survival at the small town of Kislovodsk in the Caucasus. As with all the Romanovs, her very life was now in great danger. The Parisian joke was not funny. Many of the Romanovs might be politically insignificant, quite harmless, but so, as Sandro would remark, was Marie Antoinette.

CHAPTER EIGHT

"The Mood Smells of Blood"

MARCH–OCTOBER 1917

I**N SPRING AND SUMMER** 1917, the Romanovs increasingly became a collective scapegoat, both for public opinion and for official action. Revolution fed upon the hatred of the masses for those whom they perceived as their oppressors. The Provisional Government, although spasmodically, unevenly and without any real zeal, started to persecute them.

The family had grown to huge size, sixty-five, including the Leuchtenberg cousins; of these eight lived outside Russia safely beyond reach of harassment. The others were at growing risk, although most were slow to perceive how great that risk really was. The most conspicuous targets were the former tsar and his family, but no one was truly safe.

Before the outbreak of the February revolution, Miechen, the formidable Grand Duchess Maria Pavlovna, had taken herself to the resort town of Kislovodsk in the foothills of the Caucasus mountains, known for its curative hot springs and mineral waters and its invigorating mountain air. Her son Andrew, who suffered from a "delicate chest," joined her there, accompanied by his mistress, Kshesinskaya, and their teenage son Vova. The dancer's second grand duke, Sergei

Mikhailovich, already discreetly dressed in civilian clothes, a novelty for grand dukes, was at the station in Petrograd to see her off. Early in the revolution the dancer had lost her Petrograd palace. The first Romanov or quasi-Romanov palace to be occupied and confiscated, it was now being used by Lenin as Bolshevik headquarters. Sergei was able to rescue some of the furniture temporarily by putting it into storage, but it did little good for Kshesinskaya. She would never see Petrograd again.

Grand Duke Boris telegraphed his mother from Tsarskoye Selo on February 24th to tell her of the riots in Petrograd. Miechen chafed at being so remote from the center of power and at her inability to engage in the backstage politics she so loved. But the Caucasus lay on the fringe of the empire, close to the border, and the ship traffic on the Black Sea provided the possibility of quick departure if it should prove necessary.

Kislovodsk remained as serene as ever. The heavy fist of Bolshevism did not strike it until early the next year. Officers continued to wear their tsarist insignia; soldiers saluted generals; ladies in fancy dresses strolled in the parks with their children and dogs. Another Petrograd celebrity came to town, the great singer Chaliapin. But ugly rumors of what was now erupting in much of the nation began to circulate locally, and in early March Andrew found this more than talk when revolutionaries temporarily stopped his private train on his return from an excursion to Tiflis, three hundred kilometers further south toward the Turkish border, where he had gone to see Nikolasha at army headquarters.

Miechen occupied a rented villa in town, comfortable enough but by her standards extremely modest. One evening while she, Andrew and friends were playing cards, an agitated servant came in to announce unexpected visitors. Two representatives of the Provisional Government, one military, the other civilian, each wearing a large red rosette upon his chest, had come to search the house. The grand duchess received them with dignity and grace, in the same regal manner she had used with foreign ambassadors in her St. Petersburg salon. The two visitors then began to open drawers and to remove letters and papers at random. Because they claimed to have found "compromising letters," they placed the grand duchess under house arrest. This was March 14th. She would remain in confinement until June 6th.

In May Miechen wrote to her close English friend, Bertie Stopford, complaining bitterly of her situation. She had not, she said, been out of the house for more than two months and she had confined herself to her bed-sitting room. As Stopford remarked in his memoirs, this experience came after "never in her life having been denied anything." Miechen began to complain about her health. Her heart troubled her, she said, yet she remained restlessly ambitious, eager to get into the political world. Once freed of house arrest, she took the precaution of obtaining permission from the then Minister of Justice Kerensky to go to Finland if she wished. She did not avail herself of that opportunity, although Kyril and Ducky were now there. By splitting themselves geographically, on the fringes of the empire, the Vladimirovichi were thinking strategically.

Bertie Stopford, socially well connected in London, served nominally as an official diplomatic courier, carrying messages back and forth between high officialdom in Russia and England, but he had time to look after Miechen's affairs also. Stopford, who seems to have been extremely fond of Miechen, calling her *his* grand duchess, took the lengthy and dangerous train ride down from Petrograd to Kislovodsk in order to see her, bringing with him, stashed in his boots, a large sum of money in new Revolutionary one thousand ruble notes, which she had never seen before. The cash was intended only to cover her current expenses. Miechen still expected to return to Petrograd before long and had left behind most of her clothing, furs and jewelry. In Kislovodsk she and Stopford walked and took drives together, and the Englishman stayed long enough to celebrate Miechen's nameday (the anniversary of the saint whose name she bore) with her on August 4th.

He noted approvingly that "ever since her release she has received marks of sympathy and courtesy from all classes." Miechen's health seemed on the mend. She was taking mineral baths for her heart. She was well looked after by "a few old servants" and a family of a dozen Cossacks whom she recruited locally to serve as bodyguards. Boris, with his mistress, had by now joined his brother, Andrew, and their mother. Kshesinskaya wrote repeatedly to Sergei Mikhailovich in Petrograd, unsuccessfully beseeching him to join the Kislovodsk group too.

On August 4th, a priest came to the house to sing the Te Deum; "we sat down twenty-eight to luncheon on the veranda at three tables," Stopford recalled. Miechen asked him, when he returned to England and if he had the opportunity to do so, to convey "her deepest affection" to King George and Queen Mary, and to say "how she envied everybody who lived in a country where there were policemen." A month later, she had cause to reiterate that thought. In the middle of the night she and her household were awakened by members of a Committee of Workers and Soldiers who came to the house and spent nearly four hours opening everything, searching everything and turning the whole house into a shambles.

In Petrograd, Bertie Stopford and Boris were able to gain entry into the Vladimir Palace and to the safe in Miechen's Moorish boudoir. From it they took jewelry and cash. The jewels Stopford carried back to London and put in a safe deposit box under the grand duchess's name. Miechen would never wear those jewels again nor enjoy the profits from their sale. But her children would benefit from the money, and a tiara from the collection would become part of the British royal jewels, frequently worn by Queen Elizabeth II.

In Kislovodsk the Romanovs were waiting, for exactly what they did not know, idly occupying themselves with tea parties, luncheons, cards and conversation. The atmosphere was increasingly one of tension and menace. People lived day to day, even hour to hour. Everyone gave up going out after dark. And the incidence of random visits by soldiers and revolutionary soviets increased. These searches inevitably seemed to lead to the loss of valuables, so the Romanovs began to hide what they could.

Yet all this was but a mere taste of what was to come.

⟨≈⟩

Petrograd offered little security to any Romanov, except perhaps Bimbo. House arrest and exile to some remote spot might descend on any. The Crimea, always a favorite spot, now beckoned not simply because of its customary attractions but because, on the southern edge of Russia, it seemed serenely remote from military or political conflict or intervention. Twenty Romanovs therefore now moved there, to pause and to ponder the next move while living in a comfortably familiar and seemingly secure setting.

Soon after her farewell to Nicky, Minnie was persuaded that Kiev, now exploding into chaos, overrun by bands of soldiers who had deserted the dissolving Russian armies, was no longer safe for her. The Provisional Government said she could go to the Crimea. The Bolsheviks were ready to prevent it if they could but they were not able to enforce their will. They were not yet in power.

Sandro orchestrated Minnie's departure from Kiev now as he had her earlier trip to Nicky at Mogilev. He again arranged a special train, assembled on a deserted siding in a forest outside the city, and he was able to persuade a small group of loyal troops to man the train for its dangerous journey to the south. Years later, Nicky's younger sister Olga, who accompanied her mother, remembered the departure vividly. The imperial travelers, arriving in small groups in order to avoid attracting attention, clustered silently at the train siding.

It was a bitter night. I wore nothing but my nurse's uniform. To avoid all suspicion I had not put on a coat when I left the hospital. My husband covered me with his greatcoat. I had a very small dressing-case in my hands. I remember the moment when, looking upon that small case and my crumpled skirt, I realized that I owned nothing else in the world.

Olga's house steward had refused to risk sending any jewels to her in Kiev, and so now her faithful maid, Mimka, volunteered to travel alone back to Petrograd to try to retrieve at least some of the valuables left in the house there.

At every station on the journey to the Crimea, crowds of refugees tried to force their way onto the train, repelled only by the sight of the bared bayonets brandished by the escort troops aboard. The journey took four days. The train stopped at a siding short of the Sevastopol city station and the group disembarked, now protected by a detachment from the military aviation school of Sevastopol which had been founded by Sandro. "When we left the train I saw a group of unkempt and untidy sailors staring at us," Olga writes. "It was sheer anguish to be aware of their hatred. . . . Nicky's sailors had been my friends since my childhood. It was a shock to realize that they were now enemies."

The group arrived at the end of March 1917 to take up residence, not at the imperial palace, Livadia, where Minnie might have chosen to go, but to the richly ornate Ai Todor, the palace owned by Sandro, about five miles from Yalta. The family began to gather, Minnie and Olga, Sandro, and Xenia coming later with all their children. Xenia came directly from Petrograd, as did her daughter and son-in-law, Irina and Felix Yusupov. On the train the Yusupovs whiled away the time by playing cards and eating the food they had brought with them. Their numerous pet dogs swarmed all over the car and their yelping was a constant annoyance, as people inadvertently stepped on one every few minutes. At the railway station in Bakhchisarai, the ancient capital of the Crimean khans, twenty-two miles east of Sevastopol, they were surprised to find motor cars waiting to take them to the southern shore of the peninsula.

Nikolasha and his wife Stana established themselves at their palace of Chaeer. Nearby at Dulber were his brother Peter and his family. "It was spring," Olga writes, "and the park rioted in blossom. Somehow there was hope."

Loyal retainers and officers clustered about the family, forming a sort of screen for them, encouraging and enabling them to continue something of the illusion of past power and privilege. The Provisional Government seemed happy enough to let them be, not really knowing what to do about them and having plenty else to think about. The worst aspect of the situation was the uncertainty about the members of the family not there, especially the emperor. Rumor abounded. The tsar's cousin, George Mikhailovich, back in Petrograd, wrote maliciously to his daughter that now the Ai Todor area had a "colony of grand dukes and grand duchesses and one fine day they all will be arrested and sent to different places." He said that *he* was not going to make the mistake of joining them.

For the first weeks of March and April, the Romanov Ai Todor colony lived relatively peacefully, and the gloomy prophesy of George Mikhailovich went unfulfilled. They walked, gardened, fished, played tennis and went on picnics. Outwardly at least all was agreeable and civilized. Xenia reported to Bimbo that they were all leading a "quiet life, not seeing anybody and are glad to be all together. It is the only consolation in our difficult time."

However, coexistence in the Ai Todor colony was not simple. Xenia had to tolerate her philandering husband Sandro; Minnie had to accept the hateful commoner Kulikovsky, and to face Nikolasha, whom she believed had persuaded the emperor, her son, to abdicate.

Olga and Kulikovsky lived separately from the others in a small house at the Ai Todor estate, and her first son, Tikhon, was born there in early August. Olga was the first grand duchess to nurse her own child and to cook for her family, even baking cakes. She did not complain; she enjoyed such ordinary tasks, having never had much relish for imperial splendor.

Until the summer of 1917, the Crimea remained sheltered from the political storm raging elsewhere in Russia. The Romanovs living there did not realize the extent of the violence, and Minnie complained that she should never have allowed herself to have been persuaded to come south, that it was not necessary; instead she should have gone to Tsarskoye Selo to join Nicky and his family. But Olga's loyal maid, Mimka, returned from her trek with no jewels; thieves had taken them. Tsarskoye Selo also was no longer as Minnie had known it. "So," Olga tells us, without jewels "dear Mimka brought just everything that caught her eye—a huge hat trimmed with ostrich feathers, a few dresses, and a silk kimono somebody had brought me from Japan years ago. She also brought my little Maltese poodle."

Indeed the lull soon ended. In the middle of the night, a group of sailors from the Sevastopol Soviet, profoundly suspicious of Romanov loyalties to Russia, searched Ai Todor, looking, they said, for firearms and the "secret telegraph" supposedly connecting the Romanovs to the Germans. They burst into Minnie's private apartments while she was lying in her bed. They opened all the drawers and cupboards, threw around the clothing, tore up the carpet, thrust bayonets through the upholstered furniture looking for concealed valuables and tossed all the dowager's papers and correspondence into bags for removal. They took her diaries and her Bible also. The furious and courageous Minnie unleashed a stream of invective, responding so vigorously and vehemently to the intruders that they never came to her large jewel case.

Sandro came in and persuaded the sailors to leave the old woman alone. Later Olga helped her mother hide her jewels.

We transferred everything to small cocoa tins ... we hid those tins in a deep hole at the bottom of a rock by the sea-shore. Because of the many holes in the face of the rock we marked the one in which we had hidden the jewels by placing at the front of it the white skull of a dog.

One day we arrived to find the skull lying on the beach. We didn't know what to think. Had somebody discovered our hiding place? Or had the wind just blown it to the ground? I still remember the cold drops of perspiration forming on my forehead as I watched my husband sticking his hand deep in every possible hole in the rock-face. What a relief when he finally pulled a cocoa tin rattling with jewels out of one hole!

As for the Bible, many years later Minnie received a package in the mail from a Danish dealer in rare books. He had found her Bible for sale in a Moscow book stall. She died with that Bible clasped in her hands.

The local Yalta Soviet, the new legislature of the revolutionary masses, put the family under house arrest. For a while people from the outside could still visit the palace and one of them recalls, "I brought them any eatables I could find—a cake, a pound of sugar, sometimes a little white bread—very useful presents at a time when the family were kept on short rations and what food there was came from the 'pot' of the sailors." Minnie herself wrote that she was hungry all the time. The family joked about the "wiener schnitzel" they concocted of cabbage and carrots.

King George V wrote Ambassador Buchanan of his shock "to hear of the harsh treatment to which the Empress Marie and her family have been and are being subjected." He continued, "I beg you to protest on my behalf against this attitude towards my mother's sister who has lived for over 50 years in Russia and done everything in her power for the good of the country. . . . I cannot exaggerate my feelings in this painful matter."

Buchanan replied that he had already been pressuring the Provisional Government to give proper protection to the dowager empress and to allow her to correspond freely with Queen Alexandra. Buchanan saw Felix Yusupov, he said, whenever the latter came to Petrograd, in order to get firsthand news of the dowager, and Yusupov had never mentioned any problems about food or money. Buchanan remarked that food was scarce all over the country and possibly "Her Majesty may not have been able to obtain some of the articles of food to which she is accustomed."

Sandro understood how serious the situation was and both his appearance and behavior reflected that. His son Fedor noted that he had changed a lot; he had stopped smiling, became "awfully silent" and very irritable.

The people of Yalta and other small resorts in the area, aside from the local soviets, felt indignant about the way the Romanovs were being treated. The southern Crimean coast was very different from the rest of Russia: There were no factories and therefore no workers, and the peasants were represented solely by self-sufficient Tatars, farming in the mountains. The population of the towns consisted either of the upper classes, people who had fled the capital, or the people who had for generations been providing for the well-being of those people. Large groups were not gripped with a sense of grievance, and people in the street were openly expressing their sympathy for the Romanovs.

Romanovs could not visit Yalta, the only town easily accessible. The local Soviet explained the quarantine by claiming that "counter-revolutionary emissaries" were around. Twenty-three sailors were now posted at Ai Todor. Some of them seemed only too glad to humiliate the Romanovs, and Sandro wrote ruefully that this showed how little he had learned about the navy from his long shelves of books about it. The family were indignant at their arrest, but they appreciated how much better it was to be in the Crimea than in Siberia.

On August 1st, Nicky and his family were taken from Tsarskoye Selo after four months of confinement within the iron fence of the Alexander Palace. A secret train marked "Red Cross Mission" took them to Tobolsk in Siberia, an inhospitable land to which Nicky and his ancestors had sent criminals, rebels and revolutionaries.

❦

The first Romanov to flee Russia was Kyril. Demonstrating foresight or perhaps the same sheer luck that had saved him during the explosion of *Petropavlovsk,* he left for Finland in June. He took his pregnant wife Ducky and their two daughters with him. Kyril and Ducky had a relatively comfortable and easy train ride from Petrograd to Finland, only a few hours. But the legend grew, and was apparently accepted even by some of the family, that Kyril heroically escaped Russia by crossing a frozen Gulf of Finland by foot, carrying his wife with him, a feat hard to imagine in the heat of June. Even by the time Kyril left, communications among the family, as everywhere in Russia, had broken down, and most knew nothing about the whereabouts and activities of many other family members.

Kyril chose his destination well. Finland was then slipping into an amorphous political order. Still nominally a Russian province, it was enjoying increasing independence. German interest in Finland during World War I was growing. A pro-German faction in Finland had persuaded the Germans to bring Finnish youth to Germany for military training, and some even wanted to establish a Finnish monarchy with a German prince crowned as king. Indeed, if the war had not ended with the military and social collapse of Germany, Prince Friedrich Karl of Hesse, brother-in-law of the kaiser, would likely have become King of Finland. For a Romanov refuge, Finland was safer than Petrograd yet conveniently close to Russia.

But the collapse of Russian monarchy had unleashed in Finland both a nationalist movement for secession and massive social unrest. By the fall of 1917, Finland had its own soviets, dominated by left-wing radicals. Many Russians still in Finland, especially soldiers and sailors, hoped for an uprising of the lower classes analogous to what was happening in Russia itself. Other Russians there were political conservatives, persons of wealth and position, most of them seasonal residents, owners of summer houses.

For Kyril, Finland proved a perfect choice. He had both left Russia and yet not left it. Finland was so close to Petrograd that it would be easy for him to slip back if the political winds seemed to be blowing in the right direction. He could readily keep in touch with events in the turbulent capital. After the abdications of Nicholas II and Michael, Kyril was finally first in the line of succession, if one over-looked his marriage to a divorced first cousin, an act forbidden by the Orthodox Church. A decision of the Provisional Government or some other whim of fortune could take him to the Winter Palace and the re-alization of his greatest desire.

In Finland Kyril first stayed in Borga, a small town on the Gulf of Finland just east of Helsinki, where Ducky gave birth to a boy on August 30, 1917. The family moved to the nearby estate of Haikko, loaned to them by friends, where the long-awaited male offspring was baptized Vladimir in honor of his grandfather. The priest who offici-ated was summoned from Petrograd, and he brought with him a christening bowl from the Winter Palace and the imperial register. Vladimir thus became the last Romanov to be carried on the family roster. His grandmother Miechen and his uncle Boris were named his godparents in absentia. Old customs could thus be honored. But or-dinary life was not easy. Kyril himself had to go out and scour the market for provisions. Ducky wrote letters to relatives abroad be-seeching them to send food tiny Vladimir could eat, reporting that she could get none there.

In the first weeks of summer, George Mikhailovich also went to Finland, but, unlike Kyril, he would return to the capital later—under escort. George, estranged from his wife, was separated by the war from all his family who were living in England. He corresponded frequently with his daughter, Xenia (not to be confused with Nicky's sister), telling her what was happening.

> My dearest soul, my lovely, my own Xenia!
> . . . We have to change everything to a new system. Almost all of the servants have departed for their respective provinces; they all have returned to their villages. . . . I cannot pay them any wages and that is why I fired them. . . . I cannot attain permission to leave for England. All of these new ministers are afraid of each other. . . . The kikes have created the revolution and the Russians thought they would fix up everything very nicely, but of course they will not be able to fix up everything very nicely. . . . They have completely forgotten God. And people who forget God are sooner or later, but certainly, punished by God. What scoundrels are in the English government, they will not allow me to go to England; they want to please the Russian revolutionaries and for this reason are not allowing honest people to come to England. . . . The main rascal is the local English Ambassador Buchanan; he turned out to be a horrendous villain and is constantly helping our revolutionaries secretly.

George Mikhailovich had written to ask British permission to visit his family in England, proposing to travel incognito under the name of "Mikhailoff." But Buchanan had his instructions. The Foreign Office told him that "You should discourage the visit of the Grand Duke George to England. The presence here of Grand Dukes is not desirable at present."

George Mikhailovich pointed out the fact that the British had traditionally offered political sanctuary to those needing it. In the past, these refugees were opponents of tsardom; the anarchist Prince Peter Kropotkin, among others, had found safety in England. But now the British showed themselves unwilling to provide the same haven for proponents of tsardom. Furthermore the British government was extremely sensitive to the deep public hatred of Germany in their country, created at least in part by their own wartime propaganda and even affecting their own royal house, who were of course as German in blood as the Romanovs were.

The dowager empress, on the other hand, would be a different case, the Foreign Office declared. After all she was the sister of Queen Alexandra, a Dane by birth, widow of the late tsar, and strongly anti-German. Ambassador Buchanan was reporting to London that the Provisional Government was prepared to allow certain members of the Romanov family to go abroad; the dowager was free to go whenever she pleased, whether to England, Denmark or Finland, and he began to report regularly on the state of her health, knowing of Queen Mother Alexandra's intense concern about her sister.

The only happy grand duke in the spring and summer of 1917 seemed to be Bimbo, comfortably raffish in his appearance and behavior, out on the town, pursuing his old routines, dining regularly in solitary splendor at his favorite restaurant, the chic Dinon. Bimbo was even considering running for the constituent assembly to promote the republican cause there. His brother Sergei Mikhailovich was strongly skeptical of the direction of Bimbo's liberal politics:

A Russian is so uncivilized, so much of a savage, that now he can lead only two kinds of life: either under the baton of a strong authority, fearing punishment, or in a complete anarchy under the motto 'Grab everything which does not belong to you.' This behavior is now being demonstrated on the railroads. How do people understand freedom? . . . The trains are not running—kill the station manager; the train goes too slowly—unhook the car carrying food.

Sergei Mikhailovich and others still hoped for restoration, but Bimbo was writing to his friends in Paris:

If I am elected to the famous Constituent Assembly, I will vote for a Republic. And this is why! Who are the candidates for a Monarchy? First of all, the Grand Duke Michael. He is another edition of his brother without the learning of Nicholas, without a bit of character, and married to a woman from the legal world [a lawyer's daughter] of Moscow. She was married twice before, and that does not count her love affairs. This Natasha Sheremetevsky [Countess Brassova] is an intelligent but evil woman, and her friends are interlopers and shady characters. The next candidate is Kyril, a pompous idiot. . . . Then there is the man, that Music-Hall lover, that Boris, who is well-known in Paris. Finally we have Andre the Gigolo [Grand Duke Andrew], the lover of my brother's mistress, the dancer [Kshesinskaya]. To Hell with all of them!

Far away from Petrograd, southwest of the Caucasus, Dmitri still languished in his Persian exile. Having got news about the revolution, he wrote to his young half-brother, Prince Vladimir Paley, from Kazvin, "God help us, the Russians. . . . The *ancien regime* could not have lasted for much longer. The catastrophe was anticipated. It has come. Now one should hope that free Russia will reach her ideals. I only wish they would spill as little blood as possible!"

Those who met Dmitri in Persia around this time understood that his situation was "difficult and extremely delicate" and noticed that he "behaved himself with great tact and dignity." Some welcomed him as one of the liberators of Russia from Rasputin's yoke. Others saw him as a participant in murder and refused to meet him. Some scorned him; one European diplomat remarked, "He is not the Grand Duke Dmitri, just little Captain Romanov." Sometimes soldiers would address Dmitri as "Captain," sometimes, after looking around timidly, as "Your Imperial Highness."

On March 1st, the Petrograd Soviet had issued their notorious Order #1 directed to the whole Russian army, informing the soldiers that they were to form committees to regulate the life of their units. Weapons too were to be controlled by the committees. And because soldiers possessed equal political rights with the officers, now they no longer needed to salute them. Discipline started to collapse.

Disorder spread inevitably to all fronts where Russian troops were fighting. By June 1917, the Cossacks occupying Isfahan in Persia had stopped mounting guard or saluting their officers. They took to highway robbery and drunken debauchery. Before autumn the Russian garrison was demoralized and the position of its officers became pitiable.

Dmitri moved to Teheran, where he stayed with the commander of the Cossack Persian Division, but he would spend days and nights with his Russian and foreign friends in small gatherings and at parties given in his honor. In conversation, Dmitri would repeatedly tell what he remembered about the court and the tsar's headquarters, of the dismissal of Nikolasha in the summer of 1915, and of the Romanov family pleas to the tsar to keep the grand duke as commander-in-chief.

Rasputin's murder seemed to haunt Dmitri. He would return to the story of Grishka's terrible role whenever he could but would never discuss the murder itself, saying that he was sworn to silence. So he would always abruptly stop his narrative at its most dramatic point.

Dmitri would never part with his revolver, and he openly declared that it was the weapon by which Rasputin had been killed. In a strange association he would boast that he himself was an excellent shot and would gladly demonstrate his skill in the garden. With this kind of talk people could not help wondering whether, after all, Dmitri was the wielder of that weapon used against Rasputin, and not just a passive conspirator. Dmitri pointed out that his father Grand Duke Paul had made Dmitri swear by the memory of his late mother that he had not killed Rasputin. But Paul had not been present at the murder, and when he made a public statement on the issue, Dmitri came out with an enigmatic remark: "I don't understand why Father should speak for me. I am not saying what he says. I am keeping silent."

Dmitri was received by the shah in private audience and subsequently invited by the British Minister, Sir Charles Marling, to stay at the British Legation in Teheran. Revolutionaries among the Russian troops in Persia were outraged by the cordial way in which the British diplomat treated a "representative of the dynasty," and a delegation visited Teheran to protest. Sir Charles received the soldiers politely, gave them tea, listened to their grievances, said that the British Mission was always happy to be hospitable to its allies, and then, making his goodbyes, presented each of the soldiers with cigarettes. Dmitri remained a guest.

Marling became a father-figure for Dmitri. He would scold the young grand duke when the latter would return from the club at 10 A.M. after a night of revelry, barely in time to have morning coffee with his host. Dmitri at that point saw only two ways of fighting the anguish of exile: carousing and meditating. He used both extensively. In spite of a shortage of funds, he would gamble and lose at the Teheran Club. When the terrible year of 1917 finally ended, at midnight on December 31st Dmitri made three wishes, the first being for "greatness of spirit" (relating to his studies of esoteric Eastern philosophies), followed by two others: the restoration of monarchy in Russia and a "quiet life."

On September 18, 1917, Dmitri wrote to his half-brother Vladimir from Teheran with bitterness and fatalism, "As before, I don't know when I will leave; as before, I don't know what I will do now. I have to arm myself with patience and keep my nose clean." To his diary he confided, "Only God knows when I will be able to leave this foul country."

Vladimir Paley, in his mother's eyes Russia's greatest poet since Pushkin, was, in 1917, a young man of twenty, entering adulthood with a strong inclination towards mysticism, a member of the "decadent" generation who combined a sense of hedonistic self-indulgence with political cynicism. On June 21, 1917, he wrote in his diary:

> What an awful, difficult time! We all live by gossip, suggestions, hopes—and memories. . . . Actually, nobody knows what he wants and [each] is scared of what his neighbor wants. Petrograd is experiencing a lull, but the mood is nervous—it smells of blood. The city is unspeakably dirty. Chaotic crowds, disorder, anarchy. In one word—revolution. . . . The most humanistic soul must now agree that Russia *cannot* live without a baton. It needs a policeman and not freedom. . . . If a new tsar comes, he will be extremely cruel.

The fate of all the Romanovs in Russia was directly connected to the events in the seething capital. Alexander Kerensky had shouldered aside Prince Lvov and now headed the Provisional Government. Thin and intense, wearing military uniform without insignia, Kerensky's power lay less in his appearance or title than in his ability to exploit the spoken word; he was an impassioned orator, a man for the times.

Kerensky's speaking was less suited to parliament than to the street corner; his style was emotional rather than reasoned, he spoke in slogans rather than of programs. Kerensky was more performer than politician. When he was young, growing up coincidentally in the same town, Simbirsk, as Lenin, Kerensky had wanted to be an actor, and in his maturity his speeches were performances. When he was finished, and had left the platform, he would often break down in tears, faint, and his aides would administer restoratives.

But Kerensky truly wanted to effect change for Russia; he saw Bolshevism as a profound threat to the Russia he loved. He crushed the July Bolshevik uprising and declared a hunt, which proved to be unsuccessful and not too energetic, for the coup leaders, primarily Lenin, who had fled to Finland. Yet nobody could abolish the soviets that now began to form an alternative structure of government throughout Russia. These councils of workers, peasants and soldiers, springing up everywhere from Petrograd to the Crimea, declared a witch-hunt on everyone perceived as an enemy of revolution. The Romanovs were leading targets.

In the last days of August 1917, army commander-in-chief General Lavr Kornilov made matters worse for the Romanovs. Fully perceiving the impotence of the Provisional Government and wanting to save Russia from the radicals, Kornilov marched his troops towards the capital. Following events from Teheran, Dmitri welcomed Kornilov's desperate lunge. "Finally, here is a man who at the risk of his own skin has decided to go from words, disputes, meetings, rallies, conferences—to deeds!" In order to crush Kornilov and stay in power, Kerensky appealed to the revolutionary consciousness of the soldiers' soviets, now almost in full control of the army. The revolutionary army suppressed Kornilov's uprising but ultimately failed to rally behind Kerensky, and because the Kornilov attack was generally and correctly perceived as an attempted counter-revolution, its failure bore heavy consequences for the monarchists.

In September and October rain fell heavily, more than usual. Cold damp winds swept in from the Gulf of Finland. After the bitter winter of 1916–17 with its record-breaking cold, the late autumn of 1917 continued as bad as it could be in Petrograd in that season, in weather and in mood. Mud that nobody cared to clean covered the squares, the streets and the sidewalks. Few lamps brightened the streets, partly because the city feared German zeppelins, partly because fuel was so scarce. In the shortening days of autumn, darkness fell at three and lasted until ten the next morning. Private houses had electricity only from six P.M. until midnight; candles became prohibitively expensive and kerosene hard to find.

Food rations sank to one quarter pound of bread per day and two pounds of sugar per month, but the sugar was virtually unavailable. In the market, meat and even vegetables commanded enormous sums, and people, even the comfortable middle class, began to peddle their treasures in order to buy.

Thousands of hungry, often barefoot, soldiers deserted the front and, keeping their arms, headed for the cities. Petrograd swarmed with thugs and gangsters, which forced apartment dwellers to stand guard with guns. Strikes shut down factories and paralyzed the railways. In the countryside, peasants began to loot and torch manor houses and to kill landlords. Russia, having gone through a swift transition from autocratic monarchy to parliamentary liberalism, and then to mob rule, was now descending to an even lower circle of Hell, civil war. All seemed a gathering chaos of cries and screams, the rush of looters, the crack of rifle shots. Bolshevik leaders like Leon Trotsky and Lev Kamenev spent twelve hours a day haranguing the crowds. The crowds listened.

On the night of October 24th, a squat middle-aged person made his way by foot from the working class Vyborg district to the Smolny Institute, a school for young women. The man looked like an amateur detective, perhaps even a cuckold chasing his unfaithful wife. He sported a red wig and wore a long overcoat; more than that, his face was bandaged, as if he had been in an accident or had just left the chair of an incompetent dentist. He looked so grotesque that only by pretending to be drunk did he escape arrest by a Cossack patrol.

That Cossack patrol made a fatal mistake. The man who had chosen such a ludicrous disguise was Vladimir Lenin, also now known as the Old Man, leader of the Bolsheviks. Lenin's role in 1905 had been inconsequential, and in February he and his Bolsheviks did little to bring down the monarchy; it seemed likely then they would vanish from the political stage. But in March 1917, the man who would become one of the major formative figures of the twentieth century, icon for millions and devil incarnate for other millions, suddenly had sprung out of obscurity, and the Russian revolution had its own Robespierre.

Lenin hardly looked charismatic. Short, broad shouldered, walking with a curious crab-like gait, he had become bald at twenty; his beard and moustache were red. His most remarkable feature was his eyes, of an unusual golden blue sheen, "the eyes of a lemur," someone once observed, and his habitual squint seemed only to increase their penetrating thrust. Strong willed and selfish, Lenin expressed both a passion for ideas and a cool detachment from human relationships. His moods were as changeable as Petrograd's weather. Fits of enormous energy and feverish activity bordering on mania followed periods of deep depression, with headaches and insomnia and the animal-like desire to slip away to a secluded spot in the woods and sleep there under a tree.

Lenin had a particular reason to hate the Romanovs. In 1887, his adored older brother, Alexander, had plotted to assassinate Alexander III. The police caught him and he was hanged at Shlisselburg fortress near St. Petersburg.

Lenin felt a deep desire to avenge his dead brother. The rage of the hungry mob had brought down the Romanov monarch. Lenin's vengeance would extinguish the Romanov dynasty.

One of his political rivals called Lenin a "fencer," saying that his major talent was the ability to concentrate all his energy at the right moment for attack. His ruthlessness plus his understanding of what the Russian people now wanted above all else, peace with Germany, would propel him to victory.

On that October night, Lenin reached the Bolshevik premises safely. There he expressed his will with Caesarian laconism: "Take the post-office, the telephone station and the telegraph. Secure the bridges over the Neva."

Lenin planned and directed the coup of October 1917 from Bolshevik headquarters at the Smolny Institute, since the time of Catherine the Great St. Petersburg's most fashionable school for "noble maidens." The two Montenegrin sisters, the grand duchesses Militsa and Anastasia (Stana), had softened some of their mountain rusticity there nearly thirty years before. Now, in corridors where no male voices had ever been heard except those of priests or very occasional visitors, hundreds of armed men were rushing in all directions, shouting, arguing and jostling one another. The first groups of people arrested by the Bolsheviks began to arrive. The coup had been launched, undertaken with an iron hand.

Bands of radicals put the Winter Palace under siege; the attack lasted until 2:10 A.M., when the palace yielded to its assailants. Sailors and soldiers climbed a marble staircase and rushed into a small hall decorated with gold and malachite where a small group of frightened elderly gentlemen sat, members of the Provisional Government. On a long table covered with a green cloth they had laid out pens and ink bottles, and papers covered with futile appeals and doodles drawn in despair. They were arrested and taken away across the Neva to Peter and Paul fortress for incarceration. Of all the senior members of the government in Petrograd, only Alexander Kerensky had been able to escape, allegedly dressed in women's clothes, leaving in an automobile lent to him by an American friend.

The mob began to loot the palace, their commissars making only a halfhearted effort to stop them. They began grabbing small sculptures, silver candlesticks and snuff boxes, bedsheets embroidered with the imperial monogram, blankets and clothing. For these ragged people, clothing was the most precious item. A witness saw two soldiers tearing off Spanish leather from the sofas. They wanted to make new boots from it. The old palace servants in their blue livery stood in a state of shock, feebly protesting, "No entrance, gentlemen, it is not allowed, no . . . "

Then the mob went after the wine cellars housing one of Europe's largest and finest collections. A great drinking frenzy began and spilled out of the palace onto the streets. Soon drunken figures lay comatose in shattered glass everywhere on the crimsoned snow. Bolshevik headquarters, desperate to stop the orgy, sent in troops with strict orders: destroy all the wines. The Red Guards smashed barrels and crushed bottles, walking knee-deep in wine. They too became drunk, simply from the smell.

On October 25th, that same day of Bolshevik victory, Vladimir Paley, living in his father's palace at Tsarskoye Selo, confided to his diary, "A mess again. People are saying that the Bolsheviks have occupied the State Bank, that Foreign Minister Tereshchenko has disappeared, Kerensky is either at the front or in the Kingdom of Heaven (which I doubt). Machine guns are on the streets. Thank God, it is quiet at Tsarskoye."

Four days later, Paley wrote his journal entry to the roar of artillery fire and the ringing of church bells. The Bolsheviks were fighting against troops loyal to Kerensky; some shells hit the streets of Tsarskoye Selo. "Lord, save and forgive us!" The next day Grand Duke Paul was arrested by a commissar and a group of sailors, who came to his palace at Tsarskoye and took him to Petrograd for interrogation and incarceration.

The Bolshevik coup d'état in Petrograd grew into the third Russian revolution. The Romanovs survived 1905 handsomely. February 1917 shattered their political power and position. October 1917 confiscated their wealth and put their very lives in jeopardy.

CHAPTER NINE

❧

Firestorm

OCTOBER 1917–JANUARY 1919

LENIN WON POWER IN RUSSIA because of three things. First, he promised to end war with the Germans. The "grey coats," who had been called upon to die at the front for their "Serb brethren" and for the Black Sea Straits promised to Russia by the Allies, now simply wanted to go back home. Second, for most, home was the countryside. There they wanted land from the landlords. And third, they wanted vengeance upon the former upper classes. Lenin was ready to give them all three: peace, land and blood.

Immediately after his seizure of power, Lenin started negotiating with Germany, but the enemy wanted too much and the war continued amidst a gathering chaos at home. Quickly Lenin moved to confiscate large estates and nationalize the banks. This wiped out all the paper wealth of the former rich and essentially reduced them to such property as they could carry in their own hands. But Lenin's major instrument of introducing revolutionary order was terror.

In the Crimea, sailors and workers, the new Russian political elite, were believed to be "walking in blood up to their knees." Rumor rested upon fact. On one day, February 23, 1918, in Simferopol one hundred seventy officers and middle class civilians were summarily shot. Sailors of the Black Sea fleet thrust their officers alive into the ships' furnaces, sometimes first tying them to planks and pushing them in inch by inch. Sometimes they simply tied stones to their feet and threw them into the water offshore. Long after, deep below the surface yet clearly visible, one could see the hands of the corpses waving and gesturing as the currents eddied and flowed.

The imperial army had dissolved with revolution; in this new war, the fighting was done by *ad hoc,* brand-new units; the new "Red" Bolshevik regime was pitted against groups of counter-revolutionaries. These "Whites" formed a miscellaneous body with a wide range of political views from conservative monarchists to former terrorists; they were schoolboys, intellectuals, Cossacks, army officers—all united only by their desire to crush the Reds. The symbolism of colors went back to the French revolution, red having then been the color of the revolutionaries, white the color of the Bourbon loyalists.

On all fronts of the civil war the Bolsheviks seemed to be losing. The non-Russian borderlands to the far west seethed with local nationalisms and, taking advantage of this, General Nicholas Yudenich established a base in Estonia and prepared to march on Petrograd. A White army emerged in the Don Cossack area of southern Russia, under the command of Lavr Kornilov. Siberian Omsk had become a focal center of anti-Bolshevism led by Admiral Alexander Kolchak, who brought his formidable talents for fighting at sea to fighting on land. The situation in western Siberia and in the Urals was especially bad for the Bolsheviks. Though Yekaterinburg, where Nicholas and his family were now imprisoned, was itself a Bolshevik stronghold, newspapers there announced, "The Revolutionary Red Urals are in mortal danger."

On May 1, 1918, on the eve of a jubilant parade celebrating the international workers' holiday, Lenin ordered and personally participated in the destroying of a memorial to Grand Duke Sergei that had stood at the place of his assassination at the Kremlin gates. The same year Lenin ordered destruction of other monuments to the Romanovs, to Alexander II at the Kremlin and to Alexander III near the cathedral of Christ the Savior. Instead, a monument to Karl Marx arose in the heart of Moscow. Lenin planned to build others, to Marx's closest friend and sponsor, Friedrich Engels, and to leaders of the French rev-

olution, Marat and Robespierre. But a war of statuary could not satisfy Lenin's need for vengeance. He had to decide the fate of Nicholas
II himself.

For several months the Kremlin had been discussing what to do
with the former tsar. Trotsky proposed an open trial, broadcast by
radio to the entire nation. Lenin liked the idea but remarked grimly,
"There might not be enough time."

In early July, the Kremlin leaders discussed the problem of what they
should do if Yekaterinburg had to be abandoned. The leading Red in
the Urals, Philip Goloshchekin, rushed to Moscow for instructions.
Yakov Sverdlov, Lenin's right-hand man, told him, "If you can organize
a trial, then organize it, but if not, well, you know what that means."

On July 16th, the editors of a Danish newspaper queried Lenin.

"Rumor here going that ex-tsar has been murdered. Kindly wire
facts."

Lenin immediately replied.

"Rumor not true. Ex-tsar safe. All rumors are only lies of capitalist
press."

Around the same hour he sent a coded telegram to Yekaterinburg
ordering the execution of Nicholas and his entire family. No one was
to be spared.

On July 17th, at half past one A.M., the family and its small suite
were awakened and taken to the basement of the Ipatiev house.
Nicholas carried Alexis. Suffering from his terrible disease, the
fourteen-year-old boy could not walk. Finding herself in an empty
room, Alix said indignantly, "What, there isn't a chair? One isn't even
allowed to sit down?" Two chairs were brought. Nicholas put Alexis
on one; Alix sat on the other. The Bolshevik commissar Yakov
Yurovsky ordered the others to stand in a row. When the group had
taken their places, Yurovsky called for the firing squad.

Men carrying guns entered the room and Yurovsky announced to
the tsar, "Your relatives in Europe are continuing their aggression
against Soviet Russia. The Ural Soviet has therefore decided that you
must be shot."

"What? What?" Nicholas exclaimed in disbelief, turning toward his
family. The detachment fired. Nicholas was shot by Yurovsky himself.
But then bullets began to bounce through the room, ricocheting off
the women. Yurovsky did not know that the grand duchesses had
sewn diamonds into their clothing. They had, therefore, to be finished

off with bayonets or shots in the head. The bodies were then loaded into a truck, taken to a forest and buried there.

The news would trickle out only over many months, and indeed many would not believe that all had died for many decades, until testing of the bodies after the fall of the Soviet Union would ultimately remove all doubt. Those not killed by bullets were finished off by bayonets.

Nicholas and his family were not the first Romanovs to die at the hand of the Bolsheviks. The first was Grand Duke Nicholas Constantinovich, the shadowy figure from the past whom Alexander II had exiled for theft to Central Asia forty-four years before. Extravagant and outspoken, he died in Tashkent in February 1918 in circumstances still unknown, probably at the hands of local revolutionaries.

Grand Duke Michael, "the last tsar," suffering from gastric ulcers, hemorrhoids and constant harassment by the Bolsheviks, was arrested on March 9, 1918, and with his British secretary, Brian Johnson, sent to the town of Perm in Siberia, 160 miles from Yekaterinburg. Rumor in Petrograd had it that on the train the two were made to stand during the entire journey of several days. On the night of June 13th, they were seized at their hotel and taken to the woods outside of town. The carriages stopped and Michael's jailers offered him a cigarette. He accepted it politely. As he smoked, one of the group shot Johnson in the temple. With outstretched arms Michael ran to his friend. Three bullets were fired into the grand duke and he was dead. The chief assailant then went immediately to Moscow, and Sverdlov took him straight to Lenin so that he could report all the thrilling details directly.

Another group of the Romanovs was taken to the town of Alapayevsk, a secondary manufacturing center 120 miles from Yekaterinburg. Ella, Sergei Mikhailovich, Paul's son Prince Vladimir Paley and three sons of K.R.—Ioann, Constantine and Igor—comprised the group. The Bolsheviks believed Alapayevsk to be "the strongest and most trustworthy citadel of Communism in the northern Urals." Like Yekaterinburg, it was an industrial center and the local workers, who labored under appalling conditions, were ardent followers of the Reds.

The Romanovs were placed in an old school on the outskirts of the town. The school was fairly small, consisting of only six rooms, the furniture basic but scanty. Each prisoner received an iron bed. In late May, the situation did not look too bad for them. Although they were kept prisoners by the local soviet, they were allowed to walk in town and even to talk to people, mainly to the youngsters who would come to school to play soccer, skittles and other games with the younger Romanov princes. In the imperial family, exercise had always been an important part of the routine for young males, and the Romanovs were now glad to have that opportunity. Also soccer was relatively new to Russia, and the cosmopolitan princes were ready to share its secrets with the eager provincial teenagers.

The Romanovs were preparing to spend a long time in Alapayevsk. They planted flower and vegetable gardens near the school and spent many hours working there, the kind of plain activity that Alexander III would have heartily approved. On rainy days the prisoners read Russian novels to each other.

But gradually the regime toughened. The local soviet decided that the Romanovs were too privileged to be served precooked meals and started instead supplying them with the raw materials, ordering the prisoners to cook for themselves. Then they were forbidden to take walks. The school was encircled with a barbed-wire fence and even small trenches. The soccer games stopped.

Late in the night of July 17th, the secret police suddenly came to the school. They informed the Romanovs that because of "an unexpected attack on Alapayevsk by White troops, it was resolved to remove them to a safer country place." In half an hour, the prisoners were on their way toward some abandoned mine shafts in the woods.

At shaft #7, the deepest and longest unused, the carriages stopped. The Romanovs were blindfolded and ordered to walk across a log placed over the sixty-foot-deep mine. Grand Duke Sergei Mikhailovich, the oldest man in the group, was the only one to disobey. He threw himself at the guards and they shot him to death immediately. The others fell into the deep shaft. The guards then threw down heavy timbers and hand grenades after them. When a local peasant crawled to the edge of the shaft, soon after the execution, he heard the faint sound of hymns being chanted far below.

When the Whites found the bodies, they discovered that the Romanovs had died in a protracted agony from thirst, hunger and wounds. Prince Constantine's mouth and stomach were full of earth with which he had been trying to suppress his thirst and satisfy his hunger. Prince Ioann's wounded head had been bound by Ella's monogrammed handkerchief. They also found a medallion with the picture of Mathilde Kshesinskaya signed "Malya," and a key ring holding a charm in the shape of a potato. The potato was the code name used by the Romanovs for girlfriends; a jealous Xenia had maliciously given the charm to Kshesinskaya in the good old days, three revolutions ago. And she had given it to Sergei, her lover.

Fourteen Romanovs had died within one week, between July 13th and July 18th, 1918. Most of them had been born in the same place, St. Petersburg, and they died in the same area, the Urals, whose gems had so often ornamented their palaces and persons. All in all, the Bolsheviks had thus far captured and slaughtered an emperor, an empress, four grand dukes, five grand duchesses and four princes of the blood.

The Crimean colony of the Romanovs found themselves almost totally isolated from the rest of the world, the last to get the news of the extermination of so many family members. Nor had their relatives elsewhere in Russia any idea of what was happening to them.

Minnie, in the Crimea, was able to get a letter to her sister, Queen Alexandra, using Danish channels. The letter was dated February 29, 1918; the queen did not receive it until mid-June and she immediately wrote to her "darling Georgie boy" (as she habitually addressed the reigning monarch) to express her great distress. [Aunt Minny's life is] "too awful & they [have] nearly starved & have not got a penny left. . . . I quite tremble to think of her future . . . and God only knows where she is at this moment."

The Sevastopol Soviet, jealous of their Yalta counterparts, moved the Crimean Romanovs from Ai Todor and Chaeer to Grand Duke Peter's home, Dulber, maintaining that Dulber with its high walls was easier to defend than Ai Todor, open on all sides, and they prepared a chart which they showed to Sandro of where machine guns might be strategically placed. Dulber was large, more palace than villa, and now a potential fortress.

Shortly after the move, a strapping six-foot-four sailor named Zadorozhny was posted at the palace as representative of the Sevastopol Soviet. Olga recalled:

He was a murderer but a charming man. He never met our eyes. Later he confided that he could not bear to look at those he would have to kill some day. As time went on, however, his manner became much kindlier. Yet, for all his good intentions, it was not Zadorozhny who saved our lives in the end but the fact that the Soviets in Sevastopol and Yalta could not agree as to which of them had the prior right to chop our heads off.

Yalta kept trying to take charge; Sevastopol resisted, successfully because of walled Dulber and the determination of the sailor Zadorozhny. Sandro writes that as Zadorozhny put it "in his colorful way, every one of his boys would have liked to shoot a grand duke but not before the order was given by the Sevastopol Soviet."

Olga and her husband and baby remained in a small house at Ai Todor. Because her name was now Kulikovsky she was allowed the freedom to come and go from the estate. She and her husband were thus able to take a pony cart out to collect both food and information. Olga had all the freedom of being a commoner but at the cost of having no special protection. Alone at Ai Todor, she and her little family were cut off from the rest of the Romanov colony and at the mercy of any roaming marauders.

At Dulber no one was allowed to move beyond the front lawn. The dowager indignantly refused even to leave the house. She was not at all fond of the two "black sisters," Stana and Militsa, but the greater crisis seems to have smoothed over that old tension. The family now stood together. Everyone's mood became grim; they lived in expectation of being searched or moved again or even taken away for the ultimate punishment. Perhaps what was worst was the uncertainty and the feeling of helplessness.

The sailors forming a guard functioned both to protect the imperial family and to keep them from escaping. They acted rudely and appeared to be brutal, yet ultimately they proved to be saviors, keeping the family out of the hands of those who would have killed them immediately. Minnie handled all this with supreme grace and dignity; she remained cheerful and optimistic. She refused to recognize the danger of her situation. When a group of Bolshevik inspectors arrived one day and took roll, each member was obliged to answer with "Here!" Thus "Citizenness Maria Fedorovna Romanova" was called in turn. When the exercise was over, Minnie held up her little dog and shouted, "You have forgotten someone, put his name down too."

But this was mere bravado and the facade was brittle. Minnie's emotions were childishly mercurial, reflecting the stress she really felt;

she was prone to laugh but also to cry. One day suddenly she even experienced an uncharacteristic spell of weakness and had to be helped when walking. Her favorite dogs were ailing too, and that provided one more source for worry and sorrow for the old lady.

When the Bolshevik Government took Russia out of the war in March 1918 with the treaty of Brest-Litovsk, the German army came to occupy the Crimea. The Yalta Soviet decided that they should execute the Romanovs before the Germans arrived. A detachment of troops left Yalta for that purpose, but the guard of Sevastopol revolutionary sailors at Dulber who did not want to kill the Romanovs—at least yet—were able to fight them off until German troops, on a dramatic rescue mission ordered by the kaiser himself, arrived at dawn, after a forced march from Simferopol, just as the palace gateway was being battered down by the Bolsheviks from Yalta. Thus an idiosyncratic wall of the amateur architect, Grand Duke Peter, unique among Romanov Crimean palaces, laughed at by the family when he built it, proved to be a lifesaver.

The German presence brought order and some sense of security to the Crimea; the occupiers reopened the banks and restored train service; they behaved very politely, not wanting to alienate the population. They allowed those Romanovs wanting to leave Dulber for their own palaces to do so; at the same time they allowed the remaining Bolsheviks to leave the Crimea safely. Nonetheless, despite the new seeming stability, the rich slept with loaded guns within reach, and every refugee hid or buried his treasures. Worn and gray faces showed the high level of anxiety.

For the Romanovs it was a terrible thought that their German enemies should now become saviors. Of all the charges leveled against the Romanovs, the one that was most unfair was that they were not fervent Russian patriots. The family had done its best to repudiate all its relationships both with the German people and with German culture; they now identified Germany with Prussia and with the house of Hohenzollern, and for most Romanovs these feelings of animosity ran deep.

Even those who were Romanov only by marriage showed intense loyalty to their adopted country. No one could have hated the Germans more than did the dowager empress, remembering from long ago the Prussian seizure of part of her beloved Denmark. Now, with the Germans at the gate of Dulber, Minnie declared that she would not receive the German commander since she considered that Germany and Russia were still at war. The German ambassador to the nominally independent Ukraine wanted to protect the Romanovs, although the family made clear that they had no wish for such protection. When a German general in dress uniform jingling with medals presented himself in an official call to Nikolasha, Stana, his wife, reportedly drove him away at the end of a broom. And Nikolasha sent word that if the Germans wanted to see him as a prisoner of war, he was ready to obey. But if this were just a social visit, he could not receive them.

The Germans suggested that Nikolasha should have a reliable guard. The grand duke replied that he did not require a German guard and asked whether it was possible to form a Russian one. The bewildered Germans agreed, but they set up their own patrols on the roads leading to the Romanov estates.

Olga said, "Here we were the Romanovs, being saved from our own people by our arch-enemy, the Kaiser! It seemed the ultimate degradation."

Nicholas II might have chosen death over rescue by the German kaiser. When, in a letter sent during the war, Wilhelm referred to the ties of friendship and blood that united his dynasty, the Hohenzollerns, with the Romanovs, the tsar remarked, "All that is dead and buried now." Nicholas thought it insulting that Wilhelm should even offer help. Others in the family too had always disliked this brash and superficially clever cousin once described as "a man of overbearing good will, demanding nothing but mutual love—but *demanding* it!"

Wilhelm personally had nothing to do with the German arrangements for Lenin's March 1917 secret trip from Switzerland through Germany back to Russia with the purpose of fomenting trouble there, and doubtless the kaiser would have agreed with Churchill's description of Lenin as "a plague bacillus." But Wilhelm's own power was severely ebbing as the war rushed to its close, and the German revolution ultimately forced him to flee his country and seek refuge in Holland.

The Germans on their side, apart from family concerns, did not necessarily welcome any involvement with Russian royals. Some reacted strongly to Romanov Germanophobia and expected a Bolshevik government to be friendlier. The German government limited its official concern to German princesses who had married into the Romanov family, including of course the empress, born Alix of Hesse-Darmstadt. But by the time the German Embassy in the Bolshevik capital, Moscow, began to press the Bolshevik government on this matter, it was already too late.

German concerns became less and less about politics and more and more about food. By the early summer of 1918, that nation's cupboard was almost bare, its people on the verge of starvation. With as many as five competing armies rampaging across the rich black earth of Ukraine, grain did not flow back to Germany from that source as the Germans had desperately hoped it would after peace was signed with Russia.

Two peripheral Romanovs, then living in Kiev, were ready to be useful to the Germans in any way they could. They were Duke George of Leuchtenberg, first husband of Nikolasha's Stana, and George's brother Duke Nicholas. Both were grandsons of Emperor Nicholas I. Duke George, who had lived in Germany for the past ten years, not only suggested to Berlin that he organize a pro-German anti-Bolshevik army in Ukraine, he also had kept the Germans informed about what was going on in the Romanov colony in the Crimea.

In the early summer of 1918, the Crimean Romanovs knew that Nicky's younger brother, Michael, had been exiled to Perm in Siberia, that others including Ella had been taken across the Urals, and that Nicky and family had been removed to Yekaterinburg. Minnie, always speaking optimistically, maintained that some day her son would rejoin her. In the last letter she had been permitted to send him, November 21, 1917, she recalled that a year had gone by since he and young Alexis had come to visit her in Kiev. "Who would have thought then of all that was in store for us, and what we should have to go through. . . . I live only in the memories of the happy past and try as much as possible to forget the present nightmare."

The Kremlin shocked the world by announcing in late July that the former tsar Nicholas Romanov had been executed but that his family was safe. Here is the first ambiguity about the end of Nicholas II and his family. Eventually the whole world would know that they had all been brutally shot and stabbed to death in the basement of the Ipatiev House in Yekaterinburg. But the account of these squalid and lonely deaths was so piecemeal and so slow to come out that people could long ask, did it really happen? The muddle of information permitted no emotional focus and no catharsis for the survivors. The contrast with the public murder of Alexander II was stark.

Whereas the news of the death of Nicholas II shocked and appalled the elite of old Russia, among the people few expressions of grief or sympathy showed themselves. One former courtier in Petrograd went for a long trolley ride the day after the news had broken. A passenger read aloud a report and it was received by the other passengers "with base comments, especially from the young: 'High time,' 'Go on, reign some more,' 'Hey, brother Romanov, so this is where your dancing has led you!' Older people were silent."

The revolution had swept away all tsarist censorship, freeing journalists to titillate a public avid for information about the Romanovs. Rasputin and the imperial couple had become favorite subjects. Pamphlets, sometimes pornographic, circulated in the millions, many of them describing the purported lecheries of Rasputin in lurid detail, including cartoon images of his cavorting in bed with the empress.

Many Russians, even those who should have known better, had already come to regard Alexandra as a pro-German traitor. Subsequently, in the popular imagination, sexual vice came to be linked to the taint of treason. Thus, as British historian Orlando Figes aptly points out, the pamphleteers helped to build an image of tsardom as evil and alien to Russia, a new image immensely destructive to old notions of the quasi-divine father figure.

By October 1918, the Germans had made plans to rescue the Romanovs from the Crimea before Bolshevik or Ukrainian nationalist troops could move into the area.

But, in November, Germany was forced to sign an armistice with the Allies and to withdraw its troops back to the homeland. The Leuchtenbergs fled Kiev together with the retreating Germans and settled down in Bavaria, where they had lived before. The Germans, overwhelmed by other matters, forgot the Romanovs. Revolution in Germany and the collapse of the Hohenzollerns rescued the Crimean Romanov colony from Germany. Instead they would face a Russian firestorm together with the rest of the nation.

❧

Russia embarked upon an orgy of destruction, the deliberate crushing of a culture, the civilization of imperial Russia. With the Bolsheviks in power, any act of violence seemed justifiable. The revolutionaries rejected everything created by or belonging to the "exploiters." They put religion into this category and so the onslaught began against monasteries and churches. Some were destroyed totally; others were locked up and left to decay; some were turned into museums or even warehouses. Mobs of peasants sacked and then destroyed, sometimes mindlessly, sometimes with meticulous thoroughness, the country mansions of the aristocracy. Mobs used fine carpets to start bonfires. Objects of art were smashed and burned: rare books, tapestries, sculpture, rare plants in hothouses, all destroyed. A shell of blackened walls with piles of gray ashes would be all to remind a viewer that once a house had stood there.

The rage of the assailants did not stop with the great houses but extended to the outbuildings as well. Farm implements and machinery, herds of oxen, studs of workhorses and thoroughbreds alike, forges, shops and mills were targets for elimination. The seed corn of an agricultural civilization, and all that the black earth had yielded over the generations, was swept away in the mad frenzy. The Bolsheviks could not have stopped this, even if they had wanted to do so; they did not fully control the countryside until 1920, the end of the Civil War in central Russia.

In Russia's cities, the story was similar. At best some of the great urban palaces were turned over to hospitals, orphanages and sanatoriums, in which cases at least the magnificent exteriors were largely untouched. But the contents totally vanished in bonfires, wanton destruction or in the hands of thieves. All the Romanov palaces in the Crimea, and many elsewhere, would meet this fate.

The nation's new leaders in the Kremlin did not direct this terror aimed at people as well as property, at Russia's carriers of culture, who were killed, imprisoned, exiled or just silenced. The people of the lower classes acted on their own initiative. Peasants burned unique libraries as revenge against an elite which had kept them illiterate, oppressed and humiliated for centuries. The people of the old regime were so much hated that all things touched by them were also hated. The radical revolutionaries even wanted to throw away the classics of Russian music and literature but were checked by the enlightened intervention of Lenin, Anatoly Lunacharsky and some other members of the older generation who bore sentimental memories of it.

Never before had Russia suffered so greatly. In the cities, people were dying of starvation. Horsemeat had become a delicacy; sometimes people in Petrograd would buy meat only to discover that the "veal" they thought they were getting came with a dog's tail. At the Kremlin, Lenin and other Bolshevik leaders ate red caviar, but it was accompanied by thin soup, millet kasha and salted beef.

The severe character of the Russian climate was badly suited to political and social mismanagement and turmoil. Survival demanded careful use of resources. For most of the year, houses and apartments required heat. In the cities firewood became precious, and people began cutting down trees lining the boulevards and feeding furnaces with wooden doors and furniture. We cannot know how many unique books were burned during these times to feed the primitive but efficient furnaces people made that were called *bourzhouiki* ("bourgeois ladies").

Disease spread like fire in a dry forest. Cold and hunger sped them along. Typhoid killed more people than bullets did; the worldwide influenza pandemic that had swept in from Asia killed millions more. Criminal gangs terrorized the cities, and city dwellers did not dare to leave their houses after dark. Yet during the night it was also dangerous to stay at home; this was the time when the secret police would pick up their victims and carry them off to prison, sometimes to death.

In the countryside it should have been easier to feed one's family and to find firewood. But the whole of rural Russia had become a battleground, and roving armies were combing the villages for anything of value, leaving the peasants to die of starvation and spilling the blood of those who objected with even more ease than in the cities. Beside the Reds and the Whites, dozens if not hundreds of small armies were fighting for living space from the Baltic to the Pacific. Anarchists, nationalists, local warlords and bandits formed these small armies. Known under different names but united under the term the "Greens" (from the color of the steppes and forests where they found shelter), they were the worst, perpetrating pogroms against the Jews, shooting at random anyone who looked prosperous or intellectual, raping and looting with wild abandon.

With the exception of Petrograd and Moscow, all the big Russian cities experienced an unceasing progression of invasions. From 1917–20, Kiev, the "Mother of Russian cities," saw fourteen different regimes. The Reds occupied it five times; the Whites, twice; the Poles and the Germans, once. The others were invasions by local warlords.

The warfare itself had become utterly cruel, even medieval. In an age of rather advanced military technology, all these armies, the Whites included, relied upon primitive, age-old weapons. The saber was at least as popular as the gun. Horses pulled machine guns. Decisive battles were planned in candlelight by yesterday's lieutenants, drunk on moonshine. The few tanks and armored trains looked like extraterrestrials. Electricity was as forgotten as morality and the value of a human life.

Meanwhile, in areas under Bolshevik control the Red Terror knew no mercy. The Bolsheviks shot suspected conspirators, captured White soldiers, and even took civilian hostages. Lenin stood firmly behind these actions, but their administrators were Yakov Sverdlov and Leon Trotsky. Both were Jews, themselves victims of severe discrimination; both had joined the revolution in their youth; and neither had had any career but that of revolutionary. Both seemed made of iron. Sverdlov was in charge of the soviets. Trotsky commanded the armies. Both advocated total destruction for the territories loyal to the Whites; both had personally decided on the execution of thousands.

If there could be a person more frightful than either Sverdlov or Trotsky, it was Felix Dzerzhinsky, the head of the CheKa, the direct forerunner of the KGB. In the cells of Moscow's Lubyanka, he applied fiendishly imaginative tortures to his many victims. Polish-born, an ascetic and a sadist, Dzerzhinsky was known to the party as "Iron Felix." With his thin pale face and exhausted expression, he reminded one of a monk of the Inquisition.

People of stature and wealth started fleeing Russia by the thousand. But successful flight demanded audacity, imagination and perseverance. Old Countess Kleinmichel, of a distinguished and very rich family, was shrewd enough to anticipate the worst. As the great houses fell to thieves and arsonists and as the owners and their servants were attacked, imprisoned or killed, she closed her shutters, locked her doors and put up a large printed notice:

No trespassing! Property of the Petrograd Soviet!
    Countess Kleinmichel has been imprisoned in Peter and Paul Fortress, and this property has been requisitioned by the People's Government.

The Countess meanwhile continued to live quietly inside, methodically sorting her belongings, packing and carefully preparing for flight abroad.

All over Russia the rich hastily and secretly went through their possessions, selecting the most valuable and most easily portable. This was not a "rainy day" they faced, it was a deluge, but nobody could possibly smuggle away as much as was needed to provide for a comfortable life ever after. With real estate, bank accounts and securities confiscated or made worthless, jewels as the most concentrated form of wealth became the best carrier, and at least for a while jewels could keep people alive in exile, be it Constantinople, Harbin or London. Gems lost their magic and were prized solely for their monetary value. Now only the prosaic matter of survival counted: medicines, bribes for border guards or daily bread.

Refugee owners of jewels became smugglers. Hiding jewels became a high art, a virtuoso performance, in which skill and luck were mixed. A lady-in-waiting to the empress wanted desperately to keep a large diamond brooch with the imperial initials. It had been part of her court dress. "I have received it from the emperor's hand; I must keep it." She sewed the brooch into her daughter's teddy bear. When Red soldiers came to search the nursery, one picked up the stuffed bear and said, "Aha, a toy! Sometimes we find other toys inside. Give me some scissors."

"No," the bright little girl shouted, "You cannot cut up my teddy bear!"

"Take it, take it," the soldier said, although knowing perhaps only too well that his suspicions were correct and that the child, made wise by terror, was concerned by something more important than the well-being of her toy.

The Reds quickly became expert in discovering hidden jewels, and some owners could not resist boasting about how clever they were in finding unusual hiding places; later they would learn to their sorrow the perils of indiscretion. It became a race between the ingenuity of the concealer and the imagination of the searcher as all the obvious places, both portable and stationary, were exhausted. Kshesinskaya hid her money in the frame of a window; she put her jewels in a hollow leg of her bed, tied to a string so that she could pull them out quickly. Ladies soon learned that a jar of cold cream was not a good place; soldiers would routinely put their fingers in to explore. A bar of soap, on the other hand, hollowed out inside, hard to penetrate, could easily conceal a large pair of pearl earrings or some other treasure. One man, a scholarly looking fugitive, took a long treatise on philosophy, cut out most of its pages and put currency in the space. Whereas his person was searched thoroughly, his book warranted only a passing glance from the guards inspecting all the passengers on the train in which he was traveling. He got his money to his destination.

Successfully fleeing abroad with jewels required even more imagination and good fortune since so many were doing it and places of
concealment were so limited. A commissar on the border of Soviet
Russia with Ukraine in 1918 boasted that he had arrested five people
in one week who had tried to hide diamonds in the spouts of teaket-
tles. One successful smuggler boasted that she had got her diamonds
out by swallowing them.

For many of the privileged class it was a last minute unanticipated
departure. They did not have time to think of what was best to bring
or how best to do it. Vladimir Nabokov, the writer, remembers a "farsighted old chambermaid in our St. Petersburg home [who] had swept
off a dressing-table into my mother's suitcase when packing it for our
hurried departure in 1917." What was brought along in haste would
often prove to be the refugee's greatest asset.

With some ingenuity people could still get out of Russia because the
Red Terror was, in its early months, as yet imperfect in its efficiency.
Refugees found several major gateways to physical safety. Foremost,
for three reasons, stood the Black Sea ports. First, they were situated
on territory controlled by the Whites. Second, maritime transporta-
tion, despite all the natural perils of the sea, furnished overall the
safest and certainly the cheapest means. Third, on the Black Sea coast,
White generals could stage some sort of organized evacuation.

Finland, where many rich Russians already owned summer houses,
offered another option, only a few miles away for those still living in
Petrograd. Semi-Russified yet quasi-independent, it seemed both a
good temporary refuge and a logical bridgehead to Western Europe.
In wintertime, camouflaged in white clothing, shivering against wind
chills of minus forty degrees, struggling with bundles laden with their
most precious possessions, hearts pounding with fear, Russian aristocrats fled over the snowy forested ground. But the land space separating Petrograd from the Finnish border was closely guarded. A narrow
arm of the Baltic Sea could not be as tightly watched and it provided
an alternative route. In the winter the sea froze, not with a smooth
surface but in rough ridges and hillocks of mixed ice and snow, with
treacherous gaps of half-frozen water opening here and there between
the ice masses. Yet despite the difficulties, sledges could get through
and there were always guides ready to provide this service—at a price.

Of course the traveler had to accept his guide on faith. Sometimes
luck prevailed, but sometimes not, and the guide would betray his

charges to the Red authorities. The Bolsheviks might be able to pay more than the fugitive could afford. "Any way you look at it, escape from Bolshevik Russia is about as perilous as going unarmed into a tiger's cage. Yet people dare it, and we did," writes Anna Vyrubova, former intimate friend of the Empress Alexandra and fortunate survivor.

If you were a Romanov, you could at least entertain other possibilities. A young aviation officer came to Grand Duke Paul and tried to persuade him to fly out of Russia, suggesting that he could land his aircraft on Paul's lawn at Tsarskoye Selo and that the Grand Duke, his wife, Princess Paley, and their children, with some luggage, could all be flown to Stockholm in four hours. "My machine," he insisted, "is like a regular room with arm-chairs in it." The idea was too much for the irresolute Paul; he would not hear of it.

"My dear friend, you see me touched to the bottom of my heart but what you propose is out of Jules Verne! How could we disappear without being seen, even with the fewest possible preparations? We are under watch, spied upon, kept in sight by our servants. We should be caught in the act and our fate and yours would be still harder than at present."

A Danish diplomat proposed that Paul should go to the Austrian Embassy in Petrograd, then under the protection of neutral Denmark and flying the Danish flag; he should hide there until he could leave with a convoy of Austrian prisoners being repatriated. Paul said he would rather die than put on an Austrian uniform, even for five minutes. He would live to regret his stubbornness.

Soon after the successful Bolshevik coup of November 1917, the Petrograd newspapers had published a decree summoning all the Romanovs to report to the dreaded CheKa. Those who did this had to promise not to leave the city. That was all that was required of them initially. But very soon the Romanovs who registered were summoned again, now to be sent away.

In April 1918, three grand dukes, Uncle Bimbo, his brother George Mikhailovich and their cousin Dmitri Constantinovich, were sent into exile at the town of Vologda north of Moscow by decree of Petrograd Bolshevik leaders Zinoviev and Uritsky. Bimbo proudly declared that it was the second exile in his life, but he was not complaining, quoting the words of his grandfather, Nicholas I: "Every one of us should remember that only by his own behavior can he justify his origins as a grand duke."

At Vologda the three were arrested in early July and brought back to Petrograd, "for their [own] safety," the Bolsheviks said. Joined by Paul, the four grand dukes were thrust into Shpalernaia Prison. This was a time when in the city the "want of food [was] terrible," Paul's daughter Marie wrote to the Swedish crown princess. Friends collected money and food, which they deposited at the Danish Legation, and Danish Minister Scavenius was permitted to visit the imperial prisoners three times weekly, taking food packages with him.

Bimbo, although not at all well, seemed to take the imprisonment rather lightly, joking with the guards and telling them that he was taking advantage of his enforced leisure to write a book about duck hunting. He said to Minister Scavenius that he was sure that he would be released soon, although the Dane had no idea "on what His Imperial Highness bases this conviction." Paul's wife, her own existence increasingly precarious, visited him regularly; the others could look forward only to their walks, twice daily, from ten until eleven and from two thirty until four.

George Mikhailovich was still writing to his daughter Xenia in England, now putting on the upper righthand corner of the paper, "Petrograd. Jail." In one letter he made a little sketch of his cell so that Xenia might be better able to picture his situation. Rumors ran that the prisoners might be freed; others said, no, only Paul and Dmitri would be. George wrote that his happiest hours were now those when he slept, for "while I am sleeping I am not thinking."

The celebrated writer Maxim Gorky, longtime supporter of the proletariat and backer of Lenin, now felt a sense of revulsion against the Bolshevik terror. He was able to save some of the Romanovs; he told Grand Duke Michael Alexandrovich's wife, the ailing Countess Brassova, that she would be arrested if she did not leave her hospital bed, and so when the CheKists came for her, she was gone. Princess Paley interceded with Gorky on behalf of her husband, Grand Duke Paul, although she saw the writer as an "evil genius." To her, "he was all the more dangerous by reason of his gift for describing with a certain picturesqueness the misery of the Russian people and the alleged tyranny of the autocratic regime." She swallowed her scruples to beg for her husband.

In January 1919, Gorky decided to approach Lenin on behalf of the four grand dukes imprisoned in Petrograd. Lenin, preoccupied with preserving the precarious revolution, had no wish to see him but did so reluctantly, listening to Gorky going through his plea in his heavy Volga accent, coughing with embarrassment.

For Lenin, Gorky was a difficult case. As the only widely known writer of the Russian working class, he could not be ignored. As Gorky went through the merits and human frailties of the grand dukes in question, he came to Bimbo.

"Grand Duke Nicholas Mikhailovich is a historian," he said.

"The Revolution does not need historians," Lenin barked.

Gorky was shocked but unabashed. Lenin was unpredictable. He pushed and pushed and finally Lenin yielded. He promised to instruct the CheKa to release the four grand dukes.

Gorky rushed to the Nikolaevsky Station to catch the night train to Petrograd, carrying the precious document signed by Lenin. The station had been named after Tsar Nicholas I, under whom the first Russian railroad between the two capitals had been built, designed by the engineer father of the celebrated American artist Whistler. Tolstoy chose it for one of the opening scenes of *Anna Karenina*, the place where Anna met her fateful love, Vronsky. But Gorky would have no occasion to reflect on these matters.

Hurriedly making his way down the platform to his car, Gorky suddenly spotted an evening newspaper headline: "Four Former Grand Dukes Shot in Petrograd." He nearly fainted.

On January 28, 1919, the four grand dukes had been told to go outside to the prison courtyard, where they were made to strip to the waist and then executed by a firing squad. Bimbo was holding his favorite Persian cat until the final shot. The common grave into which the four bodies were thrown already held several corpses at the bottom.

CHAPTER TEN

"Open the Gates!"

FEBRUARY 1919–FEBRUARY 1920

LENIN'S FEAR OF A ROMANOV RESTORATION explains the execution of the four grand dukes. Yet none of the four had any prospective role in the White movement. Nikolasha was a different story. At the beginning of 1919, right-wingers in the White camp had begun to view Nikolasha as potential commander-in-chief of the White armies and even as "dictator" of the liberated territories of Russia.

Several groups at different times approached the grand duke in the Crimea. The first appeal had been for him to lead the armies in Ukraine, the south of Russia, and the lower Volga region. Others believed that Nikolasha should not waste his prestige at the local level but instead wait to enter the national scene when the four major White leaders—Kolchak from Siberia, Denikin from the south, Yudenich from the Baltic and Miller from the north—might converge as they approached Moscow.

Nikolasha was reported to refuse all these suggestions, purportedly regarding them as reckless. But this judgment of his attitude belongs to General Denikin, who was his competitor at the time and therefore cannot be entirely trusted. Reliable evidence shows that at least once Nikolasha was more than ready to agree to take a command if it had been offered to him. One of the attempts to sound him out was made by a person whom Nikolasha trusted entirely, George Shavelsky, the last chaplain of the Imperial Army and Navy.

Father Shavelsky arrived at the Crimean palace of Dulber on November 6, 1918, Nikolasha's birthday, to find the grand duke finishing breakfast with his brother Peter and a group of Denikin's officers. Shavelsky found the grand duke looking remarkably energetic and dressed in uniform for the first time since he had been put under house arrest. Nikolasha embraced the priest with tears in his eyes. The faithful Peter followed suit.

The priest stayed with the grand duke for six days and had a good chance to assess his situation. At the same time, a conference of anti-Bolshevik politicians was underway in Romania at the town of Jassy. The Romanovs in Crimea optimistically believed that the conference would recommend that Nikolasha lead the army in a new crusade.

Some were already speculating about the consequences of this. Would Nikolasha become the next tsar? If so, since he was childless, next in succession would be his brother Peter, followed by the latter's son, Roman. The family discussed who should accompany Nikolasha on his campaigns, fearing that the "black plague," the two Montenegrin ladies with their immense capacity for political intrigue, would be among that number. Nikolasha was apparently hoping for an invitation from Jassy and only too ready to accept it.

No other Romanovs emerged as important figures in the White camp. The dowager would not serve even as a titular leader. She talked of her poor Nicky as if he were still alive. And in conversation she would often make unfavorable comments about her daughter-in-law Alix's obsession with "crazy, dirty, religious fanatics." These remarks could also be interpreted as an indirect reproach to Nikolasha, well known for his own intense religiosity and propensity for mystics.

Nikolasha now even had his own Rasputin, Captain A. A. Svechin, a seeker of prophecies, introduced to him by his stepson, Sergei Leuchtenberg, who may have hoped to use the man as a tool in some future power struggle. Shavelsky, a good Orthodox priest, was disgusted to learn that Svechin had recommended to Nikolasha a mystic in Yalta, Mother Evgeniya, who claimed that it was revealed to her in several visions that the grand duke would be the savior of Russia.

On that night of his birthday, Nikolasha told the disgusted Father Shavelsky that he too should submit to the will of God as manifested through Mother Evgeniya. The priest thought Nikolasha spoke as if he were in a delirium; clenching his teeth, Shavelsky nonetheless managed to interject into Nikolasha's monologue the suggestion that men should not look for miracles and prophecies. The grand duke did not like this Orthodox instruction, and the next morning Svechin reproached Shavelsky, who had spent a sleepless night thinking about the fateful attraction mysticism seemed to exercise for the Romanovs.

The Jassy Conference finally could agree on only two points: the desirability of Allied intervention in the civil war and the indivisibility of Russia. When discussing candidates for the future "dictator" of Russia, nine voted for General Denikin and only four for Nikolasha. The Romanov cause was lost once again. When General Alexander Lukomsky, a representative of Denikin, visited Dulber, Nikolasha received him warmly and with great tact, not wanting to create any problems for the Whites. But Nikolasha, like the rest of the Romanovs, was simply not wanted by a Russia convulsed with violence. The family was beginning to recognize that the Romanov name had become anathema. They could not help wondering what their fate would now be.

Meanwhile, in Persia, Dmitri found himself on the margins of the great revolution, but directly in the middle of the renewed "great game," the ancient Eurasian rivalry between Great Britain and Russia. Russian disengagement from Persia had already started by the end of 1917. A witness at Tabriz wrote, "The Russian soldiers wandered through here by the thousand, sold their rifles, ammunition, stores, horses and, in fact, anything that would fetch money." On June 10, 1918, General Baratov issued his last order to his Special Caucasian Cavalry Corps troops, comparing his farewell to "closing the eyes of a beloved deceased person." Baratov helplessly watched the disintegration and death of his army.

The British became alarmed because the collapse of the Russian Persian front meant that the way was open for Germany and her allies to march to British India through northern Persia. Furthermore the increasing importance of petroleum gave new strategic meaning to this part of the world. More than one hundred thousand German and Austrian prisoners were interned in Russian Turkestan. It was at least conceivable that these experienced soldiers could be reorganized by the Germans (or by Bolsheviks now preaching world revolution) into a formidable force that could advance to Kabul and, in the old British nightmare, southward across the Khyber Pass into India.

The British decided to support anti-Bolshevik secessionist movements in the Caucasus and Russian Central Asia, and dispatched a military mission to take Baku, the capital of Azerbaijan. By the summer of 1918, the Bolshevik regime in Baku collapsed, and the British occupied the city. Temporarily, Bolshevik power was ousted from the Caspian region, and Dmitri, opponent of the Bolsheviks, found himself the first Romanov to support the British in getting control over Central Asia. Radical newspapers even labeled him "the British candidate" for the Russian throne. Indeed in moving to Teheran in the summer of 1917, he had left the Russian zone of occupation for the British sphere.

Dmitri would remain there as a guest of the British Minister to Persia, Sir Charles Marling, for a year and a half. In his strong affection for Dmitri, Marling even tried to get the grand duke a commission in the British army, appealing directly to the king. Marling said that the young man was willing to serve in any capacity with his present Russian rank of captain. Marling remarked that Dmitri, a man of "exceptional intelligence and capacity," held decorations for distinguished war service and that he was "devoted to the Allied cause." But London brushed off the request, replying that various acts of Parliament prohibited any but British subjects from entry into commissioned ranks of the army. The alternative was an honorary commission "which would of course confer on him no powers of command, [and] would merely render him a supernumerary, a position which would be inconvenient for us and not very palatable to him."

Marling retorted that Dmitri did not expect anything but an honorary commission; "his only wish is to get to the front with our army." But the War Office was ultimately unwilling even to offer him an honorary commission. Dmitri was shocked by such coldness. He had harbored the illusion that his military career could restart in Britain. "A little humiliating," he wrote in his diary with barely concealed rage—in English. "Could it be the vengeance of Rasputin's ghost?"

When the British Foreign Office recalled Sir Charles Marling from his Persian post at the end of 1918, Dmitri left also, traveling by ship to Bombay where he contracted typhoid and nearly died. During his illness Lady Marling nursed him, he said, "as a mother would nurse her dear child or a woman in love—her lover."

For some time the British had been trying to persuade the dowager that it was time for her to leave Russia, and King George had sent a message on November 19, 1918, urging her to leave the Crimea secretly "in a very fast vessel." The king assured the dowager that a British battleship would lie across the Black Sea at Constantinople for her use as transport to England.

The king, who had been told by British military intelligence on August 31, 1918, of the fate of Nicholas, Alexandra and their children, sent his message secretly by hand via a British naval officer, Commander Turle, who was accompanied by a Russian officer who could act as interpreter if necessary. The two sailed by destroyer from Constantinople to Yalta and landed at dawn on the Crimean shore. The destroyer then withdrew from sight of shore. Minnie asked her British visitor many questions on the state of affairs and then declared that she had no intention of leaving the Crimea at present.

"Her Imperial Majesty also said that from information She had received She had reason to hope that the Emperor is still alive. It was clear that this view was not shared by the Imperial Family or the entourage," Commander Turle reported to his commander-in-chief, who so informed the king.

The king of Italy, whose queen was the sister of the two Romanov Montenegrin ladies, had also offered sanctuary and made his yacht *Trinacria* available for an imperial escape. Militsa and Stana took advantage of the British visitor to send greetings to their father, King Nicholas of Montenegro, exiled in France, as well as messages of thanks to Victor Emanuel for his offer, but said that they too planned to remain in the Crimea.

A second British naval delegation then sailed to Russia aboard HMS *Canterbury*, which docked at Sevastopol in late November 1918, and dispatched another mission to the dowager at Ai Todor, a journey by road of nearly four hours. Minnie told the British that the king of Romania said he was anxious for her safety and begged her to leave in a small yacht he had had sent over. The British warned that Romania was unsettled, the railroads disorganized and food in shortage. The dowager replied that "*nothing* would induce her to go to Romania in that little ship, but with HM The King of Italy's special offer [of any palace in Italy] and a battleship [promised by the British] the question was quite different."

The empress was agonizing. She had always encouraged all Russians to be confident and to remain in Russia. How could she now leave? She believed that the Bolsheviks were "cowards, ready to flee at the sight of an Allied flag." Her English visitor retorted that the going was now good because things were quiet and she could leave from Yalta, announcing that she was merely going to Italy for a visit. Battleships were now available but might not be later. Furthermore he argued that scarcity of food and fuel for the Romanovs was likely to recur.

"Her Majesty stated that she would never believe that the Czar was dead, and therefore did not like the idea of going away. To which I replied that if she would accept the offers made, she would only be in Italy, and should circumstances arise calling her back, a vessel could easily be placed at her disposal for this purpose." Minnie seemed to waver.

The next month Commander Turle returned. Sandro told him that the empress had recently sent a message to General Denikin to the effect that if her presence in the Crimea were an embarrassment to his cause, she would be willing to leave. Sandro, nervously trying to speed up the process, for he was far less optimistic than his mother-in-law, took the opportunity to get a message to Britain's Queen Alexandra: "Please ask Mama and family to come to England without delay." Still Minnie hesitated. Sandro, his son Andrew and Andrew's wife, meanwhile, left Sevastopol on December 26th aboard HMS *Foresight*. Sandro was heading for Paris.

An awkward situation was developing for the British. The British Foreign Office asked the Royal Navy "not to facilitate the journey of prominent Russians to England without first referring to them for instructions . . . [pointing out] that the presence of these persons is most embarrassing in the present circumstances." The Foreign Office did not want the British Government to be linked in any way to the Romanovs. This put the Navy in a dilemma because "on 18th December, Queen Alexandra sent a message through the Admiralty to the Dowager Empress of Russia, requesting her to leave Russia at once for England *and to bring everyone she wished.*" By this time the Foreign Office had refused to grant an entry visa to Sandro, who now wanted to come to London from Paris.

Minnie's younger daughter, Olga, pregnant again, apprehensive about the Bolshevik advance and exhausted by Minnie's tyranny, traveled from the Crimea to the Caucasus with her husband and baby, taking a steamer across to Novorossisk on the eastern coast of the Black Sea where General Peter Wrangel seemed to be doing well against the Reds. Perhaps the Caucasus could be held if the Crimea could not. Minnie's dislike of Olga's husband surfaced strongly in her argument with her daughter that Olga's duty was to remain with her, not to go with her husband. "It was a sad and bitter way to say goodby. I wept as I left her. She was so angry. She said she would never forgive my husband. And I, knowing what the dangers were, wondered if I would ever see her again."

The frightening news came that the Red armies in a new offensive were now approaching the narrow entrance to the Crimean peninsula and there was little to stop them. King George thereupon instructed the Admiralty that the dowager empress and her party should be taken off by warship "whatever they themselves might want." By staying in Russia Minnie was risking not only her own life but those of her family. She refused to believe that nineteen Romanovs, including both her sons and five grandchildren, had already been caught and killed by the Bolsheviks.

On April 8, 1919, Minnie embarked on the battleship *Marlborough* and the Bolsheviks crossed the gateway to the Crimea, the isthmus of Perekop. The empress had agreed to leave but only on the condition that the British take aboard their ships all the sick and wounded and all other people in Yalta wanting to get out of Russia. Minnie said that a Russian empress could not flee if so many Russians were abandoned. Before her departure, the old lady insisted on saying her prayers for the last time in a Russian church, St. Alexander Nevsky. The town magistrate announced that all churches were closed. Whereupon Minnie's loyal Cossacks declared that they would actually break down the doors with their own fists if necessary. The church was opened and the empress was able to pray as she wished.

Bending their instructions in order to meet the demands of the dowager, the British managed to gather the requisite number of ships to take aboard all in Yalta wanting to leave, and those who were to go gathered on the mole. "It was a sad sight: all those refugees, most of whom were old and sick, and all of whom were crushed by grief at leaving their homeland, sitting on bundles and rugs (trunks were forbidden) as they waited to be taken aboard the steamers." Instead of the *Marlborough* sailing first as had been the plan, the ship lifted anchor only after the last steamer had embarked its crowd of refugees. And so the dowager, "like a mother, covered the retreat of her children."

Just as the *Marlborough* was pulling away from the shore, a Russian ship passed close by, her decks lined with scores of imperial guardsmen. The tiny empress, dressed all in black, stood alone at rigid attention at the stern of the battleship as the guardsmen burst spontaneously into a thundering chorus of "God Save the Tsar." For the last time the imperial anthem was sung to a Romanov in Russia.

Nikolasha and Peter transferred to another British battleship, *Lord Nelson*, at Constantinople, and the ship took them to Italy. The others traveled to Malta, where they spent a few days of rest as guests of the royal governor. The *Lord Nelson* then came to take them on to England.

Minnie now seemed to have recovered something of her customary high spirits. To the amazement of the ship's company she was a lot of fun.

> One fine evening she sent for the Captain and demanded that there should be dancing on the quarter-deck. In vain to point out to her that wartime routine was still being observed and that all officers were already in bed or on watch; brushing aside every objection she insisted that the officers be collected and the Marine band routed out to play dance music whilst she herself supervised the festivities from a perch on the after-capstan.

When Grand Duchess Olga, the tsar's younger sister, arrived in the Caucasus in 1919, having both escaped her mother and the Bolsheviks in the Crimea, she found temporary lodging in the home village of her Cossack retainer, Timofey Yachik, who would ultimately spend his life as a Romanov servant. Olga was perhaps the only Romanov who seemed at ease with common people, to know how to talk to peasants and to gain their confidence and friendship, and these qualities made her new life easier for her than it was for others in the family.

Olga, her husband, their baby son and her maid, Mimka, traveled in the Caucasus mountains by train, cart and finally by foot. En route aboard the train, the news got out that the tsar's sister was among the passengers. "At every halt, and there were many of them, crowds of peasants would bunch together, craning their necks to stare at a tiny woman, in rough torn clothes, with a crumpled kerchief on her head, who sat by the window, a baby in her arms. They stared silently, unsmilingly."

In the village of Novo-Minskaya, Yachik knew they would be safely looked after by his family. About six weeks after they arrived, Olga, with the help only of a village woman, gave birth to her second son. Not for her the traditional Romanov names of Alexander, Nicholas, Constantine and the like: Wanting to be closer to the common people, she gave him a peasant's name, Guri.

At their rented hut, Olga and her husband planted and tended a garden, ground corn and baked bread. Kulikovsky labored at a nearby farm in order to earn some money. But in the end of 1919, the tide of the war changed and the Red armies drew near this rural haven. Four Cossacks joined Olga and her family, scooping them up: the couple, the two babies and Mimka. For weeks they were on the run, heading for the coast of the Black Sea. It was winter; traveling by foot they had to spend nights in deserted barns. Olga worried that her newborn would not survive the terrible privations of the journey.

When they arrived back in Novorossiysk, they found the city jammed with anxious, hungry and sick refugees. Its huge port, full of piers, warehouses and cranes, also now housed people, who filled the piers and the embankment. Some were living in tents; at the entrance to each tent a bunch of garlic was hanging, a traditional remedy against all sorts of epidemics. Olga did not have enough money even to buy milk for her children, but she found refuge in the Danish consulate. If her father's subjects were rejecting her, her mother's people were not.

Typhus was raging and even some at the Danish consulate were infected. "We, who were all right, gave up our beds to the sick and slept on the floor. I was terribly worried about my husband and babies. I didn't care about my own life. I had seen such horrors that something seemed dead inside me. But I had to get through somehow." The pharmacies, running out of medicines, sold Orthodox amulets, and people were instructed to tie their sleeves tightly at the wrist so as to prevent lice from creeping in. Former ladies-in-waiting were sleeping on the floor, with eleven former aristocrats sharing one room. A feeling of doom was spreading all over the city, like typhus itself. And increasingly people were desperate to get out.

The commander of the British cruiser *Cardiff*, who happened to be an old friend, got wind of Olga's presence in town and invited her to his ship. After tea on board, the grand duchess was tactfully presented with a length of navy-blue cloth, enough to make clothing for the four members of her family, and she was relieved that they could be respectable again. On a February morning she was able to arrange passage for her little group aboard a merchant ship that would take them to Turkey and safety. King Alexander of Yugoslavia invited Olga to make her new home there, but her mother, the dowager, now settled in Denmark, always possessive of her youngest child, wanted Olga to be with her.

We got [to Copenhagen] on Good Friday, 1920. I was happy to see my mother again, but we all felt sad. Deep within ourselves we knew what we never dared put into words—that the remainder of our lives would be spent in exile.

Unlike other members of the family, Olga was a realist.

Dmitri's sister, Marie, having divorced her Swedish prince and returned to Russia, had married Prince Sergei Putiatin in September 1917 at Pavlovsk Palace in the presence of her grandmother, Queen Olga of Greece, who would not leave Russia for another year. Putiatin was the son of a commandant of Tsarskoye Selo, a friend of Vladimir Paley, and a relative of Princess Olga Putiatina in whose Petrograd apartment Grand Duke Michael had abdicated the tsardom. Grand Duke Paul, Marie's father, was then under house arrest at nearby Tsarskoye Selo and not permitted to attend the ceremony. Aside from anything else marriage may have provided the young grand duchess, it enabled Marie to drop her title and the Romanov name, now considered "indecent" by the public. Putiatins were far less conspicuous than Romanovs.

Nine months after her wedding, Marie bore a son, Roman. He was baptised July 18, 1918, the day after the murder of the emperor and his family at Yekaterinburg and the very day of the violent deaths at Alapayevsk of more Romanovs. But those at the baptism knew nothing yet of those terrible events.

Marie, like so many Romanov women, seemed to be the decision-maker in her family, and she declared it was time to try to leave Russia. She believed that doing this with an infant would greatly increase the risks. Because she had initiated the divorce, Marie had been forced to leave her little Swedish prince, Lennart, with his father. Now, for the second time she abandoned a son. Little Roman stayed with his father's parents.

Marie took her husband out of Russia, choosing the southern route via Ukraine. She writes grippingly about her dangerous journey through the uprooted humanity of war and revolution, and she would retell the melodramatic story many times.

They embarked on a train that crawled, making frequent stops, aggravating the anxiety of the passengers. At almost every station, groups of armed soldiers boarded the cars, entering the compartments and checking the documents of the passengers. "We had no documents; we trembled, therefore, every time the train stopped," Marie remembered. But the conductor, as she tells it, proved to be a new friend. As soon as soldiers came aboard the train, he was always by the door, finding some reason for preventing them from coming into Marie's compartment. Sometimes the excuse was a sick woman whom no one should disturb; sometimes it was engineers going to their assignments. "My heart beating frantically, I listened to the heavy steps and the loud conversations in the corridor, expecting every time that the explanations of the conductor would be disregarded; but this did not happen." After two nights and a day of intense apprehension on the train, the most dangerous part still lay ahead.

This was Orsha, in today's Belarus, jammed with refugees, many of whom were sick, all of whom were terrified. Officials guarding the frontier between Russia and the German zone took malicious delight in harassing those wishing to pass. Since Marie and her husband were without documents and without shelter in a town completely strange to them where they knew no one, they could not stay. Nor could they return.

Marie suggested they go straight from the station to the frontier and try their luck there. They hired a carriage which took them to the frontier gates just outside the town. Marie vividly remembered the rough dusty road under a scorching sun and the endless horsedrawn carts filled with refugees, mostly peasants seeking safety.

Marie had no clear plan of action, no real idea of what they should do. "Each one of us realized that we were voluntarily walking straight into the lion's den."

Their driver, moving along awkwardly between the pedestrians and the carts, finally stopped and pointed to a fence blocking the road. This, he said, was the frontier.

Marie got out of the carriage. On her left by the side of the road she saw a low, unpainted wooden shed; in the open door, his bulk filling it entirely, stood a massive figure, well turned out in uniform and shiny new boots. He was holding a long whip, with thin leather ends "curling on the floor like live snakes." The soldier's cap was pushed back, and a lock of hair escaped from it and fell on his forehead. His round shaven face exuded smugness. Although the man contemptuously refused Marie's attempt to pass the frontier without a permit, she nonetheless determined to try. "Come what might, we had to get on the other side of the Bolshevist fence. Our whole future, our life, depended on it."

"Listen!" she said intently, taking a huge gamble. "Don't you see the *droshky* there? We have all our luggage on it and we have no money." Marie opened her shabby purse. It contained only an old cigarette case and a handkerchief.

To her amazement, the guard relented. "All right, go on."

In a trice they were on the other side of the Bolshevik fence. Ahead of them stretched a no-man's-land perhaps a quarter of a mile wide, separating Bolshevik Russia from freedom. Many people were crowded into this space, and apparently they had been there for a long time. They were holding permits to leave Russia but not to enter German-held territory. In her pocket, Marie carried a bar of soap that contained sealed within it a Swedish document identifying her as a former royal princess. Desperately she hoped that this would secure her admittance into the German zone. It was all she had.

Moving up to the fence, she saw German soldiers and officers walking about and Marie thought, "So short a while ago we fought against these men, and now I am forced to ask their protection against my own people." Dragging out from memory her German, Marie called, "Please, couldn't you come to the fence? I must speak to you."

Finally a man who appeared to be in charge, with a young and pleasant face, came over, and Marie said to him, "Owing to a stroke of luck, we have succeeded in passing the Bolshevist frontier, but we have no papers, no passport, no permit of departure, no visa. If you refuse to let us in we shall have to return to the Bolsheviks. . . . In the name of God, let us in."

"I really don't know what to do with you," the officer said irresolutely. Marie then cut open the bar of soap, took out her Swedish certificate, rolled it into a tube and pushed it through the fence. The man took and read it, scrutinizing Marie's face. Their eyes met.

"Open the gates," he ordered the guards.

The soldiers obeyed. The key clicked loudly once, twice, the bolt groaned, and both halves of the gate swung open. They all entered and "it was just as terrifying, just as simple, and just as wonderful as a miracle."

Although it was the camp of the enemy, "even the air seemed lighter," she wrote. Dinner that night was from the German officers' mess. "In my whole life I have never eaten anything better than the thin bean soup splashing at the bottom of those enamel pans. . . . Thus ended August 4th, my saint's day." Even the luggage ultimately made it. Marie possessed great powers of persuasion, at least as she tells it.

Marie's journey continued south through the German zone to Kiev, antechamber to irreversible emigration. To refugees Kiev seemed like a city reached not by train but by time machine, a step back into a past, a past now totally vanished in Russia, where officers still wore tsarist shoulder straps, where police patrolled the streets, where real food was to be had.

Novelist Michael Bulgakov wrote:

All through the summer of 1918 the cab-drivers did a roaring trade and the shop windows were crammed with flowers, great slabs of rich filleted sturgeon hung like golden planks and the two-headed eagle glowed on the labels of sealed bottles of Abrau, that delicious Russian champagne. All that summer the pressure of newcomers mounted—men with gristly-white faces and gray-ish, clipped toothbrush moustaches, operatic tenors with gleaming boots and insolent eyes, ex-members of the State Duma in pince-nez, whores with resounding names. Billiard players took girls to shops to buy them lipstick, nail-polish, and ladies panties in gauzy chiffon, cut out in the most curious places.

Marie recalled, "In the dining room of our hotel stood a table of *hors d'oeuvres*, overloaded with good things to eat. Plates piled high with white and black bread stood in front of each diner and in the steaming hot soup floated large pieces of meat. The smell alone made one's mouth water. I cannot understand how we did not die that day from over-eating."

It is difficult to express in words what we were experiencing that day! We were alive, out of danger. He who has not lived through such a moment does not know what it means actually to enjoy life. . . . Like a blind person who suddenly has seen the light, I rejoiced in everything. . . . Lord what a day that was!

Almost everyone in Kiev may have "hated the Bolsheviks, but not with the kind of aggressive hatred which spurs on the hater to fight and kill, but with a cowardly hatred which whispers round dark corners." Kiev also carried the less attractive past, that which had brought forth the deluge of revolution. A refugee from Moscow, when politely told by a waiter that he must wait a bit for his fried potatoes, exploded in a paroxysm of rage. A witness wrote, "A young busboy stood by the wall and sarcastically pursed his lips, observing the scene which was better than any new Soviet poster depicting the hydra of capitalism and counter revolution."

For Marie, real safety was not to be found in Kiev. A nervous tension, like the heavy stillness before a thunderstorm, vibrated in the air. The metallic gray Germans with their spiked helmets and furious moustaches were there in the summer of 1918 as predatory occupiers, seeking to exploit the fruits of the rich Ukrainian earth to feed the hungry population of blockaded Germany. The war was still raging in France; the future of Ukraine seemed quite uncertain.

Marie decided that having fled the Bolsheviks successfully, she and her husband should remove themselves as soon as possible from any chance of new disaster. "We should move on, farther south, nearer to the sea, to the frontier, and wait there." Marie went to the cosmopolitan seaport of Odessa, where they felt they could relax a bit and recover from the ordeals they had endured. Ships were taking refugees out across the Black Sea.

Sitting in Odessa and pondering her next move, Marie received a letter from her first cousin, Queen Marie of Romania, who used an agent to track her down. Spectacularly beautiful, flamboyant, passionate and impulsively generous, Marie of Romania now was offering her namesake a haven in that country and also the means to get there. Marie of all European sovereigns seemed to have the greatest sympathy for the plight of the Romanovs, possibly because her own life in tumultuous Romania had not always been easy. The queen's people in Odessa arranged that Marie, her husband, two officers and a recently-employed elderly maid would travel to Romania in a special railway car reserved for them. The countryside was in chaos, with bands of soldiers of highly uncertain allegiances wandering about; a private car was thus a necessity for security reasons.

Marie, half-sick with fever and shivering with cold, for winter had set in, reached the border in the evening. She then sent for the guards riding the train to ensure her protection, wanting to say goodbye and thank you. A half a dozen men entered the railway carriage and filled it with their heavy winter uniforms, their fur caps, the jingle of their rifles. They carried with them the smell of Russia in autumn, of wood smoke, of leather boots and gunpowder. In the dusky compartment, lit by a single candle, only the contours of their figures and faces could be discerned.

Marie was so agitated that she could not utter a word. These strangers, people she had never seen before, felt closer to her now than her own kin, and part of her very being. Wanting to etch their faces forever in her memory, Marie picked up the candle from the table and held it before each face in turn. The tiny yellow flame lit for a second the short haircuts, the weathered complexions and the heavy moustaches.

Marie wanted to say something meaningful, so that they too would remember her, but she could not say a word; only tears, bitter tears and comfortless, rolled down her cheeks.

Thus a grand duchess said goodbye to Russia.

Kyril had left Russia as early as the summer of 1917, but the place where he lingered, Finland, had dissolved into increasing social disorder; by winter of 1917 the Finns had their own Red Guards and White opponents. Forty thousand Russian troops remained in Finland, many of them pro-Bolshevik. Finnish Communists, assisted by Russian soldiers and sailors, staged a putsch and captured Helsinki and much of the southern part of the country. The Baltic fleet had regularly used Helsinki as a nearby port of call, and sailors now formed the drunken engine of the revolution. The Red Finns were slaughtering "counter revolutionaries" with gusto; people could be arrested simply for smiling at some oddly dressed Red Guardsman on the street. Plunder and political pogrom occurred right in the neighborhood where Kyril was staying, Haikko, but he remained untouched. Once, sailors searched Haikko, but the owners said that the grand duke and his family were not there. Kyril later gave another explanation: One of the "little brothers," as the sailors customarily addressed one another, had at one time served under Kyril on the cruiser *Oleg* and out of respect for that experience persuaded his comrades not to search thoroughly for a grand duke in a Finnish manor. That Kyril and his family, by good management or just by good luck, survived the chaos raging around them without mishap is truly extraordinary.

People outside Russia expressed concern for Kyril's well-being. On February 27, 1918, the grand duke got word from Helsinki that the French government was willing to take him and his family to safety. Several days later the Swedish King Gustav V proposed the same. Kyril refused these offers; he still hoped for an early collapse of Bolshevism and a return to glory.

Early in April 1918, over the objections of Finnish Whites who sensed that Germany was now losing its war against the Allies, German units under General Rudiger von der Goltz landed in Finland and captured Helsinki, demanding the withdrawal of the Russian Baltic Fleet to Kronstadt. By the end of April, they had successfully expelled Russian Communist troops from the country, and for several months Finland became in effect a German protectorate. The Whites, with Germans standing behind them, executed eight thousand Reds and put eighty thousand into camps, where nine thousand more died of hunger or disease.

The Germans were especially interested in any Russian royalty who might be both pro-German and harbor their own political ambitions. Certainly Kyril's strong Germanophilia, so unlike most of the rest of the family, did nothing to make things more difficult for him. The German foreign ministry had kept a detailed file on the activities of Russian royalty before and during the war. Kyril was of the greatest interest to them because he was so high in the line of imperial succession and so friendly to Germany.

In June 1918, General von der Goltz talked to noblemen and officers close to Kyril about possible military collaboration in an offensive against the Bolsheviks in Petrograd. But the German was disappointed, complaining to Ludendorf that "this part of the Russian Imperial house has forgotten nothing and learned nothing."

Ducky, as a princess of Great Britain and first cousin of King George V, tried to exploit Kyril's position in Finland in two very long letters she wrote the British monarch, although with blatant insincerity she opened by saying that "neither Kirill [sic] nor I have the slightest wish or intention of playing a political part," offering herself simply as the "mouthpiece of real Russia." Ducky was flatfooted in her approach, berating England for supposedly inviting the Bolsheviks to the Versailles peace conference, "a crime such as history has never known," and accusing

England of failing to understand the true nature of the Bolsheviks who are "nothing but the scum of the earth."

After irritating with her belligerence a king whose disposition was notoriously bad, Ducky then softened the tone, asking for British assistance in a campaign to capture Petrograd for the White cause by equipping the troops of General Yudenich. Yudenich wanted to approach the capital from the west to complement the White armies approaching from other directions. Kyril had a representative at Yudenich's headquarters.

Ducky asserted that

Russians, Finns, & Balts are ready all to march together against the enemies of humanity & civilization but without food we can do nothing. Petersburg at the present moment has reached the limit of human endurance. . . . Is England who has ever been the first to raise an indignant protest against cruelty oppression & tyranny now going to remain not only an impassive onlooker but, by her trying to recognise the Bolsheviks as a government, a partaker in the most heinous & monstrous enterprise that ever the world has known?

The king replied to the grand duchess six weeks later. His words were coldly official. He denied that England had invited the Bolsheviks to the peace conference: "We fully recognise who, and what they are. We are appalled at and outraged by their revolting crimes, and realize that they are daily becoming an international danger—a danger from which it behoves us to defend our own land."

Furthermore, the king pointed out, British food and British weapons and munitions had for some time been on their way to the Whites. He might have added that British material assistance to the White cause was greater than that of any other foreign power. The king recognized the desperate straits of the people of Petrograd and also understood, he said, "that if [the capital] were occupied, order restored and the starving population supplied with food and clothing, an important step would have been taken in the regeneration of Russia." But ships were in short supply, efforts had to be coordinated among the allies, and "I must add that the lack of any united action of the Russian people themselves adds to the complexity of a problem which seems to be almost insoluble."

Britain did not support a military expedition against Petrograd, and thus a chance to crush the Bolsheviks there was lost. Nor was the Finnish leader, General Gustav Mannerheim, willing to get involved in the Russian civil war, and he too failed to support the Whites when his intervention might have mattered. Lord Curzon, British Foreign Secretary, had made it quite clear to Mannerheim that "he could not look for British support or approval if he undertook such an operation."

The British minister in Helsinki, Lord Acton, wrote to the king at the end of 1919 to tell him about Kyril and Ducky.

> I was very much struck by the attitude towards me of the Grand Duke Cyril, who ostentatiously turned his back upon me. He is reported to be pronouncedly anti-Entente, and to resent our alleged action in fathering the first Russian Revolution of Prince Lvoff and Professor Miliukoff. In consequence of the Grand Duke's attitude, I somewhat hesitate to call on the Grand Duchess at Borga, where they are staying, as I am not sure of my welcome in so far as he is concerned.

The diplomat added that Ducky "looked aged and battered, and has lost much of her beauty, which is not astonishing considering all that she has gone through."

Three months later, Acton reported the collapse of White Russian forces in Karelia, Archangel and Murmansk and that Kyril and Ducky were, he learned, intending to try "to proceed to France through Germany, and [there to settle] down at their house in Paris. The Grand Duke constantly sends me indirect appeals for a bottle of whiskey, to which I have so far turned a deaf ear."

In 1920 Finland finally signed a treaty with Soviet Russia guaranteeing national independence, and Kyril left Finland, not for France but directly for Germany, where he had always felt so comfortable. He realized that he would not soon be receiving a summons to return to Russia and take the crown.

❧

Throughout her life, ambition had guided Kyril's mother, Miechen. This is why in 1917–19 she was disregarding reality, pursuing the ultimately hopeless goal of making her son Kyril tsar of Russia. For this she jeopardized her own life and those of her two younger sons, Boris and Andrew, who faithfully stayed with her in the turbulent Caucasus.

In August 1918, the Bolsheviks arrested Boris and Andrew one night but the two slipped away in the confusion reigning at Bolshevik headquarters. The Vladimirovichi then decided to flee Kislovodsk for the countryside in the hope of finding White forces to protect them. Their unexpected benefactor turned out to be Colonel Andrew Shkuro, leader of a band of fanatically loyal local Cossacks from the Kuban who called themselves "The Wolves." Shkuro did not pay his officers; they supported themselves by pillaging, paying particular attention to wine cellars, the Kuban being a wine-growing area. Even other White officers preferred to keep out of the way of Shkuro's people. But Shkuro sheltered the fleeing Vladimirovichi.

It was well the Romanovs left Kislovodsk when they did, only weeks before the Red Terror struck there in the fall of 1918. The Bolsheviks took one hundred and one people to the mountains, told them to dig an enormous pit, and then started shooting. The next morning a local watchman came to the site of the execution and nearly fainted at what he saw. An arm in priestly vestments was "sticking out of the ground and it moved trying to liberate the whole body." What the watchman did typified the days of Russian civil war. He trampled the arm down "as quickly as I could." Later he whined, "How could I possibly save that man with all those Reds around?"

But even Whites were seldom keen to help or even to identify themselves in any way with any of the Romanov family. Andrew had tried twice unsuccessfully to join General Denikin's White army. The little group of Vladimirovichi decided to go to Anapa in the north Caucasus, near the Kerch Straits separating the Crimea from the Caucasus, an ancient fortress town, just north of Novorossiysk, where conditions were reported to be good and the seaside location might make it easier to get out. They traveled by carriage, train and finally a small, dirty and old fishing boat named *Taifoun*. Other refugees did not know whether the grand duchess would condescend to journey in such a humble craft, but she boarded it resolutely declaring, "What a wonderfully picturesque setting!"

Sitting in a deck chair placed on the bridge, she watched the others crowd aboard. Luckily the weather was calm and the seaworthiness of the vessel was not tested. They all reached Anapa safely, despite darkened lighthouses and floating mines, but they felt as if they were moving tenuously between life and death. This was October 22, 1918.

Kshesinskaya wrote that they put up at the Metropole, the only hotel in town. The lavatories were frozen, winter had come early, but the rooms were adequately furnished and "not too dirty." The dancer was even able to find a masseuse, essential, apparently, for her well-being.

In a few months, Boris left the group and left Russia, accompanied by his mistress, Zinaida Rashevskaya. Before he left he tried to persuade his mother to come abroad with him but, much distressed at his decision, she declared that she was not yet ready to leave. She told a British officer that she thought it her duty to stay in Russia and that she would leave only if absolutely necessary. As long as the Vladimirovichi had a chance of realizing their ultimate ambition, the grand duchess wanted to be in Russia. Coordination with Kyril in Finland was difficult but not impossible. Even Dmitri in Persia at the height of the civil war in the summer of 1918 was getting letters from Kyril.

Miechen spent fourteen months in Anapa hoping for a turn of the revolutionary tide. In the meantime her health was deteriorating. When invited to take tea aboard a visiting British warship she had to decline because her legs were not up to climbing aboard. The weather grew cold and typhus continued to rage. Miechen and Andrew celebrated the new year, 1920, in a railway car parked in the station, dirty, exhausted, half sick, sitting on hard wooden seats but drinking champagne. Still the grand duchess hoped that the White forces now under General Wrangel might yet be successful in crushing the Bolsheviks. When the general himself warned her that the situation was becoming hopeless, she finally consented to leave.

By the first days of 1920, it became obvious that the Whites had lost the civil war. By March most of the Caucasus had fallen to the Bolsheviks. General Alexander Kutepov informed his commander, General Denikin, that it was no longer possible to resist the Reds. At Novorossiysk a British squadron stood by, able to board five to six thousand refugees. But there were many more Whites who knew that if they stayed ashore they faced instant death from the Red Army. The city also swarmed with desperate civilians. Many who wanted to leave could not do so. The fight for a place on a boat became a desperate struggle for survival. Everything that could float was pressed into service, all vessels packed, passengers clinging to one other. But inevitably not everyone could go. Waiting crowds remained on shore, sitting on bags or lying in exhaustion, opening cans and packages of food, cooking over little fires, crying out to the ships moored just beyond reach in the harbor. Those who could swim jumped in the water and headed for one of the ships. Others, anticipating death from the Reds, committed suicide on the pier.

But Miechen and Andrew were spared all that. They embarked exactly one month before the evacuation of Novorossiysk started. They became the last grand ducal Romanovs to leave Russia, waiting at Anapa in the north Caucasus for a ship that would take them directly to France or Italy, not wanting to land at Constantinople where they would need visas, a hotel, and would have to wait for another ship. A direct passage might also spare them the indignity of delousing in Constantinople, to which Miechen particularly objected. The Italian liner *Semeramida* brought Miechen back into the old world of grand luxury that she once had known so well and relished so greatly. As Kshesinskaya, who, with her son Vova, was still with them, wrote:

We embarked on February 13, 1920. This was the day we left Russian soil, since the ship, though anchored in a Russian port, was foreign. After so many hardships, a first-class cabin seemed a place of incredible luxury! But we really thought we were seeing a mirage at dinner: clean table-napkins, glasses, knives and forks! We uttered "ohs" and "ahs" of enchantment. We were rather embarrassed at having to sit at table in our shabby clothes; but when the impeccably dressed waiters began to serve us we felt as if we were in another world! Our state of mind can easily be imagined when it is realised that there was also the thought that we were at last safe, with nothing more to fear from the Bolsheviks!

Kshesinskaya gratefully presented the captain with a pair of Fabergé cufflinks.

When their ship arrived in Venice, Miechen left the little group and went directly to Switzerland en route to France, in an attempt to repair her shattered health. Andrew and his Mathilde celebrated the golden memory of an earlier visit to that city, nineteen years before, by going out to dinner with their son Vova.

The grand duke and his lady had little money that night in Venice and their clothes were decidedly shabby. Vova refused to take off his overcoat because his suit was in such a sorry state. Only by choosing very carefully from the menu would their cash be sufficient for the meal. But Andrew, as a way of raising their confidence, as well as conveying a message to the waiter, carefully placed in conspicuous view on the top of the table a heavy gold cigarette case. The event would symbolize the life that lay ahead for all Romanovs: a vestige of wealth, an urge to spend, an air of bravado.

PART THREE

Abyss

Anguish is my companion.
> —Princess Natalia Iskander
> Moscow, 1997

CHAPTER ELEVEN

⁓

Stateless

R AGE AND FEAR, GRIEF AND APPREHENSION crowded the minds of the Romanovs and thousands of other Russian refugees as they slipped away from home and fitted as best they could into new lives abroad. Defeat in the civil war had left a simple but bleak choice for all who survived in Russia on the White side: death or exile.

As we have seen, few refugees carried any resources except what they had within their minds and could conceal on their persons. Among them Romanovs were singularly ill prepared for living in the practical world. Grand dukes and grand duchesses had never had to take care of themselves, let alone earn a living or even handle money. They scarcely knew a ruble from a kopek. Romanovs had never been trained for anything except for leading the lives of royal persons, and the men for exercising at least nominal military command. But who in the European world would now need the dubious skills of these four generals, two admirals and one captain?

On the other hand, at least the Romanovs were familiar with a world beyond Russia and knew other languages. They would not be sealed into the enclosed linguistic envelope that many of their less cosmopolitan fellow refugees were forced to endure.

People from all walks of life now fled Russia. The major centers of Russian emigration were understandably those old favorite haunts, Paris and Berlin. But Prague and Belgrade, Sofia and Riga also lured refugees. Some places treated Russians better than others did. Russians found England the worst place to go to, despite the British tradition of hospitality to political refugees. The British were still reluctant to grant visas, especially to Romanovs, and Russians in London were always the last, it seemed, to get jobs. The British were also unwilling to let Russians freely move to the Dominions, Australia or Canada, for instance, delaying or not issuing visas, sometimes accusing applicants of communist sympathies.

As for France and Germany, most Romanovs, despite their German descent, felt culturally much more at home in the former than in the latter. They tended to move on to Paris. Russian refugees had always perceived Paris as a political haven. Lenin himself had spent three and a half happy years there. At times Paris had been home to as many as twenty-five thousand Russian Bolsheviks, Mensheviks, Socialist Revolutionaries and Anarchists. Artistic refugees as well found a home in this splendid city. American artists, writers and musicians, for example, bored back home, came looking for excitement and creativity in a cheap and bohemian life. In the 1910s, Grand Dukes Andrew and Boris had walked along the same streets as Lenin; now they could run into Hemingway, Picasso or Gertrude Stein. Russians formed only one strand in a gaudy cosmopolitan Parisian life.

By the early 1920s, a Soviet observer of the Russian presence in Paris described the city as having become "an archaeological museum of Russian reaction." The novelist Vladimir Nabokov speaks of a dead civilization, "almost Sumerian" in its remoteness from the Russia that evolved after 1917. The Frenchmen among whom these Russians were living were for the latter mere illusions, as Nabokov says, "as flat and transparent as figures cut out of cellophane, and although we used their gadgets, applauded their clowns, picked their roadside plums and apples, no real communication, of the rich human sort so widespread in our own midst, existed between us and them." Europeans on their part were quick to stereotype and to belittle the Russian arrivals: "nostalgia, fatalism, balalaikas, lugubrious songs of the Volga, a crimson shirt, a frenzied dance—such is the Russian emigration." Yet the emigré Russians brought with them the higher culture of the Russian nation, a culture that had been in full bloom at the time of the assault. 1917, and the unusually cruel and bloody civil war it unleashed, had set loose a tide of people flowing across Russia, leaving a nation they were convinced now lay in the hands of a small group of evil, even maniacal, persons, dedicated not simply to destroying a political and social order but to razing an entire civilization.

Few major intellectuals chose to remain in the Communist world. The Russian creative force, embodied in painters, poets, philosophers and historians, had fled the land of Lenin, transferring itself to the banks of the Seine. Paris may have remained for them a space detached from the roots that had sprouted the culture they were now trying to express, but the new environment did offer complete mental freedom.

At first, members of the imperial clan sought merely to exist; trauma kept them mute in their struggle to build new lives. Grand Duchess Marie likened it to sleepwalking for several years; "we lived side by side with life but were afraid of meeting it." Many other Russian refugee aristocrats, particularly the men, never recovered from the shock of being plucked out of their home environment. The real strength of refugee families seems to have emerged from the women who, in some cases, experienced an odd sense of liberation. Women who had never before cooked took it up with enthusiasm, consulting books they had used previously only to instruct servants. They began to use the skill of their hands, trained for embroidery, for more practical work. They went out of the house to find jobs. Men, usually untrained for any career other than the military, emasculated by the loss of power as well as the loss of wealth, were more reluctant to accept the fact that the golden years they had known were gone forever. The Romanovs themselves reflected this widespread pattern among emigrés: strong women taking charge in an often desperate situation.

No one knows how many Russians in all fled the homeland. Perhaps one million, perhaps many more. We are interested here in seventeen, the senior Romanovs, the grand dukes and grand duchesses who escaped the revolution.

These seventeen included Minnie, the dowager, and her two daughters, Xenia and Olga, plus Xenia's husband Sandro. The latter three were Romanovs by birth, and they can be classified as Alexandrovichi, descendants (by marriage in Sandro's case) of Emperor Alexander III. Then came Miechen (Maria Pavlovna the elder), the Grand Duchess Vladimir. Miechen and her three sons, Kyril, Boris and Andrew, were the Vladimirovichi, descendants of Alexander III's next younger brother; Kyril married to Ducky was the only one of the three to be wed at the time of escape.

Next in closeness to the imperial line came the two Pavlovichi, the children of the murdered Grand Duke Paul, Marie and Dmitri. Following them in seniority came the Nikolaevichi, cousins of Nicholas II: Nikolasha and his wife Stana, the Montenegrin, and Peter, his brother, married to the second Montenegrin, Stana's sister, Militsa. Finally, on the far fringes of the imperial relationship came Olga of Greece, a Romanov grand duchess by birth, and Mavra (Elizabeth Mavrikievna), widow of the Grand Duke Constantine, K.R., and a Romanov only by marriage.

Of our seventeen, eleven had passed through Constantinople, swiftly fleeing from the Black Sea area to move on to Western Europe. That great city now became the main checkpoint to the West. Those Russians in Constantinople did not much enjoy it, finding it backward and crowded with narrow, congested and dirty streets, but the city soon took on a Russian accent, so numerous did the Russian diaspora there become. After the final exodus from the Crimea, on November 19, 1920, one hundred twenty-seven ships of all kinds were anchored in the Bosporus, with White soldiers and civilian refugees aboard. All were overladen, some dangerously so. One steamer carried eleven hundred passengers instead of its normal number of two hundred. One hundred fifty thousand troops alone had been evacuated in the final flight. Fortunately no storms arose and the Black Sea, sometimes dangerously rough, remained smooth during the epic crossing. God smiled; no ships foundered.

Now Russian flags waved everywhere above the ships crowding the strait. The evening prayer, sung by thousands of sailors and soldiers, broke the stillness of the Bosporus every night, the watery expanse magnifying the sound to glorious proportions. The Turks, themselves defeated in the Great War, treated the Russians surprisingly well and smiled acceptingly when their uninvited guests would rest on the stairs of mosques. They would even allow the Russians to enter Hagia Sophia, which before the Ottoman conquest of 1453 had been the major cathedral of Eastern Christianity. Greeks and Armenians, old foes of the Turks, were still banned from this enormous mosque.

But despite the Turks' friendliness, most of the exiles soon left Istanbul. No opportunities existed there for them, and Turkey seemed an alien land. Private individuals proceeded to western Europe, French visas being most sought after. Russians still regarded Paris as the center of civilization, especially in contrast to the ferocious Stone Age into which Russia had fallen, or to the sleepy lands of the former Ottoman Empire.

Two royal sisters, Alexandra, queen of England, and Minnie, empress of Russia, bought a house together, "Hvidore," in their home country, Denmark. Here they are enjoying a game of billiards.
[Royal Danish Library]

The exiled empress dowager in old age at Hvidore, c. 1925.
[Royal Danish Library]

Minnie being helped from her car by one of her faithful cossacks.
[Royal Danish Library]

Grand Duchess Maria Pavlovna Jr., later called Marie, here dressed for her marriage to Prince William of Sweden, 1907. [Royal Danish Library]

Marie at the opera, c. 1935. Somehow she managed to make ends meet; the king of Sweden certainly helped. [Royal Danish Library]

Grand Duke Dmitri Pavlovich at the Stockholm Olympics, 1912. He had the reputation of being the best horseman in the Imperial Guards, yet in Stockholm he came in only seventh. [Royal Danish Library]

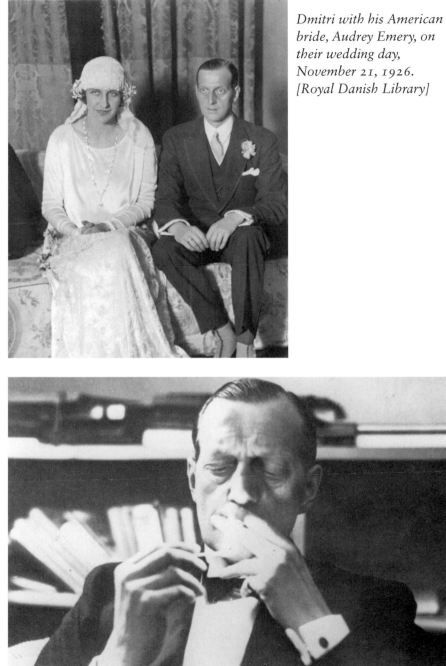

Dmitri with his American bride, Audrey Emery, on their wedding day, November 21, 1926. [Royal Danish Library]

Dmitri near the end of his short life, c. 1940. [Royal Danish Library]

*Grand Duke Michael Alexandrovich and Grand Duchess
Olga Alexandrovna, younger siblings of the future Emperor
Nicholas II, in high spirits. [Krasnogorsk]*

Olga Alexandrovna in her wartime nurse's uniform. [Krasnogorsk]

Grand Duchess Olga planting tomatoes on her Canadian farm; her older son is helping. [Hoover Library]

One of the last photographs of the last grand duchess, Olga, c. 1959. [Royal Danish Library]

The bogatyr Grand Duke, Nicholas Nikolaevich (Nikolasha), c. 1910.
[Krasnogorsk]

Grand Duke Kyril Vladimirovich, would-be emperor, in his lonely exile,
c. 1935. [Royal Danish Library]

The Grand Duchess Victoria (Ducky).
[Grand Duchess Leonida Georgievna]

Vladimir Kyrillovich at the age
of 21, in Paris, 1938. [Grand
Duchess Leonida Georgievna]

Three generations of Vladimirovichi: George; his mother, Maria
Vladimirovna; and his grandmother Leonida, widow of Vladimir
Kyrillovich, at the Donskoi Monastery, Moscow, June 1, 1992.
[Alexander Zakatov]

The Vladimirovichi with the Patriarch of the Russian Orthodox Church, Alexis II.
[Alexander Zakatov]

Natalia Androsova, the Princess Iskander, 1947.
[Princess Iskander]

Natalia Androsova, Moscow, 1997
[Pleshakov]

Of all the eleven Romanovs who had traveled via Constantinople in 1919–20, one had a particularly tough experience: Grand Duchess Olga, Nicky's younger sister, a Romanov pariah since her love match with the commoner Colonel Kulikovsky. Having fled Novorossisk on board a merchant vessel, she and her family had reached Constantinople after a two-day journey. The ship's passengers, not allowed within the city, were taken together with thousands of other refugees to the nearby Prinkipo islands in the Sea of Marmora. There the first order of the French authorities was to fumigate the refugees' clothing. This was scarcely unreasonable. War-torn Russia was now a potential source of every possible epidemic. But the refugees worried that their tattered clothing would not survive the rigors of fumigation.

Olga did not try to use her title to gain any special treatment. As a result, the new outfits she had sewn out of the cloth given her by the officers of HMS *Cardiff* shrank abominably from undergoing delousing. And this was but one difficulty. Life at Prinkipo was hard; the islands may have been a place of real natural beauty, but they were isolated, with inadequate food, inadequate water and horrifying sanitation for their many temporary residents.

Eventually Olga was able to reach Copenhagen, but the way to freedom was not easy for anyone. With few exceptions, Russian refugees found themselves pretty much on their own, as refugees so often are. The British and American governments disengaged themselves quickly from the problem. France did remain actively concerned, along with the newly born League of Nations. The League appointed the famous Norwegian Arctic explorer Fridjof Nansen to be High Commissioner for Refugee Affairs, and the refugee passport, the essential document for stateless people, came to be known as the Nansen passport. It was, wrote novelist Vladimir Nabokov, "a very inferior document of a sickly green hue, its holder little better than a criminal on parole who had to go through the most hideous ordeals every time he wished to travel from one country to another, and the smaller the countries the worse the fuss they made." Even Romanovs had to carry these wretched Nansen passports, their passes to security in glamorous European capitals.

The Romanov in exile with the highest position and prestige was Minnie, the empress dowager. She had accepted help from her foreign royal relatives, but this dependence almost immediately caused problems. Her nephew King George V was determined to keep Minnie's arrival in England in 1919 as low-key as possible. The Queen Mother Alexandra went to the wharf at Portsmouth to greet her sister but no press were allowed. And the king ordered that "no one should be at the Railway Station [in London] on Empress Marie's arrival except the Members of the Royal Family."

Grand Duchess Marie, Minnie's niece, who did go to the station, although she received no invitation to do so, remarked that all "the brilliance and bustle were gone, and the feeling of welcome, even if only official, was somewhat lacking." The station was virtually empty. The empress seemed unchanged, dressed as always "in her little black tailor-made suit with a small hat trimmed in sequins. Around her neck she wore a short feather boa pinned together at the throat." Marie carried away a sense that the empress was received by her British kin with mixed feelings: "The impressions we brought away were painful."

Minnie settled into royal comfort with her sister Alexandra at Marlborough House, but it seems that the old intimacy between them began to fray under the burdens of age and the strains of the new relationship. Alexandra was seventy-four, Minnie already seventy-three. Minnie was no longer an empress, Alexandra was still a queen and the mother of a reigning monarch. Alexandra was invited to lavish dinner parties and other glamorous events; Minnie languished at home. Minnie was not accustomed to being either a permanent guest or a poor relation. Now she was both.

For fifty years the two sisters had cultivated their deep friendship intensely but at a comfortable psychological, and usually geographical, distance. Until the war ended the opportunity for corresponding, the two wrote or telegraphed virtually every day. They met each other yearly at least, but usually in Denmark, their childhood home, in a house that Minnie and Alexandra had bought together as a summer retreat, not thinking that for one of them it would become a place of permanent exile. The two sisters had acquired the house in 1907, just after the death of their father, King Christian IX, because they would otherwise have no home in Denmark for their yearly reunions.

As she grew old, Alexandra's vagueness and increasingly severe deafness made it difficult for anyone to communicate with her easily, and this tended to make even Minnie impatient with her. Minnie clung to the illusion that her old world still existed; she spoke of Nicholas II and his family, and of Michael, as if they were all still alive. So confident were her words that people sometimes believed her, thinking that she had private information to back her assertion. Discreetly each sister complained that the other had changed, and sadly neither understood why their relationship was not what it used to be.

The British royal family encouraged Minnie to return to Denmark; her constant presence was a political embarrassment, a reminder of a relationship some Romanovs believed the House of Windsor would prefer not to have. Minnie recognized this and wrote graciously to Queen Mary, "I am more than sorry that I might have caused involuntary trouble to you, but I hope & trust that my absence will help to calm everyone. Everyone has only been kind to me & I have never even heard an unkind insinuation of any kind. With God's help things will blow over and I will return. I promise faithfully not to go near Buckingham Palace as long as my presence there might be misconstrued."

She returned to Denmark, at first to live with her nephew King Christian X. That relationship rapidly became strained. Christian was responsible for his aunt's bills. Minnie was impulsively generous and could not be trusted with a checkbook; Christian was intensely frugal. She would give money to virtually anyone who asked and then find herself penniless. In 1923, King George V set up an annuity for Minnie, which he supplemented after his mother's death two years later. The annuity yielded ten thousand pounds yearly which, if not lavish by royal standards, helped substantially to maintain Minnie's Danish exile in some comfort.

Minnie had found after a year that she could not live in a wing of the Amalienborg Castle, home of her nephew, the King of Denmark, because he complained about the size of her electricity bill. So in 1920, she settled in the house she and Alexandra owned at Hvidore, on the northern outskirts of Copenhagen.

Hvidore, which means "white gravel beach," refers to a sandy spit of land at the foot of a low rise where the house stands. Minnie and her sister could walk to the beach through a small tunnel under a road running parallel to the shoreline. They enjoyed strolling along the shore, picking up shells and bits of amber. Thirty servants, indoors and out, kept it running smoothly, and the establishment allowed Minnie to live with great dignity. Built around a large marble-floored, domed, two-story center hall, almost every room of the house provided a view of the sea. To the south one could see the spires of Copenhagen's churches. Directly across the water, at night, sparkled the lights of Sweden. To the north lay Elsinore. Light flowed throughout the house from its great windows, even on the gloomiest days of winter. And from a glassed tower on the roof, sheltered from wind and rain, the two ladies could sit, watch the sea and survey miles of wooded coast. The view was what had originally persuaded them to buy the Hvidore house.

They had spared no cost on the furnishings and appointments, primarily supplied and arranged by Queen Alexandra, who had a greater interest in such matters than did her younger sister. Plush carpets, carved Brazilian rosewood furniture, lace curtains and silken draperies, supplemented by a lavish array of bibelots, statues, silver-framed photographs, paintings and plants, filled the house in a quintessential expression of overstuffed late Victorian taste. Alexandra had an English-style billiard room designed for her husband, King Edward VII. The king visited Hvidore only once, but the two sisters themselves enjoyed many games of billiards there. Above a fireplace they had a Danish motto inscribed in the stone, "East or West, Home is Best." Before the war, it had become the custom of the two sisters, both widows, to spend a couple of months in the early autumn there.

Hvidore was far smaller than what either of the sisters was accustomed to elsewhere, but Minnie long before said, "Hvidore is quite perfect as it is. Here we have everything we need. At Gatchina I have 400 [actually 700!] rooms, but I never use more than two of them and only occasionally enter a few of the others."

Still, Hvidore was built as a warm weather residence; it had no fireplaces or stoves. At best one could "warm one's hands on the columns in the central hall, because the chimneys and ventilation ducts from the kitchen went up through four of the columns." The sisters had installed electric fireplaces, but they were not adequate for the rigors of the Danish winter, with a frigid wind whistling off the water. Minnie's daughter Olga complained that during the winter of 1927–28 even the kerosene heaters they had brought in could not keep the house warm. But Minnie would rather be cold at Hvidore than return to Amalienborg Palace and her frugal nephew Christian.

After some consultations with the Danish royal family, Sir Frederick Ponsonby, a confidential secretary to King George V (as well as to his father, Edward VII, and his grandmother, Queen Victoria), arranged that a Danish naval officer, Captain Andrup, be appointed to manage Minnie's finances and to make sure that her annuity income was handled prudently. Andrup allowed the empress to spend only the amount remaining every month after paying the salaries of her retinue and the expenses of her household.

Through the years the empress had managed to hold on to the jewels she had brought from Russia. In exile they formed the only tangible reminder of the great wealth she had enjoyed in the past and she seemed quite resolved to keep them. Jewels became important to sustaining Minnie's ability to create her own world regardless of harsh realities. Just as she did not want to accept that her two sons and five grandchildren had been killed by the Bolsheviks, she did not want to recognize that she was no longer incredibly rich.

Reason would have declared: sell the jewels and invest the capital for income. But Minnie displayed the bravado typical of Romanovs in exile: She held on to her fabulous treasure and kept it securely in a large box underneath her bed. The existence of the jewels was well known to the Danish king, who openly expressed his covetous interest, and to the House of Windsor also, whose power over Minnie had become substantial. Queen Mary—"May" as the family called her—was well known for her fondness for jewels and well known also for her avidity as a collector.

Unlike Queen Mary, Minnie had little use now for jewels. She had no official functions to attend; she did not even go to parties. Throughout the 1920s, most of the news the dowager got was sad: Kyril telling her that her sons were dead and claiming the crown for himself; a fake "Anastasia," a Polish adventuress claiming to be Nicky's youngest daughter who had miraculously survived Yekaterinburg, reminding Minnie of her five missing grandchildren. Only the death of her mother-in-law might have provided some grim satisfaction. For the family, Princess Ekaterina Yurievskaya's death put an end to an embarrassment. Yurievskaya died on February 15, 1922, on the Riviera, forty-one years after her husband's brutal murder in the snows of St. Petersburg, just as, according to gossip, she was spending down the last of her fortune.

Whereas the death of Yurievskaya brought Minnie no sadness, the death of Queen Alexandra in November 1925 brought profound sorrow. Despite the clashes of their later years, the two had remained extraordinarily close emotionally, and shared personal grief had further bound them together. Even before the revolution, both had lost adult children. Minnie's third son, George, died of tuberculosis. Alexandra's oldest son, the vapid Prince Eddy, Duke of Clarence, Heir Presumptive to the throne of Great Britain, died young, perhaps of syphillis. Both Alexandra and Minnie also lost infant sons, each named Alexander. Both had to endure widowhood.

Olga and her family moved in with Minnie when she returned to Hvidore. The dowager who had so disliked Kulikovsky did not much like her grandchildren, Tikhon and Guri, either. Always quick to explode in anger as well as laughter, in old age Minnie became despotic. "Can't you keep those boys under control?" she would ask Olga sharply when the children were playing noisily. If Olga had permitted her to do so, Minnie would have treated her as badly as Queen Alexandra treated her daughter, Princess Victoria. Victoria remained a body servant and companion to her mother as long as the old lady lived and as a result became an embittered spinster. Olga was too tough to allow that to happen to her. She enjoyed her husband and children, and she found great satisfaction working with her hands. She relaxed by painting, mostly flowers, but also local Danish scenes and nostalgic Russian landscapes with monasteries and religious pilgrims.

Xenia had always been Minnie's favorite daughter. She had accompanied her mother out of Russia to England, taking with her her younger boys and a large number of servants. Because she was a royal relative, King George V provided her a rent-free "grace and favor" house owned by the crown, Frogmore Cottage, on the grounds of Windsor Castle. By this time Xenia's marriage, to all effects and purposes, was over. She traveled on the continent to visit her many children and of course included visits to Denmark to see her mother. She spent no time with Sandro.

Minnie kept to her quiet routine as her health began to fail in the mid-1920s, not long after Alexandra's death. Remembered fondly by older Danes as their Princess Dagmar, Minnie sometimes moved through the streets of Copenhagen, invariably escorted and supported by a towering bearded Cossack. She attended the Russian Church in Copenhagen. Speaking Danish and English but Russian less and less, she still insisted that "in a Russian church I will talk only Russian." People besieged her at church with requests for money, and she never refused anyone. When the Soviets claimed the church as their property and attempted to turn it into an annex to their diplomatic mission, Minnie engaged one of the best Danish lawyers and won a case in court for the church. Despite attacks of lumbago and increasing arthritis, she proudly attended the first service after its reopening.

Olga was terrified by her mother's firm and outspoken anti-Bolshevism and worried constantly that the Soviets would try to kidnap her. When the Soviet government officially requested on November 7, 1924, that the empress be expelled from Denmark, the Danish premier proudly told the Soviet envoy that the whole Danish nation would rise up to resist any such action.

Minnie's royal relatives were often insensitive to her feelings: She had been a fabulously rich reigning empress and was now an exile, living under relatively modest circumstances. She clashed with her Danish royal nephew over politics as well as money. When Christian invited the king and queen of Italy to pay a state visit to Denmark in the early 1920s, the dowager was furious because Italy had given diplomatic recognition to the Soviet government. Well aware of her attitude, the Danish king did not invite his aunt to the gala banquet honoring the visitors. Instead he sent her a telephone message saying that he and his guests would call on her at Hvidore in the afternoon. His anger knew no limits when the royal party was greeted at the door by the dowager's footman saying, "Her Imperial Majesty deeply regrets that, being indisposed, she does not receive today."

After the bitter winds of the winter of 1927–28, and the renewed aches and pains of old age, Minnie took to her bed in what became her last illness. Two weeks before her death, she could not sleep and lost her appetite. The doctors had to give her sleeping pills. She died on October 13, 1928, the same month thirty-four years after her Sasha. She was eighty-one years old.

Suddenly the Russian exiles realized how important and admirable this tiny lady had been. Never involved in politics, except for her firm stand against the Soviets, she preserved the dignity of the throne and upheld the imperial tradition. Now she was no more, the last woman of her generation in the family, leaving both the Romanovs and Russia abroad bereft.

Russians from all over Europe now came to Denmark to pay their last respects. The brilliant imperial elite regiment, the Horse Guards, whose honorary chief Minnie had been, could send only one representative; they were poor and could not afford the travel costs for others. Copenhagen lowered its flags for its Princess Dagmar. Pictures of the empress, shrouded in black, stood in store windows. The flower shops were booming, selling wreaths. Red and white, the colors of Denmark, prevailed.

Minnie's body was left on view at Hvidore for several days after her death. Olga and Xenia, and the prodigal son-in-law, Sandro, with their son Nikita, stayed at Hvidore. Kyril, Dmitri and Marie, joined by junior members of the family, would come later, to the church.

After six days, the body of the empress was taken from Hvidore to the Russian church in Copenhagen where she had often prayed. The church was so filled with flowers that it looked as if it had been decorated for a wedding instead of a funeral. The tiny coffin, almost child size, was draped with the flag of St. Andrew. The guards were Russian. Before the coffin was taken away, members of the guard put flowers on it with a ribbon saying, "From the soldiers of the last guard."

On October 19th, at ten o'clock, the funeral mass started and lasted for two and a half hours. Access to the church was limited, by invitation card only. Kyril assumed the role of head of the family and greeted all the guests at the church entrance. Nikolasha did not attend, perhaps because of his own poor health, perhaps because he anticipated the prominent role Kyril would play there.

Among the royalty who came to the funeral were the King of Norway, the Crown Prince of Sweden, the Duke of York (future King George VI of Great Britain), and the entire Danish royal family. Kaiser Wilhelm's only daughter, Viktoria Luise, was there. All were of course related to Minnie by marriage or by blood. But they had come not simply from a sense of family duty. With Minnie, the whole spectacular second half of the nineteenth century was going—she had been a living link to Queen Victoria, Alexander II, Alexander III, Bismarck, Napoleon III. No queen would ever be trusted with such sacral authority as Minnie had been; no royal would ever live in more luxury than Minnie. Very few would retain so much dignity when deprived of both.

The whole congregation, according to the Russian custom, held lighted tapers while the priest prayed that "the Little Mother of Russia would in heaven some day see the victory of truth and justice." After the service, the coffin was carried in the royal hearse to the railroad station, followed by the kings and princes on foot while the ladies drove, escorted by royal guards and hussars.

The destination was Roskilde, a small town in the western suburbs of Copenhagen, whose only distinction is the cathedral there that holds the tombs of Danish royalties. The Romanov family rode in the first two cars of the funeral train. The body lay in the third car, and other Russians had the last two cars at their disposal.

At Roskilde, soldiers lined the flag-bedecked streets, while fir twigs on the pavements muffled the sounds of the great procession. The coffin of the empress, banked by wreaths, was placed near the tombs of her father and mother. While the organ played, the coffin, draped with Danish and Imperial Russian flags, was carried in by Guards officers, preceded by a procession of Russian priests holding icons and followed by Minnie's two faithful giant Cossacks, who had all morning mounted guard over the coffin in the Russian church.

Maria Fedorovna wanted to be buried at Roskilde beside her father, King Christian IX, but only temporarily. The last imperial Romanov woman firmly made it known that, "when things settled down," she should lie at Sts. Peter and Paul Fortress beside her Sasha.

After her mother's death, Olga wrote from Hvidore on October 26th that "my soul feels so peaceful—for everything was exactly *peaceful* and in the way she would have wanted it herself. The Danes reacted in a very moving manner—a lot of sympathy and kindness was demonstrated. We have so many letters that we could not answer them all, so we had to express our gratitude through the newspapers."

Xenia wrote to Queen Mary, "You know how much we loved our mother & how we clung to her always & how in these cruel years of exile more than ever. She was *all* that was left to us—everything was centred in her—our home, our country, all the dear past. . . . The light of our life is gone. . . . And now we are going through another ordeal—looking through all her letters, papers & belongings, dividing these between us & picking to pieces with our own hands our last "home" & then in a month Olga and I will have to part." *Belongings* carried a special meaning to the royal addressee, for it meant Minnie's fabulous jewels.

The dowager's younger daughter Olga often had seen her mother anxiously looking at her jewel box containing those favorite pieces that Minnie had been able to take out of Russia when she left. When the dowager was still alive, several of her relatives did not conceal their interest in the collection. The old lady might have foreseen trouble in the future.

Her nephew, Danish King Christian X, had started hinting that Minnie should sell the treasures and give him a fair portion as a payment for his grudging hospitality. Minnie's expansive son-in-law, Sandro, ever the imaginative entrepreneur, wrote to her suggesting that the sale of some of the jewels would enable the Romanovs to open a paper factory and thus recoup their fortunes. King George V wrote to his aunt suggesting that she deposit the jewels for safekeeping in a London bank vault prior to selling them. Queen Mary was undoubtedly eager to add Minnie's treasures to her already formidable collection. Perhaps she was also annoyed by the fact that the box now contained some beautiful pieces bequeathed to the dowager by her own mother-in-law Queen Alexandra.

Queen Mary well understood that jewelry has always been an important prop in the drama that is royalty, of the pageantry that gives life to the institution, substance to the abstract. Her photographs, circulated all over the world, illustrated her immense and imposing jewel collection, including some of the largest stones in the world, diamonds like the Koh-i-noor and the Star of Africa. For state occasions or official portraits May would wear a diamond tiara, a collar of rows of diamonds, below that another necklace, opera length, of pearls. She would also wear a diamond stomacher and various jeweled orders including the Garter sash. She saw this stunning array as part of her proper role as royal consort. Jewels transcend the person of the monarch as symbols of the splendor of what the monarch represents and as statements of the wealth, hence the power, of the royal person.

Today Queen Elizabeth II has probably the world's largest single collection of jewelry, in part because of her grandmother's interest. Elizabeth is documented as having worn at various times "fourteen tiaras, thirty-seven pairs of earrings, one hundred and five brooches, fifty-eight necklaces, thirty-seven bracelets, six pendants, fourteen watches and fifteen rings." Other jewels, not necessarily to her taste and therefore unworn by her, supplement the collection. Crown regalia of course belong to the nation, but the rest is personally owned by the monarch; some of these gems are designated to be worn only by a queen. A number of the finer pieces in this magnificent collection were owned earlier by Romanovs.

At the time of the revolution of 1917, the Romanov jewels probably had constituted the single finest collection in all Europe, even better than that of the British royal house. Queen Victoria had not concealed her envy of the jewels her Romanov daughter-in-law Marie of Coburg brought to England. Marie may have been Alexander II's only daughter but she was a mere grand duchess; Minnie had been a reigning empress, and what she had been able to take with her from Russia to Denmark represented her favorites.

Minnie would not sell. On this she was adamant. Her large jewel box remained in her bedroom until the day of her death. Neither the petty and quarrelsome King Christian X nor the enterprising Sandro had ever even seen its contents. Neither had any of the Windsors, except possibly Minnie's sister Alexandra.

When Minnie died, the fate of the box was sealed. Xenia, a hostage of the Windsors, upon whom she depended entirely for support, arrived at Hvidore during her mother's last illness and kept a close eye on the box. Olga did not care; she was losing a mother and the idea of checking the box, she said, did not occur to her. Xenia allowed a British agent to take it away secretly. When, two or three days after Minnie's death, King Christian arrived at Hvidore to claim the treasures, to his rage he learned that he was too late. The box was already on its way to England.

Sir Frederick Ponsonby, private secretary to King George, had arranged that Sir Peter Bark, a former Russian finance minister and now a governor of the Bank of England, should go to Denmark, ostensibly to attend the funeral of the empress but actually as Ponsonby's private emissary acting on behalf of the British king. His mission was to get the jewels. And, since Bark was himself a Russian and an expert in financial matters, presumably his words would be more persuasive than those of someone else.

Bark reached Hvidore even before the funeral and was able to persuade Xenia that it would be safest if the jewels were sent directly to the British monarch, who would keep them and perhaps even arrange for their sale on behalf of Xenia and Olga, Minnie's two heirs. Without even consulting Olga, Xenia yielded to Bark. Bark then went off to attend the funeral ceremonies while a messenger secretly left for London carrying the sealed jewel box with him. Ponsonby was in London to receive the box and to place it, still under seal, in the safe at Buckingham Palace.

No one made an inventory of Minnie's jewels until the box was later opened at Buckingham Palace. Among them was a brooch set with diamonds, a small V-shaped tiara with a large center sapphire, a cabochon sapphire brooch surrounded by two rows of diamonds with a pearl drop hanging from a diamond, and Minnie's favorite pearls, a four row choker of one hundred sixty-four pearls interspersed by twenty diamond-studded vertical bars between every two pearls at the front, and between every three pearls at the back. The largest of these pearls were the size of big cherries. The octagonal clasp was formed by a large sapphire surrounded by two rows of diamonds. All told the box contained some seventy-six pieces, some of which were virtually priceless.

King George fell ill for some months and the whole matter of how to dispose of the jewels had to be postponed. Ponsonby wrote that Queen Mary, recognizing the financial anxieties of her Romanov cousins, agreed to give an allowance to Xenia and Olga to tide them over until the jewels could be sold.

Ponsonby erred. Olga never received a penny. Because of her marriage to a commoner whom her royal relatives had disliked and would never accept, Olga had often been treated poorly by her mother. Her older sister also was in the habit of acting on Olga's behalf, or in her name, without even informing her.

British historian William Clarke reports that London experts appraised Minnie's collection at one hundred fifty-nine thousand pounds. Sales proved to be slow; the great depression may have sapped the strength of the market. The total yield by the end of 1934 was reportedly one hundred thirty-six thousand pounds, not far off Clarke's report of the jewels' value. But this estimate may not have been correct. One can certainly question whether the jewels were sold under the best conditions for the seller. Members of the Romanov family believe that Buckingham Palace commissioned Clarke's research.

Clarke argues that Queen Mary is documented as having paid fair prices for everything she bought, but certainly the circumstances of the sale raise questions of conflict of interest. The amazing feature of all this, as Clarke admits, is that the House of Windsor allowed the whole matter to fester for so many years and never told Olga, Xenia and their heirs what precisely had happened. Therefore we do not know for sure how much money the jewels yielded, nor do we know where all the money went. The facts we know are that Olga received nothing, Xenia sixty thousand pounds, and Queen Mary some magnificent jewels. Thus the death of the empress dowager became even more depressing for the Russians, accompanied as it was by another humiliation at the hands of the British.

The ancient dislike that many Russians felt toward the British gripped Minnie's son-in-law Sandro. For him it was humiliating, he said, as a grandson of Emperor Nicholas I who had fought the British in the Crimean War, to be rescued from the same Crimea by a British warship. On the voyage out of Russia across the Black Sea, early in 1919, he mused unhappily, "Here you are . . . a refugee accepting the hospitality of your royal British cousin, saved by his men from the fury of your own sailors, drinking the health of His Britannic Majesty while your own Emperor has been shot and your brothers are nightly awaiting their doom!"

Nonetheless Sandro promised Minnie that he would go immediately to London to report at length to Queen Mother Alexandra on the family's experiences during the revolution. Without power, without money, his first concern had to be clothing; King Edward VII had made correct dress a matter of great concern at the British court, and it remained so under his son. If Sandro were to be received at court, he must be properly dressed. He had only his uniform to wear, and that would not be appropriate. He kept his civilian clothing in his Paris apartment, but he would need to pay the overdue rent if he wanted to get access to his trunks there. He lacked the cash to do that.

The terrible clothing dilemma was solved because the British refused to grant the grand duke an entry visa. Sandro had applied for one at the British Embassy in Paris, saying that he had been "travelling under British protection," as indeed he had aboard HMS *Foresight* leaving the Crimea. The embassy checked with the Foreign Office, which in turn referred the matter to the court. King George V raised the question with Prime Minister Sir Arthur Balfour, who was "of the opinion that these Grand Dukes should not be allowed to come to England, as wrong impressions would be caused and the presence of these Grand Dukes would be attributed to the influence of the King."

King George sent the British ambassador in Paris, Lord Hardinge, to explain to Sandro why he could not visit England at this time. Hardinge then reported to the king that he was received by Sandro at the Ritz,

in the most friendly manner. . . . I experienced but little difficulty in explaining to His Imperial Highness that the political situation in England rendered, from the point of view of public opinion, a visit undesirable at the present moment, and I took care to emphasize the fact that this opinion emanated in no sense from Your Majesty, but that it was the considered view of Your Majesty's Government and did not apply specially to the Grand Duke Alexander, but to all Russian Grand Dukes. He said that he quite understood and did not seem to be in the least perturbed by what I had said, and expressed the hope that the time was not far off when all such objections would be removed and he would be able to travel freely to England and elsewhere.

But the incident confirmed Sandro's belief that England was no friend to the Romanovs and that family ties really meant nothing.

At this time, January 1919, Xenia and the dowager were still in the Crimea, and the ambassador comments caustically in his dispatch that "I cannot say that I was much impressed by [the] explanation of His Imperial Highness having left his family."

Sandro, as always witty and cynical about himself as well as others, affected a cool and worldly sense of detachment. While his wife and mother-in-law "continued to believe in the impeccability of the World of the Romanoffs, I knew that all our truths were lies and all our wisdom just one colossal conglomerate of vague illusions and stale platitudes. . . . And there I was, a man of fifty-three, without money, occupation, country, home or even address," as he would write in his memoirs.

The grand duke now bitterly regretted not having taken the advice of friends who had wanted him to invest at least one-quarter of his fortune outside of Russia. An American businessman had, in February 1915, urged Sandro to give him a few hundred thousand dollars of capital to invest on his behalf in the United States. "I stand and fall with Russia," Sandro said—"dramatically," in his words.

Now Sandro had enough cash to get him through two months at the Ritz, not in his accustomed suite but in a mere "cubbyhole," as he puts it. His valet remained at the hotel with him, and Sandro did his best to pretend that life had not changed. He anxiously awaited news from Russia about his brothers and cousins still there and said, "the revolution had taught me that the absence of news invariably means bad news." He was quite correct; while he waited, all were killed.

Despite his polite assurances to Lord Hardinge, Sandro was bitter that now he could not enter a country where his cousin was king and where he had spent more than twenty summers of his life.

Wanting to plead Russia's case at the Versailles conference, he was not even able to see Arthur Balfour, Woodrow Wilson or any other statesman of consequence. When he was trying to get an appointment with Foreign Secretary Balfour, Sandro says he caught sight of Balfour leaving his hotel room via a fire escape, letting an embarrassed assistant make explanations for his employer's inability to meet the grand duke. When the assistant asked if Sandro wanted to leave Balfour a message, Sandro replied, "Yes, by all means. Tell him that a man of his age should use the elevator."

But in the spring of 1919, Sandro could not have the luxury of dwelling on his complete lack of success in playing statesman. Of greater importance was his urgent need to pay his shoemaker, his haberdasher and his tailor, not to mention the Ritz. The immediate answer for the grand duke lay in selling the valuable collection of ancient coins he had brought with him out of Russia. Years ago he had begun to assemble the collection from finds he had made on the grounds of his Crimean estate, Ai Todor. He then began to finance digging expeditions across the Black Sea in Anatolia, hiring German scholars to mine the area of Trebizond and other ancient sites of Greek and other early civilizations. Even before this extension of his sphere of search, his father disapproved of the extravagance.

> Just think, Sandro, of the opportunities you are missing. Why, if you would invest but a fraction of what it costs you to dig in the Crimean soil into sound preferred stocks and government bonds, you would double your annual income and never be in need of cash. If you don't like stocks and bonds, buy oil lands, buy copper, buy manganese, buy real estate, but for Heaven's sake stop spending good money on these boresome old Greeks.

Sandro later wrote that if he had followed his father's advice, he would simply have amassed more pieces of paper in a safe-deposit vault to which he no longer had access. And the destruction wrought by the revolution had made these certificates of dubious value to anyone anyhow. A tailor on the Rue du Faubourg St. Honoré would hardly exchange a pair of flannel trousers for the promise of a Caucasian oil lease.

Sandro did not like being without a job. He had been a naval officer, he had briefly run the Russian merchant marine and had assumed command of the air force during the world war. He had always done something—not well, he cheerfully admitted, but at least he had maintained a level of activity. Now he found it depressing to wake up in the morning and face a day with only a social engagement or two on his calendar. So he tried to get a job.

When he approached friends who might be able to offer him one, they laughed. "The very idea of hiring a grand duke struck them as a ridiculous notion," he wrote. They simply assumed that Sandro and his family would eventually inherit, from imagined bank accounts and investments, a vast sum of money, once the tsar was declared legally dead. One banker, who did take Sandro's desire seriously, questioned his credentials. Shaking his head sadly, he said,

> I am afraid that you are going to find it rather difficult to sell these qualifications of yours. Your administrative experience might be used by an empire, but where are the empires? The steamship companies are losing money steadily, and would not even dream of building additional craft. As for languages, permit me to be frank and brutal: you are entirely too old to become a teller in our foreign department.

Sandro had ended up as roving lecturer, a pursuit well suited to his debonair conviviality and restless temperament. He was able to generate a small income and invariably attracted the attention of the press. He made his first trip to the United States for a speaking tour in 1928, followed by several more visits. On arriving in New York in 1928 to begin his first tour by speaking at Town Hall on the subject, "Out of My Life," Sandro predicted to the press that a spiritual revolution would topple the Soviet regime within a few years. But he went so far as to say that the revolution had its "benefits as well as its drawbacks" and maintained that the challenge of a new life for the former aristocracy had demonstrated its good qualities. Sandro told the New York reporters that he had been forced to start his life all over again and that the experience had given him the idea that spirituality should triumph over materialism. He declared that he had "found more satisfaction in my new life than in the old. I am free; that is the great thing in my life. There is nobody above me except God, and He is the best commander I can have. I don't need anything any more except a little to eat and drink."

Despite professing this fondness for a simple life, Sandro always traveled First Class and drink included wine. He had little liking for American Prohibition ("water is not adapted to my nature") but he did not drink spirits. On the question of vodka in Russia, Sandro reminded the press that Nicholas II had abolished the production and consumption of vodka during the war; some even said this was one of the causes of the revolution. The Soviet government had restored the vodka industry despite the bad impact on the people, deriving a huge income from liquor sales.

Sandro's hatred for the Bolsheviks did not win out over his sense of national pride. He ultimately would shock some Americans by applauding the economic development of Russia pushed by the Soviet government, and he thoroughly approved of the regime's independence of foreign financial assistance in its drive to build new factories and to put tractors on farms.

After a dinner speech, a man sitting next to Sandro, whom the latter knew to be a descendant of a nineteenth-century railroad baron, said, "with an air of thorough disgust, 'A strange speech for one whose brothers were killed by the Bolsheviki.'"

The grand duke replied, "You are quite right. But then we Romanovs are a strange family. The greatest of us killed his own son because the latter tried to interfere with his Five Year Plan," referring to Peter the Great, who ordered his son killed because he opposed his father's reforms.

Sandro took up writing, with some success. In the spring of 1933, he died of cancer, having continued to write until the end—up early in the morning, devouring American, British, French and German newspapers, fighting pain, reluctantly accepting medication. He published two memoirs. The first, *Once a Grand Duke,* sold well. Its sequel, *Always a Grand Duke,* did not, perhaps because he was too ill to write the second without a lot of help. For a joint biography of the two sisters Minnie and Alexandra, both of whom he had known well, he got no farther than assembling materials.

Sandro's last words were written appropriately at Monte Carlo: "I am going home. I have one, for the first time in sixty-seven years. Not much of a home—just big enough for me and my future." Sandro was buried with the rites of the Orthodox Church even though he had asked not to be. Family tradition prevailed over individual preference.

❦

In January 1919, Sandro encountered his younger cousin Dmitri in the lobby of the Paris Ritz. He had not seen him for several years. Sandro saw Dmitri enviously as a young and handsome man, "gleaning the admiration of women, his whole life before him." Indeed Dmitri would become the most socially conspicuous post-revolutionary grand duke.

After his near death from typhoid, Dmitri had sailed from Bombay to France via Egypt on a painfully slow steamer, accompanied only by his valet. He was traveling as an official member of the staff of Sir Charles Marling. who had been recalled from his diplomatic duties in Teheran. Dmitri had been cut off from most news of home and family. He knew that his sister had remarried; he did not know that she had given birth to a child and had escaped from Russia. Arriving in Paris on November 28, 1918, he felt alone and miserable. The last time he had been there was June 1914, on the eve of the war. He was then an officer of the Guards, fabulously rich, and had come to meet his father. Now he wore an alien, British, military uniform, having finally accepted a loathsome honorary commission, of no use in restarting a military career in Britain, a hope he had cherished. He had no money, "no home and even no motherland," and his father was jailed in Russia.

Dmitri for the first time grasped the scale of the terror then raging across Russia. Not only was his father in prison, but his half-brother, Prince Vladimir Paley, had also disappeared, and so reportedly had his sister. In London, Dmitri received a telegram from his sister in Romania. He now knew that Marie had survived but that his father had met a firing squad. The young duke confided to his diary in disgust, "I feel such a brute. When I think of all the terrible things they went through while I lived in Teheran like a son in [Marling's] family, playing polo and riding and enjoying life."

Marie, after her nursing career and her second wedding, and her escape from southern Russia, had found that, of all the royal families in Europe related to the Romanovs who were still sitting on thrones, only the Romanian sovereigns offered "real sympathy and understanding." She went first, late in 1918, to Bucharest, newly freed from German occupation,

> with the single, very much weather-beaten suitcase I had brought
> with me out of Russia; the toilet articles were the same nickel-

topped things I had used during the war. I possessed one or two wornout dresses made over from my pre-war wardrobe, and hence more than four years old; thick cotton underwear, no silk stockings, and a few miscellaneous articles such as handker-chiefs, the initials of which had been cut out with scissors.

Because of her former status in the Swedish royal family, Marie had been able to use diplomatic channels to smuggle her jewels from Pet-rograd to Stockholm, but until she could retrieve them, she was de-pendent upon the generosity of the Romanian cousins.

Bucharest is not, nor was it ever, one of the most opulent or cos-mopolitan cities in Europe, and yet the liveliness, order and prosper-ity of the city, in contrast to the Russia she had just left, overwhelmed Marie. She felt that she was in Europe again, connected with culture in a way in which Russia had not been since the beginning of the war. And wartime Russia had not been nearly as isolated as Russia became with the outbreak of revolution.

Queen Marie greeted her guests affectionately and gave clothing to the grand duchess. The queen's exuberance was intoxicating, and she was a woman of great beauty; she was warm and fearless, altogether far more attractive a personality than her sister Ducky, married to Grand Duke Kyril. Kyril, icy and detached, had chosen a congenial mate.

Queen Marie admired herself enormously, but in such a childlike and naive way that many people found it charming. "Often when speaking about herself she would sound as if it were some other supremely beau-tiful and fascinating creature she was seeing and describing." Her prob-lem was her desire always to be center stage. To seek such prominence and "to be brilliant is not always an advantage for a Queen in the dem-ocratic age," her Russian namesake shrewdly judged.

The grand duchess applied for a French visa, which took a long time to arrive. Gradually she came to realize how little the world thought of the Romanovs, and she reached the conclusion that "we had outlived our epoch and were doomed." She began to understand that she needed a new attitude, a new sense of pride, because her old sense of security and superiority was utterly gone. As long as Marie remained in Romania she was sheltered by the fact that she was the queen's cousin. In Paris it would be starkly different. There she would be an ordinary exile. And the ordinary was totally bizarre to a Romanov.

Before the revolution, someone else had always paid her bills—in Sweden, the equerry in charge of her household; in Russia, the superintendent of her brother's business office. Marie knew approximately how much jewels and clothing cost but had not the slightest idea of the price of bread, meat or milk. She did not know how to buy a subway ticket; she feared entering a restaurant alone, not knowing how and what to order there or what to give as a tip. Although she was then twenty-eight years old, in practical matters she recognized that she was still a child and had to learn everything from the beginning, just as a child has to learn to cross a street before going to school alone.

In Paris, Marie felt particularly sad, for she associated the city with memories of her father who had lived there in exile and who was now lying in a common grave in Russia, killed by the Bolsheviks in January 1919. Marie decided to make London her new home and on her arrival there she and Dmitri had a joyful reunion. Dmitri had money in England transferred from the sale of his palace in Petrograd, but the rubles he had received had immediately depreciated in value and he was now drawing down his capital rapidly. He had been living at the Ritz since his arrival in London.

For grand dukes, regardless of the current size of their purse, the Ritz in whatever city they found themselves was the residence of choice. Marie found a furnished flat for herself and her husband because she thought the Ritz too expensive for them, but they nonetheless continued to eat their meals with Dmitri at the hotel. Marie and Dmitri talked together for hours, days and weeks and of many things, but never of the reasons for the great debacle, of what happened in Russia and why. She would have liked to have done so; Dmitri seemed to prefer his dreams.

Marie lingered in London, savoring its sense of tradition. Her Swedish royal relatives brought her the jewels she had managed to send to Stockholm. These jewels had remained in the same wrappings in which they had been spirited out of Russia, concealed in ink bottles, paperweights and imitation candles. Outstanding among them was a magnificent sapphire tiara made by Cartier in Paris and given Marie by her father, Grand Duke Paul. These now formed Marie's total material wealth.

She did not want to sell the jewels and did not think it necessary to do so because she still thought that her circumstances were temporary, that the Bolsheviks would soon be overturned and that she would soon be able to return to Russia. More than that, these brooches, bracelets and tiaras were now her only physical link with her grand-mother and great-grandmother. When the inevitable happened and she had to begin selling, "each time that I was obliged to part with a piece of jewellery I remembered its history, and, when it passed into the hands of the buyer, a bit of the past went with it."

Instead of selling all the jewels at one time, amassing a sum of cap-ital and investing it for a regular return, Marie sold them piece by piece, an exceedingly painful process emotionally and probably less profitable in the long run financially. Ultimately the market would be flooded with Russian jewels, and the sellers were convinced that the dealers came to an understanding not to bid against one other. The dealers often knew the stones well, having originally sold them to the Russians. The line of patter the desperate sellers heard became all too familiar. The jewels were "either too big or too small, cut when they ought to have been uncut, or vice versa, and they were never well enough matched." Times were hard, customers rare, or at least so the jewelers maintained.

In defense of the jewelers, the jewel market was plunging into cri-sis. Not only were former royalty selling, but also the many aristo-cratic families all over Europe, newly uprooted and impoverished by war and revolution. Furthermore, the Bolsheviks, desperate for hard currency, began to sell what they had been able to seize.

For Marie another, more devastating, blow fell with a letter bearing the terrible news that her one-year-old baby, Roman, had died from an intestinal disorder. Unlike her cousin Olga, who took her tiny sons through dreadful privation and danger to safety in exile, she had left Roman with her husband's parents when she fled Russia. Guilt pre-vented her from telling her friends. Meanwhile her older son, Lennart, in Stockholm, was now ten years old, and Marie was forbidden to see him because of the divorce and her remarriage. Divorce had caused her to abandon her first son; her decision to flee Russia as quickly and comfortably as possible had made her leave the second.

At the end of 1919, Marie decided to find a job, to fight apathy and depression but also to make money. The only talent she thought she could exploit for that purpose was knitting and embroidery. She made hand-knit sweaters and even dresses. The market for these elegant gar-ments was good, but she could not charge enough to compensate her-self adequately for the enormous amount of time she had to spend making each one. Because Paris was the center of style in clothing, her opportunities seemed greater there. Furthermore Marie thought she could live more cheaply in France than in England. She moved back to Paris in 1921 and Dmitri followed. He allowed a champagne company in Rheims to use his name; she began to work as a designer for Coco Chanel.

Chanel had begun as a designer and dressmaker, but her great success derived from brilliant entrepreneurship. Chanel's "fierce vitality" attracted Marie; here was a woman whose power was based not upon position but solely upon personality and ability. Beginning with the Russian folk art that she knew from her own experience, Marie drew inspiration for clothing designs from a wide variety of sources such as Persian rugs, tiles and miniatures, and Chinese porcelains. Chanel and the public received her work enthusiastically.

Meanwhile Marie's second marriage, to Sergei Putiatin, gradually deteriorated. She referred to it as "a fundamental difference in attitude," although she sustained a good relationship with the Putiatin family and continued to help them financially. It seemed that although Marie was willing to work to earn money, Putiatin was not. Yet although money was scarcely in great supply, neither Marie nor her husband ever had to perform humble household tasks. They did not cook, clean or wash dishes; servants did these chores. Marie employed an eccentric butler named Karp, a Russian who had left the home country long ago and had earlier worked in one of the grand ducal houses in Paris. Karp looked, appropriately, like a fish, and performed the role of the perfect servant, although he padded about in ancient carpet slippers and, while serving a dinner party, did not refrain from occasionally slipping a witty remark into the table conversation.

In contrast to his energetic sister, Dmitri led the life of an idle playboy, though in 1921 he turned thirty. He said himself that he was living in a "feverish idleness." In the mornings he would rise late and usually had visitors, most often a former officer of the Guards with whom he would exchange gossip. After lunch, the grand duke would play golf or go to his club, and in the evening return home "only just in time to change for dinner." He spent his nights carousing in expensive restaurants or less reputable places, causing the emigré community to refer to his "lechery in pigsties." Tolstoy's granddaughter, Vera, saw Dmitri at Monte Carlo, sitting alone in a corner watching people play roulette. He had no money to join in.

Marie, deeply troubled about her brother, mused about him:

Nobody had had an easier, a more brilliant debut in life than he.
He had had a large fortune with very few responsibilities attached
to it, unusually good looks coupled with charm, and he also had
been the recognized favourite of the Tsar . . . there was no young
prince in Europe more socially conspicuous than he was both in
his own country and abroad. He walked a golden path.

Even Marie, who probably loved her brother more than anyone
else, admitted that he had failed to use his talents and opportunities.
Dmitri had left the Russia he knew before the disintegration of culture
and behavior. The revolution did not harden him; he saw little directly
of it, "he had not looked into its sordid face," Marie remarked.

Dmitri remained an immature and unfulfilled man, one who did not
know what he really wanted. "Reticent and morose," he behaved like
a spoiled child, contemplating his life with indolent self-pity, making
no attempt to improve his situation. His relations with Felix Yusupov
had sharply deteriorated. During the first months after Rasputin's
death, they had still been friendly, but Felix's constant talk about the
murder angered Dmitri, who believed that they had agreed not to talk
about it.

Felix had opened a couture house in Paris which he named "Irfe"
after his wife, Irina, and himself. The beautiful Irina, granddaughter
of Alexander III, modeled the gowns herself. Another of Felix's ven-
tures was a restaurant, La Maisonette. Then Felix, having failed to get
enough customers to sustain these enterprises, published in 1927 a
successful book about Rasputin that gave him the opportunity to present his own version of Rasputin's murder and made him some money.

Although Felix had lost one of the world's greatest fortunes in the
revolution, he was never poor. He held property in western Europe
and he carried into exile not only his wife's extraordinary jewels but
also two of his favorite Rembrandts, *The Man in the Large Hat* and
The Woman with the Fan. He had boldly cut them out of their frames,
rolled them up and carried them with him on the long train ride to the
Crimea, and then aboard the *Marlborough*, out of Russia. He subsequently sold the paintings to the American collector Joseph Widener.
Today they are part of the permanent collection of the National
Gallery of Art in Washington, D.C.

Dmitri considered Felix's book recounting the assassination the disreputable act of a greedy man. If Dmitri had chosen to write one himself, it would have been an even greater bestseller, but he never even considered the idea. Then, in 1934, Felix got more money by successfully suing Metro Goldwyn Mayer for the movie *Rasputin and the Empress* which he claimed falsely portrayed his wife as having had an affair with Rasputin. Much later, in the early 1950s, Felix would write an autobiography, *Lost Spendour*, in which he would dismiss Dmitri as "extremely attractive: tall, elegant, well-bred, with deep thoughtful eyes . . . but the weakness of his character made him dangerously easy to influence."

In February 1920, Dmitri and Felix had exchanged letters that essentially ended their friendship. Felix complained that Dmitri, formerly such a close friend, now looked at him "almost as an enemy." Dmitri, deeply hurt, felt it was his duty to respond at length. He wrote that the murder of Rasputin would always trouble his conscience and that was why he never talked about it, whereas Felix was not just recounting the story but actually boasting! And now he was planning to go to America to raise funds, telling people, "Look at me—I killed Rasputin!"

Dmitri felt so angry that he even reminded Felix that had it not been for Dmitri's royal participation in the conspiracy, Felix would have been "hanged as a political criminal." But, being fair, Dmitri admitted that his presence at the murder had providentially led to his exile from Russia and escape from death during the Terror. "So, we are quits," Dmitri concluded firmly, bringing an old friendship to a close.

Early in 1921, Dmitri fell in love with Coco Chanel, with whom Marie was still working. Coco had met Dmitri at the Ritz. The grand duke seemed to bring Coco good luck. It was then that she brought onto the market her famous Chanel No. 5, her most famous and enduring product, a perfume labeled revolutionary because it departed from traditional formulas based on natural odors. Pleased with her new triumph, Coco spent a happy summer with Dmitri at a villa near Arcachon on the shores of the Bay of Biscay. The couple fished, walked, played with Coco's numerous dogs, and saw as little of their friends as possible. Once back in Paris, Dmitri introduced several high-born Russian ladies to Coco to work as sales assistants at her salon. Of humble background herself, she had always harbored a desire to patronize, and thereby humiliate, aristocrats.

The newspapers announced that Coco would marry the grand duke. But unlike his cousins Boris and Andrew, Dmitri was not prepared for "morganatic liaisons," as he put it. A marriage did not take place. Coco sighed, "These grand dukes, they are all the same, an admirable face behind which there is nothing, green eyes, broad shoulders, fine hands . . . the most peaceful people, shyness itself. . . . They drink just not to be afraid. Tall, handsome, superb these Russians are. And behind that is nothing: hollowness and vodka."

❧

The Romanovs were not intellectuals, nor were they artists in any serious way, but some of them maintained strong and informed interests in the arts. Part of the grand ducal role after all had been to be patron. Even before 1917, Paris had established itself as a foreign showcase for Russian music, for Russian dance, and for Russian opera; much of this being subsidized from fat grand ducal purses. In Paris, Scriabin had played his own work for piano; Kshesinskaya had danced *Coppelia*; and the great Chaliapin had electrified the public with his majestic thundering *Boris Godunov*. Russian artists in painting, like Chagall or Kandinsky, as well as in music, like Stravinsky, were pushing into and even seizing world leadership in new and exciting fields of modernism.

Long before the deluge, Grand Duke Vladimir Alexandrovich and his wife, Miechen, came to Paris especially for *Boris Godunov*, and after the second act went backstage to congratulate the assembled company, admiring the costumes and the scenery and speaking to each of the singers individually. For the Parisian public, therefore, the Russian aristocracy came to be known for its cultural interests as well as for its love of a good time, an exuberant extravagance being common to both.

But Miechen this time did not have the opportunity to indulge herself in the artistic delights of Paris she had so enjoyed in the old days. She died on August 24, 1920, at Contrexeville in southern France, the first Romanov to die in exile after the revolution. Organizing her escape after first bravely suffering three nightmarish years in revolutionary Russia, she seems then to have decided to die. Even before the fall of White Crimea, this iron lady sensed that the cause of the Whites was lost, restoration of the Romanovs impossible, and she left with no purpose in life. At least she died in comfort, surrounded by her family, and until the end tried to take good care of them, giving each a spectacular set of jewels, smuggled from Russia for her by her English friend, Bertie Stopford, and kept in a safe deposit box in London. Her only daughter, Helen, who had survived the revolution by being with her husband in Greece, was to get the diamonds, Kyril the pearls, Andrew the rubies, and Boris the emeralds. The emeralds were the most precious part of the grand duchess's collection, and they were to be for Boris because he was his mother's favorite.

Kyril visited Paris often and ultimately took an apartment there. Andrew and Boris embraced the city. The pensive Andrew was a cosmopolite who enjoyed dividing his time between Paris and the Riviera, where he had owned a villa long before the revolution. In the south of France, Andrew had no need to deplete his resources by living in a hotel; he could keep on his servants and solve the cash flow problem, at least temporarily, by taking out a mortgage on the property. But later, according to rumor, the gambling tables at Monte Carlo would put a further strain on Andrew's finances. Both he and his Mathilde liked to gamble, and it was commonly said that she lost her fabulous jewel collection at the roulette wheel. Kshesinskaya, having dragged three Romanovs through her bed, had decided to marry the only one of the three now still alive. She and her son, Vova, then eighteen, settled permanently with Andrew.

Unlike so many great performing artists, Mathilde also was a gifted teacher. Opening a ballet school in Paris, she became a great success in the classroom, and among her pupils was the future star of British ballet, Margot Fonteyn. In addition to being fun for Kshesinskaya, the school had the advantage of providing an income for the grand ducal family and cushioned for them the rigors of exile.

Feuds and factionalism had always torn the ballet world. Presumably Andrew and Mathilde now felt some satisfaction at the collapse of their artistic arch-enemy, Vaslav Nijinsky, always a subject for their jealous intrigues. Russia's greatest male dancer was now insane. But Diaghilev, the impresario, another of Andrew and Mathilde's *bêtes noirs,* had made a triumphant return to Paris in December 1919, giving a gala benefit performance for Russian refugees. He and his company were privileged guests in Monte Carlo, on close terms with the ruling family there. King Manuel of Portugal, the Duke of Westminster and Daisy, Princess of Pless, were among the many social luminaries attending these performances. Kyril and Ducky came too, and Grand Duke Michael Mikhailovich ("Miche-Miche"), who had been banished from Russia so long ago by Alexander III, was there with his wife, Countess Torby.

The grand dukes were glad to mix with the European *beau monde* at Diaghilev's parties. The roles had been reversed: Diaghilev now was patronizing the Romanovs, in a sweet revenge. And abroad he could act without the restraints, imposed even on him, by Russian conservatism. His homosexuality now became much more public; he could even flaunt it. After a London performance of *The Triumph of Neptune*, a critic wrote with wry humor that the company was "greeted with many floral tributes, even the female dancers receiving some."

Boris was as happy as Andrew to find himself in the familiar atmosphere of Paris, although by now he was a person tied by marital bonds. In 1919, he had married Zinaida Rashevskaya, with whom he had fled Russia. Unlike Mathilde, whom the family tolerated, Zinaida they regarded as disreputable, vulgar and low born, although she was the widow of an army officer. She was never accepted by the family. This was not just a Romanov prejudice; few emigrés seem to have had a good word for Zinaida. Nonetheless Boris seemed both happy and financially at ease. Although the generous Queen Marie of Romania was constantly helping her Vladimirovichi relatives, people generally believed that Boris's money came from his wife.

Boris had once been described as "Russia's favorite spender." His exuberant public manner had attracted the occasional attention of the newspapers well before the revolution. His career had been long in the making. Once in St. Petersburg Boris had been forced to apologize to an old lady of high rank from whose house, as he departed after a visit, he had insisted upon taking along a bowl of goldfish to which he had taken a sudden strong fancy. His hostess complained to the empress.

Now, exiled from his Russian playgrounds, Boris started looking for new places to have fun. In the winter of 1925, he and Zinaida, who claimed a professional interest in dressmaking, sailed for New York, she reportedly bringing as many as three hundred dresses and he twenty-two trunks of personal luggage. New York Congressman Fiorello LaGuardia objected strongly to the visit, suggesting that Boris really might have no money of his own but be traveling with tickets given to him by rich Americans, implying that other Romanovs had recently done this.

LaGuardia referred scornfully to "these repudiated, unemployed and shiftless dukes and archdukes" who might want to see a monarchy established in the United States, and that "people clamored and paid admission for the purpose of curtseying and kissing the hand of these pretenders in a manner so un-American that it would have been shocking were it not so ridiculously stupid." LaGuardia urged that "the same rigid application of the immigration law that is generally applied to arriving aliens should be applied to these roaming royalists who come here to collect funds to destroy organized governments and to prey upon the credulity of social climbing dupes."

On its editorial page a year earlier, the *New York Times* had already taken a critical view of the Romanovs. Although the deaths of the tsar and his family were certainly cruel, nonetheless

> except to the comparatively few Russians who prospered under the old regime the Romanoffs [*sic*] were not attractive personages, and the murdering of them was not appreciably more horrible than thousands of other killings of which the Bolsheviki have been guilty. . . . It is more than doubtful if the Grand Dukes, even the best of them, are the proper persons to give Russia the sane rule which it lacks now—and always has lacked.

In a New York interview at his suite in the Ritz Carlton, the insouciant Boris did little to influence for the better the attitude expressed by the *Times,* saying that he had come to the United States solely to see friends and to enjoy life, to have a good time. When asked about politics, he expressed no interest except to remark that he believed that the Russian people would eventually choose a monarchy again since they were most accustomed to that form of government. And if the old regime should be restored, he would expect to return to soldiering in Russia, the career for which he had been trained. When a reporter asked if it were true that Henry Ford was one of the chief financial supporters of the movement to restore the monarchy to Russia, Boris replied, "Who is Henry Ford?"

CHAPTER TWELVE

❧

"We Should Act!"

M ARIE AND SANDRO WERE THE ONLY grand ducal Romanovs who tried to get a job. Others still hoped to return to Russia and resume their lives of privilege. Most of them did nothing to promote political change in their homeland. Only two Romanovs decided to challenge the Reds: Nikolasha and Kyril. For them at least, in the early 1920s, the time seemed right for direct action.

In April 1919, Nikolasha had moved from Yalta to Genoa, to live in Italy as a guest of his brother-in-law, King Victor Emanuel. The king's wife, Elena, was Montenegrin, a sister of Stana and Militsa. Restless, like his fellow exiled kinsmen, and not wanting to be a political embarrassment of any kind to his Italian hosts, Nikolasha then moved across the French border to Antibes in 1922 just as Mussolini was seizing power. There on the Riviera he lived close to his brother, Peter, assuming the surname Borisov, after the name of his estate back in Russia, Borisovo.

Still interested in politics, Nikolasha felt he needed to be close to Paris in order to stay in touch with the different emigrant groups. As a former commander-in-chief of the Russian army, Nikolasha was well connected to the French military and even granted a marshal's pension by a grateful French government, remembering 1914. In May 1923, the grand duke took up a stubbornly reclusive life in a small country house in a chestnut and pine grove at Choigny, near Choisy-le-Roi, some twenty miles outside Paris. There he lived with only his wife and a handful of faithful and extremely conservative retainers.

The house may have been small and simple, even shabby, but like the old soldier himself it radiated dignity. An allée of Lombardy poplars in rows of military precision marched up to the front door. Life at Choigny contained none of the splendor of Imperial Russia. Guests to the house were received modestly, the dining table was covered in oilcloth, and the grand duke wore clothing that obviously had been darned. Yet despite his lack of money, Nikolasha converted an outbuilding on the estate into a chapel tended regularly by a priest visiting from Paris. Religion was integral to his life. Nikolasha found the godlessness of Communism as distressing as any other aspect of it. He judged the Communists to be morally bankrupt and stoutly expected that the underlying faith of the Russian people in the Orthodox Church would ultimately destroy the Soviet regime.

Nikolasha's cousin Kyril, soon to become his arch-enemy, was now dividing his time between Paris and Munich. He could occasionally be spotted on the streets of Paris, described by an unfriendly observer as a tall, pale, slightly round-shouldered man with a long limp face and little dark moustache, standing out from the crowd by his slow self-assured walk and general air of disdain. Kyril preferred Germany to France; he and Ducky held property there given them by her mother. Kyril's tastes were German, and Ducky, although a granddaughter of Queen Victoria, was nonetheless, like her mother, Marie of Coburg, a strong Anglophobe.

Kyril presented himself as a sportsman. He liked to talk about his hobby, racing cars. Yet he also affected grand ducal pomposity, an arrogance fed by his intense awareness that he was now number one in the imperial succession, all his competitors conveniently taken care of by Bolshevik bullet or bayonet.

In 1922, a mysterious character from Russia's civil war stoked the fire of Kyril's political ambitions. Ataman Grigory Semenov wrote to Kyril from the Far Eastern Russo-Chinese borderland proposing that the grand duke come to the area and proclaim himself the "Ruler of the Amur." The Russian Far East was so remote from the power centers of the nation that Semenov and others could hope that the Bolsheviks would be unable to establish themselves there.

Semenov was one of the more colorful figures of the anti-Bolshevik movement in Russia. Leader of the Trans-Baikal Cossacks, dark, thickset and physically powerful, he was a war hero and had been awarded not only the St. George Cross but also the St. George Sword, a rare distinction. Semenov had served during the war as a junior officer with the Ussuriisk Cossack Division, the so-called Yellow Cossacks, actually Russo-Mongols, notorious for their ferocity. Their very name had provoked terror.

In 1918, Japan's intervention in the Russian civil war was the only attempt by a foreign power to dismember the nation at a time of its great weakness. Other powers, the United States included, sent expeditionary forces to Russia but with no intention of keeping them there. Semenov, however, collaborated with the Japanese in establishing their zone of occupation in Russia's Far East, betraying his oath of allegiance to Russia. Semenov was primarily out for himself. He terrorized Siberia east of Lake Baikal, hijacking trains and looting towns. He was known for loving bloodshed and plunder, but an aura of outlaw romance also clung to his name.

In January 1920, the self-proclaimed "Supreme Ruler of Russia," Admiral Kolchak, defeated by the Reds in western Siberia, named Semenov commander-in-chief and the supreme civil authority of the Russian Far Eastern borderland. The triumph of the Reds and the end of the civil war had given this brigand new prominence.

In addition to Semenov's invitation to Kyril, the "Assembly of the Land" (*Zemsky Sobor*), ancient Russian analogue of a constituent assembly, gathered in Vladivostok in the summer of 1922. They wrote the dowager empress and Nikolasha asking them to choose a sovereign for the Far East, even sending two generals all the way to Europe to talk to them about the restoration of the House of Romanov. But no military leader of any standing wanted to talk to Kyril. So however disreputable Semenov may have been, his current appeal to the grand duke set Kyril moving, for one very simple reason: His was the only appeal Kyril had ever gotten from anybody of any political importance.

During their first years of exile, political restoration was very much on the minds of many Romanovs. The Soviet system had not yet proved its power or even viability, and the monarchist heritage seemed too rich to be discarded so quickly. However, the wider emigré community did not want to hear anything about monarchy. The anti-Romanov mood was expressed, among others, by a famous poet, Zinaida Gippius, now in Paris. When asked in 1921 to collaborate in the publication of a new emigré newspaper, Gippius wrote that she could participate only if the newspaper were "democratic, equally unsympathetic towards Bolshevism *and* monarchism."

A proliferation of parties, groups and individuals was coming out with different schemes for saving the motherland and overthrowing Bolshevism. Russian emigrants tried to organize themselves for political purposes. In 1921, they established a Supreme Monarchist Council in Berlin. This body did not have any particular affiliation with the Romanovs, although it showed two sentiments: interest in Nikolasha and disgust for Kyril.

In principle, monarchical restoration is possible in two ways. One way could be called Napoleonic: a charismatic pretender hoping to seize supreme power launches a successful military coup. None of the Romanovs ever came close to achieving Napoleon's example. Some of Europe's other deposed royals tried. For example the young, recently dethroned Hapsburg emperor of Austria-Hungary, Charles I, in 1921, slipped into Hungary in disguise, carrying the passport of an officer in the English Red Cross, and tried to ignite a restoration movement there. Ousted by Admiral Horthy, several months later Charles returned to the country by plane and marched on Budapest with a small monarchist army, only to be defeated in the suburbs of the capital and forced to flee. But if Charles was no Napoleon, Kyril was even less so.

Though Kyril was inspired by Semenov to launch his quest for the Russian throne and seriously considered that idea, Kyril did not go to the Far East, a territory still only feebly controlled by the Kremlin. Semenov was a bandit, ultimately too disreputable for Kyril to trust. The grand duke did have other options, though. Soviet Russia lacked stability. In 1921, even the firmest supporters of the revolution, the sailors of Kronstadt, had staged a powerful mutiny. And new chances for an anti-Bolshevik popular uprising came with reactions to the brutal Soviet collectivization of all farmlands.

The second way could be called Bourbonic: exiled royals patiently wait until they can return on the coattails of an invading army. Kyril hoped somehow for a triumphant return to his country in due time, like the Bourbons. But, unlike the Bourbons, no foreign power then— or ever—wanted to restore the Romanovs.

On August 8, 1922, Kyril published a manifesto to the Russian people, declaring his status as claimant to the throne. In it he claimed that he prayed the emperor and *tsesarevich* were alive. If not, he said, then the All-Russia Assembly of the Land (*Zemsky Sobor*) would choose the tsar, as in 1613 when the first Romanov had been crowned after "the Time of Troubles," when the previous Rurik dynasty had been extinguished. In the absence of any news about the "salvation" of Grand Duke Michael, Kyril announced that he, "Grandson of the Tsar Liberator," Alexander II, would be regent.

On the same day Kyril solemnly addressed Russian soldiers in exile "I pray to God that, according to my request, His Imperial Highness Grand Duke Nicholas Nikolaevich [Nikolasha] will become commander-in-chief of the Russian army." Kyril knew only too well how limited a support he enjoyed and in this fashion was actually proposing that he and Nikolasha rule together.

Kyril, ever the Germanophile, was now living mainly at Coburg near Munich in Bavaria, where Ducky had spent much time as a child. The little colony of Russian emigrants there formed the core of his support, although Duke George of Leuchtenberg, a minor Romanov who lived there too, remained Kyril's bitter enemy. Bavaria was the place where Hitler was soon to spring into politics by staging his unsuccessful Beer Hall Putsch on November 9, 1923. Some wealthy White Russian emigrés, attracted to the intense anti-Communism of the Nazis, would back them financially, and that support would prove crucial to the success of the movement. Ducky herself became an enthusiastic supporter of the Storm Troopers and was seen at several of their meetings. She posed for a photograph alone with a smiling Hitler and, as early as 1922, Hitler allegedly visited the couple at their Coburg home.

Ducky, known for her strong will, ambition and resourcefulness, was believed to be the driving force behind Kyril's political aspirations, as his mother had been earlier. Ducky was not popular even within the circle of Kyril's closest advisors. Her inability to speak Russian well was one reason for this, but most disturbing to them was her driving ambition. The wiser of Kyril's advisors were urging him not to rush his career. "You should be like an icon, and when the time is ripe, people will take you and carry you to the throne themselves." But even if Kyril could wait, Ducky longed for the throne immediately, at any cost.

The would-be tsar was desperately trying to secure the support of the military leaders who still controlled the exiled White troops, now organized in the Russian All-Military Union (ROVS) and who represented the only organized force of any consequence among the Russian emigrés. Kyril particularly sought out the leader of the ROVS, General Peter Wrangel, a distinguished soldier and man of imagination, iron will and stalwart honor. Wrangel responded that the future of Russia had to be decided by its people. Wrangel did believe that monarchy was the best form of government, but he sharply disappointed Kyril by accusing him of acting rashly, saying that he wouldn't be able to support Kyril.

The Supreme Monarchist Council in Berlin agreed with Wrangel, telling Kyril it believed his suggestion to lead the monarchist movement was premature. But neither they nor Wrangel could reject him altogether, for technically speaking, he was first in the order of imperial succession.

. However, a top secret document of Wrangel's headquarters reveals that the Supreme Monarchist Council did not object to Kyril's bad timing so much as to Kyril himself. They remembered that during the first days of revolution he had marched his unit under the red flag to the revolutionary duma in Petrograd. Furthermore they scorned Kyril because of the failure of his mother to convert to Orthodoxy before Kyril was born, a serious impediment for the throne of Russia. Miechen had not had herself baptised until 1908, long after all her children had reached maturity. It is unlikely that she then experienced any sudden conversion of faith. By that time everyone in the family knew that the heir, young Alexis, was a hemophiliac and unlikely ever to become tsar. That fact had vastly enhanced Kyril's chances, and Miechen had responded to the new situation. And finally the Council was deeply concerned with the matter of Kyril's controversial marriage to Ducky, wrong in the eyes of the Church on two counts: She was his first cousin and she had been divorced; "Therefore this marriage would require imperial permission." The Council planned eventually to force Kyril to abandon any claim to the throne and had already voted this, eleven to five. The Council saw Nikolasha as the only monarchist leader, the proper regent. The documents indicate that at this point in the Russian emigré world, only Munich and Budapest, relatively small communities, supported Kyril's claims.

As the monarchists started scrutinizing the survivors among the members of the dynasty their judgments were harsh, even of Nikolasha. The old soldier was "legendary in his stinginess," and some could not forgive him for having telegraphed Nicholas II, begging him "on my knees" to abdicate. Although Dmitri got grudging praise for his "patriotic participation in the murder of the vile creature who was strangling Russia," Rasputin, he was dismissed as a tool of the Freemasons and a gigolo supported by the "kike tailor" Chanel. Boris, like Dmitri, was perceived as being manipulated by Freemasons and

Jews. Andrew was married to Kshesinskaya, apparently regarded as bad enough in itself. Sandro had deserted his wife and children for "a French adventuress." Marie, although still married to Prince Putiatin, had become "the mistress of an American." These middle-aged Romanovs were the worst: "lechery, mixing with Jews, bankrupt." The possible tsar should therefore be selected from others, for instance the "wonderful youth, Prince Roman Petrovich," son of Grand Duke Peter and nephew of Nikolasha. The bickering led inexorably to a conclusion that the rules of succession would need to be changed altogether. This demanded revolutionary thinking on the part of monarchists, but they were not revolutionary thinkers.

When Kyril met the representatives of Wrangel in January 1923 at Cannes, he did not impress them favorably. They did not like his excessively casual sporting attire, his golden bracelet, his nervous tic, his face "expressing both fierce anger and weakness." Kyril said that the throne belonged either to Nicholas II, the *tsesarevich,* or Grand Duke Michael—all "absent right now"—or to himself as the next closest in line. He said that the Assembly of the Land should announce that Nicholas II and his family had been killed and then introduce him to the throne.

With a malicious smile, Kyril remarked that Nikolasha was apparently waiting for the people to come to the Kremlin and kneel there before him. "Would the grand duke really live to see that day?" he asked sarcastically. Nikolasha, he sneered, was in the hands of the Freemasons acting through the "black menace," Stana.

Meanwhile Nikolasha was continuing to lead the life of a virtual recluse, and even his ardent followers, General Wrangel among them, had to glean information about the grand duke's views and activities from incidental conversations with members of his entourage, with his confessor, for example, the Reverend Spassky. The priest reported in November 1923 that Nikolasha exuded energy, showing interest in everything connected with Russia, participating vigorously in all meetings and talks, contrasting sharply with his behavior in the Crimea in 1918 where Spassky had also seen him. Sometimes, however, Nikolasha would summon his priest and ask him to talk, not about politics, but "solely about God."

Nikolasha's entourage feared Wrangel and did everything they could to compromise him in the eyes of the grand duke. Jealous, they knew only too well that, unlike themselves, Wrangel was a man of independence and of deeds. His sense of initiative certainly compared well with Nikolasha's. The British thought highly of him, and after the civil war, a Foreign Office official commented that "there can be no doubt that General Wrangel is most energetic and if he had been in command of the Volunteer [White] Army from the beginning, it might have reached Moscow."

Nikolasha, always cautious, believed that any discussion of the imperial succession should wait until such time as Nicholas II, Alexis and Michael could all be declared officially dead. He expressed doubts that the Romanovs would ever be invited to return to Russia and thought that if they were it should be the result of an election. And indeed he wondered whether Russia would ever be a monarchy again. Outside intervention in Russian politics would be highly inappropriate, the grand duke declared. The Soviet regime he thought vulnerable to foreign intervention, but foreigners could never establish any kind of government in Russia that would capture the confidence of the Russian people.

Kyril strongly disagreed with his cousin, thinking it possible to reestablish an autocratic monarchical government for Russia outside of Russia and then to transplant it there when the time was right.

Kyril's behavior galvanized Nikolasha into action.

In August 1924, Kyril had sent a letter to Grand Duke Nicholas, addressing him as "Dear Uncle Nikolasha." In the letter Kyril said that he was now convinced that the tsar's family and his brother Michael had been killed and that therefore he had decided to declare himself "Emperor by Law." Kyril pointed out that Nikolasha, although himself silent, was lending his name to different individuals and organizations proclaiming him to be the national leader, thus creating a schism between the two of them. Kyril demanded that Nikolasha declare "the principle of legitimate monarchy," in other words, recognize Kyril.

Back in 1922, Kyril had established a Council for Building Imperial Russia, recruiting Andrew, Dmitri, Miche-Miche and Sandro as grand ducal representatives of the dynasty. The Council comprised forty-four members, and by August of the next year Kyril had his representatives in more than two dozen countries, including France, Britain, the United States, and even China and the Dutch East Indies.

Kyril wrote to "dear Aunt Minnie" that he had been driven by his conscience to assume the title. But Kyril's declaration shocked and dismayed Minnie, who allowed no prayers in her household for the re-

· pose of the soul of Nicholas II, insisting that some day her son might return to her. "My heart was painfully depressed," she said, "nobody is in a position to deprive me of the last gleam of hope." Having reopened the wounds of the unhappy old lady, Kyril declared his "son-like love" for her and begged her "not to abandon him."

On October 20, 1924, Nikolasha made public a letter he had received from the dowager. Minnie wrote,

> Painfully did my heart shrink when I read the manifesto of Grand Duke Kyril Vladimirovich who has proclaimed himself the Emperor of All Russia. . . . Until now there is no precise news about the destiny of my beloved sons and my grandson. . . . So far there has not been a single person who could have extinguished the last beam of hope in me. I am afraid that this manifesto will create a schism and by this not improve, but on the contrary worsen the situation of Russia, tortured enough without that.

In a brief commentary on the letter, Nikolasha rejected Kyril's grand pronouncement and said that only the Russian people should decide the future state system of Russia.

Even those who were not particularly partisan to the cause of any other Romanov found Kyril's declaration of leadership to be offensively abrupt. In the family and beyond, Kyril was never popular and Ducky even less so. But he remained as always quite unflappable, humorless and self-important, seemingly totally unable to cultivate even the family, let alone the general public.

Grand Duke Dmitri too had received an appeal from Kyril to recognize his imperial claims. He told several people that he planned to turn him down and appeared glad to hear that Kyril was ineligible for the throne because his mother had not been Orthodox when he was born. Visiting Choigny, according to Nikolasha and Stana, Dmitri spoke "with indignation about Kyril, about his policy, disastrous for the monarchy." Then, only three days later, in October 1924, Dmitri wrote to Metropolitan Antony, "I recognize His Imperial Highness Grand Duke Kyril Vladimirovich from now on as Emperor of All Russia and obey Him as my true and natural Sovereign."

Dmitri's actions demonstrated that his own judgment was scarcely firm; the relationship between him and Kyril had always been complex. Trying to explain his waverings to acquaintances, Dmitri argued that although Kyril had behaved incorrectly, even badly, if one supported the principles of legitimacy, one had to back Kyril once he had made his declaration.

Among those whom Dmitri talked to about this was General Baratov, his former patron in Persia. To Baratov, Dmitri said that he too had succession rights and "that's why if I had not recognized Kyril, he could have said that I had not done so out of sheer selfishness." Indeed, Dmitri was now number four in the succession line, immediately after Boris and Andrew, who were totally uninterested. Dmitri's claim, unlike those of Kyril or his brothers, was without any religious or marital blemish. His father was a grand duke, his mother a princess of Greece and Orthodox. Furthermore Dmitri had not yet married and thus had the real possibility of enhancing his position by marrying a woman of royal blood. But indecisive Dmitri had never shown any interest in ascending the throne.

Baratov felt sad. He believed Dmitri the "most suitable and the most prepared" of all the Romanovs left to occupy the throne, but he thought, like Grand Duchess Marie, that Dmitri had missed a golden opportunity when "fortune was smiling upon him." He blamed the young man for being distracted by a "sordid dalliance with Chanel, and lechery and debauchery in Parisian pigsties!"

Meanwhile Nikolasha, disgusted by Kyril's behavior, announced on November 16, 1924, from Choigny that he was assuming the supreme leadership over all Russian armed forces, with Wrangel staying as commander-in-chief. He emphasized that his decision had followed the letter from the dowager, and he asked emigrants to unite behind all those "who think like Her Majesty and myself." Nikolasha created his own treasury and began to solicit contributions.

Kyril's supporters began to counterattack. They falsely accused Nikolasha's treasurer of appropriating Russian gold in Japan belonging to all Russian emigrants, a substantial sum kept there by the Russian government during the world war to pay for miltary supplies. The "Kyrilists" also told German politicians that Nikolasha had always been a bitter enemy, a "devourer" of Germans, and therefore was undeserving of their support. While it was true that Nikolasha detested Germans, he had traditionally disliked all foreigners.

Nikolasha disliked politics and those who went in for it. He informed the ROVS generals loyal to him that he did not want the Russian army in exile to get politically involved in any way. "The army,"

Nikolasha declared, "should be *la grande muette* [the great mute]." As his own record demonstrated, he had always been loyal to this principle. This was true even in 1916 when Nikolasha had mutely watched Nicky drag the throne and the dynasty into disaster.

But Nikolasha now recognized that he had to articulate a political platform, remembering that a lack of guiding principles had disabled the White movement during the civil war. His inclination was, as always, to offer a carrot to people he needed. In 1914, he had issued a manifesto to the Poles, promising them a better life. In 1925, he gave a series of interviews to the American press, saying that he favored the restoration of law and order in Russia but that Russians should choose their own form of government guaranteeing personal freedom, law and property rights. Industry, becoming private again, still had to reconcile property rights with the interests of workers. The grand duke suggested a social democratic monarchy, an idea that Kyril would snatch away from him in the future. As for his own role, "I am no pretender," he said, "nor am I an emigré in the old French interpretation of the term. I am merely a citizen and a soldier, anxious to return home in order to aid his fellow-citizens and his country."

General Wrangel was entirely loyal to Nikolasha, although the grand duke never entirely trusted him. In December 1924, Wrangel traveled to Berlin to try to unite the exiles under Nikolasha's political leadership. While he was unsuccessful, he was able to undercut any support for Kyril.

Meanwhile the international environment was bad for all Russian monarchists. Political realities dictated that Soviet Russia was an entity that had to be acknowledged. Left-wing parties in western Europe advocated full diplomatic recognition. On March 16, 1921, the British rang in a new era by signing a commercial treaty with the Soviets. Again the Romanovs grimly saw London abandon the anti-Bolshevik forces.

Then, in April 1922, with the Rapallo Treaty, Moscow and Berlin, both disinherited by the Versailles settlement, signed an agreement, giving the Soviet Union additional international status. The same year, Edouard Herriot, a rising star of French politics, visited Russia for a month and reported favorably on Lenin's "New Economic Policy," his successful attempt to revive market economy agriculture while the nation recovered from war and revolution. American writer Lincoln Steffens, who visited Soviet Russia in 1919, was widely quoted when he said, "I have been over to the future and it works." Steffens and

Herriot were followed by many visitors who returned proclaiming the glories of the Soviet system.

The Romanovs watched the growing global acceptance of the legitimacy of the USSR in frustration and fury. Princess Paley addressed Fridjof Nansen of the League of Nations, complaining that British Prime Minister David Lloyd George was talking to the "ferocious beasts" who had stolen everything from her. The Romanovs suspected Windsor intrigue lying behind their own dynasty's misfortunes. A rumor circulated through the family that while the dowager and her relatives were being taken from the Crimea to Western Europe aboard the battleship *Marlborough*, the captain had received secret orders to return his passengers to Russia, and that only the intervention of indignant Queen Alexandra had prevented the betrayal.

Kyril liked to think that the British were responsible for Minnie's hostile attitude toward his claims, using the "grannies and aunties" of the greater European royal family to encourage the dowager empress to resist his attempt to recreate Russia's monarchy. Kyril remembered the frosty reply Ducky had received from King George V to her impassioned pleas for British aid and intervention when he and Ducky were still in Finland. The British did not want, Kyril said, to see a successful restoration movement, for they were afraid Russia would become strong once again. Having won the great game by default, the British did not want to reopen the contest.

The Romanovs had one more reason to feel bitter toward the Windsors. The Windsors treated them very differently from other displaced European royalty. Long before, the Bourbons, and later Napoleon III and the Empress Eugenie, had found sanctuary in England, and Manuel II of Portugal had also been able to take refuge there.

Indeed, the Hapsburg Emperor Charles I, who had waged war against the Allies in 1916–18, had subsequently received British protection. A British warship, ironically the same *Cardiff* whose officers had been so kind to Grand Duchess Olga, had even taken Charles, so recently an enemy, to a safe haven on the island of Madeira. Why should the British now treat the Romanovs, wartime allies, worse than wartime enemies?

The Romanovs did not yet know that they were in new danger. Recent British, German and French dealings with Moscow, endorsing the legitimacy of the communist regime, had encouraged a reassured Kremlin to take a more militant stance toward all exiles. The Soviet secret police dispatched its agents to Western Europe.

In the summer of 1921, Moscow decided to kidnap Nikolasha and possibly Kyril and Dmitri. The Soviet government aimed to take the grand dukes to the dungeons of the secret police, torture them, put them on public trial and then kill them. The Soviets had executed Romanovs but never before tortured or extracted confessions from them. In the case of Nikolasha, the Soviets had strong motivation; the old soldier had started to fight their regime from abroad in earnest, and they saw him as more dangerous than any of the others.

On March 9, 1923, the indefatigable General Alexander Kutepov, hero of the White army, a capable general, fearless soldier and "knight of honor," as his men called him, had gone to talk to Nikolasha. At that time, the grand duke was refusing to see anybody, believing that after the deluge the Romanovs had no moral right to interfere in politics. However, Kutepov's reputation as iron general and man of deeds served him well. Nikolasha decided to make an exception to his rule and to listen to Kutepov.

Their first conversation proved a disaster. Nikolasha refused even to discuss the issue of his participation in the political struggle. But very few things could stop Kutepov when he had made up his mind. He insisted on a second meeting on March 28th. Although the short-tempered Kutepov had used harsh language in his arguments with the grand duke, Nikolasha nonetheless liked him for his straightforwardness. The grand duke finally agreed to return to the battlefield. He let sixteen emigrant groups unite around him. Nikolasha, moved to action by Kutepov's dreams, decided to create an anti-Bolshevik underground in Russia and chose Kutepov to head it, as well as Nikolasha's intelligence unit.

Wrangel disliked this idea immensely, thinking that no underground was possible in the Soviet domain of terror and fearful that Moscow might entrap the grand duke. He therefore fired Kutepov as his deputy at the Russian All-Military Union. Now Kutepov would run Nikolasha's new Fighting Group instead. It was a small elite body consisting of the most trusted, most energetic and most purposeful men and women he could find among the emigrés. Only thirty-two people in all served during its entire five-year life span.

Nikolasha began to spend a lot of his own money establishing communications with people in Russia and sending agents there. To the struggle he had to bring all his resources. The grand duke knew only too well what the risks were; the Reds were ruthless and he had challenged them directly himself, provoking a very likely revenge.

The French secret police, knowing the danger the grand duke faced, guarded his estate at Choigny night and day. Even familiar faces had to submit to interrogation in order to gain entry; the closest advisors carried identification cards with a seal, bearing the signature of the grand duke and also that of the French secret police boss. The precautions taken by the French police were prompted in part by Nikolasha's popularity in France. Knowledgeable Frenchmen appreciated his contribution to the Allied war effort in 1914–16. Some, at least, remembered that it was Nikolasha who had saved Paris.

But Kutepov insisted that the French security measures were not enough. He supplied Choigny with Cossack guards, later reinforced by several officers loyal to Kutepov personally. Kutepov had a keen sense of the importance of military camaraderie and the shared ordeals of the past. The guards got their instructions from him personally, and he supervised them closely, unexpectedly checking their alertness at any point, day or night. He warned his people that assassination attempts were likely and he stationed guards not only inside the walls of the estate but also around them. They patrolled the land and the house itself continuously.

Never before had any Romanov, in Russia or abroad, taken such precautions. But Kutepov and Nikolasha also knew only too well that there were few barriers that Soviet agents could not penetrate.

No one at Choigny suspected that Wrangel was correct and that Nikolasha's idea of building a monarchist underground in Soviet Russia had been planted by the Soviet secret police itself. The Kremlin, unable to get at Nikolasha easily, the man who was not only the most popular grand duke with the Russian military abroad but also with secret monarchists in Russia, turned to provocation. The best minds in the Soviet secret police created an operation called *Trest* (the word means "trust," in the sense of monopoly). The CIA would make a study of *Trest*, and in 1999 it was still being studied in Russian schools of foreign intelligence as a masterpiece of deception.

Operation Trest was conceived by the counterespionage department of the Soviet secret police, its name now changed from CheKa to OGPU. Its goal was to undermine the monarchist movement both in Russia and abroad. The Soviet's idea was simple: to convince the leaders of the Russian emigré community that a powerful anti-Soviet organization, embracing bureaucrats and the military, had been built clandestinely in the USSR and wanted to unite its efforts with those of Russians in exile in order to overthrow the communist regime.

Exiles dangerous to the Soviet regime had to be persuaded that *Trest* was in dire need both of high-level contacts and a leadership that could operate only on the territory of Soviet Russia. The OGPU needed bait for their trap.

In late fall of 1921, Alexander Yakushev, a former tsarist bureaucrat and now a Soviet agent, traveling in Europe on business as an executive of a Soviet foreign trade commission, had visited his former student, Yuri Artamonov, in Tallinn, Estonia, and told him of a powerful monarchist underground called *Trest*, of which he was a part, flourishing in Soviet Russia.

Artamonov was now the Supreme Monarchist Council's delegate stationed in Tallinn. He became the major channel of communication between *Trest* and monarchists in Berlin and Paris. Through him, Soviet intelligence officers arranged their visits to the European capitals, penetrating the circles of White Guards there.

A number of emigrés, General Kutepov among them, were duped by the Soviet secret police lie and began to plan cooperation between the Romanovs and *Trest*. Officers of the Polish and Finnish General Staffs were also persuaded that *Trest* was genuine. In their correspondence, the naive and good-willed emigré conspirators used a primitive code. Thus Nikolasha became "the Junker," his planned political center was a "firm," Russian military organizations were "brokers," Nikolasha's Choigny estate was "Vienna," and so forth. Kyril received the code name "Zinger."

Moscow was taking Nikolasha even more seriously than many of the emigrés were. Some pointed out in irritation that *Trest* could not be very shrewd if it did not perceive Nikolasha's weaknesses as a leader. But Moscow was pushing, having set its heart on getting the grand duke. The Soviets desperately wanted to weave Nikolasha into their fake conspiracy. The Kremlin even sacrificed its interest in Kyril for the sake of winning Nikolasha's confidence, and the *agent provocateur* from Moscow maintained that all communications with Kyril should be banned.

The naive emigrés, on the other hand, were afraid that if Nikolasha got involved, his entourage would eventually manipulate *Trest*. In other words, people like Artamonov were ready to believe more in *Trest* than they did in Choigny. They therefore planned to surround Nikolasha with *Trest* people. To allay Nikolasha's suspicions, they planned to induce Dmitri to persuade Nikolasha to deal with *Trest* and to open the gates of Choigny to its people. This was before Dmitri sided with Kyril in the issue of imperial succession, at a time when Nikolasha still listened to his younger cousin.

In late 1922, Yakushev, the Kremlin's *agent provocateur,* had stolen his way into Grand Duke Dmitri's confidence, and Dmitri, fascinated by Yakushev's romantic picture of the anti-Bolshevik underground, gave him an encouraging letter to deliver to the political council of the *Trest* and also recommended that Nikolasha meet with Yakushev. The OGPU desperately wanted direct conversations with Choigny.

Moscow had become terrified by the unintended consequences of its success. Believing that *Trest* was a reality, Nikolasha had created Kutepov's Fighting Group of terrorists, ready to take the lives of already paranoid Soviet potentates. The Kremlin decided that it had to penetrate Choigny, first to learn of Nikolasha's plans and then to do away with the grand duke. The grand duke hardly ever left the estate, and so it was impossible to assassinate him in any other place. *Trest* and its advocates abroad pushed to have a representative permanently stationed at Choigny.

In 1923, the Kremlin partially succeeded. On August 27th, Nikolasha received the agent Yakushev at Choigny and enthusiastically talked with him for three hours.

Yakushev, not only an undercover agent but also part of the former imperial establishment, was thrilled. He was impressed by Nikolasha's looks: "He has not changed much since I saw him in 1917 in Tiflis. The same infintely tall body, but he now has artificial teeth and looks younger."

Nikolasha twinkled.

"So, have you come to make sure I am not disabled by palsy?"

Embarrassed, Yakushev presented his proposal.

"Your Highness, you are an enormous trump card for us, but you are the last we have and we cannot take any risks. There is danger of premature action on the side of the emigrants."

Nikolasha frowned.

"Nobody will persuade me to act prematurely. I am waiting for the call of the whole of Russia."

Yakovlev also hoped to get Dmitri involved in the conspiracy. But as soon as Yakushev suggested that Dmitri could become Nikolasha's deputy and presumed successor, the Romanov patriarch exploded.

"I will have no relatives involved! Dmitri Pavlovich? A womanizer! How could he possibly be a tsar! Kyril Vladimirovich? Nobody takes him seriously. His enterprise is a failure. He also has been suffering from a tic since he was in the drink. A nice tsar—grimacing and shaking like a clown!"

Of course the Kremlin was delighted to know that the Romanov family had splintered and was not opposing the Soviets with a powerful and united front. But the Soviets were also alarmed by Nikolasha's readiness to act. The report that his wife, Stana, trembling with enthusiasm, was saying that "it's time to pack" to go back to Russia, was bad news. Stana was known to exercise strong influence on her husband.

The timing was exceptionally bad for the Kremlin.

Yakushev visited Nikolasha in 1923. Two years before, Lenin had announced a "New Economic Policy" (NEP), stimulating both private farming and petty entrepreneurs in the cities. He had launched the NEP to quell mutinies breaking out all over the country. Peasants were killing commissars and refusing to supply the government with grain. In 1921 the most loyal units of the revolutionary army, the sailors of Kronstadt, had revolted, demanding "Soviets without communists," that is, civil rights without the new tyranny. Lenin understood that for a time he must put his iron hand within a velvet glove.

As a result of the NEP, Soviet Russia had recovered swiftly from the civil war. Peasants enthusiastically farmed the lands of the former landlords. Tens of thousands of city dwellers joined the ranks of the "Soviet bourgeoisie." Beef returned to the markets and boots to the shops. Life became tolerable. Lenin saw the NEP as a temporary retreat, a pause for the regime to regain its strength.

Nonetheless the new situation looked dangerous to the Kremlin. The Bolshevik leaders rightly suspected that the economic independence of the peasants and of the "bourgeoisie" would inevitably evoke longing for a full-scale market economy and for political freedoms. They feared that a comeback of the Whites would have been welcomed by millions. With their own hands, Bolsheviks had thus created an environment favorable for restoration!

Then there was also the troublesome matter of a struggle for power within the Kremlin itself. Lenin suffered his first stroke in 1922, and after that could not rule either the country or the party. His disciples and friends, demonstrating surprisingly little interest in his fate, had begun quarreling with one another, taking sides, and scheming over the question of who would be the future leader of Russia.

Stalin won out over the others very unexpectedly. The great influenza pandemic in 1919 had conveniently taken care of his chief rival, Yakov Sverdlov, whose primary memorial would be Yekaterinburg, renamed Sverdlovsk. Another major candidate, Leon Trotsky, was so self-assured that he failed to watch out for Stalin's progress. The result for him was exile and ultimate murder. By the time of Lenin's death in January 1924, Stalin had become the first among equals—the leader of the party, but very far from being a dictator yet.

The wily Stalin could not be sure of his personal victory, and he expected unrest within Russia fomented by Trotskyites and others opposed to him. What frightened him most was the possibility that domestic opposition and emigré military leaders would meet and unite their efforts, possibly supported by some Western powers.

Within the country Stalin relied more and more on the secret police as a tool in his struggle for supreme power. The OGPU, with its headquarters in the massive but squat Lubyanka not far from the Kremlin, was instrumental in insuring the stability of the regime. Its head, Felix Dzerzhinsky, was patiently and relentlessly trying to seize the leaders of Russia abroad, keeping control of all top secret operations within his own hands. Stalin followed the OGPU activities in Europe impatiently. He had high hopes for *Trest,* alarmed as he was by secret police reports that confirmed his worst fears: Local branches of OGPU from all over the country reported popular hatred toward the Bolsheviks. Former members of the imperial elite were attempting to organize themselves. Many small monarchist groups formed in Petrograd and Moscow. The secret police were frantically trying to keep up with developments and files swelled in the Lubyanka.

The regime learned that the peasantry, still the backbone of the nation, was the least reliable segment. The Archangel OGPU branch office reported that local peasants were saying that "the British will land in Archangel and then Soviet power will be done for." Peasants in Severo-Dvinsk gladly anticipated terror against the Bolsheviks. "All Communists, Comsomol members, and Pioneers will be either shot or hanged and this is the right thing to do, for it is God's punishment." The "Old Believers," religious fundamentalists, insisted that they had mystic knowledge proving that Soviet power would fall in 1933, "and then Russia will be governed by a tsar again." This was bad enough for Stalin. Worse was that people in Russia seemed to know precisely who would be the next tsar. The answer was uniform: Nikolasha.

When in March 1921 the Soviet press reported falsely that Niko-lasha had died in Lausanne, Muscovites felt heartbroken. "There is one *good* Romanov less. . . . He was a kind and sweet person." Un-fortunately for the Bolsheviks, however, Nikolasha was very much alive and his image as the "good Romanov" persisted. Within three months of Lenin's death in April 1924, an exciting rumor spread all over Moscow that Nikolasha had sent a special manifesto to the cap-ital of Soviet Russia. Nikolasha's mere name could provoke a signifi-cant stir, filling the Kremlin with suspicion and fear.

For his part, the old soldier could now be optimistic about the prospects of his cause in Russia. Lenin's NEP had opened a window of opportunity for restoration. Military analysts in Nikolasha's circle did not hesitate to pronounce that Soviet Russia was undergoing a cri-sis. Stabilization of the regime was only superficial. In the summer of 1921, the Bolshevik leaders were forced to admit that "the central area of the Russian republic was surrounded by an almost unbroken ring of peasant uprisings." As late as that autumn, the Cossack areas, especially in the Don basin, had dozens of guerrilla groups, some of them consisting of several hundred men. In one month alone, May 1922, the secret police had arrested 350,000 political suspects. White generals believed that the NEP not only "has not reached its pro-claimed goal, to strengthen Communism, but has also caused the weakening of the Soviet regime."

Nikolasha and the White generals abroad received much evidence of the grand duke's popularity inside Russia. A peasant from the Yeka-terinoslav area, for instance, wrote that "People say that soon we will have Nicholas Nikolaevich. Inhumanity comes to an end, though right now more and more blood is spilled." But Nikolasha and Kutepov wanted more than this secondhand evidence. They dispatched people to Soviet Russia to make direct assessments of the situation.

Their agents normally crossed the Polish border and then headed east, disguised and dressed as peasants, having memorized invented biographies. The physical strain alone was challenging. Agents had to cover huge distances by night, walking in the fields and in the woods, never using the roads. One of them remembered, "At any rustle or if a dog barked or if the moon came out from the clouds, I had to lie prone. My feet were tangled by rye and bindweed. My clothing, even underwear, was completely wet." Having penetrated as deeply into Russia as they could, these men would start talking to peasants and soldiers, sounding out the situation, exploring the social tensions, assessing the state of military equipment, the morale of the army and the police, the food supply, the general mood. The task was always dangerous; one never knew whether he was asking questions of the wrong person, a secret police agent, for instance. Yet some were successful.

Even if *Trest* orchestrated several of these visits, the OGPU still could not control the flow of other agents moving secretly from the Polish border to Moscow or Petrograd. In September 1923, one of these agents reported, "The name of Grand Duke Nicholas Nikolaevich is surrounded with love and respect. I have passed through many villages. . . . He is especially revered by former soldiers." Presumably such information was passed to the Kremlin, inflaming Soviet anxieties.

In the second half of 1923, having already amassed considerable information, Nikolasha and Kutepov decided to activate their plan to overthrow the Bolsheviks. They knew that Lenin was now extremely ill (actually totally incapacitated), and the regime itself looked internally unstable. On the other hand, Nikolasha's age was of concern to him and his supporters. In 1923 he was sixty-seven, and the Romanov males were not known for their longevity.

Nikolasha's concept of restoration totally excluded foreign intervention. He was deeply patriotic. He and his advisors, both generals and intellectuals like philosopher Ivan Ilyin, planned as follows:

> Moscow is the key to Russia. . . . Moscow should become the center of counter revolution. Therefore a conspiracy should be organized there and with extreme caution, using the experience of revolutionaries themselves. It is possible to buy loyalty of the military and of the bureaucracy, as Napoleon bought Talleyrand and Barras. Of special interest are new generals who have risen from the lower classes. They are ambitious and ignorant. People like Semyon Budhenny, the famous cavalry leader [also proverbially dullwitted] will yet serve the tsar.

Strikes would start in the major industrial centers. "The most prominent leaders of the Soviet regime" would be assassinated. Uprisings then would start in other big cities. Communists would be exterminated, the police disarmed, barricades in the cities built. A peasant uprising would join the counterrevolution. Nikolasha's troops, consisting of White emigrés, would liberate some area bordering upon Poland or Finland. Nikolasha would then step on Russian soil and from that time lead the struggle in person.

In the fall of 1923 Nikolasha and Kutepov thought that their plan was already underway, but this was an illusion that the OGPU was elaborately creating. Still unable to kidnap or kill Nikolasha, the Lubyanka was preparing a tighter net for him. Kutepov's people went to Moscow and liked what they saw; *Trest* looked impressive. Kutepov's agents reported, "The things I have seen at our friends this time make me appreciate anew how active, talented, and endowed with extraordinary organizational skills the leaders of *Trest* are." The agents became so excited that they worried they would miss the *coup* in Moscow and begged Yakushev "not to deprive us of the joy of participating in armed struggle." Yakushev sardonically promised to grant that wish. *Trest* started sending intelligence reports to Kutepov concerning the Red Army. The reports were disinformation but looked genuine, listing many figures like numbers of tanks and armored trains and even the current whereabouts of major army units.

Kutepov agreed to represent *Trest* in Paris, and on November 5, 1924, he arranged for Yakushev to visit Choigny. The visit was a disaster for the Soviet spy. The major purpose of Yakushev's Choigny visit was to empty Nikolasha's treasury. He said that *Trest* needed ten million dollars, a huge sum those days. Nikolasha refused, but what dismayed Yakushev and his Kremlin masters was that Nikolasha and Kutepov were insisting on the immediate use of terror, arguing that political assassinations and sabotage could provoke the desired social detonation in Russia. The horrified Yakushev did his best to persuade Kutepov that violence was totally unnecessary and that *Trest* should be given time to grow quietly. But the grand duke was listening to Yakushev with growing distrust.

The grand duke's uneasiness was explained by a disaster that had occurred some time ago, the Soviet capture of the pre-revolutionary terrorist, now anti-Bolshevik Boris Savinkov. By 1921, Savinkov had emerged as one of the most prominent leaders of the anti-Bolshevik struggle. Long before the revolution he had been a terrorist, working against the imperial government. For his role in the murder of Grand

Duke Sergei just inside the walls of the Kremlin, he had been arrested by the tsarist police and sentenced to death. He escaped to Switzerland, where he started a new career as a novelist, writing under the pen name of Ropshin, specializing in description of the Dostoevskian souls of Russian terrorists. *The Pale Horse,* its title taken from The Book of Revelation, became a huge success. In World War I, Savinkov served in the French army and returned to Russia after the February revolution. By August 1917, he had risen to become Deputy Minister of War in Kerensky's government. When the Bolsheviks came to power, Savinkov staged conspiracies inside Russia and stirred the refugee community in Europe. Savinkov caught the attention of Winston Churchill, who wrote vividly of "this strange and sinister man. Small of stature, moving as little as possible and that noiselessly and with deliberation; with remarkable grey-green eyes in a a face of almost deathly pallor; speaking in a calm, even voice, almost a monotone." Boris Savinkov had dedicated his career to conspiracy.

Savinkov swallowed bait dangled by *Trest*'s twin, another fake underground group, *Syndikat*. In August 1924, he crossed the Soviet border into Russia in order to lead a purported anti-Bolshevik underground. He was arrested and given a show trial at which he publicly confessed. Nikolasha couldn't help wondering whether he was walking into the same sort of trap. To probe *Trest*'s authenticity, the grand duke kept insisting on terrorism and sabotage.

The Kremlin and the Lubyanka, having conferred, decided that either Nikolasha or Kutepov, preferably both, had to be liquidated immediately. Officers of *Trest* informed Nikolasha that it was necessary to send to Moscow "one of the most outstanding representatives of the army, so that that person would live here for a while and learn more about ideas and ideology of the party and its attitude towards the White army and then return." Neither Nikolasha nor Kutepov liked the idea. *Trest* leadership then decided on blackmail. *Trest* operatives wrote to Kutepov, "We have reasons to believe that the party [i.e., *Trest*] would accept General Wrangel, who is very popular here, as its leader and break up with the grand duke." This was a poisoned arrow. The schism between Nikolasha and Wrangel was widening. Wrangel intensely disliked Kutepov's secret dealings with Russia and did not conceal those views. The only person to mend the situation, Kutepov's *Trest* correspondents told him, is "you." *Trest* agents proposed that Kutepov meet its leaders at the Neman (Niemen) River in

Poland, between the villages of Stolbtsy and Rodshkovo, not more than twenty-four miles from the Soviet border. For a while Kutepov hesitated. He even marked the place of this dangerous rendezvous on a map of Poland. Eventually, he did not go.

The Kremlin did not despair. Now it turned to Nikolasha as prime target. Of course, it was impossible to imagine the grand duke making a risky journey to the Russian border, with Kutepov so stubbornly concerned about his security. The imaginative OGPU conceived another plan. *Trest* operatives informed Kutepov and Nikolasha that the leaders of the monarchist underground wanted Nikolasha to move from Choigny either to England or to Germany, for it would be "easier to communicate with *Trest*" from there.

The Soviet plan was simple. Because Choigny was like a fortress, it was impossible to penetrate. Kutepov's security service did not earn its bread for nothing. But if the grand duke were to take a journey either to Britain or to Germany, it would be infinitely easier to kidnap or assassinate him at a railway station or even on the doorstep of Choigny.

The plan did not work. Nikolasha felt comfortably protected at Choigny. The idea of going to another country seemed bizarre to him. Instead, he sent a message that he regarded as top secret and ordered his aide, "Let Kutepov transmit the message orally, without any documents. Let them take notes while he talks." The message in question was a plan for military intervention. Nikolasha did not believe in the magic of foreign bayonets. He thought that the Bolsheviks should be defeated by Russians. Ideally, the intervening force would consist of one hundred thousand, but scraping together that number of men from the Russian community abroad would be extremely difficult. The minimal number was fifteen thousand in the Far East, in Manchuria, and twenty-five thousand in Finland. Both armies would strike "when an uprising occurs in Russia," and their numbers would swell from the disaffected in the homeland.

With Moscow terrified by the prospects of uncontrolled terrorism and perhaps even military intervention carried out by the fanatic monarchists, Yakushev returned to Choigny to see the grand duke in the summer of 1925 and tried to persuade him to listen solely to *Trest*. Nikolasha felt somewhat uneasy about the visit. No doubt the fate of Boris Savinkov, who had committed a problematic suicide in a Soviet jail in May, was still very much on his mind. He curtly responded, "I trust only Kutepov. Kutepov and none other!"

The nervous Yakushev made a slip. He referred to the fighting going on between armed Moslem groups in Central Asia and the Red Army there, saying that it was exactly the kind of help *Trest* needed. Nikolasha's eyebrows rose sharply. His motto had always been "Russia single and undivided."

"I am afraid of separatism," he curtly remarked. "Anyway, the Moslems will trust me."

And then Yakushev made a third mistake. Wanting to ravage the grand duke's purse, he begged for money again, saying that it was needed in order to ruin Soviet currency. Nikolasha met the request with an icy silence.

The atmosphere warmed slightly during lunch, attended by Stana. She looked extremely well, her beautiful eyes still shining like black olives. She even kissed Yakushev on his bald spot, saying, "You just cannot know how precious you are for me." Nikolasha remained withdrawn.

Several weeks after the meeting between Nikolasha and Yakushev, in September 1925, the monarchist movement lost a prominent figure, Sidney Reilly, an international adventurer of Russian origins, a fierce anti-Bolshevik conspirator in 1918–19, a man of many wives and mistresses, and a British master spy. Like Savinkov with *Syndikat*, Reilly had succumbed to the enticements of *Trest*. He was lured across the Soviet border in September 1925, to disappear forever in the labyrinths of the Soviet secret police.

But the truth about *Trest* was still not exposed.

Throughout 1925, Wrangel openly expressed his doubts to Nikolasha and others about *Trest*, but many others refused to share his skepticism. Vassily Shulgin, one of the two monarchists who had extracted an abdication from Nicholas II, risked his own life to check the authenticity of *Trest*. Shulgin had a personal reason to return to Russia: He desperately wanted to find his son, who was allegedly a patient in a mental asylum. The Soviets gladly permitted Shulgin to visit secretly in December 1925. Of course the poor man never found his son, who had been long dead. But he did verify *Trest*'s credentials to his own satisfaction and even wrote a book complimenting the Bolsheviks on their controversial but impressive economic performance. He sent the manuscript to *Trest* for clearance and the Kremlin liked the flattering tone of it immensely. Shulgin became an ardent endorser of *Trest* and criticized Wrangel for labeling it a trap.

In 1926, Yakushev saw Nikolasha for what would be the last time. Choigny now seemed hostile to him. Nikolasha received Yakushev dressed in an old jacket. His boots were covered with mud. Apparently he had just been for a walk within the protected walls of his estate. His first words to Yakushev were, "We should act, act!"

"Unthinkable, Your Highness. No sooner than in two years."

"Nonsense," Nikolasha snorted.

Yakushev then proceeded to the major errand he had been assigned by the Lubyanka. He suggested that Kutepov should visit Russia to assess the situation for himself. Kutepov refused. Alarmed, Yakushev kowtowed to Nikolasha, begging him to write a manifesto for the Red Army and also to give *Trest* a token of his friendship, his own portrait. Nikolasha obliged with both, the portrait being an inspiring one of the grand duke on horseback.

Operation *Trest* seemed to be doomed. The Kremlin did not succeed in capturing Kutepov or Nikolasha; one could scarcely interrogate a portrait in the dungeons of the Lubyanka. Desperate, in March 1927, Yakushev again suggested that Kutepov visit the Soviet Union. Again Kutepov declined the invitation.

Reilly remained the only prominent loss among the monarchists. Choigny remained closed. The old soldier was too shrewd to expose himself in such fashion.

The shocking truth about *Trest* finally emerged in April 1927 when two Soviet defectors fled to Finland and revealed the story. Enraged, Nikolasha and Kutepov ordered an all-out attack. This time they sent terrorists into Russia.

Their "Fighting Group," as it was called, was almost like a religious order. All its people were volunteers, with a missionary zeal. Former White officers saved their own money for three years, economizing fiercely, in order to equip themselves to enter the Soviet Union on a secret combat mission. Nikolasha lacked money even to pay their expenses. Before each mission Kutepov would bless each volunteer personally, never betraying any emotion, just giving his orders briskly and shaking hands. If he thought a person were not ready for the mission, which was, after all, almost suicidal, he would not hesitate to cancel the operation completely.

On June 7, 1927, one Kutepov group threw a grenade at a very minor meeting in Leningrad, and the same summer Kutepov's people were able to explode a bomb in a reception office at the Lubyanka in

Moscow, the heart of the Soviet secret police apparatus. These were impressive, but isolated acts. Bad luck gripped Kutepov's people. Eighty percent of them died, and many of them died the most horrible death imaginable at the hands of the Soviet secret police.

In early summer 1928, Kutepov sent another group with the ambitious goal of assassinating one of the leading Soviet officials, Nicholas Bukharin, who mixed with people more easily than the rest of the top echelon of the Kremlin. The terrorists failed. But *Agent Provocateur* Yakushev was so frightened by the long arm of Nikolasha that he left Moscow in panic and for a while lived anonymously in a refuge provided him by the OGPU.

On the morning of January 6, 1929, the patriarch of Russian literature, Ivan Bunin, who had met Tolstoy and had been friendly with Chekhov, summoned his wife, Vera Nikolaevna, to his room. Bunin was heartbroken; he had just learned that Grand Duke Nicholas Nikolaevich had died.

Some years earlier, when the grand duke had fallen seriously ill with pneumonia, the *New York Times* commented that "everyone who admires manliness, dignity, and high ability when found in the descendant of kings had to be sorry to hear of it." The newspaper continued wryly by saying that "for a Russian grand duke, [Nikolasha was] a truly remarkable man." In 1929, at age seventy-two, Nikolasha had come down from Choigny to enjoy the milder climate of the Riviera.

Russian Orthodox Christmas fell on January 7th, coinciding with the requiem of the grand duke. His body stayed at Villa Tenard, a plain white house standing inside the grounds of a big estate, with an officer in Imperial Russian uniform posted at the door. Mourners crowded the antechamber. Within, Nikolasha lay in a deep oaken coffin resting on low benches placed within a hall with three windows and a high ceiling. The doors of the hall were covered with red velvet; the body was dressed in a black *cherkesska,* the Cossack uniform. The grand duke looked very thin, his chest sunken, and his enormous height now accentuated by death. His head seemed shrunken, and his face no longer resembled those in his portraits. Nonetheless Bunin found Nikolasha in death to evoke not horror but admiration. "Lying in the coffin, long, meagre, red-haired. With the chest of a chicken. But the fist is *that big!* And this huge fist grasps a cyprus cross, like a cudgel. Splendid! What a tsar-like corpse!"

Cossacks stood at attention on both sides of the coffin and a huge wreath stood by its cover; a metal plate fastened to the cover said in Latin letters: Nicholas NICOLAEVITCH. (The Frenchman who had made the plate thought "Nicolaevitch" was his last name, which is why the patronymic was engraved in capital letters.) A table with icons stood in the corner of the room. Everything was quiet and plain. A young man sat reading the Psalter.

Like others there, Bunin was in tears. "When I saw him forty years ago at a railway station in Orel where he was pacing the platform— he was bringing home the remains of his father—splendid, young, with reddish curly hair, could I have ever thought that our lives would cross and I would bow to his remains at Antibes?"

Just before the requiem mass began, the widow, Stana; her brother-in-law Grand Duke Peter; her sister, his wife Militsa; and their children entered the room, all dressed in deep mourning. A priest with a reputation for always conducting the service properly arrived from Cannes. A Cossack choir sang. After the requiem, Peter and Militsa came to the coffin, knelt, prayed and kissed the cross and the hand grasping it. Then Nikolasha's nephew Roman and nieces Marina and Nadezhda; his stepson, Prince Sergei of Leuchtenberg; and his stepdaughter, Princess Helen came to the bier. After the family, the public was allowed to approach to pay their respects. Many brought wreaths. Those who could not afford a wreath brought bunches of white carnations.

Peter, resembling not his brother but his uncle, Alexander II, appeared overcome and frequently used his handkerchief. One can only wonder who grieved more: Nikolasha's emotional twin, Peter, or his powerful widow, Stana. Finally Peter and Militsa bowed to everyone and left. Peter would die two years later, in 1931, also in Antibes, as would Stana, in 1935.

In its obituary the *New York Times* called Nikolasha "the natural head of the family" and judged his behavior, unlike some of the other Romanovs, exemplary. Indeed Nikolasha had never lost his dignity under the most trying circumstances: when the tsar removed him from the supreme command, when the Bolsheviks imprisoned him in the Crimea, when the Germans sought to rescue him from the Bolsheviks, when he was obliged to flee his homeland on a British warship, when he lost his grand ducal wealth.

Many European nations sent military officers to represent them at the old soldier's funeral. British Major General Knox, who had known Nikolasha well during the early months of the world war, wrote of his old comrade, "with him dies a true son of Holy Russia, and the greatest of his generation of Romanovs."

Joseph Stalin undoubtedly rejoiced at Nikolasha's death. With the old grand duke gone, a Romanov restoration became unlikely. But Stalin lived in a nightmare of paranoia, and a man in Paris frightened him. This was Alexander Kutepov, Nikolasha's old comrade-in-arms.

After the exposure of *Trest* as a Soviet ruse, Kutepov directed the Fighting Group, although his agents were none too successful. Stalin even found them somewhat useful as a pretext for tightening his political control over the nation. The terrorists so far appeared to be poorly connected in Moscow and thus had no special access to potential targets. But who could guarantee that one day they would not be lucky? No member of this small elite Fighting Group, Nikolasha's brainchild, knew about anything more than his own mission. No torture could therefore yield to the Kremlin the complete knowledge of the Group. With Nikolasha's death, in 1929 Kutepov became the sole keeper of its secrets.

Kutepov claimed that he now worked with the posthumous blessing of the Grand Duke Nicholas Nikolaevich. For Kutepov, and many others, Nikolasha's blessing had been equal to God's will. Kutepov, of solid build and hearty manner, courageous and energetic, was a soldier, not a statesman. But Kutepov looked dangerous to Stalin, a potential organizer of a Russian putsch. He was not an imagined enemy or a mere suspect. He was a mortal foe, a mortal foe with strong and stable monarchist sympathies. Nikolasha was dead; Dmitri politically inactive; Kyril only a mock emperor. These facts were good news for Stalin. But monarchism as a motivation and even as a political force was very much alive.

In 1930 Stalin ordered a military operation known as *Spring*, in which the OGPU arrested five thousand former tsarist officers then serving in the Red Army. Simultaneously, Stalin directed an attack on the monarchist generals in Paris. Kutepov's people knew how vulnerable he was to kidnapping or assassination. They feared that Stalin's agents were following him and asked the general to give them a phone call each time he returned home.

Stalin wanted Kutepov brought to Moscow alive. He had someone close to Kutepov working secretly for him. This was General Steifon, Kutepov's chief of staff during the Civil War and now a close associate at ROVS. Steifon, on Kutepov's behalf, had made several clandestine trips to the Soviet Union and brought back very encouraging news. There was in Russia, he declared, a viable underground with which ROVS could work. Despite the bitter lesson of *Trest,* Kutepov rejoiced. He did not know that Steifon had long ago been recruited by the Kremlin.

On Sunday, January 26, 1930, slightly more than a year after Nikolasha's death, Steifon told Kutepov in Paris that two representatives of the anti-Bolshevik movement in Russia urgently needed to talk to him. Kutepov responded with excitement. Only a day before he had expressed a desire to go to Russia and lead the uprisings of the peasants outraged by Stalin's genocidal collectivization. When Steifon told him that the two representatives from Russia were waiting outside in a taxi, Kutepov decided to see them.

Actually the two in the taxi were Soviet agents. A third conspirator, dressed as a French policeman, had been placed close enough on the street so that when a bystander saw Kutepov bundled into the taxi, the kidnapping could be passed off as a police arrest.

The car with Kutepov in it rushed to the English Channel, where he was drugged and taken aboard the Soviet freighter *Spartacus.* But his kidnappers miscalculated, and the dosage proved too strong. Although the outside world would not know it for a long time, Kutepov scored the final victory by dying aboard the ship when it was still one hundred miles off Novorossiysk. Ironically Kutepov had been among the last of the Whites to evacuate that seaport in 1920.

Death at sea saved Kutepov from the dungeons of the Soviet secret police, but people in Paris did not know this. General Evgeny Miller, Kutepov's successor as head of ROVS, himself a notable commander of White forces during the civil war, exclaimed, "The worst thing for Kutepov's wife is that she does not know how to pray for him, as a living man or a dead one." Emigrés in Paris could imagine the terror and anguish of Kutepov in the torture chambers of the Lubyanka. All felt a cold shiver of horror.

For the whole previous decade the Kremlin had seemed to belong to a remote barbaric peripheral world, buffered from central and western Europe by a cordon of states like Poland, Hungary and Romania. The *Trest* operation frightened many, but after all the Kremlin had captured Savinkov and Reilly on its own territory. Stalin had seemed to be on the defensive.

The kidnapping of Kutepov signified that no one was safe any longer. Murderous Soviet agents were living in Paris, moving around on the streets, drinking and eating in cafes and restaurants alongside the Russians of the emigrant community! What was even more terrible was the sudden knowledge that the community had been penetrated to its very core by the Soviets. Your lifetime friend with whom you might have shared the trenches of the great war and then the battlefields of the civil war could be secretly planning to kidnap or kill you! The Soviets suddenly appeared to be omnipotent. They could take people at will right in the heart of Europe, and a great fear descended upon the Russian exiles. Grand Duke Peter's family took comfort in their own two cossacks, armed with sword and pistol. The French police increased their protection of all the Romanovs in France.

The Romanovs living in Paris, at last feeling that they must speak for the community, sent a collective letter to the French government asking for help. An associate of Grand Duke Andrew gave the letter to Prime Minister Andre Tardieu himself. When the man handed over the letter, Tardieu bent over to his ear and whispered, "Captain, I beg you to tell General Miller [head of ROVS], and only him, that our thread of investigation leads directly into General Kutepov's office at the Rue de Colisée!"

Stalin probably hated Miller as much as he had Kutepov. The mild and affable Miller, unexpectedly and reluctantly finding himself Kutepov's successor as head of ROVS, lamented that he was alone, that the treasury of the organization held only thirty francs, and that he had not the slightest idea what Kutepov's secret operations had been all about. Nonetheless he quickly pulled the organization together.

Miller despatched agents into Soviet Russia again, even while the Great Terror raged there, although fewer than before. Some survived to return and report. Miller closely followed events in the USSR and reacted quickly to them. In the summer of 1930, for instance, he received intelligence from the Soviet Far East about peasant unrest caused by Stalin's brutal land collectivization and immediately held a conference to weigh possible military intervention in the area, under the leadership of White General Mikhail Diderichs.

Stalin, having failed with Kutepov, still wanted to bring an ROVS leader to Moscow, to extract everything he knew and to kill him properly, that is, with the maximum pain. Kutepov had been too lucky. With Miller there would be no overdose. On September 22, 1937, General Miller disappeared, again in broad daylight on a busy Paris street.

That morning, a Soviet plant in the ROVS office, General Nikolai Skoblin, had informed Miller that two "Germans" were waiting to see him. Miller smelled a rat and took the precaution of leaving a note with his secretary to be opened in case he failed to return. Miller left the office, but the secretary failed to take the matter seriously. When, later in the day, the alarmed staff began to question Skoblin about where Miller had gone, the traitor ran out of the office and fled abroad. Having accomplished his purpose, he would later be murdered by the Soviets in Spain.

Miller was brought to the Soviet Embassy, carefully sedated, put into a large wooden crate and taken by truck to the port of Le Havre. The truck was later identified as bearing the license plate 235X CD, registered some five weeks earlier in the name of the Soviet ambassador to France. At Le Havre, the Soviet vessel *Maria Ulianova* sailed for home unexpectedly early.

Miller survived the journey, unhappily for him. In Moscow he was brutally interrogated and then shot. The Romanovs were frightened by what happened to Miller because grand dukes and grand duchesses were, after all, still conspicuous. Everyone knew who they were. In France, the police went out of their way to help. Police agents would often shadow the Romanovs. From time to time, discovering a new Moscow agent, they would inform the Romanovs to be careful of that person. The family took what precautions they could against the possibility of kidnapping. But they did not have the resources for adequate protection.

The family of Nikolasha's late brother Peter, exhausted by the strain of constant fear, decided to leave France. Queen Elena of Italy invited her sister and family to come to Rome, where they could be safely sheltered. They thereupon abandoned their villa at Antibes and left in a hurry. They had no interest in politics, only in survival.

CHAPTER THIRTEEN

❧

"Always Be Visible"

NOT ALL THE ROMANOVS HAD GIVEN UP POLITICS. Those who continued a political life had to struggle with a difficult question. How could one possibly survive and defeat the Bolsheviks? Who were possible allies for that effort? The western European nations did not want the Romanovs back on their throne. Contrary to Romanov hopes, the Soviet Union, despite its famines and purges and the suffering of its people, remained stable. Other nations had no intention of intervening there. And in the early 1930s a younger generation of Russian exiles were looking for something more than daydreams of past glories that they scarcely remembered, or wreaking bloody vengeance that seemed to be more costly to the perpetrators than to their targets. The Young Russians Movement sprang out of a craving to create a political group that could carry the exiles back to Russia. To many of them, Italian fascism seemed an attractive model. Fascism did have room for monarchy, and this was of interest to at least some of the Romanovs.

The Young Russians' founder was Alexander Kazem-Bek, a young aristocrat born in 1902. His ancestors had moved to Russia from Persia in the early nineteenth century and joined the ranks of imperial high society. Kazem-Bek's grandfather had married Leo Tolstoy's sister. After the revolution, Kazem-Bek's family left Russia hurriedly, and the precocious Alexander began to dabble in politics, founding an association of generals' sons.

In 1923, Kazem-Bek had tried to solicit the support of Nikolasha, that most inspiring of living Romanovs. The grand duke refused even to receive a youngster of such uncertain motives. Kazem-Bek then wrote Nikolasha's rival, Kyril, and suggested that he accept for Russia the Italian model of a monarch presiding over populist institutions. Kyril expressed interest. One cannot say that the grand duke was then being overwhelmed by attention from younger exiles. Better this adventurous Kazem-Bek than no one.

"Adventurous" was perhaps the most charitable thing one could say about Kazem-Bek. He had the reputation of a "careerist and opportunist." Yet everyone, even his ill-wishers, grudgingly agreed that he was a "smart boy."

The Young Russians movement preached Orthodoxy, nationalism, monarchism and peasant collectivism. Kazem-Bek acknowledged that in the revolution the Russian people had sided with the Bolsheviks. Therefore a new monarchy for Russia must capture their allegiance by preserving the social gains of the lower classes in Russia. Kazem-Bek advocated a monarchy for Russia, with Grand Duke Kyril as tsar, but one preserving the social gains the Soviet system had achieved for the lower classes.

On January 20, 1936, Kazem-Bek boldly declared:

> We believe in Russia. We watch what is going on there. We know that monarchy can be reborn only through Russia alive, through Russians living on the Russian land. . . . [Others] would like to build monarchy by whining memories and weeping about the past—a great past, but the past nevertheless. And you forget that in spite of unacceptable government, in spite of disgusting authorities, Russian life is constantly evolving; Russia is being renewed; it grows and strengthens, and the Russian people are being revived with her.

Terror or no terror, Kazem Bek proclaimed, millions of Russians had climbed the social staircase. Peasant girls, before 1917 doomed to bleak lives in patriarchal village households, were now becoming engineers, pilots and factory managers. Russia had emerged as a significant industrial and military power again. This was a phenomenon in which *all* Russians could take pride.

Kazem-Bek liked Italian fascism because it would allow him a position of power in a new Russia following the Italian triad of monarch, leader and nation. He aspired to be a Russian *Duce*. Indeed in 1935, at the height of the popularity of the Young Russians, crowds of youths with outstretched right arms would chant at rallies in Paris, "Glava! Glava! Glava!" ("Leader! Leader! Leader!") as Italians were then shouting "Duce! Duce! Duce!" in Rome beneath Mussolini's balcony.

Again inspired by Mussolini, Kazem-Bek encouraged his young followers to dress uniformly in dark blue shirts though, impoverished, all of them could not afford to do so. The emblem of the Young Russians was an orb, symbol of monarchy, topped by a cross, standing for Russian Orthodoxy, or, as Kazem-Bek put it, "the predominance of the spiritual over the material." The official color of the party was blue, for some reason identified with "reconciliation and the cooperation of national and social elements."

Most of the Young Russians were like Kazem-Bek, men in their twenties and early thirties blaming their parents for having lost Russia, restless and eager for political action, and wanting to build a new relationship with the motherland.

Sixty years later, in her Paris apartment, Grand Duchess Leonida, daughter-in-law of Kyril and Ducky, would recall that "at that point everyone was a Young Russian." Now more or less forgotten, then the movement was the only real organization for Russian monarchism not simply a fringe group. The Young Russians were a virtual political party, supported by most monarchists and most of the Orthodox clergy in exile.

Grand Duke Dmitri, surprisingly enough, given his reputation as eternal playboy, allowed himself to be named chairman of the Council of the Young Russians. This body formed the nominal collective leadership of the party, and on it Dmitri represented the dynasty and, even more specifically, "Emperor" Kyril. Perhaps Dmitri now turned to politics and the possibility of a public life because his private life was collapsing.

On November 21, 1926, he had married a commoner, an American heiress from Cincinnati named Audrey Emery. They were wed at the Russian church in Biarritz, his bride having previously converted to Orthodoxy. By this morganatic marriage, Dmitri not only prejudiced any prospects for the succession himself but also barred any of his future offspring from consideration. Had he chosen instead to marry royalty, his claim to the imperial throne would have been stronger than that of anyone else.

Audrey's father, John Josiah Emery, had died in 1908, leaving his daughter with a multimillion-dollar fortune. Audrey was very attractive, and her beauty and wealth combined to make her one of the most eligible and sought after American women in France. The romance between Dmitri and Audrey was quick. After their marriage they settled in London where they had a son, Paul, in 1928, named for his murdered grandfather, the Grand Duke Paul Alexandrovich.

The couple also spent time in Biarritz and at Neuilly-sur-Seine. To many observers, the hasty marriage seemed the result of Dmitri's cynical hunt for economic security. But his old friend, General Baratov, took the marriage as a good sign. He hoped that the young man would now cease his debauchery, quoting the old Russian proverb, "You change when you marry." "Now it is my greatest hope," Baratov sighed, "with the birth of his child, particularly because it is a son!"

However, that proved to be wishful thinking. Family life did not go well. Audrey, little Paul and Dmitri fled to America in 1932, looking for a happier life together. Dmitri did not like New York, although he was impressed by its skyscrapers and the new Empire State Building, then the world's tallest building. What he liked best was Florida with its palm trees, cactuses, exotic flowers and—last but not least—fishing in the Gulf Stream. But America did not help Dmitri and Audrey. The marriage, Dmitri's attempt to build a normal family life, fell apart by 1933, and four years later the couple were formally divorced. Dmitri returned permanently to Europe.

Europe, though, did not help to cure his ennui. He met no new person to care about; his friendship with Felix was over; his relationships with other Romanovs were formal and detached. Dmitri also felt estranged from his European royal relatives. When he attended the funeral of King George V in London in 1935, he found himself assigned to walk with an Albanian prince in the last row of the royal cortege.

But Dmitri had begun devoting more and more of his time to politics. In his speeches he stressed that however notorious Stalin's regime was, Russians abroad should welcome a strong Russia. For oldtimers, this was blasphemy. To conservative ears, Dmitri sounded like a revolutionary. Yet his attitudes were consistent with his past. His participation in the murder of Rasputin in 1916 could be interpreted as a manifestation of a long-standing, although repressed, desire to lead as a grand duke should. Dmitri shared the basic premises of the Young Russian movement, allowed Kazem-Bek to use his name, and publicly argued that any foreign intervention against Soviet Russia should be prevented, saying that a defeat of the Red Army would be a "horrible blow against Russia and Russian national honor."

Of course Dmitri gave Kazem-Bek prestige by endorsing him. For Russian exiles, whenever a grand duke participated in some event, it became a special occasion. The Romanov charisma was still intact. On Easter, Christmas and New Year's Day, Russian emigrés would try to visit a grand ducal house, if only to sign the guest book. When a young boy from a good family living in Paris met the still reprobate Grand Duke Boris around 1935, he was nonetheless so impressed by the imperial aura that he kissed Boris's hand.

Despite Kyril's posturings and pretensions, Dmitri in the 1930s had become the most elegant and regal of all the grand dukes—and "for me," his son says, "the perfect gentleman." Certainly he looked the part. Now approaching fifty, he remained strikingly handsome. Instinctively he seemed to understand the mystique of royalty, that it is best to withhold part of oneself. He always kept a distance between himself and the world. Some said the reserve in his face bore the stamp of Rasputin's murder.

At Young Russian ceremonies attended by thousands, Kazem-Bek would stand at the grand duke's back as if to express the relationship between him, the leader; Dmitri, a Romanov; and the audience, the party. Dmitri and Kazem-Bek were on good terms. They were friends as well as political allies. And undoubtedly the young men in blue shirts were attracted to the aura of Dmitri, the story of his involvement with Rasputin, his imperial blood and his romance with the glamorous Coco Chanel as well.

Dmitri was not only attracted to the Young Russian message of patriotism and hope, but also found his association with the organization a means of quiet revenge against Kyril. Dmitri had never really liked Kyril and the whole Vladimirovichi clan, and only his sense of duty and loyalty to monarchical principles had motivated any association with them.

Kyril cautiously supported the Young Russians, although offering them any support at all was costly to him since it alienated his con-

servative White adherents. On December 23, 1931, Kyril issued a
New Year appeal that provoked enormous controversy, declaring:

> Capitalism has degenerated into another way for a small minor-
> ity to enslave people. [Although] communist authority is
> doomed, the nation has survived under the onslaught of destruc-
> tive forces. Now it recovers. Authority has tried to hide the na-
> tion under the mask of 'USSR,' but in the souls of the Russian
> people the sacred name RUSSIA is gleaming brightly. Do not
> events in the Russian land prove that? Is it not the construction
> which is underway there the cause of the Russian people itself, its
> true desire to rebuild the Motherland?

This kind of talk enraged many monarchists. The behavior of the
Young Russians was appalling to them. At their meetings the Young
Russians would even sing songs glorifying the Red Army, for instance
the widely popular (within the Soviet Union) song about the Soviet Air
Force, "Higher and higher we send our birds into flight."

The legendary White general, Andrei Shkuro, rescuer of the
Vladimirovichi in the Caucasus, sent an impassioned letter of com-
plaint about Kyril to his younger brother Grand Duke Andrew, widely
circulating it among the emigré community. "I have just read the New
Year appeal of Your August Brother to the Russian people," he wrote
on February 1, 1932, from Belgrade.

> My heart ached; my soul boiled. . . . I cannot keep silent. . . . You
> have known me for more than ten years. I am not only an officer
> of the old Imperial Army, I am also the only officer in the whole
> army who had the privilege, perhaps accidentally, to save from in-
> evitable death several members of the Imperial House of the Ro-
> manovs. . . . By my word of honor, when I started reading [the
> proclamation], I was sure that the document would be signed
> "Stalin" and suddenly . . . "Kyril." Your Highness, for God's
> sake, what's going on? Where are the three hundred years' history
> of the House of Romanov, where is God, where is God's mercy,
> where is all the mysterious charm which has always been invol-
> untarily, in imagination, associated with the name "Tsar.". . . For
> six years I have been fighting for Russia's honor . . . tens of thou-
> sands of corpses cover my path, starting from Poland, Galicia,

Hungary, Romania, Persia, finally the Caucasus, the Don, the Terek, Yekaterinoslav, Kharkov, Voronezh . . . and all that what for, what for? . . . Cannot we think that this is done by Moscow's will, that only Moscow wants to discredit the Tsar by the mouth and hands of the Tsar himself? Cannot we think that the circle of Your August Brother has concealed Bolsheviks within it?

The delicious irony is that the tough old general, merciless leader of the looting "Wolves" of the Civil War, was absolutely right. Kazem-Bek, always standing at the back of Grand Duke Dmitri, and, alternatively, working with Kyril, was Stalin's secret agent.

At four P.M., July 31, 1937, at the height of the Great Terror in Soviet Russia, Alexander Kazem-Bek was spotted at the expensive Paris Cafe Royale talking to an extraordinary emissary from Moscow. His companion was old, exceedingly well dressed and wore the badge of the Legion of Honor in his lapel. He was none other than Count Alexis Ignatiev, a former Imperial Russian general and military attache in Paris, now a prominent figure in Stalin's military establishment. Any meeting with a Soviet official was anathema to the emigré world.

The emigré witnesses to this recklessly incautious meeting (and there were five of them, including the former Russian ambassador to Austria-Hungary) insisted that Ignatiev was instructing Kazem-Bek about something and that, when the two became aware that they were being watched, they reacted with extreme nervousness. Scandal erupted; ultimately the Young Russians accused their leader of being a Soviet agent.

Kazem-Bek's explanation was weak. He announced that the Young Russians had received a long-awaited signal from Soviet military who were preparing a coup against the Bolsheviks and seeking support from monarchists. But during this summer of 1937, the Soviet Union was undergoing the most ruthless, merciless and thorough of all purges. The notion of an anti-Bolshevik coup being possible in such an atmosphere at such a time was absurd.

Recent purges of the top military leaders in the USSR had probably prompted Kazem-Bek's urgent meeting with Ignatiev. For fifteen years he had been insisting that the Red Army was a healthy force providing Stalin with his major support. Now everything Kazem-Bek argued seemed to be totally wrong. Three weeks before his meeting with Ignatiev, Soviet newspapers had announced the arrest of the leading Soviet marshals, including the brightest star and darling of the army, Tukhachevsky, all now accused of being German spies, plotting to overthrow the Soviet government.

Analyzing Kazem-Bek's behavior, the Young Russians and other emigrés found that it accorded with their image of a Soviet agent. Kazem-Bek had "infiltrated an organization," Kyril's legitimist movement. He was "provoking actions doomed to fail," his notion of combining tsarism with populism. He had "undermined faith," in Kyril and his cause. Kazem-Bek could be defined as an "agent-theoretician," a person working inside an organization in order to subvert and destroy it. Even his meeting with Ignatiev, although it proved his undoing, accorded with the first rule of conspiracy, "Always be visible."

Soviet Russia may have been enthusiastically perceived by rank-and-file Young Russians as a potential social-democratic monarchy and as a great power recovering its might, but even so the vast majority of emigrants had good reason to believe it remained a domain of terror. Any hint of Stalin's hand within the Young Russian movement was anathema to its members. Kazem-Bek's career as a political leader in the exile community was now over.

Although the French had identified Kazem-Bek as pro-Soviet, thus unreliable and eligible for detainment, he was able to get an exit visa and sailed to America, where he would end up in the 1940s as a teacher of Russian language and literature at Connecticut College. There, in New London, no one knew anything of his flamboyant past. Kazem-Bek had trouble living on the salary of a junior faculty member and constantly complained. The college physician told the president that her professor of Russian was a "first class neurotic who takes it for granted that whatever he needs will be provided no matter at what cost." But Kasem Beg (as he spelled his name in America) endeared himself to his teaching colleagues by his "energy and gusto. . . . He gave marathon dinners which were legendary for exuberance and variety of both food and drink."

In September 1956, Kazem-Bek abruptly defected to Moscow, flabbergasting his friends in New London, and in Russia he subsequently publicly denounced the United States as a "land without culture." In Moscow he was given an important job with the Patriarchate, in the

KGB-infested Department of Foreign Liaison, working closely with Metropolitan Nikodim, an energetic church leader believed to be a major KGB agent. Kazem-Bek remarried without divorcing his wife, Svetlana, who remained in America teaching his college courses for him. When Kazem-Bek went to Paris, on his first trip abroad in years, his old friends refused to see him. When he died shortly thereafter, the KGB took all his papers, and even today they remain locked in the vaults of the Russian secret service.

Ultimately neither Dmitri nor Kyril got any mileage out of the Young Russians. Though the organization did provide Stalin with first rate information about Dmitri and Kyril, it proved not of much use because Dmitri seemed not to want to be an emperor and there was not much to be known about Kyril. The self-proclaimed Russian emperor was a sphinx without the riddle.

Kyril and Ducky had moved to France in the mid-1920s, where they bought a house in the village of St. Briac on the coast of Brittany. St. Briac was only four hours by train from Paris and it was conveniently situated on the Channel. Ferries from nearby St. Malo ran frequently to England. St. Briac was a quiet place from which one could get out quickly and easily. The grand ducal house was charming but modest, tucked away at the back of the village; its seclusion offered security, supplemented by the local police, who kept a protective eye on the house. For the imperial couple, money was obviously not abundant; they employed only a housekeeper and a man to help in the garden. Russians from Paris would occasionally come down to lend a hand. Life was simple.

St. Briac had become a post–World War I haven for elderly Britons trying to live comfortably—with servants—on retirement incomes, among them many who had spent their working lives in India. The community, both French and foreign, was proud to have a resident grand duke and grand duchess. They found Kyril abrupt, reserved and unbending—in short, "difficult." Ducky, on the other hand, although she may have appeared to be haughty, was not, and she was careful to conceal her Anglophobia. Her regal grace and cultivated manners made her many friends. If she spoke English with a gutteral German accent, so did Queen Mary. She was polite to retired colonels and their wives, and they much appreciated such attention from a Princess of Great Britain and granddaughter of Queen Victoria. The ladies curtsied and everyone remembered to call her "Ma'am." The republican French were less serious about it, but they did address both Kyril and Ducky as "Altesse" (Highness). Everyone was careful not to ask too much about the old days.

The imperial couple played bridge and attended parties. Here they celebrated their twenty-fifth wedding anniversary, allowing an American acquaintance to throw a party for them. None of the Russian ecclesiastics in Paris would consent to proclaim Kyril and Ducky's imperial titles at the celebratory mass; they therefore brought a compliant priest all the way from Belgium for the occasion. The Russian guests felt humiliated that an American should be the host, distributing fruit baskets and a photograph of the imperial couple to all who came.

Ducky painted and gardened. She delighted in organizing amateur theatricals, the most ambitious being a performance of *Sleeping Beauty* for which she recruited the help of a Russian ballet teacher in nearby Dinard. For her friends Ducky would demonstrate the steps of the *polonaise* as it had been danced in the Winter Palace. Kyril golfed and everyone in town recognized his small sporty dark green Amilcar; he was still able to indulge his passion for automobiles. But his unhappiness was apparent. Photographs say it all. Village rumor had it that Kyril slipped off to Paris for an occasional fling, and Ducky confided bitterly to her sister, Queen Marie of Romania, that the marriage was over. Nonetheless the imperial couple preserved a facade of unity.

Kyril's political life was also a charade. Kazem-Bek had abided by the agent's motto, "Always be visible"; Kyril applied this principle to royalty in exile. He had established a mock court in the house, keeping a schedule, receiving respectful visitors, issuing proclamations, and giving out titles, including naming his son, Vladimir, a grand duke, although, as a mere great grandson of an emperor (very few people would consider Kyril a true emperor), Vladimir would properly have been known as "prince." Critics suggested that Kyril was actually selling awards and titles.

Part of the charade was Kyril's "court circular," a newsletter sent out every month to the emigrant community. November 30, 1930, for example, described a monarchists' reception in Paris attended by "Their Majesties" (Kyril and Ducky) and twelve hundred guests. However "Their Majesties" could not have paid the tab. The harsh reality was pointed out by Sandro, who attended the reception and said later of his cousin that "the would-be Emperor of Russia ... [could not] write a check for as much as one thousand dollars ... [he lives] from month to month, depending on the generosity of [his] impoverished supporters or the bounty of [his] reigning relatives, [his] revenues from both sources failing to cover the bills."

In 1936 the mock court collapsed. Ducky died of a stroke on March 2, at the castle of her daughter, Princess Maria zu Leiningen, at Amorbach, Lower Franconia. She was buried in her native Coburg. Kyril himself had been ill for several years, with progressing atherosclerosis, and, although he had found other *amours,* he seemed never fully to recover from the emotional shock of losing his wife, upon whom, in the Romanov pattern, he was greatly dependent. But he did survive long enough to attend the wedding of his daughter Kira in the spring of 1938.

Kira married Louis Ferdinand, "Lulu" as he was called, son of the former crown prince of Germany and grandson of the last kaiser, whose blessing Kira received when she visited him in exile. Lulu had been born in 1907 and at the age of ten was commissioned as a lieutenant in the Prussian Imperial Army. Visiting America in 1929, already a celebrity in American eyes because he was a Hohenzollern and the kaiser's grandson, Lulu made himself famous by taking a job for a time at a Ford automobile plant in Detroit and cultivating friendships with people like Franklin D. Roosevelt, Charlie Chaplin and a French-born movie actress, Lili Damita, who would later become the first wife of Errol Flynn.

Some now liked to see political significance in the marital union between Hohenzollern and Romanov, two of the major deposed European imperial houses, but the event remained a mere historical footnote. After the wedding, Kyril declined rapidly and died in the American Hospital in Paris on October 12, 1938. He was buried next to Ducky in Coburg.

❦

For Dmitri, the death of Kyril, whom he so much detested, was still a sad event, for it reminded the grand duke of his own mortality and at a time when his health was deteriorating rapidly. Now Dmitri, the most fashionable Romanov, was conspicuously absent from Paris, struggling, like a Thomas Mann character, with tuberculosis in a Swiss sanatorium.

Dmitri's had been an unhappy, lonely and unfulfilled life. When doctors told him he was seriously ill and had to slow down a bit, he was plunged into despair. In his diary he wrote, "I will never play golf again. This is horrible." Dmitri saw his only child, Paul, for the last time in 1939 in Genoa for three days before Paul and his mother sailed home aboard the *Rex* to America. Paul remembers that his father took him to a toy store, where they bought many lead soldiers to while away the long ocean voyage and to make seasickness more endurable. The toy soldiers were also to remind the boy of the military tradition of his family, and the last words Dmitri had for Paul were "always love your mother and be a good soldier!"

Dmitri deplored the new Romanov disunion, with many family members carping at each other and a general lack of civility prevailing. When he received a letter from Kyril's son and heir Vladimir, Dmitri was irritated by the fact that the letter was typed. "He is an asshole—he could write it himself. His uncle Grand Duke Andrew Vladimirovich who always types—even he thanked me very politely in a hand-written letter. . . . I wanted to respond to Vladimir by a typed letter too and then decided against that—he is just a fool!"

Dmitri was sarcastic about Vladimir's elevation of some people to pompous titles. Of one of K.R.'s sons, he wrote that Gavriil Constantinovich had been granted the title of grand duke in violation of every possible rule. "I think he will not write to me, fearing that I will not address him 'Le Grand Duc Gabriel.' This is a title which I really don't recognize and will not recognize the right of Vladimir Kirillovich to give it!!!"

When the French arrested Alexander Kazem-Bek in 1939, Grand Duke Andrew wrote a "malicious" letter to Dmitri in Paris. Andrew had always been unhappy that his son, Prince Vladimir Krasinsky (Vova), a prominent Young Russian, was close to Dmitri and Kazem-Bek. Jealous for years, Andrew now took special pleasure in telling Dmitri that all Kazem-Bek's papers had been confiscated by the French police. Dmitri was terrified. The last thing he now wanted was to be associated with a man identified as a Soviet agent. Dmitri instructed his friends in Paris to move his own papers to a "secure place."

Yet Dmitri forced himself to be cheerful. He would send his friend and secretary Kozlianinov a postcard showing a young man alpine skiing, flying in the air over the snows of Davos in the bright rays of the sun. Dmitri wrote, "What a marvelous picture and what a jump!" He would also send Kozlianinov a Wagnerian photograph of sharp mountain tops, black forest and low clouds that he took himself from his balcony. "I think it's not worse than a professional one," he boasted.

World War II found Dmitri in Davos. Just before the German blitzkrieg struck the French, Dmitri was giving thought to buying a small chateau in France, and he asked Kozlianinov to approach real estate agents. He judged his health to be improving but chafed under his medical regimen and isolation from world events. "Our life here reminds me a bit of a golden cage. We read sometimes with joy, sometimes with a feeling of deep anxiety and pity mixed with anger the recent reports from the Finnish front where an historic struggle of armed communism is on against old European civilization." On April 10, 1940, on the eve of the collapse of France in the German onslaught, Dmitri would remark, "Everything starts looking petty in comparison with world events!"

Triumphant Germany was free to trample on all of Europe. The world the Romanovs had known again changed dramatically. The ultimate irony occurred in May 1940. In 1919 the British had come to the aid of their recent enemy, the Hapsburgs. Now it was the turn of another former enemy, the Hohenzollerns. The new British prime minister, Winston Churchill, sent a message approved by King George VI to the eighty-one-year-old Kaiser Wilhelm in Doorn saying that if he would like to escape the Nazis and choose asylum in England, he would be received "with consideration and grace" and the Royal Air Force would send a plane to Holland to get him out. The ghost of Nicholas II stirred indignantly in its unmarked Siberian pit. The kaiser thought over the British invitation and decided to decline it. Other royals now in danger would not be as fortunate as the kaiser. No airplanes were offered to them. Exiles in a Nazi-dominated Europe, the senior Romanovs—Boris and Andrew in Paris, Vladimir at St. Briac, Olga in Denmark, Militsa in Italy—were again facing a threat to survival. Dmitri in Switzerland was spared the humiliation of Nazi rule, but he did not live to rejoice in its collapse.

On March 5, 1942, a day when the British bombed Paris heavily, Grand Duke Dmitri died at his Davos sanatorium. He was only fifty. His health had been sharply declining since August 1940. In the autumn of that year he underwent an unsuccessful operation and had been confined to bed for three months afterward. In January and February 1941 two more operations followed and the doctors spoke optimistically, hoping that the lung that had been especially touched by disease could be cured.

Dmitri's death drew little comment or attention; even the Romanov family was silent. His chief mourner was his sister Marie. The world was far too preoccupied by enormous events to have much time for such a figure of the past.

CHAPTER FOURTEEN

✦

"Escape Contact with Allies at Any Cost"

O N JUNE 22, 1941, AT DAWN German tanks began to roll across the frontier of the Soviet Union; the invasion of Russia had begun. The short alliance between Moscow and Berlin, the raptors tearing eastern Europe apart, was now over. Hitler was simply doing what he had always proclaimed to be his intention, getting *lebensraum* (living space) in the east. But when Stalin's staff dared break the news, he refused to believe it.

Many in France were already collaborating with their German occupiers, including Dmitri's former love, Coco Chanel. The German invasion of the Soviet Union split the Russian emigré community into two parts. People like Ivan Bunin regarded the German attack with disgust, feeling that German boots were trampling on the soil of *their* motherland. Others saw fresh opportunity to bring down the Bolsheviks, and they stood up for collaboration. Vladimir, claiming to be the Head of the Russian Imperial House, was one of them.

At the end of June he issued a proclamation that left little doubt about his political sympathies:

In this severe hour, when Germany with almost all the nations of Europe has declared a crusade against Communist-Bolshevism which has enslaved and which has been oppressing the peoples of Russia for twenty-four years, I address all loyal sons of our

Motherland with an appeal: help as you can the overthrow of
Godless Bolshevik power and the liberation of our Fatherland
from the horrible communist yoke.

Vladimir later insisted that he had no illusions about Hitler, but
these words carry no hint of any reservations whatsoever about the
leader of the "crusade" against Bolshevism. This "crusade" would
cause twenty-eight million Russians to die.

Many in the Romanov family disagreed sharply with Vladimir's
stance. Young Prince Nicholas, grandson of Grand Duke Peter and
Grand Duchess Militsa, remembers that for him, "Russia did not exist
until June 1941, then Russia became *my* country; the regime faded
into unimportance."

The Romanovs began to receive apocalyptic news from the Russian
front. The Germans seemed invincible, their forces victorious everywhere. The Soviets bombed Berlin, but the Nazis moved rapidly to occupy most of European Russia. The Red Army seemed unable to hold
its ground before the Nazi onslaught; the news reached Paris that Russians were setting their forests afire just as they had burned Moscow
in 1812 when Napoleon entered the city. The Nazis held Leningrad in
the iron grip of siege, and Hitler boasted that he planned to destroy
the city utterly and build a water reservoir on its site. Nazi bigwigs
were already distributing amongst themselves the palaces of the
Crimea. Hitler would of course have Livadia.

During the war, some Russian exiles became active in the European
resistance movement. The symbolist poet Elizaveta Skobtsova, who
had entered the Church as Mother Mary, sheltered Jews and died in a
gas chamber. The Germans executed Princess Vera Obolenskaya, also
a member of the resistance. General Anton Denikin resisted German
attempts to draft his name for the anti-Soviet crusade. Prince Vladimir
Krasinsky, the son of Kshesinskaya and Grand Duke Andrew, was arrested in German-occupied Paris on the day German troops crossed
the Soviet border. Because he had been a Young Russian, he was regarded by the Nazis as pro-Soviet. He would spend one hundred nineteen days in a concentration camp at Compiègne before being
released. When his son was arrested, Andrew felt heartbroken and forgot his customary pride, making repeated visits to German Police
Headquarters like hundreds of other anxious parents. He also sought
help from the distinguished leaders of Russian emigration like former

ambassador to France, Vassily Maklakov, only to find to his dismay that the Whites had not forgiven Vova's Young Russian past. Maklakov smoothly said that "Your Highness will understand" that they could not help.

On November 9, 1943, Vova's uncle, Grand Duke Boris, died, a fact briefly noted by the newspapers and Vichy radio. He was sixty-five; his widow Zinaida was his only survivor. The obituaries called him "a man of generous tendencies, who tipped shopgirls with twenty dollar bills." Boris, the quintessential grand duke, alive or dead, always supplied good copy for the press.

On a summer day in 1943, at a villa in Lucca, Italy, the phone rang. Queen Elena was on the line to speak with her sister, Grand Duchess Militsa, the widow of Grand Duke Peter and Russia's "black plague" of long ago. The conversation was in Serbo-Croatian, a language the two sisters used together only in extraordinary circumstances. "You must leave immediately," the queen said, "a storm is coming from the south. Either come to Rome or go to Switzerland."

The Germans were coming.

Militsa and her family chose to go to Rome, thinking it safer "to face the wave and dive under it rather than run the other way." They traveled under police protection to the Villa Savoia in Rome, an Italian royal residence. The king and queen themselves then fled the capital, although the king confidently told Militsa, "It's a matter only of a few days." Militsa, her children and grandchildren were the only royal relatives staying in the city. The Germans rolled in and the Romanovs hunkered down, not knowing what to expect. Militsa's two young grandchildren, Princes Nicholas and Dmitri, did not leave the house; the family knew that they were vulnerable to being picked up by German patrols looking for any able-bodied young men to dig trenches on the front line.

In February 1944 a police officer came to the house.

"The old lady is not safe here; the Germans are asking questions."

Militsa was a courageous woman. She had already experienced a German occupation, in the Crimea in 1918. But the Nazis were much more fearsome than Kaiser Wilhelm's soldiers. The grand duchess wavered but soon left for the convent of the Sacred Heart, at the top of the Spanish Steps. The rest of the family moved in with Swiss friends whose house was flying the Swiss flag. Soon after a German colonel appeared there in full dress uniform. "I shall be very brief. I know where the grand duchess is and *they* do too. She must go to the Vatican, and I can organize this myself." The colonel, it seems, was actually an anti-Nazi Austrian with strong monarchist sympathies. He arrived in a German jeep and drove the grand duchess to the Vatican with one small bag, straight to the left door of St. Peter's.

Since the time of Nicholas I, the Romanovs had had a chilly attitude toward the Vatican. Although occasionally they had audiences with the popes (Grand Dukes Sergei and Paul saw Leo XIII, and Grand Duchess Olga Constantinovna, later Queen of Greece, had tried to engage the pope in a friendly theological argument), no love was lost between the Holy See and the Romanovs. The Vatican had no reason to like Militsa's sister, the queen, either; the House of Savoy had bitterly fought the temporal authority of the papacy.

But they granted asylum to Militsa, and to Militsa only. She may have been safe, but her children and grandchildren began "a most unpleasant experience," moving from house to house in an attempt to stay beyond the reach of the Germans. The family relationship with the House of Savoy was key. As Romanovs they were not potential pawns, but as relatives of the Italian monarch they were.

On June 3, 1944 the Allies liberated Rome, and the family's ordeal was over. On June 6th, the Allies landed on the beaches of Normandy. In that same June, Soviet troops liberated Odessa. But in flight the Germans left everywhere in Russia a horror of destruction, often wanton. Nazi vandals devastated Romanov palaces that had survived the revolution, civil war and Soviet neglect.

The Nazi war on Russian culture was even worse than that of the Bolsheviks. They made Pavlovsk, that gem of Russian neoclassicism, a burned out shell. At Tsarskoye, the Germans did their best to erase the Catherine Palace but were careful first to take at least some of its treasures along with them in retreat. The unique and priceless Amber Room, its walls formed by sheets of carved amber of all possible shades, disappeared. Given to the Romanovs by the Hohenzollerns, it presumably now lies at the bottom of the Baltic Sea or perhaps forgotten in some deep abandoned German salt mine.

From Scotland, Grand Duchess Xenia wrote, "It hurts to think that nothing has been spared by the enemy (*beasts*) and all those beautiful palaces & lovely spots exist no longer & everything is now a mass of ruins! Gatchina Palace has also been burnt down & as to Peterhof— nothing is left of it."

By the summer of 1944, the Germans were in retreat on both fronts, east and west. Withdrawing from the territories they had occupied, they took hostages with them. Having been deported from France to Germany in 1944, Vladimir Kirillovich, the only son of Kyril and Ducky, was living under surveillance at his sister Maria's house in Amorbach, behaving with utmost circumspection.

The young Vladimir was the only Romanov of particular interest to Hitler. After Kyril's death, Vladimir, born during his parents' Finnish exile, assumed the role of the Pretender. Vladimir had received an education in some respects like that of the older generation of Romanovs. Local schools for Vladimir were out of the question, both inappropriate for an imperial heir and insecure. Ducky worried a great deal about the long arm of Stalin. Vladimir had tutors; his studies emphasized languages and he would gain fluency in the four tongues the Romanovs conventionally learned: English, French, German and, of course, Russian. He was offered a scholarship to study at Winchester, one of the leading British public schools, but Ducky turned it down. She did not want her son to become an Englishman. For a time, after his formative years, Vladimir attended a Russian school in Paris, and King's College in London (1937–38). But of course he was not able to have the traditional career in the military that male Romanovs traditionally pursued.

Unlike his father, Vladimir did not assume the title of emperor but satisfied himself with the title of head of the imperial house. With his mother and father dead and he himself only twenty-one, Vladimir felt alone and uncertain. In December 1938, shortly after Kyril's death, the leading European newspapers announced that Vladimir would go to Berlin to conduct secret talks with Hitler. "Reliable sources" there said he was to discuss with the Führer the future status of Ukraine.

The newspapers said that an expeditionary force formed of Ukrainians was to be created to cross the Soviet border through Romania and Poland. Vladimir would be proclaimed Emperor of all the Russias on two conditions: Vladimir's Hohenzollern brother-in-law,

Lulu, would assume a regency for a time; and a proven pro-German *hetman* (leader) would be appointed for Ukraine.

The legacy of Grand Duke Kyril's lifelong sympathy toward Germany was making his son's position very delicate indeed. Several of Kyril's former close associates from the period in which he and Ducky had known Hitler in Munich were now working for Alfred Rosenberg, the person who was preparing the Nazi blueprints for the future of Eastern Europe and Russia. Rosenberg had been an advocate of an independent Ukraine for years. Such a nation, the Germans thought, would be an excellent check on Russia and serve perhaps even as a way to eliminate Poland.

Kyril was the only Romanov of his generation who had not disliked the former kaiser, Wilhelm. Both his daughters had married German princes, and Lulu was the putative head of the house of Hohenzollern. If there were any Romanov with a pro-German family background it was Vladimir.

Two days after the rumors about Vladimir's flirtation with the Nazis were reported by the press, on December 16, 1938, the Romanov made it known through interviews, radio and his uncle Andrew that he had no intention of becoming a puppet emperor. He said he was going to Germany only to spend Christmas with his sister Maria, Princess of Leiningen. He emphatically stated, "I have never been approached nor would I ever lend my name to any act tending to dismember the Russian empire." Nonetheless, Vladimir maintained a close relationship with German royalty. Marriage had made Kaiser Wilhelm an even closer relative. To the extent that the Hohenzollerns cooperated with the Nazis, Vladimir was drawn into the net.

The British were anxious lest Vladimir be manipulated by the Nazis and used to advance German interests in Russia. The Palace wrote to the Foreign Office to inquire if any Imperial Russian funds on deposit in England were available to subsidize the young grand duke to live in England instead. The Foreign Office reported that they were not aware of any such funds except possibly the so-called "Baring balances," explaining to the king's private secretary that these were funds deposited by the Imperial Russian Government during World War I to meet their commitments in Britain and had remained untouched ever since, mainly because the Soviet Government, who had "a plausible legal claim to them in English law, have hitherto not seen fit to claim them, for reasons of their own . . . [and] it would be hardly possible to use any part of the balance for the Grand Duke." But in any case the government did not know the amount because "the banks are sworn to secrecy in such matters."

The British worried that if they made any official overtures to Vladimir, they risked offending the Soviet Government, and this they were not prepared to do. The solution was to have the young grand duke brought to England as a relative of King George V in "some purely private family arrangement." And this is what was done discreetly.

Vladimir went to England in early 1939 and worked there for a short time at an automobile plant as an ordinary mechanic, assuming the name Mikhailov, following the example of his distinguished ancestor, Peter the Great, who had worked as a carpenter in England using the same surname. For Peter the Great, with his fascination with Europe and maritime power especially, England had seemed a reasonable choice. For Vladimir to go to a country that had always been hostile to Romanovs and that disliked his father Kyril, in particular, the choice was rather strange. Was it because of the example of mixing with the common people set by his Hohenzollern brother-in-law Lulu, who went to work at a Ford plant in Detroit? If so, why didn't Vladimir go to America?

Vladimir explained that he just wanted to see what the life of a working man was like. This sounded most implausible. Soft and spoiled, already a *bon viveur*, the "heir" to the Russian throne whose chief interest had been driving expensive motorcycles, wanted to mix with British factory workers? Was it simply because he needed money? Certainly he was broke and without any prospects for employment. In any case the job lasted only a few months. Summer came and Vladimir returned to France.

The full story presumably lies in the archives of British intelligence, which are closed. But we do know that some influential Englishmen saw a possible future political role for Vladimir in Russia. They assumed that if he were educated in Britain and became personally conversant with British monarchical democracy, he might become more friendly to Britain. "Might it not be worthwhile making of him an English gentleman?" one man wrote to the king. This was of course just what Vladimir's mother had *not* wanted.

We also know that in Paris Vladimir's uncle, Grand Duke Andrew, had commented on the occasion of his nephew's first visit to England, "I knew that important Intelligence Officers would accompany my nephew and that Vladimir's trip to London did not have studies as its purpose, it is just a pretext, I know all about it, but I cannot talk for understandable reasons." Andrew, always discreet, understood British interest in Vladimir on the eve of war. And Vladimir had his own reasons for repairing relations with the House of Windsor. Without British support, no imperial restoration in Russia was likely.

By the late 1930s, the intelligence community of Europe had realized that Russia would be part of the next great European conflict. In that situation it was vital to collect all the trumps related to Russia. Vladimir could be a valuable asset—first the heir and then the only pretender to the Russian throne. At least two secret services had started a battle over the royal pawn. One was the British; the other was Nazi. In the background lurked the Soviet.

Meanwhile the young Vladimir was eager to assert his leadership in the Russian community abroad. In a letter to the new leader of ROVS, General Alexei Arkhangelsky, on February 6, 1939, Vladimir said that "when the time comes, I will call everybody to fulfill his duty to the Motherland."

In the summer of 1939, Vladimir returned to France to take a long vacation at the family home in St. Briac. The German secret services were suspicious of his relationship with the British. "I do not exclude," one of the officers wrote, "that his coming to [continental] Europe is explained by the need to fulfill the errands of the British." But local people in St. Briac took a different view. While there, Vladimir had a long visit from a German friend whom everyone in town knew to be a member of the Hitler Youth. The two young men traveled all over Brittany together by motorcycle, and later some people interpreted the trip as having had the sinister purpose of mapping the bridge and road network for the benefit of the Germans. Later such detailed information would have been valuable to the German High Command. Were the Nazis winning out over the British in the control of Vladimir's allegiances?

Gestapo chief Heinrich Mueller wrote to the German ambassador in Paris, "[Vladimir] Romanov favors Germany. His father also expressed sympathy toward National Socialism. The Führer . . . demonstrated his willingness to let him move to Germany and also to grant him some financial benefits."

The outbreak of war in the early autumn of 1939 caught Vladimir at St. Briac. The Germans attacked Poland in September, and with

France fighting Germany, Vladimir could no longer visit there. Temporarily his options were only France or England. He volunteered to serve in the French army, but he was turned down for political reasons. The British did not want him either. King George VI did not want his cousin to return to England, remembering that he had taken "a great deal of trouble to get this penniless young man some employment, with good prospects, and he showed himself to be altogether unsatisfactory."

Sir Alexander Cadogan at the Foreign Office took the view that "even in the event of a revolution in the Soviet Union there would be [no] chance of the Romanovs returning to the throne." Others in England were not so sure and thought it wise to reserve that as a possibility. Vladimir, they thought, could be useful.

Vladimir had been waiting for Hitler's invitation to proclaim himself Emperor of Russia. He was more confident in 1944 than he had been in 1939 that this would happen. Now all the major right-wing emigrant groups supported him. In a letter to the Supreme Monarchist Council on September 21, 1942, when the Russians were fighting the Germans to a standstill at Stalingrad, Vladimir complained that the Axis powers had not appreciated his willingness to cooperate with them. He referred to his appeal of June 26, 1941, in which he had urged the Russians to support Hitler's war against the Soviet Union. Now he believed that participation of the Whites would have allowed Berlin to concentrate on the Western front.

Vladimir clearly hoped for the defeat of the Allies. He also wrote that the "major struggle against the universal evil is waged by Germany," while Stalin was supported by "World Jewry." Vladimir called for cooperation among the "three boldest and biggest nations—Germany, a restored Orthodox Russia of the Tsars, and Japan." But, he complained, he could not "act" until the leadership of Germany or Japan addressed him.

Several Russian military groups emerged at this time, close to Vladimir and also trusted by the Germans. The First Russian National Army was one such group. Under the leadership of Boris Smyslovsky, a former captain with the tsar's guards, it began to take form in July 1941, only weeks after the German invasion of Russia had begun. After 1917, Smyslovsky had managed to get a Polish passport and to attend a German military academy. He assumed a German pseudonym, von Regenau. His group, the First Russian National Army, remained small, only six thousand men. Eighty percent of its members were prisoners of war or defectors; most of the officers were White emigrants of the older generation.

Von Regenau–Smyslovsky himself was also an officer in the German military intelligence, the infamous *Abwehr*. Most of his White Russian subordinates were *Abwehr* people too. In February 1945 he was promoted to Major General and assumed a second pseudonym, Holmston. The *Abwehr* knew by that time that Soviet intelligence had a clear idea of the real identify of "Colonel von Regenau." Von Regenau's path would dramatically intersect with that of Vladimir.

The Nazis had brought Vladimir to Germany in order to have him readily available should they find a use for him. The idea of using a would-be or dispossessed monarch was not alien to the Nazis by any means. Hitler kept a close eye on pro-German royalty. When Edward VIII abdicated because of his wish to marry a woman unsuitable to be queen of England, the twice-married American divorcee Wallis Warfield, Hitler invited Edward, now the exiled Duke of Windsor, to visit Germany with his bride. The duke was well known to have Nazi sympathies. Lavishly entertained by Nazi moguls like Goering, the Windsors were finally received at Berchtesgaden by the Führer himself, although they were kept waiting while Hitler finished his afternoon nap. Knowing how annoyed and hurt the duke had been by the disrespect shown to his beloved Wallis and the British monarch's refusal to allow her to be addressed as "Royal Highness," the Nazis provided enthusiastic crowds at railway stations to chant, "We want the duchess!"

When the war broke out, Hitler considered the idea of placing the duke back on the British throne as his puppet king. The German secret service even developed a plan to smuggle the Windsors from Portugal to Spain and then to Germany. Hitler's intermediary with the Duke of Windsor was a mutual relative of Windsor and Vladimir, Carl Eduard, Duke of Saxe-Coburg-Gotha, an ardent Nazi and now a uniformed party member.

Given prewar speculations about Vladimir and the Nazis, the grand duke may well have been the designated puppet monarch for a new Ukraine. Throughout the war years, Alfred Rosenberg continued to plan an independent Ukraine allied with Germany. In June 1943 he visited the Crimea and spent a night at Livadia, appreciatively sampling there some of Alexander III's wines.

Hitler was eager to exploit anyone of prominence whom he thought he could bend to his will. He suggested to Felix Yusupov and his Romanov wife Irina that, lavishly supplied with money, clothing, and jewels, they become official hosts for him to important guests in occupied Paris. Felix, though tempted, turned the offer down.

But the war was coming to an end with Soviet triumph, and Vladimir decided to try to escape from Germany. If Soviet troops should catch him, it would be the end. Later he said, "When in spring of 1945 the whole apparatus of National Socialism fell apart and we had no contact with Berlin, the local military gave me some gas (I had come from France in my own car) and I decided to drive south, to get out of Germany into Switzerland. I went through Austria to the Swiss border where I stayed in a small town."

This was Feldkirch, close to the border of the tiny quasi-independent Principality of Liechtenstein and the place where the last Hapsburg emperor, Charles I, had issued a manifesto in 1919, denouncing the new republican government of Austria and then fleeing into exile— with British help.

In the spring of 1945, this area of Austria was flooded with thousands of fleeing refugees, who were bombed and strafed from the air and in a panic left their belongings behind. As a result, "All roads and forests to the west from Vienna were covered with suitcases, bundles, and coats." On April 14, 1945, in the final days of the war, Vladimir checked in at the Zum Loewen Hotel in Feldkirch. He had to think now of his survival, fearing both the Soviets and the Allies. The Austrian Archduke Albrecht of Hapsburg was with him, as well as several White emigrants sharing his concerns. They all waited nervously.

At noon, May 2, 1945, Sergei Voitsekhovsky, an associate of Vladimir and a former head of the Russian emigrant community in Warsaw, arrived at the village of Nofels, near Feldkirch. Voitsekhovsky had at one time been Kutepov's representative in Poland, involved in the *Trest* operation in the 1920s. In Nofels he met the commander of the First Russian Army, the man of many names, currently General Holmston. Holmston was also on the run, having fled the eastern front with seventy-three officers and four hundred men. Holmston told Voitsekhovsky that he was determined "to escape contact with the Allies at any cost" and that he would set a time for crossing the border depending upon the rate of advance of Allied forces in the region. Holmston's interest seems to have been saving his own skin.

At eight P.M. artillery fire in Nofels broke the stillness of the night. The guns belonged to the French. Two days earlier, on April 30th, French troops had crossed the northwestern frontier of Austria and, after a short fight, occupied the town of Bregenz. Holmston could now hear a battle raging between the attacking French and the Germans retreating into Feldkirch. The arrival of the Allies was imminent; they would reach Nofels in no time.

Holmston-Smyslovsky did not hesitate, always reminding his officers of the motto of the German General Staff Academy, "Make a decision! Even a bad decision is better than nothing!" He ordered his men to prepare to cross the border from Austria to neutral Liechtenstein immediately. Driving conditions on the alpine roads were never good, especially at night, and now it was snowing. Holmston-Smyslovsky summoned an officer of the German border guard and asked him how he would react to their passage. The officer was cooperative; he seemed to understand the anxiety of these Russians in German uniform. He even volunteered to accompany them to the frontier.

The column set off, headed by the general's car. His aide was crouched on the running board, leaning against the fender, holding an automatic rifle. He was ready to shoot if necessary. In one of the cars at the rear rode Grand Duke Vladimir.

When they arrived at the frontier, the German border officer accompanying them ordered the gate in the barbed wire to be opened to let the convoy through. They could see light coming from the Swiss checkpoint ahead; the Swiss had assumed responsibility for the security of Liechtenstein during the war. It was midnight, May 2nd.

Holmston-Smyslovsky assigned a truck with the convoy to drive at the head of the column, and he ordered that the convoy was not to shoot in any circumstances, even if the Swiss border guards did so.

As the truck roared through the checkpoint, the Swiss opened fire. The general shouted to the truck to stop and the whole convoy came to a halt, now out of Austria. The Swiss commanded in German, "Hands up! Let one person come!" The general's aide, who could be clearly seen in the lights of the car, put down his weapon and went to the checkpoint, followed moments later by the general. He returned in five minutes saying, "They will accept us." The convoy moved into a Liechtenstein village, and the general was invited to stop at the local inn while the Swiss border commander sought instructions from his superiors as well as from Vaduz, the capital of the principality.

The officer demanded to see a list of those wanting to cross the border. The list included General Holmston-Smyslovsky, along with various officers, soldiers and their families. It also included the Russian Committee in Warsaw, a much odder group—Sergei Voitsekhovsky, the sometime Warsaw resident, but also Vladimir Kirillovich and his suite, Archduke Albrecht and his suite, two Polish officers, and *a British officer.* Nazi collaborators and their ilk, fleeing the Allies, seemed to have every reason to be there. But a British officer looked strikingly out of place in this company. On May 2nd, there were no British troops in the Feldkirch area; this was the French zone of occupation. But in the area there were two teams from the most controversial of all British secret services, Special Operations Executive (SOE), created in July 1940 to organize sabotage in Axis-held territories all the way from France to China. In its five years of life, SOE had trained and equipped more than nine thousand agents and dispatched them to foreign lands. The SOE had an Austrian subsection, with two teams rather unsuccessfully fighting the Gestapo there. Yet one of those teams, GREENUP, was instrumental in securing the surrender of the local German administration in the area, in Innsbruck, about one hundred miles from Feldkirch. A second team, DOCTOR, was also in the Tyrol, near Kufstein and Kitzbuhl, sixty miles from Feldkirch. Put together the teams constituted five men, none of them British (one Austrian, two Belgians and two Americans). To local German officials, any one of these men could have passed as a British officer. The SOE officer, whoever he may have been, presumably joined Vladimir's group shortly before the crossing of the border and persuaded Vladimir that he would be a valuable escort.

Vladimir's situation was perilous; he was very possibly playing a double game. Now, in deciding to travel through Austria, he had leapt from the German frying pan into the British fire. The intelligence service with which he had been associated in 1937–39 and perhaps even later could now do a nightmarish thing—turn him over to Stalin. That would surely have meant torture and execution. Though Feldkirch itself was technically in the French zone of occupation, the British could do there fairly much whatever they wanted.

As soon as Vladimir reached Switzerland, he would be out of British control and could go to his Aunt Beatrice, Ducky's younger sister, a Princess of Spain, who lived in Madrid. Therefore the British had to find a way to keep him from leaving Austria.

Voitsekhovsky nervously asked the Swiss officer whether there was a chance of deportation of some members of the group back to Austria. No, the officer said; everyone could stay in Liechtenstein. But he did want to check again the members of the last group, the Russian Committee in Warsaw.

At dawn he suddenly announced that he had changed his mind, ordering Grand Duke Vladimir and Archduke Albrecht into a car. Others in the royal entourages were put into a truck. Four armed Liechtensteiner policemen boarded the truck too, ordering everyone to lie on the floor and stay there, even when the truck was bumping. One hour later, both car and truck, Vladimir and his group, were back in Austria, under Allied control.

German Field Marshal Albert von Kesselring, when he arrived in Feldkirch early on the morning of May 3rd, decided to surrender, and at ten A.M. French troops entered the town. But during the next several days, Soviets too were cruising the area, easily persuading the Allies to hand over POWs, including many Whites, to Stalin. In May–August 1945, the Allies turned over more than two million two hundred thousand Russians to Soviet custody. Most of them had not been collaborating with the Nazis, but many were nonetheless killed immediately. Later, others were either shot upon their return to Soviet soil or sent to the Gulag.

The British surrendered to the Soviets thirty-five White generals—to face deaths of unimaginable horror in Soviet dungeons. These included General Andrei Shkuro, the man who had saved the Vladimirovichi in the Caucasus, and Peter Krasnov, the famous Civil War general and Cossack chieftain turned novelist, rescued from Novorossiysk twenty-five years before. Krasnov was one of the few who had fought for the Germans. The great German retreat brought him to Trieste, and from there he went to Austria and surrendered to the British. The British army drove him and other Cossack men, women and children into the Soviet zone. Meanwhile some two hundred members of Holmston-Smyslovsky's First Russian Army voluntarily agreed to return to the USSR from Austria. They were taken straight to the Gulag. In Yugoslavia, monarchist Vassily Shulgin was arrested and jailed by the occupying Soviet army.

With the British so willing to assist the Soviets in rounding up prominent White emigrés, the survival of Grand Duke Vladimir was an aberration. The Soviet secret services were kidnapping people with ease from the French occupied zone in western Austria, crossing the frontier between their zone and the French in the small hours of the morning. The best explanation for Vladimir's survival is that British intelligence decided to keep him at their disposal, just in case he might prove to be a valuable asset.

In November, King George VI received a letter from Vladimir that the King's private secretary, Sir Alan Lascelles, described as "intelligent and sensible." Lascelles reported to the Foreign Office that the grand duke "says that he could communicate to The King or to H.M.G. certain aspects of what he calls 'the Russian problem' which he thinks are unknown to them and which they might be very glad to know."

Vladimir wanted to come to England and speak directly to the king. The king demurred but suggested that someone be sent to the grand duke to "find out if he really has got anything to say that is worth hearing." After consulting with British authorities in Austria, the Foreign Office replied to the king that "our people in Austria could [not] possibly get in touch with [the grand duke] without grave risk of its becoming known to the Soviet representatives, whose minds would at once be filled with the worst suspicions." In the end, King George seemed concerned only that the Romanov know that his letter had been safely received, and that British interests were only to avoid offending the Soviets.

Vladimir would not be allowed to pass or to flee to Spain, where he felt he would be secure, for the next sixteen months, but he was not surrendered to the Soviets either. All the other Russians staying in the same Feldkirch hotel with him were given over to the Soviets, who sent them back by locked cattle cars to the Soviet Union. The Whites in 1945 might well have echoed Nicholas II after his abdication when he wrote in his diary, "everywhere is treachery, cowardice, and deceit."

CHAPTER FIFTEEN

The End of the Line

B Y 1945, ONLY FIVE GRAND DUKES and grand duchesses of the
seventeen who had escaped the Bolsheviks were still alive: Peter's
widow, Militsa; Andrew; Marie; and Nicky's two sisters, Xenia and
Olga. Militsa, who had survived the hunt by the Gestapo, fled Rome
in 1945 with her sister, Queen Elena, for Alexandria, Egypt. Her
grandson, Dmitri Romanovich, remembers the years following as
happy ones; a great reader, Militsa was contented with her books, and
Egypt, where the living was cheap and the climate agreeable, was then
a "paradise" for a foreign resident. Her death there in 1951 went virtually unnoticed by the world.

This was not the case of the last two children of Alexander III and
Minnie, Xenia and Olga. Xenia's life after 1945 is an unhappy chronicle of straitened financial circumstances and failing health. She remained dependent upon the largesse of the British royal house, and
this provided her with the shell but not the substance of a royal life.
George V had said that Xenia was his favorite cousin. They had
known each other since a visit he made to St. Petersburg as a young
midshipman. Because of her big and beautiful eyes, his nickname for
her was "Owl." Xenia had lived rent-free in royal "grace and favor"
houses since arriving as an exile with her mother in 1919, first at Frogmore in Windsor Great Park and then, after 1936, when the children
had all grown, at Wilderness House, a twenty-two room structure
next to the maze at Hampton Court.

There she lived a very quiet life, looked after by a Russian nun, Mother Martha. Xenia built a chapel in the house so that she could have services regularly under her own roof. She is reported to have remarked that the Bolsheviks had taken everything away from her but had left her "with one privilege—to be a private person," almost the same sentiment her husband, Sandro, had expressed nearly thirty years before.

Queen Mary went to see her at Wilderness House in 1946, where the grand duchess had returned after spending the war years in Scotland. The queen reported that Xenia "has a bad duodenal ulcer & suffers much and looks very ill poor dear, her son Feodore lives with her, he ought to be in a sanatorium for he is eaten up with lung trouble . . . "

The house was large, but the supply of cash was not. Queen Mary sent Xenia presents fairly regularly, and they tended to be practical: a bedjacket, housecoat, underwear and food. Xenia responded, "Oh, & here comes a chicken—now this is really too angelic of you—May dear—thank you 1000 times." During her last years, Xenia spent much of her time in bed, still looked after by Mother Martha, who was actually much more ill than Xenia.

In a secluded bedroom, beneath the soft glow of a ruby lamp that burned constantly before an icon, Xenia died, April 20, 1960, aged eighty-five. At her bedside were her daughter, the beautiful Irina Yusupov, herself now an old woman, and two of her sons, Andrew and Dmitri. The funeral provided the occasion for a gathering of the clan; Xenia's family itself was large. The White Russian community turned out in full force, as did various British dignitaries representing people like Queen Elizabeth and the Archbishop of Canterbury. The queen does not generally attend any funerals, except those of close family members. Earl Mountbatten and Marina, Duchess of Kent, were the two most prominent people to attend Xenia's funeral.

Xenia's estate was valued at $348,361, although her friends had thought her virtually penniless. In death, at the cemetery of elegant Roquebrune–Cap Martin, Xenia was finally reunited with her philandering Sandro, who had died nearly thirty years before. Her sister, Olga, was unable to come to the funeral; her life too was drawing to its end.

In 1948, Grand Duchess Olga had left Denmark in great haste—and with considerable unstated reluctance. With her went her husband, her two sons and her two Danish daughters-in-law. The family had spent almost thirty years in Denmark and regarded that country as home. Though after Minnie's death Olga had received no jewels, she did get a part of the money from the sale of Hvidore. With it, in 1932, she bought a farm in Ballerup, Knudsminde, not far from Copenhagen. Besides working the farm, Olga painted and even sold some of her paintings, as Ducky was doing in France, although they were by no means a major source of income for her.

When the Nazis occupied Denmark, German officers would visit Olga to pay their respects to the sister of the last tsar. Olga felt in no position to prevent them from doing so, though she was not happy about the situation. But there were other guests in German uniform whom Olga sincerely did welcome: Russian emigrés and Soviet POWs, now collaborating with Hitler. When the Nazi regime collapsed, some of these men returned to Knudsminde, now seeking asylum. The Soviet Mission was paying one hundred kronor to anyone reporting a "Soviet defector," and left wing Danish bureaucrats were promoting what people called "repatriation in handcuffs." Olga did what she could to prevent this, sometimes even hiding people in her attic for several weeks. She was the only Romanov to help her compatriots, clandestinely abetting their journeys to Chile and Argentina.

One episode in the summer of 1945 particularly aroused the Kremlin. Pro-German Russian Cossacks, fifty to sixty thousand in all, were interned by the British near Lienz in Austria. One thousand four hundred thirty of them were White emigrants, not even Soviet citizens. The British seemed ready to give them all to Stalin, as they had so many others. Peter Krasnov, interned with all the rest of them, made an appeal to Olga, the only Romanov who appeared to be interested in the fates of these Russians. Olga turned to her cousin, Axel, Prince of Denmark. Axel promised to help, provoking the irritation of the British as well as the rage of the Soviets.

Krasnov's appeal went for naught. He and the others were sent to the Soviet Union. The White generals were executed at Lefortovo Prison in Moscow in a manner reminiscent of the Dark Ages: They were stripped, hooked to a wall by their ribs, and left to die. Krasnov was treated more leniently: Because of his advanced age he was simply shot. Before the execution, a Soviet interrogator, mouthing an ancient prejudice, was reported to have told Krasnov, "What a foolish thing on your part to believe the British. Trading is their age-old metier. They will betray anybody and anything without blinking an eye."

Moscow, having taken care of the White generals, still sought vengeance against Olga and plotted against her. Early in 1948, a Soviet agent posing as a defector came to her farm and asked for work. She hired him. The man then went to the Soviet Embassy and claimed that Olga was attempting to keep him in Denmark against his will. The Soviets lodged an official protest. The Danish authorities, already frightened by their confrontation with the British about Krasnov's Cossacks back in 1945, decided that Olga must leave the country as soon as possible.

The announced reason for Olga's departure was her fear that the Cold War might affect Denmark and make her vulnerable to the Soviet secret police. And so in May 1948 Olga and her family sold their farm, left their comfortable Danish existence and became refugees yet again. Twenty years before, the Danes had proudly protected Olga's mother, "their" former Danish princess. Now their fear of the Kremlin's new might overrode any such feelings.

Olga's first stop was London. The previous month, Scotland Yard had contacted J. S. P. Armstrong, Agent General in Britain for the province of Ontario, asking whether Olga would be welcome in Canada. This was the place of exile the British had selected for her. Armstrong was told that it was important that Olga leave Britain "as soon as possible." Before leaving, Olga attended Queen Mary's eighty-first birthday party. When asked later whether she had brought up the subject of her mother's jewelry—in 1948 she needed money more than ever—she shook her head vigorously, saying, "Why create unnecessary bitterness?"

Olga subsequently wrote a long letter to Queen Mary from her new home, Nassaguawaya Corner Farm in Campbellville, Ontario. Unlike Xenia, who used writing paper engraved with a coronet, Olga used the cheapest quality.

We have got settled on our farm and are very happy. It is about 45 miles fr. Toronto in a very picturesque part of the country—higher up & somewhere not far from Guelph, Hamilton & the Niagara falls. Lovely country all around. Our house is large enough for us—smaller than ours in Denmark & as yet devoid of furniture—that we can get by and by. The great thing was to *find*

a farm. . . . I love Canada—the large & lovely country & the
most friendly kind & helpful people. We have many very nice acquaintances and some friends even . . . Happily my old maid
'Mimka' is quite happy here & even likes the food I cook. So that
is a great comfort. She has a good caracter [*sic*]—always good
humour & enjoys life & loves us all too. I haven't had time to
paint yet—but soon, when we get a workman & wife—the
woman can cook & do the housework—then I'll be free.

The contrast is stark. Queen Mary's childhood may not have been opulent, but it is doubtful that she ever did any housework or cooked a meal.

Three years later, Olga and her husband had to sell their farm. It
was simply too much for them to manage and Xenia wrote to Queen
Mary that it was too expensive. Olga moved into "a tiny bungalow (it
will be easier to look after) nearer to our boys & to our church in
Toronto." This was in Cooksville. She held an exhibition of her paintings in Toronto and to her delight sold twelve of them in spite of the
fact that "there are but few houses with *pictures* here—people buy
prints (they cost much less) & look quite nice."

The next year Olga wrote Queen Mary to thank her for sending her
a calendar for a Christmas present. Olga's letters were simple and matter of fact, testiments to her sturdy independence, mentioning for example that she took her collie walking early every morning before
preparing breakfast. She had no taste for the role of the piteous poor
relation, played so well by Xenia.

Olga's husband, Colonel Kulikovsky, died in Cooksville in August
1956; he was seventy-six. Olga herself fell severely ill by February
1960. She could hardly move and needed assistance to rise from her
chair. A former Russian officer, K. N. Martemianov, and his wife assumed the primary burden of her care. Her son Tikhon and his wife
came only on Fridays. The Martemianovs would spend Saturdays
with her. On other days Olga had to stay alone until four o'clock,
when the Martemianovs came. They urged her to move in with them;
she stubbornly said she did not want to leave her own house. Tikhon
said that his mother did not want to have anyone hired to look after
her. Tikhon and Guri, his brother, seemed willing to leave the responsibility of their mother to her friends.

On February 13th, Olga called the Martemianovs to tell them, "I feel
so well today; I could come to the phone myself. My legs can bend and

I can touch my head. Good night. Thank you." But the improvement was temporary. In early April, the Martemianovs took Olga to their apartment above Ray's Barber Shop in West Toronto. On April 12th, they put her in a hospital, where she felt weak and fell into apathy. Her mind was beginning to fail. She talked to her brother Michael, admired her mother's court dress, and mimicked Count Witte's disappointment at the plainness of the food provided at Gatchina by Alexander III.

But Olga had a sturdy constitution; she rallied and improved. In early June she was well enough to return to the Martemianov's apartment. Martemianov came to the hospital and said, "Your Highness, I have come to take you home." She beamed with joy, took his hand and wanted to kiss it. The weather was fine and Olga in high spirits. On the way home, in an ambulance, she joked, "I have been dreaming all my life about riding in an ambulance; finally my dream has come true!"

At the Martemianov's crowded and modest apartment, Olga said, "How good I feel. I am in paradise again." Tikhon came and brought her favorite orange-colored mug.

Again the slide downhill. On June 17th, when addressed "Your Highness," she asked, "And whom do you call Highness?"

"Of course, you."

"This is the first time I have been addressed this way."

The next day she said, "Don't call me Your Highness."

"But how should I call you?"

"As you did before."

"But I have always called you Your Highness."

"Well, call me Your Excellency then."

On her birthday, June 13th, Martemianov congratulated her.

"Don't congratulate me," she cried. "I cannot understand anything and I don't understand anything."

The doctors said she was suffering from cancer.

Another former Russian officer, Gleb Odintsov, suggested that a miracle-working icon be brought to Olga's bedside, the icon of Our Lady of Kursk. The icon had allegedly been found on September 8, 1295. The city of Kursk by that time had been destroyed by the Tatars, and people were obliged to rely upon hunting for their livelihood. A hunter had found the icon at the root of a tree, and as soon as he took it, a spring opened up under his feet. This was the only miracle-working icon of Russia abroad. It was taken from Russia on March 1, 1920, through Istanbul to Salonika (most probably out of Novorossiysk). Six months later, on General Wrangel's request, the icon was carried back to Russia, this time to the Crimea, but on October 29, 1920, it left Russia with the last White Guards.

Olga was extremely enthusiastic about the icon. She remembered that several years earlier it had been brought to Cooksville when Kulikovsky was very ill. His "gangrene" of the foot had disappeared after the icon had arrived. But the holy fathers at the Jordanville Monastery in New Jersey who now had custody of the icon answered the request made on Olga's behalf by saying that it would cost one hundred dollars to ship it to her and they were not prepared to send it without prepayment. Olga herself did not have one hundred dollars. Several former White Guard officers, old people themselves, collected money from their miserable savings and finally were able to send the requisite amount to the holy fathers.

Three visitors carried the icon to Olga's bedside on September 16th at 5:30 P.M. Seeing the new faces, Olga got very nervous, crying "Grandma! Where is the Grandma?" which is how she referred to Mrs. Martemianov. She became calm when the latter grasped her hand. The presentation of a miracle-working icon must be accompanied by an Orthodox mass. Tikhon was late for the service; Olga repeatedly made the sign of the cross; others quietly wept. When the icon was taken away, Olga asked that the light not be switched on, lay serenely in her bed and smiled.

By mid-November, in constant pain and fever, all Olga said was "leave me alone." She refused to eat and would drink nothing but water. She would not answer questions. She died on November 25, 1960.

Olga was the last grand duchess, the last link with the family of Alexander III. Russian newspapers abroad devoted much space to obituary notices. The *New York Times* ran a prominent article but erroneously showed a photograph of Olga's niece, Olga Nikolaevna, the oldest daughter of Nicholas II, murdered long ago at Yekaterinburg, not Olga Alexandrovna, Nicky's younger sister. The self-effacing Olga Alexandrovna probably would have laughed rather than been angry.

Aged members of monarchist organizations like the Union of Nobility and the Akhtyrsky Hussars, a regiment founded in the seventeenth century, which had fought the armies of Frederick the Great and whose honorary colonel Olga had been, came to grieve their grand duchess. These specters of a long gone past gathered for the lengthy funeral ceremony, which lasted from nine A.M. until after noon. Eight hundred mourners packed the small Russian Orthodox Cathedral of Christ the Saviour in Toronto on November 30th. No royals attended, but messages and flowers came from people all over the world. Olga was related to most of the royal houses of Europe. The most prominent wreath, of red and white carnations, was sent by King Frederick and Queen Ingrid of Denmark. Olga's sons Tikhon and Guri stood to the right of the catafalque. Eight members of the former Imperial Cadets, now men in their sixties, stood guard at the bier.

At the cemetery Bishop John of San Francisco pronounced the final blessing and dropped a pinch of "true Russian soil" into the grave. Thus the last grand ducal grandchild of Alexander II, born one year after his brutal murder in March 1881, went to her final rest, covered, like him, by the sheltering earth.

⟿

If Olga achieved tranquility in exile and old age, her first cousin Marie found nothing but turbulence. Restless but spirited, she had decided to try to build a new life for herself in America in the late 1920s. She had enjoyed very much an earlier visit that had taken her across the country to California. From the train window she sampled the vast North American panorama. "I was filled with exhilaration at the sight of space; the feeling of space entered into my very being. It made me breathe deeper, it gave me a sensation of freedom, it reminded me of my own country."

However, when she talked in New York about the possibility of entering business in the United States, perhaps by marketing a new brand of perfume, she got nowhere. People did not take her seriously; she had failed at her design business in Paris. She did not even get the opportunity to show her samples. But while recovering from ankle surgery, she sent off an incomplete memoir to an editor at Alfred E. Knopf, the New York publishers. Knopf rejected the manuscript, later ruing that decision. Viking accepted it, and the response was so favorable that Marie settled down to finish the book, writing in Russian, "the language in which I could express myself more easily than in any other."

This book, published in 1931 in English as *Education of a Princess*, was successful enough to be taken up by the Book of the Month Club. In the meantime Marie also got offers to work as a style consultant and dress designer. These events made her decide to return to France, wind up her affairs there, and move to America once again, creating a new life for herself.

This meant leaving her house, animals, friends and brother Dmitri, still married and in Europe. Marie found it most difficult to say good-bye to her stepmother, Princess Paley, whom she knew to be dying of cancer, although the princess was still unaware of the gravity of her own condition. This time Marie says she crossed the Atlantic with "very little luggage," no maid and only three hundred dollars in her pocket. This was all she now had; her jewels were gone. She carried her typewriter and her Russian guitar, and during the trans-Atlantic crossing worked hard at her writing. "I realized," she records, "that at the age of nearly forty I was about to change deliberately the entire structure of my existence. I had seen enough of America to know how different my life would be over there."

In New York, merchant Edwin Goodman hired Marie as a fashion consultant for his store, Bergdorf Goodman, but he seemed not to know what to do with her. Marie simply sat in the store and was gawked at; no one knew exactly what a grand duchess was other than being a very important person.

She therefore quit and, emboldened by the success of her book, hired an agent and began touring the country on a lecture circuit he organized for her. Her subject was her escape from Russia. She took along with her a young woman named Betty Tobias whom she had met in Goodman's office. Betty became secretary, companion and maid of all work to the "G.D.," as she called her.

Before beginning the speaking tour, the two went shopping at Macy's, where Betty helped the grand duchess buy fake furs. Marie could afford nothing more and knew that no one in the world would think a Russian grand duchess would wear anything but the best. Marie also bought a brown lace dress that she wore for every lecture. After some months she told Betty that she thought the dress could now stand up by itself.

People were fascinated by Marie and by what she had to say. One of the most popular lecturers in America at the time was Professor William Lyon Phelps of Yale, who invited the grand duchess to speak there. "She made a most agreeable impression," he wrote, "both on the lecture audience and on the students, and indeed on everyone she met at Yale. There was not a trace either of shyness or of condescension. Perfect ease of manner." Phelps was fascinated by Marie's English, which she spoke with "absolute accuracy, only it was almost too precise; it was faultlessly faultless."

Audiences everywhere found Marie's story, whether or not it was altogether true, moving and compelling. After a lecture in Flint, Michigan, as she was leaving the hall, a man pressed a ten dollar bill into her hand.

"Why did he do that?" she asked Betty.

"He feels sorry for you."

Although not especially tall, Marie gave the impression of being so. It was a matter of carriage and presence. Her waist was tiny, but she had "shoulders like a policeman," she would say. In her manner she was regal but simple. In America she did not mind sitting on the floor and eating an unpared apple. Yet in Europe she expected people to bow and to back their way out of her presence. Marie liked good food, and in restaurants she was always careful to tip generously because "otherwise the newspapers would report that she did not."

She was both generous and gregarious; through her speaking tours she made many friends, perhaps because so many Americans love titles. Irving Thalberg, the movie tycoon, lionized her in Hollywood. But her circle was wide. She came to know Eleanor Roosevelt well and frequently drove from New York to Hyde Park for visits.

The lectures and the book made money, but the grand duchess spent it faster than she made it. She kept a car, driver and maid in New York, in addition to Betty. And one summer, complaining that she was hardpressed for funds, she nonetheless rented the house of the great banker J. P. Morgan in Glen Cove, although she rarely used it. Marie's rights as an author were represented by George T. Bye, who charged her "the usual agency fee of ten per cent of the gross proceeds." Marie found these terms "most satisfactory," and she learned that Bye could be trusted. But interaction with the publishing world of New York was a totally new experience for Marie. She often felt uneasy. When an article in the popular magazine *Liberty* failed to appear on the announced date, she angrily wrote to Bye, "I hope very much for your sake and mine that you have not been a party to pulling my leg." To which Bye slyly answered, "I do not know of any more pleasant employment than pulling your leg."

Marie, unlike most Romanovs, was not anti-Semitic. A while into their relationship, Betty Tobias asked her, "Do you know that I'm Jewish?"

"Why do you ask?" was the answer. "If the tsar had treated Jews correctly instead of turning the Cossacks on them, I wouldn't be here and you wouldn't either."

In 1941, Marie left the United States for Argentina because she was disgusted by the wartime alliance between the United States and Soviet Union and the new warmth many Americans were expressing toward the Soviet system. She could not stay in a country that was giving arms to the regime that had slain her father. A second reason was that, although the king of Sweden, her "anchor," as she called him, quietly and regularly sent Marie money (and had provided her with a Swedish passport), she spent whatever she got as soon as she got it and always felt pressed. Buenos Aires would be much cheaper than New York.

Marie complained that Americans admired only her title and despised her for her poverty. She had many acquaintances, she said, but no real friends. She lived out the war years in South America, renting the first floor of a small house with a garden. Always resourceful, she made money by painting and doing watercolors of the interiors of beautiful houses. She also wrote articles on fashion and interior decoration.

War's end found Marie still in Buenos Aires. Her Swedish son, Prince Lennart, came there on business in 1947, doing films for Scandinavian Airlines and a marine life insurance company, work that took him all over the world. For the first time mother and son had an adult conversation together, and Marie shared her deepest feelings with Lennart. She confessed to him that she had always been lonely, felt abandoned because she grew up without a mother, manipulated by others, rootless, thoroughly at home nowhere. Marie spent much of her life looking for love, and, although discreet about it, was susceptible to affairs.

Lennart found his mother rapidly aging. Although still in her fifties, she was thin and frail, suffering from low blood pressure, duodenal ulcers and sclerosis that made her legs swell. But the grand duchess perked up sufficiently in the late 1940s to leave Argentina for Europe, where she began to travel more or less constantly, making the circuit of relatives. She carried always a voluminous amount of luggage, including much clothing, a sewing machine, typewriter, camera and photographic apparatus (she liked to develop and print her own photographs), and her paints also. Her son called it an "artistic mess." The family found Marie a difficult guest. She did not like children, even her own grandchildren, of whom she was outspokenly critical. Perhaps she had forgotten that as a child she enjoyed irritating her elders. She still grieved the death of the only person she had ever truly loved, her brother, and told Dmitri's friends that his former wife Audrey had sold his personal belongings for six thousand dollars. They were shocked by the impersonality of the act, and that Audrey, a rich woman, should have done this. Marie's own financial worries were over because the Swedish king in 1952 gave her an annuity. The arrangement was sensible. She could not spend the capital, and the income was adequate for her basic needs.

Marie died in Germany in 1958; she was sixty-eight. Despite her considerable talent, hers was a life without focus or consequence. She had consistently abandoned her husbands, her children and her various enterprises in search of something she was never able to find.

Marie's grand ducal cousin Andrew, to the contrary, had a peaceful sunset. Andrew, in Paris, was the last survivor among the Romanov grand dukes who fled Russia. In his old age, he continued to live quietly in the shadow of his wife. Kshesinskaya stopped reminiscing about her exuberant youth and her affairs with other Romanovs. Outside of school, her pleasures lay in entertaining guests, playing cards and nurturing an unimaginable number of cats. Andrew, detached from politics, cultivated beautiful Russian ladies with no romances implied, simply relishing their companionship. He would invite guests for dinner, but—mindful that he was a grand duke—only if they were of appropriate background or current standing.

When he arose on October 31, 1956, he said he felt fine, although he was scarcely robust and his eyesight had for some time been failing. That morning he worked in his study as was his custom but left the room suddenly after noon, exclaiming that he felt dizzy. He lay down on his bed and died. He was seventy-seven, old for a Romanov. In fact Andrew broke the family longevity record by six months; the oldest male Romanov previously had been Grand Duke Michael Nikolaevich, Sandro's father and Andrew's great uncle.

Andrew's protracted funeral process, as described by his widow, Kshesinskaya, in her memoir, *Dancing in Petersburg,* reminds us of that of Emperor Alexander III, except that the undertakers did their work better and the corpse did not begin to disintegrate in the interval between death and burial. For three days the body lay in state at home, with services held twice daily. Marie was the only person of grand ducal rank to attend, but others, including Xenia and Olga, sent letters of condolence. Kshesinskaya lived on until 1971, dying at the great age of ninety-nine and continuing to run her ballet school until she was ninety-two. Her one child, Vladimir, survived her by only three years.

◈

After 1945, Kyril and Ducky's son, Vladimir, was the only member of the family who was active in politics in any way. Vladimir's aunt Beatrice had married a Spanish prince, and, penniless, he moved in with her as soon as the British allowed him to leave Austria.

In 1948, Vladimir married a handsome, energetic woman, somewhat older than he. Leonida Bagration-Mukhranskaya was from an old family of Georgian nobility, distantly related to the Bagrations, hereditary kings of Georgia, which had been swallowed up by the Russian empire in 1801. The Bagrations therefore had been Russian subjects for more than a century; one of them served as a general in the Russian army that fought Napoleon, and Tolstoy wrote of him in *War and Peace*. Leonida was therefore, strictly speaking, of noble but not of royal blood. After the revolution of 1917 her family had moved to Constantinople, like thousands of other refugees, but they lived in a villa on the Bosphorus, entertaining guests lavishly, the source of their fortune unknown. Then they moved to Paris. There Leonida shrewdly made friends with Grand Duke Boris's mistress and later wife, Zinaida Rashevskaya, an outcast to all other Romanovs. Zinaida held a salon frequented by cosmopolitan *nouveax riches* who were excited by the proximity to a "real grand duke." Everyone gained. Boris loved his wife, indulging all her whims, and perhaps also made some profit from the acquaintance of unscrupulous industrialists and bankers of obscure origins.

In Nice, Leonida had met and married, in November 1933, a charming and debonair American expatriate millionaire named Sumner Moore Kirby, who had inherited a part of the Woolworth retail empire. Leonida was twenty; Kirby was thirty-nine, a man of infectious high spirits and great generosity, apparently much liked by all who knew him, which included many in the Riviera Russian colony. Kirby and Leonida produced a daughter, Helene, two years later. But the marriage failed and in 1937 they divorced. Undoubtedly Kirby amply provided for Leonida and their daughter. He would live on in France, at Montebello, his villa in the hills outside of Nice, even after the war broke out. As an American citizen Kirby was first interned by the Italians, who treated him well and allowed him to have his meals sent into camp from a nearby hotel. The Germans were not so kind. They sent him back to middle Europe as a political prisoner and he died in a camp at Leau just as the war was ending, another victim of Nazi brutality. Leonida had meanwhile moved to Spain.

When Vladimir came to Spain, his life was a mess. He had received little formal education, had no real career and was penniless. He stayed with his royal aunt, who regulated his life, making family meals obligatory and giving the young man only twenty-five dollars a month for private expenses. For a time Vladimir worked as an interpreter. But Leonida noticed the poor Romanov immediately.

On July 28, 1948, representatives of the Russian colony in Madrid came to Vladimir to congratulate him on his name day, for Russians traditionally as important an anniversary as a birthday. Vladimir rudely declared that he had no time for them because he was off to the dentist. But in fact, instead of the dentist, he had an appointment to elope with Leonida.

Vladimir's aunt, Princess Helen of Greece, heard the news immediately. Infuriated, she telegraphed all Russian bishops in Europe, and as a result they prohibited priests from marrying the elopers. But the two found a Greek church in Lausanne where they were married in the Greek, not the Russian, rite on August 30, 1948. By doing so, Vladimir effectively splintered himself off from the rest of the family. All his relatives, with the exception of his uncle Andrew, turned their backs on him. More than that, the emigré community was horrified. The shock reverberated for a long time. Five years later, an old general, Nicholas Shinkarenko, wrote to a friend, "Men marry whomever they want. But a man who marries [a person like Leonida] would have done better by marrying a Soviet DP [displaced person or refugee]. This marriage is shameful, indecent and intolerable, trampling into dirt the very heart of Russia's and the Romanovs' principles."

The newlyweds returned to Madrid, where Leonida's money allowed Vladimir to establish a court of sorts. His choice of advisors was peculiar. One of his chief aides was Yury Zherebkov, a notorious Nazi watchdog in Paris during the war who was not now even allowed to visit France. The grand duke and Irakly Bagration, Leonida's brother, who had proclaimed himself "Tsar of Georgia," allegedly began a business importing cars into Spain. Using his title and connections, Vladimir had obtained a license to bring in cars from Germany which he and Irakly later resold on the Spanish black market.

Even Grand Duke Gavriil Constantinovich, thankful to Vladimir for granting him a grand ducal title, wrote of Vladimir, "Poor soul, he has been tricked by these adventurers, Irakly and Leonida Bagration. This is very sad indeed." After five years of marriage, Leonida finally gave birth to a daughter, Maria. Vladimir's supporters expressed disappointment, for they had been eagerly anticipating a boy whose name, they said, would have been Nicholas.

The older generation of emigrants, even those who accepted his marriage, remained skeptical about Vladimir; his hopes seemed even more difficult to realize than those of Kyril. Aside from continuing questions of legitimacy, Kozlianinov, who had been Dmitri's friend and secretary, wrote, "The dynasty in Russia was supported by the nobility, its main pillar. Where will you find nobility today, even if Russia is liberated by some miracle? [Furthermore] no restoration is possible . . . without agreement and cooperation of the great nations. And they will not consider restoration in Russia, even of a constitutional monarchy."

Vladimir himself knew that his cause was shaky, and in February 1952 attempted to rally support by issuing an "Appeal to the Free World." In this proclamation, which went unnoticed despite being sent to virtually anyone of any political importance, Vladimir argued that the Soviet Union should not be confused with Russia and that being anticommunist should not mean being anti-Russian. "The Red Dictator is certainly not successor of Emperor Alexander I," and the European and American press were wrong in speaking about the "Russian menace" or the danger of "Russian imperialism." The majority of Russians, Vladimir argued, loathed the rule of Stalin and communism in general, and that was why "millions of soldiers of the Red Army went over to the Germans, believing them to be sincere enemies of Communism coming to deliver Russia and its people from their Soviet rulers." The last sentence probably referred to his own inglorious role during the war.

After a while Vladimir found it possible to return to France, from which he had been banned for his wartime collaboration with the Nazis. Playing bridge, golf, reading detective stories, sailing and gardening became his quiet routine, living either at his parents' house (which he inherited) in St. Briac, or in an apartment in Paris. Leonida owned a villa in Madrid that became incorporated into the Vladimirs' schedule.

Just as Vladimir had in World War II sought to return to Russia behind German bayonets, in the summer of 1950, with the outbreak of war in Korea, he hoped for a conflict between the United States and the Soviet Union that would bring him to the throne. In July, Vladimir was prepared to "create an executive body and also centers of communication and propaganda in case decisive events come." The decisive events for which he was waiting could only have been World War III.

Vladimir made enemies among Russian monarchists. In 1953, a former lady-in-waiting, Baroness Elena Gune, visited Vladimir and his wife and then sent them a letter of thanks for the reception. Vladimir's chief of staff sent an indignant reply. "You send your thanks for a nice reception. One could think that you as a former lady-in-waiting to Their Imperial Majesties should very well know that when addressing the Royal Persons one can thank only for a 'gracious' and not a 'nice' reception." The old lady replied vigorously. "When I returned home and went through my mail I discovered your rude impudent letter. . . . This letter has been read in Paris by all those Russians whose opinion should be of concern to you. Everyone was indignant and even mocked you." Indeed, by that time, Vladimir's name had been completely deprived of any royal charisma it might ever have held.

❧

As long as a Romanov was tsar, there was no question about who was head of the family. Today argument swirls around who has that role or indeed even concerning who is a Romanov.

Unlike his father, Vladimir Kirillovich never called himself emperor, but he irritated others in the family with his imperial pretensions. Because of the flaws to his father's claim, Vladimir had no right, they believed, to act as the head of the family and heir to the Russian crown. No descendants of other branches of the Romanovs ever recognized Vladimir as head of the Imperial House or as heir apparent.

A year after the death of the last grand duchess, Olga, in October 1961, Prince Nikita Alexandrovich, one of Sandro's many sons and a senior member of the family, made public a letter he had written to Vladimir. "Stop performing this shameful farcical charade! Stop humiliating your older relatives and their children!" Endless polemics erupted over Vladimir's behavior. Romanovs, Nikita argued, had to be called by that name and not Romanovsky, as Vladimir was insisting. The latter name had been given long ago by Tsar Nicholas I to the children of his daughter, Grand Duchess Maria Nikolaevna, from her marriage to the Duke of Leuchtenberg, "of which fact you are perhaps not even aware," Nikita Alexandrovich tartly observed.

The family felt outraged that the Vladimirovichi considered that they were now the only Romanovs, that the family, due to "improper marriages," had declined dramatically to three, what it was in the eighteenth century. The family believed that they had married no worse than the male Vladimirovichi (Kyril and Vladimir) themselves.

Nikita also averred that monarchical power now belonged to all Romanov males as a collectivity. Furthermore, Nikita argued, Vladimir had no right to call his wife and daughter grand duchesses. Contemptuously Nikita called the former "Madame Kirby," the name of her first husband, as if to emphasize that the Vladimirs' marriage was not legitimate, having not taken place in a Russian Orthodox church. Moreover Vladimir's wife, Nikita insisted, had never belonged to a royal family because the Bagration-Mukhranskis had been ordinary subjects of the Russian emperor, like other noble families.

In 1969, isolated from the rest of the family, Vladimir proudly proclaimed his only child, Maria, to be regent of the Russian Imperial Throne in case of his death. Thus Vladimir chose to defy the law decreed by Emperor Paul that succession could pass through the female line only with the extinction of the last male issue.

Maria's subsequent marriage provided a splendid occasion. The groom was Prince Franz Wilhelm of the house of Hohenzollern, a great-grandson of the last German kaiser and a cousin of Louis Ferdinand, "Lulu," who had married the bride's aunt Kyra. Once again the genes of the greater European royal family were pooled. The king and queen of Spain and a number of royal exiles from Italy, Bulgaria, Albania, Portugal and Egypt inflated the importance of the wedding with their presence.

But the union brought further grief to the succession issue and further dissention within the family. In 1976 Vladimir granted Franz Wilhelm the title of a Russian grand duke, Michael Pavlovich. Five Romanov males made an explicit and public protest to an act they considered an outrageous violation of imperial law, utterly without precedent.

In 1981, "Michael Pavlovich" and Maria provided Vladimir with a long awaited male descendant, George. The marriage, however, dissolved in divorce. The Hohenzollern reverted to his earlier name. Undeterred, Vladimir elevated his daughter Maria from prospective regent to heiress presumptive to the throne. None of the Vladimirovichi had yet even visited Russia.

CHAPTER SIXTEEN

❧

"Eternal Memory"

IF THE EARLY ROMANOVS HAD SEEN the decay of the family in the twentieth century, undoubtedly they would have been disgusted. But the passion of Peter the Great, the generosity of Catherine, the wily stubbornness of Paul, and the iron will of Nicholas I have not perished without a trace. If their descendants living abroad have lost much or all of this, the only Romanov survivor in Russia has not.

More than a century ago, back in 1874, Grand Duke Nicholas Constantinovich, a grandson of Nicholas I, was exiled to Central Asia. His crime of stealing his mother's diamonds embarrassed the family deeply and became a state secret. When the grand duke in exile subsequently fathered a son, Alexander, and married the boy's mother, a woman named Nadezhda Dreyer, the boy's birth certificate was marked "Top Secret by Decree of High Authority" on the place where the father was normally listed. But the godparents, Grand Duke Constantine Nikolaevich and Olga, Queen of Greece, were named. Obviously the subject was a person of importance.

Subsequently Alexander III granted the boy Alexander and his brother the rank of noblemen and a family name, Iskander, a Central Asian version of Alexander and identified with Alexander the Great of classical times. Prince Alexander Iskander grew to maturity, was allowed to join a Guards regiment, the Blue Cuirassiers, married and had two children, one of whom was a girl named Natalia.

Natalia was born in Petrograd on February 5, 1917, a month before the revolution dethroned her cousin Nicky. Her exiled grandfather, the grand duke, became her godfather in absentia. When the revolution got going, the Iskander family decided that it was safer to be in Central Asia and they joined the old grand duke there in Tashkent, where Natalia's early childhood was spent. She was barely one year old when her grandfather was killed by local revolutionaries, the first grand duke to die in the Red Terror. The family never discussed the circumstances of his death, and now no one knows exactly what happened.

Prince Alexander Iskander and his brother left home to join the Whites, and for a time the two Iskander princes were lost in the swirling havoc of civil war. Prince Alexander was reported missing in action. Meanwhile the revolutionaries forced Natalia, her brother and her mother to leave the grand ducal palace, but they did not persecute them. The family were helped by the fact that their name was Iskander, not Romanov, but even more by the preoccupation of the revolutionaries with their own survival in a bitter seesaw civil war.

After the war, the palace became a museum and little Natalia would visit it, aware of the fact that it had once been her home and that all its treasures—armor, sculpture, paintings—had once belonged to her family. The lavish rose garden, shielded by its high walls from Asian dust and harsh desert winds, continued to bloom. And in the cellar, a few hunting dogs still lived. Their master was gone, but they waited for his return.

Peace meant that the Bolsheviks would now have the opportunity to become interested in the Iskander family, conspicuous because of the memory of the grand duke. Nicholas Constantinovich had spent his own personal funds to build canals for irrigating the crops essential for sustaining the life of the people. But Natalia's mother knew she could expect no gratitude from the Bolsheviks and decided that she would take her family to Moscow. Giving up her husband for lost, she remarried and changed the name of her children immediately to that of her new husband. Thus Natalia dropped Iskander for Androsova.

Moscow offered new jobs and also safety in the anonymity of big city life. Former tsarist officers, bureaucrats, professors and merchants hoped to find privacy and security in the bustling new capital of the Soviet regime. The now-Androsovs found a spacious apartment, but a neighbor, apparently wanting the place himself and learning who they really were, threatened to report them to the secret police. The family fled to the Arbat district downtown near the Kremlin and to the squalor of a cramped basement apartment. Because they were neither peasants nor workers, the state gave them the status of *lishentzy,* people regarded as socially alien, having no right to vote and therefore unable to secure good jobs. Yet they survived.

Natalia had grown up to be dazzling in appearance and dashing in manner. Tall and svelte, with finely chiseled (and also very Romanov) features, she had radiant blue eyes, long blond hair and a captivating smile. Her mother, despite changing her name, never tried to conceal the past from Natalia. All the family photographs sat proudly on a shelf in the shabby Androsov apartment: Grand Duke Nicholas Constantinovich, his brother K.R. and Natalia's father, Prince Alexander Iskander. Natalia would proudly tell close friends of her real origins. Everyone was astonished; one of the friends said disgustedly, "Put those pictures away; it is indecent to keep them!" But the Androsovs were bold. Friends returning from Siberian exile, political pariahs, always knew that they could spend a few nights with the Androsovs.

Natalia perhaps inherited some of her grandfather's propensity for adventure. She did not conceal that she was a Romanov. She chose a wild career, professional motorcyclist. She joined the famous sports club Dynamo and became a prominent motorcycle racer. Then the troubles came.

It was 1939; Russia was experiencing Stalin's Great Terror, when millions were taken away to die, often inexplicably. Natalia was twenty-two. A young mechanic from Dynamo came courting her. When she boasted of her imperial lineage, he tried to blackmail her into sleeping with him. When she refused, he threatened to report her to the Lubyanka. Natalia slapped him hard across the face. He was very tall and muscular, but "I was a very strong woman," she says proudly.

Still, she panicked and burned all of her family papers. She changed her sports club and went to another famous one, Spartak. But in several weeks the Lubyanka summoned her. The secret police people were explicit. She had only two options, they said. Either she became a secret agent or she would be shot. Under the codename "Lola," Natalia began to work for Stalin's secret police.

Her Lubyanka supervisor came regularly to the Arbat where they met, not in her apartment but in the shadows of an archway outside. Years later Natalia learned that her file at the Lubyanka described her in the most flattering terms. She was young, intelligent and attractive. She had, in short, all the qualities of an excellent agent except one: She did not want the job. Her friends knew nothing of her Lubyanka affiliation. But she knew which of them would be arrested and when.

Many people found Natalia's manner pleasingly raffish; she dressed in men's jackets and leggings. She smoked. She was proud of her ancestry, especially her grand ducal grandfather and his reputation as a womanizer. She liked to whisper to guests that she was a Romanov, a descendant of tsars. Soon she became known as "the Queen of the Arbat," a district that was taking on some of the character of New York's Greenwich Village. Visitors found hers a warm hearth in a cold and gray metropolis. And she was embarked on an extraordinary career as a vertical motorcyclist at Gorki Park. She drove the machine up a wall. The secret to success, she says, was to "feel the vehicle" and to look only forward, never at the wheels.

Then the war broke out. The Germans invaded Russia. In the fall of 1941, when the enemy came very close to capturing Moscow and the Soviet Government fled, Natalia stayed in the city. She was in charge of her neighborhood fire brigade, on the alert for incendiary bombs dropped by German aircraft. When these bombs hit the ground, they whirled around sending out showers of sparks before they exploded and shot out a sea of flame. One had to catch the moment of impact and throw sand over the bomb to smother it before the explosion. Impatient Natalia would often seize the hissing bomb itself and throw it into the sand. Sometimes the white-hot bodies of bombs buried themselves deeply into the asphalt, setting even that aflame, and at night explosions and fires burst out everywhere, with people shouting and horses neighing in terror.

Natalia also joined a paramilitary militia as a motorcyclist courier. When she came to her Arbat neighborhood dressed exotically in a brown velvet jacket, army boots and breeches, some passerby, unused to such extravagant dress, detained her as a "German saboteur." Rumor then had the Germans already entering Moscow from the west. Crowds were running for the railway stations, losing their companions and their luggage in total panic and chaos.

Natalia took another job, driving a truck, delivering bread to the troops at the front and clearing snow from downtown streets afterward. She discovered that she had talent for mechanical matters and she could keep her truck in good repair. Few drivers were so adept.

As early as the summer of 1942, Stalin, now feeling more secure about the course of the war, decided that it was time to cheer up his people. He ordered more performances in Moscow: theater, concerts, opera and the circus. Natalia returned to her earlier career as a vertical motorcyclist. But the Lubyanka was not finished with her. They suggested she marry an intelligence officer and go abroad to work. She refused. In the summer of 1953, just after Stalin's death, they gave her a new assignment, promising it would be her last.

The Lubyanka suspected that an ambassador of a Western power in Moscow was a closet homosexual, an excellent subject for blackmail. Therefore the secret police constructed a trap. They knew that the ambassador was planning to take a vacation in the Crimea and that he would be traveling there by car.

On a hot summer morning, as Natalia tells it, a green Pobeda left Moscow's downtown and headed south. Two people were in the car, a handsome young man named Boris and a good-looking woman, Natalia. Being a good driver, she was at the wheel.

Young Boris was intended as bait for the ambassador. Natalia was there to portray them as a heterosexual couple. The Lubyanka thought the ambassador more likely to be attracted to a young man of uncertain sexuality than by an obvious homosexual. A married man would also be more discreet. But Natalia had another role; after all, the ambassador's sexual tastes were not proven. She too could be bait.

The ambassador was riding in a foreign car several miles ahead of the Pobeda, which was laboring to catch up to its prey. His car was fast, but his driver was a secret employee of the Lubyanka. The plan was that the two cars should meet. Suddenly the ambassador's car developed engine problems. The driver told his employer that they must stop. While the ambassador lowered his window to enjoy the fresh air and to contemplate the fields in bloom, the driver worked on the engine. Very soon he informed the ambassador that they needed a spare part without which the car could not function.

The driver began to hail passing cars, but none had the requisite part. Then the green Pobeda pulled up. "Yes," said the beauty driving it. "I have what you need." The driver returned to his engine, and the grateful ambassador invited the lady and her shy companion to join him in an impromptu picnic. Never since, Natalia says, has she enjoyed better coffee made on a spirit lamp. Boris, who spoke fluent French, acted as interpreter, and the conversation went well.

They agreed to meet again in Yalta. There, at Lubyanka expense, Natalia enjoyed the most luxurious vacation of her life, sailing along the Black Sea coast and hiking into the mountains, and even visiting the Massandra winery where she and her two companions were given samples of its famous sweet Crimean wine. The hotel where she and Boris stayed was just several miles away from Kichkine, the palace that had belonged to Natalia's great uncle, Grand Duke Dmitri Constantinovich. In the hotel the ambassador's rooms were heavily bugged. Agents had even put a microphone into a paperweight. But their work was crude. They had not even bothered to cover holes in the ceiling where they had placed more microphones.

All this was to no avail. The ambassador did not take the bait. The operation was a total failure. But the good news was that the Lubyanka kept its word, and Natalia says they never asked her to work for them again.

Her career as a motorcyclist soared. She was at the top of her profession now and toured the whole of the USSR. She used the world's best motorcycles—Harley Davidsons and Indian Scouts—but her performance, "Fearless Flight," was always dangerous. Sometimes she would spend a month in the hospital nursing broken bones. Fame brought fans. Natalia became friendly with the leading Moscow bohemians of the day, and they dedicated their poems and stories to her. In July 1964, eligible for a pension, she retired. But when she stopped performing, the world began to forget her and her life took on a smaller dimension.

Now, in late 1998, in her tiny studio apartment, the last Romanov in Russia and the only Russian among Romanovs, at the age of eighty-one lives alone with her dog. Natalia Androsova owns little of the great Romanov treasure, only her grandfather's crested silver spoons, a silver cup made for the coronation of Empress Elizabeth in 1742, a small decorative box, a cross and a tiny hinged icon. Whatever else of value she inherited, she had to sell in hard times. But material objects seem not of great importance to her.

Three years ago, in winter, Natalia Androsova found a dying puppy in the street. He was suffering from pneumonia and had been severely beaten. She picked him up, remembering the mournful howls of her grandfather's dogs when the grand duke was gone. She named the dog "Malysh" (Baby).

Malysh has grown up a healthy ginger-colored mongrel, friendly to visitors, passionately attached to Natalia. On her crutches she takes him for walks herself, even in wintertime when the sidewalks are sheathed with ice. Malysh talks to Natalia, adores Natalia, licks Natalia's plate clean. When she is out, the dog chews the front door, and an inch of wood is already gone from its surface.

Random gunfire signifies the instability of contemporary Russia, just as terrorist bombs punctuated the prolonged unrest that ultimately destroyed Romanov rule. When Malysh hears shooting in the streets, he starts whining and hides under the bed. Is Natalia herself afraid of these shots? "No," she says firmly. "I have never been afraid of anything."

Alarmed by a flicker of public interest in monarchy shown during the Khrushchev thaw, the Brezhnev leadership wanted to remove any vestiges of the Romanovs, including the Ipatiev house in Sverdlovsk (Yekaterinburg) where the last tsar and his family had been executed. By the irony of the gods, at that time the party boss of Sverdlovsk was Boris Yeltsin. The Politburo ordered the Ipatiev house demolished. Yeltsin had it destroyed at night and the site paved with asphalt.

The Soviet Union itself collapsed and Yeltsin, now the nation's chief political figure, sealed the fate of the old communist regime. Somewhat awkwardly Yeltsin fell into correspondence with Vladimir Kirillovich, and the upshot was that Vladimir traveled to Russia in November 1991. The only stipulation he made was that he should not need a visa to enter the country, his country.

The visit stirred excitement; both church and state were cordial. The official occasion was renaming the city, St. Petersburg. Vladimir visited his namesake grandfather's palace on the Neva, now the Scientists' Club, and there he sat for a while at his grandfather's desk. Seeing elsewhere a huge poster of Lenin stretching his arm toward the invisible heights of communism, Vladimir made a sad little joke. "Finally Lenin has blessed me." Leaving Russia, standing at the foot of the stairway to the plane, Vladimir crossed himself and said to his wife, Leonida, "if something happens to me, bury me here."

A few months later, on April 21, 1992, the day before Lenin's birthday, Vladimir suddenly died while giving a press conference in Miami, Florida, when he was making an impassioned plea for aid to Russia. Leonida got on the telephone to Boris Yeltsin to solicit his cooperation in the funeral arrangements. In three days the matter was accomplished and Vladimir went out in style. The three-and-one-half-hour funeral mass was held within the marble, malachite and golden splendor of St. Petersburg's vast St. Isaac's Cathedral, the coffin draped with the blue, white and red flag of Russia and the double-headed eagle of the Romanovs.

Vladimir's widow spared no expense to make the funeral a memorable one. But it was President Yeltsin and Mayor of St. Petersburg Anatoly Sobchak who made it possible by quickly granting all the official permissions. The patriarch himself presided and said of Vladimir in his eulogy, "His faith and long patience were not in vain. On the eve of his passage to the other world, he stepped on his native soil."

The vault at Sts. Peter and Paul Cathedral, traditional resting place of the Romanovs, was ready for Vladimir. Because the number of grand dukes was increasing so rapidly at the turn of the century, the Romanovs had then built an annex to the cathedral with sixty-two additional places, thirteen of which were filled before the revolution. The Soviet regime neglected them, but the tombs of Vladimir Alexandrovich, the patron of arts and French cuisine, and his younger brother Alexis, the navy man who favored fast women and slow ships, were reidentified and restored especially for this occasion. In 1995, the bodies of Kyril and Ducky were brought from Coburg to join the others. Russian flags and flowers brighten the tombs of these last Romanovs. But Minnie still lies in Denmark, yet to rejoin her Sasha.

In 1995, Russian monarchists established a Supreme Monarchist Council, trying to bind together the splinters of various quarrelsome and rivalrous groups and to propagate the idea of monarchy itself, to get Russians accustomed to the idea. The Vladimirovichi are energetically trying to implant the idea of a Romanov restoration, specifically their own, in the minds of the Russian people. If in the early 1990s this looked like daydreaming, by the late years of the decade the situation had changed significantly.

Maria Vladimirovna keeps today the title of Head of the Imperial House, although her octogenarian mother Leonida seems more interested in politics than she. For forty-four years, Leonida worked hand in hand with her husband. With Vladimir's death, she is the mastermind and major engine of the Romanov restoration movement and, during 1991–95, made twenty-six trips to Russia to push her cause.

Leonida's headquarters is her Paris home, thirty steps away from the corner of the Rue de Rivoli and the Place de la Concorde. A visitor passes through a small quiet courtyard with a white marble statue, and a tiny elevator takes him to the apartment of the grand duchess, a shrine to the last Romanovs. Leonida dresses in black and favors costume jewelry, artificial pearl necklace and earrings. Even her black slippers are studded with tiny pearl beads. She talks to people as would a charming grandmother, yet one senses an alert shrewdness and a driving ambition for her only grandchild, George Mikhailovich, born in 1981.

In the eyes of the pro-Vladimirovichi, he will sooner or later become Head of the House of Romanov. After the collapse of the Soviet Union, George was slated to enter the Admiral Nakhimov Naval Cadet School in St. Petersburg, following the precedent of his great grandfather Kyril. But the Russian military have confidentially told Leonida that the morale in all Russian cadet schools is now very low; cruelty reigns. They say it would be better for the boy to attend some military cadet school abroad, say, in Spain, and only later enter an academy in the land of his ancestors. Perhaps air or aerospace will lure George from the navy; he is said to prefer missiles to ships.

In January 1997 European newspapers announced that President Boris Yeltsin had granted the Vladimirovichi an official status in Russia, something they had wanted for years. The news proved a hoax, but the chances for restoration have begun to sprout. Policymakers are testing public opinion.

The monarchist movement in Russia remains divided. Some support holding a special popular assembly to elect a new tsar. Many dislike the Romanovs and prefer the candidacy of a grandson and namesake of the war hero Marshal Georgy Zhukov, now a student at a military school. But the best organized are those supporting the claim of the Vladimirovichi. They command twenty-three branches in the provinces and have established a Romanov museum in Moscow.

Many monarchists privately express their distaste for the pushiness and impatience of the Vladimirovichi. Even some of those sympathetic to the Vladimirovichi cause think it premature to bring the three members of "The Family," as they call them, to Russia. Their plan is to build a monarchist movement first and raise succession questions in the future, perhaps as long distant as fifty or sixty years.

Actually, the mayor of Palm Beach, Florida, has as good or better a claim to the throne than does any Vladimirovich or any other Romanov. He is a former U.S. marine, Paul Ilyinsky, the only child of

Grand Duke Dmitri who died in Switzerland in 1942. He is the only living son of a legitimate grand duke. He is a great-grandson of Alexander II through the male line—as he puts it, the only Romanov who is a "man to man to man" descendant of an emperor.

Paul's parents were married in a Russian Orthodox church, his mother having become a convert to the faith like so many other Romanov brides. Paul's only disqualification for the throne is that his mother was an American heiress, not a woman of royal blood.

But Paul Ilyinsky seems quite happy to be "Tsar of Palm Beach," as the local press calls him. He professes no interest in ruling Russia. Unlike most of the rest of the family he was friendly with Vladimir Kirillovich, just as his father Dmitri had supported Vladimir's father, Kyril. Paul is less friendly to the living Vladimirovichi. He admits that Vladimir's daughter, Maria, has a following. "She has a lot of people on her coattails," he says, but "I have not met a single one of them that I would, frankly, want to have lunch with."

Russia today has a new obsession with its imperial past in part because it was for so long a forbidden topic. The remains of the miracle-worker St. Seraphim of Sarov, the saint who helped Empress Alexandra conceive a son, were found in a sack at the Museum of Atheism in St. Petersburg and have been buried again with great ceremony. Sergei Alexandrovich, resting in pieces beneath what had become a Kremlin parking lot, was reinterred with great fanfare at Novospassky Monastery in Moscow where sixteen other, early Romanovs lie.

The most popular Russian TV anchor, Evgeny Kiselyev, reputedly one of the most influential men in Russia, has declared that

eventually it is necessary to find a way out of our endless political upheavals. There is a Spanish way. Restoration of a constitutional monarchy in Spain has promoted transition from dictatorship to democracy and even checked a military coup in 1981. [For Russia] no possible solution, no matter how fantastic and paradoxical it may look, should be disregarded. ... Remember, many people reacted in such a manner to the first cautious mentioning of a multi-party system, free elections, and freedom of the press only ten years ago.

Russia may now be a country in search of an idea, as Boris Yeltsin suggests, but Russians are clearer in what they oppose than what they support. Despite the muted suggestions of Evgeny Kiselyev and the strenuous efforts of the Vladimirovichi, the popular imagination remains unmoved. None of the three Vladimirovichi are heroic; Leonida, Maria and George are pudgy. "If you are creating a myth," writes Masha Lipman, deputy editor of a Moscow news magazine, "there should be something catchy about it. The fat boy isn't catchy."

Some Russian monarchists even say that many European princes have Romanov blood and could be considered candidates for the tsardom. Some of them might even qualify as "catchy." Prince Charles, for example, has as much Romanov blood as does pudgy George. Each carries 1/32 the genes of Nicholas I, the Iron Tsar. Charles's candidacy for the tsardom would be the ultimate triumph of the House of Windsor over the Romanovs!

❧

Though Charles has never visited Russia, from October 17th until October 20th, 1994, Queen Elizabeth II, accompanied by Prince Philip, made a state visit there. This was the first occasion in which a reigning British monarch set foot on Russian soil. The future George V attended the funeral of Alexander III in 1894, and Edward VII as Prince of Wales visited Russia many times, being married to Minnie's sister Alexandra. But when Edward came to Russia as king, he did not set foot on Russian soil; security kept him aboard ship. Instead he entertained his imperial nephew Nicholas II aboard the royal yacht anchored at Tallinn and in turn dined aboard the tsar's yacht.

In 1994, Queen Elizabeth traveled part-way by yacht and could give a dinner aboard for Boris Yeltsin. But she flew to Moscow and toured St. Petersburg. In Moscow, at a performance of *Giselle,* the Queen and the Duke of Edinburgh sat in the imperial box at the Bolshoi, below the gilt hammer and sickle still to be seen both there and on the red and gold damask stage curtain. The queen wore some of her more spectacular jewels: a sapphire and diamond necklace, ear drops and tiara, but none of Romanov provenance. The only Russian jewelry she put on during the trip was a cabochon sapphire and pearl drop brooch, given as a wedding present by England's Queen Alexandra to her sister, the future Russian empress, in 1866.

At a formal dinner given by Boris Yeltsin, after caviar and salmon, cream of asparagus soup, chicken fillets with fruit, and a strawberry parfait, the president toasted the queen. "Bearing your mission with dignity, Your Majesty, you confirm an important idea—monarchy can be an integral part of a democratic system of government, an embodiment of the spiritual and historic unity of a nation."

Queen Elizabeth and Prince Philip visited the Romanov tombs at Sts. Peter and Paul Cathedral but offered no comment. No communiqué raised the matter of Russian succession controversies.

The closest relative Prince Philip has among Romanovs is Natalia Androsova. Philip is the great nephew of the martyred Grand Duchess Ella, but she had no descendants. Philip and Natalia are both descendants of Grand Duke Constantine Nikolaevich, and are therefore Constantinovichi. It goes without saying that Philip did not see her during the royal visit to Russia. It is doubtful that he even knows of her existence.

Queen Elizabeth's Russian visit coincided with the one hundredth anniversary of the death of Alexander III, although no one officially took notice of that fact. During that one-hundred-year period, Russia and the world have changed tremendously. Two world wars dethroned four emperors and eleven kings. Most of their descendants have dispersed and gradually become ordinary citizens. In the case of the Romanovs, most are now living in the English-speaking world, identifying with those nations, not with Russia.

In St. Petersburg, the palace of Kshesinskaya, mistress to three Romanovs, now houses a waxworks museum depicting heroes of the revolution of 1917. At Nevsky Prospect, the rooms where Dmitri and Felix Yusupov played their guitars are also home to wax figures. Dmitri and Felix have become heroes to Russian gay intellectuals as a glamorously romantic homosexual couple. Nikolasha's memory is now blurred with that of his father. Was he junior or senior? Even the Grand Duchess Leonida in 1995 was not sure. Kyril is vaguely remembered as the preposterous mock emperor living in France. Other grand dukes and grand duchesses have been swept away into the mists of history.

In St. Petersburg, on July 17, 1998, the eightieth anniversary of their murder, Nicholas, Alexandra, three of their five children, and four retainers were buried in Sts. Peter and Paul Cathedral. Although the event did not collapse into a "dog's wedding" of confusion and lack of dignity as some feared it might, it had its share of ironies. President Boris Yeltsin made a dramatic last-minute decision to attend. "The shooting of the Romanov family is a result of an uncompromising split in Russian society into 'us' and 'them,'" he declaimed at the beginning of the service. "The results of this split can be seen even now."

President Yeltsin's observation was borne out by the apathy greeting the funeral cortege as it moved through the city to the cathedral, the procession outnumbering the spectators; by the beer-drinkers and the smokers among those holding coveted cards of invitation; and even by some members of the Romanov family wearing brightly colored scarves and ties instead of the conventional black. Ironically, the devout Nicholas and Alexandra went to their final rest without the full blessing of the church they so adored. The Orthodox patriarch refused to attend because of the possiblity that genetic science is wrong and that, despite the extensive DNA testing, the bones to be interred were not those of the Romanovs. The Vladimirovichi Grand Duchess Leonida, her daughter, Maria, and grandson, George, also did not attend, presumably lest they offend the church by doing so. And the military, with which the Romanovs identified so closely, sent only a poorly trained honor guard and no bands to play funeral marches.

Yet bells rang and cannon roared as they had for Alexander II in 1881 and Alexander III in 1894. And the powerful voices of the choir again soared in "Eternal Memory," as if to bear the souls of the departed to Heaven. As the coffin of Nicholas II touched the earth, the entire Romanov family present spontaneously dropped to their knees. Russia may have ended its century of "blood and violence," but will it now find "repentance and peace," as Boris Yeltsin insists it must?

NOTES

Several abbreviations are used in endnotes:

GARF	Gosudarstvenny Arkhiv Rossiiskoi Federatsii (State Archives of the Russian Federation), Moscow
RGAVMF	Rossiiskii Gosudarstvenny Arkhiv Voenno-morskogo Flota (Russian State Naval Archives), St. Petersburg
HI	Hoover Institution, Stanford CA
BA	Bakhmetieff Archive at Columbia University, New York
PRO	Public Record Office, London, UK
RA	Royal Archives, Windsor Castle
f.	"fond" (collection)
op.	"opis" (file)
d.	"delo" (folder)

See Selected Bibliography for full citations of references.

PART ONE
Chapter One
Death of a Tsar: March 1, 1881

page 4   Assassination of Alexander II: *Pravitelstvenny vestnik*, March 2, 1881; Baddeley, 106; Volkov, 20; Bogdanovich, 46.

4   "Why shouldn't I go?": Paleologue, *Roman*, 103.

4   Cossacks carried the tsar: *Alexander II*, 351–352.

4   Wedding ring: Lamsdorf, 1886–1890, 154.

4   In chaos and panic: Mosolov, 64–65.

4   Servants carrying basins: Kleinmichel, 110.

4   Young officers: Mosolov, 64–65.

5   "What have we come to!": *Alexander II*, 352.

5   The heir had arrived at the Winter Palace: Mosolov, 65; Bogdanovich, 46; Poliakoff, 131.

6   The doctors pronounced: *Pravitelstvenny vestnik*, March 2, 1881; Bogdanovich, 46.

6   Great crowd massed outside: Mosolov, 65.

7   Sergei and Paul: Poznansky, 205–206; Berberova, *Tchaikovsky*, 221.

7   Nicholas Nikolaevich Senior: Paleologue, *Roman*, 7–8.

7   Memorial mass: Paleologue, *Roman*, 108–109.
7   Grief-stricken widow: Mosolov, 66. The hatred of the rest of the family and of the court for Princess Yurievskaya is stressed in many sources. One lady-in-waiting, for instance, remarked that the last gift of Yurievskaya to her late husband—her hair—actually did not mean much, for her hair "was not particularly long or thick": Tolstaya, 214–215.
7   The funeral: Paleologue, *Roman*, 9–13.
9   Along Millionnaya: Volkov, 21–22.
10 The great squares: Almedingen, *I Remember*, 104.
11 Russians had started mining: Kornilov and Solodova, 15–22.
11 Court rituals: Viroubova, 58.
12 "The palace of Tsarskoye Selo": Christopher, 50–51.
13 The Winter Palace: Poliakoff, 82.
13 In the palace at night: Alexander, *Once*, 56.
14 Imperial reception: *ibid.*
15 "A court official": Christopher, 52.
15 Nicholas I: Tiutcheva, 35.
16 "Pumpernickel courts": Alice, 41.
16 The Great Poet Alexander Pushkin: Paleologue, *Ambassador*, I, 324–325.
18 "To the age of fifteen": Alexander, *Once*, 15–16.
18 "Laughing at poor jokes": *ibid.*
19 "An intellectual mediocrity": Marie, *Education*, 116.
19 "The comfortable products": Nabokov, 51.
20 "Snug and mellow": *ibid.*
21 For fourteen years Alexander II: Paleologue, *Roman*, 16–18.
22 The empress's rooms: Tolstaya, 167.
23 "Am I a wild animal": Paleologue, *Roman*, 70.
23 Old women: Kann, 154.

Chapter Two
The Muzhik Tsar: 1881–1894

25 6'4": *Dom Romanovykh*, 99.
25 Death of Nicholas Alexandrovich: BA, Shvartz.
26 Marriage: Poliakoff, 58–59.
26 Telegraphing the commander: GARF, f.677, op.1, d.642.
26 Musical instruments: Nicholas, 65.
27 After his father's death: Mosolov, 64.
27 "I hope it will prove": Houghton Library, Kilgour Collection, Alexander II to Grand Duke Vladimir, Jugenheim, 1 September 1868.
27 The Anichkov Palace: Kann, 41.
28 Yet Gatchina: Tiutcheva, 73.
28 "Horrible and gloomy": Bogdanovich, 54.

28 When the royal family arrived: *ibid.*, 57.
28 On March 14, 1881: GARF, f.677, op.1, d.52.
28 Pobedonostsev: Gurko, *Tsar*, 54.
28 "Keeping Russia": "Pisma K.P.Pobedonostseva k Alexandru III," 320–323.
29 "I want this": *ibid.*
29 Pobedonostsev argued: *ibid.*
29 "Made such a mess": GARF, f.648, op.1, d.52.
29 Five of the six: Bogdanovich, 55.
29 "I am my own minister": Witte, I, 328.
30 The tsar would meticulously: *Rossiiskaya diplomatiya v portretakh*, 259.
30 Among Alexander's most important childhood memories: Tiutcheva, 67; Blake, 33; Greenhill, 217.
30 "No person with a heart": Witte, I, 411.
30 "One cannot help worrying": BA, Meshchersky, Alexander Alexandrovich to Meshchersky, 9 August 1870.
30 "We have only two allies": Bogdanovich, 98; Witte, I, 420–422; Alexander, *Once*, 67.
31 "About time too": *Dom Romanovykh*, 99.
31 Negotiating with Yurievskaya: GARF, f.677, op.1, d.1146.
31 Reports about Yurievskaya: *ibid.*, d.1162.
31 Tombs: *Petropavlovskaya*, 42.
32 Relationships with ballet dancers: Witte, I, 159.
32 Nicholas Constantinovich: Witte, I, 224–225; Poliakoff, 87.
32 Alexander III and the Tolstoys: BA, Romanov; *Rossiiskie*, 289.
32 Witte's marriage: Witte, I, 472.
32 "So the prince": *ibid.*, 425–426.
33 Grand dukes often got into trouble: *ibid.*
33 Alexander III denied Nikolasha the right to marry: Bogdanovich, 99.
33 Miche-Miche: *ibid.*, 67–68.
33 Miche-Miche called "swine": Lamsdorf, 1891–1892, 80.
33 Little notes: GARF, f.648, op.1, d.52, Alexander III to Sergei Alexandrovich, 18 December 1886.
33 "Decree on the Imperial Family": *ibid.*, f.677, op.1, d.80. "Uchrezhdeniye o Imperatorskoi Familii."
35 What did a ruble buy: Chekhov, XIV, 29, 36, 58, 61, 85, 97, 186.
35 "Poor girl!": Brayley, 149.
35 Vladimir's lifestyle: Alexander, *Once*, 137.
36 The Vladimir palace: Solovieva, 83–89.
36 Window glass from Maxim's: Interview with Vladislav Kostin.
37 Moorish boudoir: Belyakova, 166.
37 The careful attention: Interview with custodian.
37 Vladimir's library: Belyakova, 171.
38 In the late 1880s: Bogdanovich, 83.

38　Gossip had it: *ibid.*, 109.

38　One gathering: Lamsdorf, 1886–1889, 143, 203–204.

38　"May she become Russian": Houghton Library, Kilgour Collection, Maria Alexandrovna to Vladimir Alexandrovich, 5/17 May 1874.

38　"We shall never have": Bogdanovich, 81.

39　"Seven puds": Kann, 279.

39　Alexis and Zinaida Beauharnais: Brayley, 229–230.

40　"We Speak Russian": Von Dreyer, 51–53.

40　Description of Paris: *ibid.*; Segel, 1–83.

40　"What a handsome man!": Mosolov, 72.

40　"Good-humored sailor": Brayley, 228.

40　La Goulue: Flanner, 49.

41　"In anything": Alexander, *Once*, 138.

41　When Sergei commanded: BA, Epanchin.

42　"I thought": Balsan, 164.

42　"The *very bad state*": Hough, 55: Balmoral, 21 September 1883.

42　"I cld. not have": *ibid.*

42　Ella's wedding: Miller, Liubov, 36.

43　Sergei Alexandrovich allegedly proposed: Bogdanovich, 68.

43　"I am enjoying raising Dmitri"; "She is so cute": GARF, f.648, op.1, d.28, Sergei Alexandrovich's diary for 1892.

43　"Can I have at least": "Net spokoistviya," 158.

44　"Noblest heart": Witte, I, 407.

44　"Ruble belonging to the state": *ibid.*, 407–408.

44　The emperor's tastes: *ibid.*, 190–191.

44　Alexander's wardrobe and orders: GARF, f.642, op.1, d.29.

44　Alexander relished: Witte, I, 409.

44　Obesity: *ibid.*, 214–215.

44　Drinking: Figes, 16.

45　Alexander at Gatchina: Witte, I, 213–214; Volkov, 24.

45　Fishing: Volkov, 23.

45　"A bit cool": "Net spokoistviya," 154.

45　Finland was known: Baddeley, 323–338.

46　"It is boring here": "Net spokoistviya," 157.

46　European bison: Interview with Mikhail Moliukov.

46　Many of the Romanovs: BA, Shevich.

46　Romanovs in the Crimea: Mosolov, 164.

47　Minnie's riding: "Net spokoistviya," 152.

48　"The evening": GARF, f.648, op.1, d.52, Alexander III to Sergei Alexandrovich, 17 November 1888.

48　Crash at Borki: Witte, I, 196–198.

48　"The children!": Bogdanovich, 83.

48　"Trials: fear, anguish": GARF, f.648, op.1, d.52, Alexander III to Sergei Alexandrovich, 17 November 1888.

48　Lavish gifts: *ibid.*, f.642, op.1, d.3329.

48 In the summer: Lamsdorf, 1894–1896, 55–56.
49 Alexander III and the King of Sweden: Nicholas, 65.
49 "Children are": Van der Kiste, *Queen Victoria's Children,* 64.
49 "It seems to me": *ibid.,* 64.
50 "Such was the majesty": Windsor, 11.
50 "Mopping his brow": Van der Kiste, op. cit., 115.
50 "Callous, obstinate": Cannadine, *Pleasures,* 28.
50 "I am really": Hibbert, 73.
51 "How dreadful": Weintraub, 116.
51 "Like a bird": Meriel Buchanan, *Queen Victoria's Relations,* 115.
51 "Kind but": Buckle, George, 337.
51 "Quite shaken": *ibid.,* 202.
52 "That horrid": Hough, 80.
52 "I have": *ibid.,* 82.
53 Yet when her teeth: Lamsdorf, 1886–1890, 21.
53 "Graceful and elegant": *ibid.,* 139.
53 When she was dancing: *ibid.,* 139–140.
53 "Empty and everything is different": "Net spokoistviya," 155.
53 "Of course": *ibid.,* 161–162.
54 The emperor would tell his wife: *ibid.,* 152.
54 "This date has been merry": *ibid.,* 150–151.
54 Bread pellets: Mossolov, 5.
54 "I do not need porcelain": Bokhanov, 22.
54 "Dear Papa": GARF, f.677, op.1, d.900, Michael Alexandrovich to Alexander III, 25 September 1892.
54 "Everything is the same": *ibid.*
54 "I took it": *ibid.,* d.935, Olga Alexandrovna to Alexander III, July 21, no year.
55 "Must have gone somewhere else": "Net spokoistviya," 155.
55 "Nicky is out": *ibid.,* 156.
55 "Which is far from being": Witte, I, 437.
55 April 10, 1892: "Net spokoistviya," 155.
55 "Doing I don't know what": *ibid.,* 158.
55 "Potato parties": *Dnevnik imperatora,* 12–13 (entries for 29, 30 January, 1 February 1890, etc.).
55 Labunskaya: Lamsdorf, 1886–1890, 241.
55 Kshesinskaya: Ferro, 19.
55 Kshesinskaya practicing: Interview with Vladislav Kostin.
56 Nicky danced for Kshesinskaya: Romanovsky-Krassinsky, 38.
57 Officers' parties: *Dnevniki imperatora,* 7–8; Lamsdorf, 1886–1890, 303–304.
57 Nicky on an Orthodox Patriarch: GARF, f.677, op.1, d.919, Nicholas Alexandrovich to Alexander III, November 1890.
57 Nicky on his visits to Egyptian prostitutes: *Dnevnik imperatora,* 36–37.
57 Nicky describing the Otsu incident: GARF, f.677, op.1, d.919, Nicholas Alexandrovich to Alexander III, 7 May, 1891.

57   Nicky in Vladivostok: *ibid.*, 11 June 1891.
58   *Yolanta* performance: Buckle, Richard, 22–23.
58   St. Petersburg's high society on Nicky's marriage: Bogdanovich, 169.
58   "Condition of the grand duke": GARF, f.677, op.1, d.934, Olsufiev to Alexander III, 3 January 1894.
58   "What a misfortune": "Net spokoistviya," 161.
58   "Torture me": *ibid.*, 159.
58   "Kiss Georgy": *ibid.*
59   "Xenia ignores me": *ibid.*, 158–159.
59   Sandro fell in love: GARF, f.645, op.1, d.7, Alexander Mikhailovich's diary for 1890, 297, 305.
60   "Gymnastic": Maylunas and Mironenko, 73.
60   Cruise to the Finnish islands: GARF, f.645, op.1, d.7, Alexander Mikhailovich's diary for 1890, 343, 367.
60   Prince Nicholas: Nicholas, 65.
61   The couple travelled: GARF, f.677, op.1, d.840, Xenia Alexandrovna to Alexander III, 12 August 1894.
61   From Ai Todor Xenia wrote: *ibid.*
62   The emperor was anxious: Lamsdorf, 1894–1896, 59.
62   Professor Zakharyin: Witte, I, 400.
62   "No. A Russian tsar": BA, Epanchin.
62   Zakharyin's own precarious health: Volkov, 35.
62   "It was like seeing": Nicholas, 116.
62   John of Kronstadt: *Svyatoi*, 69–72, 153.
63   Death of Alexander III: HI, L'Escaille, letter from L'Escaille, 1 November 1894.
63   The servants were permitted: Volkov, 36.
63   The empress: Miller, Liubov, 83.
63   "Throughout": "Net spokoistviya," 163.
63   "The sun of the Russian Land": *ibid.*, 162.
63   Rumor spread in St. Petersburg: Lamsdorf, 1894–1896, 75.

Chapter Three
Nicholas II: Family and Nation, 1894–1904

65   On November 7: BA, Kozlianinov, Box 1.
65   "Enough!": Witte, II, 6.
66   Khodynka: Maylunas and Mironenko, 145–146.
66   "Do not let": *ibid.*, 146.
66   "The heat": *Dnevniki imperatora*, 146.
66   "Actually": Vorres, 68.
66   "I know": Lamsdorf, 1894–1896, 85.
66   "My grandson": *ibid.*, 87.
67   "Don't tell me": Witte, II, 175.
67   Leo Tolstoy: "L.N.Tolstoy i N.M.Romanov," 233.

67 "This tendency": Maylunas and Mironenko, 151.

67 The tsar's uncles: Lamsdorf, 1894–1896, 88.

67 "Their favorite": Maylunas and Mironenko, 161.

67 "I was especially hurt": *ibid.*

68 In 1896: GARF, f.642, op.1, d.3325.

68 Minnie collected pictures: *ibid.*, d.3328. Katalog kartin.

68 Fabergé egg of 1895: Faberge, 175.

68 A subsequent Easter: *ibid.*, 178.

68 "You are": *ibid.*

68 "You talk to Mama": Maylunas and Mironenko, 214.

69 Once an official: Viroubova, 240.

69 At the theater: Buckle, Richard, 63–64.

69 In February 1900: *ibid.*, 46.

70 After the baby's birth: Nijinska, 112.

70 "What's surprising about that?": *ibid.*, 46–47.

70 Boris in Paris: GARF, f.654, op.1, d.14; Bogdanovich, 446.

70 Boris in the United States: HI, Tarsaidze, Box 15.

71 George: *ibid.*, letter from D. Nikitin.

71 Grand Duke Paul: *Rossiiskii imperatorskii dom*, 68–69.

71 At a Winter Palace ball: Chavchavadze, *The Grand Dukes*, 138.

71 "He has behaved": Houghton Library, Kilgour Collection, Vladimir Alexandrovich to Sergei Alexandrovich, Tsarskoye Selo, 7 October 1902.

72 "He has forgotten": Maylunas and Mironenko, 224.

72 Paul and his wife in Paris: Witte, I, 202.

72 "How painful and distressing": *Rossiiskii imperatorskii dom*, 68–69; Bing, 170.

72 "Unique personality": Marie, *Education*, 17.

72 "Cold, inflexible": *ibid.*, 18.

73 "Saw as little"; "I recall one such time": *ibid.*, 19–20.

73 "One evening": *ibid.*, 21.

73 Ilinskoie: *ibid.*, 26.

74 "When we got your letter": GARF, f.644, op.1, d.170, Dmitri Pavlovich to Paul Alexandrovich, 24 October 1902.

74 "We are so sad": *ibid.*, f.642, op.1, d.2137, Maria Pavlovna to Maria Fedorovna, 7 November 1902; also d.1535, Dmitri Pavlovich to Maria Fedorovna, 7 November 1902.

74 "The landscape": Marie, *Education*, 28.

75 "In no other great country": Charques, 24.

75 One Russian traveller reports: Almedingen, *The Emperor*, 348.

76 Barefoot children: Charques, 24.

76 "Lived in clean houses": Marie, *Education*, 246.

77 "Beggars": Zhukov, 8.

77 "That was the way": *ibid.*, 20.

77 Przhevalsky and Nicky: Rayfield, 151.

78   Badmaev and Alexander III: Semennikov, *Za kulisami*, 81.
78   Badmaev and Nicholas II: *ibid.*, 88–104.
79   "The emperor wanted": Witte, II, 45.
79   His diary entries: *Dnevniki imperatora*, 141, 207.
79   Willy in St. Petersburg: William II, 121.
79   The Prussian court: Ludwig, 26.
80   Engraving: Lamsdorf, 1894–1896, 244–246.
80   "The Admiral of the Atlantic": Ludwig, 117.
80   "He should be locked up": Mosolov, 144.
80   Sandro's toast: Lamsdorf, 1894–1896, 186.
80   Bezobrazov: Witte, II, 182.
80   "What will happen tomorrow": GARF, f.650, op.1, d.3, *Dnevnik ve-likogo knyazia Andreya Vladimirovicha*, 25 January 1904.
81   In the early hours: *Dnevniki imperatora*, 193; *Rossiiskaya diplo-matiya*, 299–300.
81   "Around midnight": RGAVMF, f.469, op.1, d.64, Telegramma Alex-eeva Nikolayu II, 27 January 1904.
81   "Now they've done it!": *Rossiiskaya diplomatiya*, 300.
81   Later in the day: GARF, f.650, op.1, d.3, *Dnevnik velikogo knyazia Andreya Vladimirovicha*, 27 January 1904.
81   "God will not let": *ibid.*, 7 February 1904.
81   Sergei in Moscow: *ibid.*, f.648, op.1, d.41, *Dnevnik velikogo knyazya Sergeya Alexandrovicha*, 17 February 1904.
82   During Kyril's naval career: RGAVMF, f.467, op.1, d.290, l.51–54.
83   Kyril had fallen in love: Van der Kiste, *Princess Victoria Melita*, 79.
83   "A languid expression": Maylunas and Mironenko, 228.
83   "The only": *ibid.*
83   Kyril's departure: GARF, f.650, op.1, d.3, *Dnevnik velikogo knyazia Andreya Vladimirovicha*, 14 February 1904.
84   Boris's departure: *ibid.*, 26 February 1904.
84   Commander of the Pacific fleet: RGAVMF, f.763, op.1, d.180, Dnevnik Vasilyeva Yu.V., l.57.
84   At eleven o'clock: *Port-Artur*, 161.
84   The sinking of the *Petropavlovsk*: RGAVMF, f.469, op.1, d.64, l.60–61, Telegramma Alexeeva Nikolayu II; *Port-Artur*, 167–168; Tomich, 54.
85   "It was bitterly cold": Cyril, 168–169; also see more evidence in: RGAVMF, f.763, op.1, d.181, l.28; *ibid.*, d.180, *Dnevnik Vasilyeva Yu.V.*, l.123; *Port-Artur*, 182–183.
85   Makarov: Benckendorf, 59; J. Miller, 330.
86   The message reached the Vladimirovichi: GARF, f.650, op.1, d.3, Dnevnik velikogo knyazya Andreya Vladimirovicha, 31 March 1904.
86   "To go abroad at such a time!": *Dnevniki imperatora*, 207.
86   "Radiant with happiness": Maylunas and Mironenko, 244.
86   Serov: HI, Tarsaidze, Box 15; Lenyashin.

87 "Dry and sardonic": Maylunas and Mironenko, 101.
88 "My greatest enemies": *ibid.*, p.314.
88 The exhibition: Buckle, Richard, 87.

Chapter Four
A Faltering Monarchy, 1905–1914

91 On January 6: GARF, f.650, op.1, d.29, *Dnevnik velikogo knyazya Andreya Vladimirovicha za 1905 god,* l.11.
91 The Romanovs suspected an assassination attempt: "Iz dnevnika velikogo knyazya Konstantina Romanova," 105.
91 "The workers' strike": GARF, f.650, op.1, d.29, *Dnevnik velikogo knyazya Andreya Vladimirovicha za 1905 god,* l.14.
91 Three days following: *ibid.*, l.17.
92 Events of January 9: *ibid.*, l.18–21.
92 Sergei's assassination: Miller, Liubov, 101.
92 Pasternak's poem: Pasternak, 432, translated by Constantine Pleshakov.
93 "What do you think": Marie, *Education*, 71.
93 Nicholas had invited: Maylunas and Mironenko, 261.
93 Weather on February 5: *Pravitelstvenny vestnik*, February 5, 1905.
93 At 7:30: GARF, f.650, op.1, d.29, *Dnevnik velikogo knyazya Andreya Vladimirovicha za 1905 god,* l.77.
94 The Black Sea fleet: *Vospominaniya*, II, 190–196.
94 "Only the devil": *Dnevniki imperatora*, 266.
94 "This scoundrel": "Perepiska Nikolaya II i Marii Fedorovny," 179.
95 He presented two recommendations: Witte, III, 41–42; Pares, 85–86; Epanchin, 326.
95 "I have a constitution": Pares, *My Russian,* 86.
95 Nicholas II replaced Vladimir: "Iz perepiski Nikolaya Romanova s V.A.Romanovym," 221–222.
95 "If the emperor": Witte, III, 41–42; Pares, *My Russian,* 85–86; Epanchin, 326.
96 "All Russia is a madhouse": Lincoln, *The Great Reforms,* 321.
97 "Nicholas, tsar": *Russkiye narodnye pesni,* 521, translated by Constantine Pleshakov.
97 Nicholas II opened: "Iz dnevnika Konstantina Romanova," 118–119.
97 "The large group": Maylunas and Mironenko, 283.
98 Stolypin: Cherkasov, 394.
99 Conference on April 13: "Iz dnevnika Konstantina Romanova," 116.
99 Conference on July 30: *ibid.*, 126.
99 Conference on August 9: *ibid.*, 127.
100 "I considered": Cyril, 180.
100 The wedding: *ibid.*, 182.
100 "How she must hate": "Perepiska Nikolaya II i Marii Fedorovny," 161–162.

100   Vladimir staged a scene: *ibid.*
101   Marie of Coburg interceded: *ibid.*, 164–165.
101   "Ta Femme": Van der Kiste, *Princess Victoria Melita*, 98.
101   Even less appropriate: "Perepiska Nikolaya II i Marii Fedorovny," 193.
101   "A clear mind": Maylunas and Mironenko, 240.
102   In 1911: Crawford, 122–128.
102   "What harm": Maylunas and Mironenko, 305.
102   Alexis had resigned: Witte, II, 388.
102   Eliza Baletta: Bogdanovich, 446.
102   Red Cross money: Kasvinov, 6–7.
102   Alexis's death: Almedingen, *I Remember,* 52–53.
103   Nicholas Constantinovich in exile: BA, Iskander, Videniya proshlogo.
103   Tigers and leopards in Central Asia: Interview with Mikhail Moliukov.
103   "Deliriously happy": GARF, f.642, op.1, d.2137a, Maria Pavlovna to Maria Fedorovna, 12 November 1907.
103   Ella: Almedingen, 58.
104   Marie in Sweden: Interview with Betty Tobias, April 11, 1996; Bernadotte, 25, 148, 164–166.
105   Dmitri spent a lot of time: "Iz perepiski Nikolaya i Marii Romanovykh v 1907–10 gg.," 190.
105   Sandro complained: GARF, f.642, op.1, d.713, Alexander Mikhailovich to Maria Fedorovna, 24 October 1907.
106   By 1909: Bogdanovich, 465.
106   Minnie and her grandchildren: Poliakoff, 291.
107   "Real flock": Witte, II, 263.
107   "Second-rate grand dukes": *ibid.*
107   "Weird": GARF, f.671, op.1, d.29, Nicholas Nikolaevich to Anastasia Nikolaevna, 6 December 1908.
107   The two sisters: *ibid.*, d.34, Militsa Nikolaevna to Anastasia Nikolaevna, 28 October 1910.
108   "Oh, these two": Witte, II, 263.
108   "We have got to know": *Dnevniki imperatora*, 287.

Chapter Five
The Great War, 1914–1917

109   On Sunday, 20 July 1914: Rodzyanko, 110.
109   "Younger": Chukovsky, 69.
109   "Flaccid": *ibid.*
109   "I welcome you": Rodzyanko, 110.
110   "Nicholas the Great": Mikhailovsky, I, 31.
111   "The all-seeing eye": Voronovich, 4–5.
111   "Bogatyr": Miliukov, II, 184.
111   Nikolasha's character: Danilov, 7, 75–76.

111 Shavelsky on Nikolasha: Shavelsky, I, 132–133.
112 "There was movement": Blucher, 37.
112 "We are happy to have made": Knox, I, 90.
113 "Lunch in Paris": Aronson, *Crowns*, 116.
113 Nikolasha's appeal to the Poles: Miliukov, II, 216.
114 "The professional character": Brussilov, 93.
114 Pinsk: Florinsky, 224.
114 Hussar regiment: BA, Sakhno-Ustimovich.
114 "The necessary measures": Knox, I, 276.
116 Self indulgence: Lebina, N.B. and M.V. Shkarovsky, 25–49; Segel, 256–313.
117 Sergei's diary: GARF, f.648, op.1, d.41, Dnevnik Sergeya Alexandrovicha za 1904 god.
117 Fedor close to his grandmother: *ibid.*, f.642, op.1, d.2908, Fedor Alexandrovich to Maria Fedorovna.
117 "Unkind and corrupted": *ibid.*, f. 645, op.1, d. 651, Xenia Alexandrovna to Fedor Alexandrovich, 9 January 1917.
118 "Come, and I will hang you": Rodzyanko, 118; Bubnov, 37.
119   "the patronage of Rasputin": Figes, 278.
119 Nikolasha's HQ: Bubnov, 28.
120 "Elusive": Interview with Prince Nicholas Romanov.
120 Every day: Bubnov, 29–30; Shavelsky, I, 121.
120 The meals: Knox, I, 45; Bubnov, 29–30; Shavelsky, I, 121.
120 Nikolasha disapproved of visits: Bubnov, 31.
120 Nikolasha's monkish existence: Shavelsky, I, 122, 297.
120 When the emperor: Shavelsky, I, 190–191.
121 "Just imagine my horror": *ibid.*
121 Rasputin and Nikolasha: Shchegolev, III, 392.
121 "Nicholas III": Shavelsky, I, 265.
121 "They left an impression": Rodzyanko, 130.
121 "You know": Shavelsky, I, 128.
121 The cabinet ministers: Sazonov, *Vospominaniya*, 364–365.
122 Dmitri: Shavelsky, I, 310–314.
122 Nikolasha accepted the order: Shavelsky, I, 306.
122 "Everything has passed well!": *Dnevniki imperatora*, 544.
122 "Why should you?": Shavelsky, I, 315.
123 "My dear boy": "Iz dnevnika A.V.Romanova," 77–78.
123 "He was loved ": Loukomsky, 15.
123 All of the grand dukes: Gavriil Constantinovich, 293.
123 Kyril's command: RGAVMF, f.418, op.1, d.363; f.406, op.9, d.1766, Polny posluzhnoi spisok.
124 Oleg's death: Gavriil Constantinovich, 262–276; "Iz dnevnika A.V. Romanova," 103–104.
124 But even worse: BA, Sakhno-Ustimovich, Box 3, Vospominaniya o mirovoi voine.

125   Nicholas Mikhailovich tried to persuade the tsar: Shavelsky, I, 340.

125   He wrote Nicholas: Semennikov, *Nikolai II i velikiye knyazya*, 63–64.

125   "England doesn't care a straw": Paleologue, *Ambassador*, II, 278.

125   "To send for Boris": *Letters of the Tsaritsa*, 359.

126   "To live long enough": Maurice Paleologue cited by Tuchman, 61.

126   Boris's budget: GARF, f.654, op.1, d.17, Otchet o prikhode . . . za 1915 god.

126   "The oftener I think": *Letters of the Tsaritsa*, 280.

126   Dmitri as Nicholas's companion: *Dnevniki imperatora*, 546–547.

126   Dmitri skillfully played: Semennikov, *Nikolai II i velikiye knyazya*, 42.

127   "Do, if only possible": *Letters of the Tsaritsa*, 307.

127   "Would be very glad": GARF, f.642, op.1, d.1535.

127   Dmitri's major peacetime regimental duty: BA, Kozlianinov, Box 1; BA, Gavriil Konstantinovich, Box 1, Memoirs, 636.

127   Dmitri in the Stockholm Olympics: HI, Odintsov, Box 3.

127   Dmitri and Kyril at Borodino: Gavriil Constantinovich, 162.

128   Paley and Rasputin: Shchegolev, IV, 264.

128   "Honorable family": Semennikov, *Nikolai II i velikiye knyazya*, 41.

128   "I would somehow": GARF, f.644, op.1, d.153, Paley to Paul Alexandrovich, 3 October 1916.

128   "I have been": *ibid.*, 15 August 1916.

128   Marie: Marie, *Education*, 180.

128   "My happiness": *ibid.*

129   The tsar's younger sister: Vorres, 209.

129   That year Repin: Chukovsky, 55.

130   "She, an Emperor's Daughter": *Letters of the Tsaritsa*, 307.

130   Olga told her mother: GARF, f.642, op.1, d.2427, Olga Alexandrovna to Maria Fedorovna, 14 November 1916, in English.

130   "I can't tell you": *ibid.*, 6 November 1916, in English.

131   "It is finished": Aronson, *Crowns*, 112.

131   The Yusupov art collection: Faberge, 66.

132   "Temporary insanity": *K istorii poslednikh dnei tsarskogo regima*, 232.

132   "His hypnotic power": Youssoupoff, *Lost Splendour*, 187.

132   Bimbo was fairly sure: "Zapiski N.M.Romanova," no.4–5, 104.

133   Felix concluded: *ibid.* Our account of Rasputin's assassination is mostly drawn from the personal notes by Grand Duke Nicholas Mikhailovich. This version seems to be the earliest and reasonably authentic.

133   Felix invited: "K istorii poslednikh dnei tsarskogo regima," 235.

133   "I am going": Voyeikov, 11.

133   Rasputin watched by tsar's police: "Rasputin v osveshchenii okhranki."

133   Rasputin's murder: "Zapiski N.M.Romanova," no.6, 98–101.

134   Rasputin's member: Mikhailovsky, I, 454.

134   Felix's letter to the empress: "K istorii ubiistva Grigoriya Rasputina," 425.

134   Ella's telegrams: Kobylin, 239.

135   "Gentlemen": "Zapiski N.M.Romanova," no.6, 98.

135   Dmitri's role in assassination: Russian newspaper *Izvestiya* (16 September 1995) reported that new documents had been found in France by Marina Grey, a historian and daughter of General Anton Denikin, proving that Dmitri had actually killed Rasputin himself. The documents were said to have come from Purishkevich's personal archive. Purishkevich had allegedly concealed the truth hoping that Dmitri would eventually become the next Russian monarch.

135   "For the first time": Marie, *Education*, 255.

135   Dmitri swore to his father: *ibid.*, 276.

135   At 2 am: Marie, *ibid.*, 274; Semennikov, *Dnevnik b. vel. kn.*, 191.

136   Felix exiled: "Zapiski N.M.Romanova," no.6, 101.

136   On December 29: *Dnevnik b. vel.* kn., 191.

136   Sandro thought: Maylunas and Mironenko, 515.

136   "A murder premeditated": Vorres, 142.

137   "Nobody has the right": Gavriil Constantinovich, 312–313.

137   Dmitri meanwhile: Semennikov, *Dnevnik b. vel. kn.*, 188; GARF, f.644, op.1, d.170, Dmitri Pavlovich to Paul Alexandrovich, December 28, 1916.

137   "God help me": HI, Baratov, Box 1, Diary, 25 December 1916.

137   "My front has been visited": HI, Baratov, Box 1, Diary, 31 December 1916.

137   Dmitri, listening: GARF, f.644, op.1, d.170, Dmitri Pavlovich to Paul Alexandrovich, January 14, 1917.

138   The party; Dmitri's drinking: HI, Baratov, Box 1, Diary, 31 December 1916.

138   Dmitri impressed: *ibid.*

138   "That mad dog": *ibid.*

138   Dmitri's fellow officers: GARF, f.644, op.1, d.170, Dmitri Pavlovich to Paul Alexandrovich, 14 January 1917.

138   Writing to his father: *ibid.*

138   After the New Year party: GARF, f.614, op.1, d.98, Dmitri Pavlovich to Vladimir Paley, 8 February 1917.

138   Sandro's ambitions: Buranov, 315.

139   Dmitri could not take Holy Communion: BA, Gavriil Konstantinovich, Memoirs, 1067.

139   Dmitri and esoteric rituals: Houghton Library, *Dmitri's Diaries*, 23 January 1917, 26 January 1917, 27 January 1917, also notes of December 1917.

139   Sandro at Tsarskoye Selo: *Rossiiskii imperatorskii dom*, 186–187.

140   Sandro subsequently: Semennikov, *Nikolai II i velikie knyazya*, 118–122.

140   French ambassador: Maylunas and Mironenko, 512.
140   Prince Lvov's conspiracy: Melgunov, 105–109.
141   Michael as a new emperor: Mikhailovsky, I, 236.
141   Dmitri marrying Olga: Interview with Grand Duchess Leonida.
141   Bimbo exiled: GARF, f.670, op.1, d.212, Dmitri Pavlovich to Nicholas Mikhailovich, 31 December 1917.
141   Kyril, Miechen and Andrew exiled: Semennikov, *Dnevnik b. vel. kn.*, 194.
141   Boris ignored: BA, Sakhno-Ustimovich, Box 2.
141   "Everything is over": Kobylin, 241–242.

PART TWO
Chapter Six
"The Crown Falls from the Royal Head"
February 22–March 3, 1917

145   On February 22nd: *Dnevniki imperatora*, 624.
146   Measles: *ibid.*
146   Riots, Khabalov: Melgunov, 140.
147   Rodzianko and Nicholas: *ibid.*; Katkov, 283–290.
147   Michael: *ibid.*; Crawford, 260–265.
149   "Take *everything*": Melgunov, 248.
149   On February 27th: Melgunov, 94–102.
149   The mood at headquarters: HI, Tal.
149   Rerouting the train: *ibid.*, 76–77; Katkov, 311; Melgunov, 171.
150   The emperor, however, was less concerned: *Dnevniki imperatora*, 625.
150   Hanbury-Williams' letter: *Romanovy i soyuzniki v pervye dni revolutsii*, 46–47.
150   Kyril's visit: Shulgin, *Days*, 143–144; Kobylin, 312; Voyeikov, 258; Epanchin, 319. People politically loyal to Kyril justify his motivations and deny particular details of the visit—especially the red rosette: Vladimir Kirillovich, 12.
151   On March 2nd: Shavelsky, II, 289.
151   Commanders of the fronts advised: *Otrecheniye*, 238.
152   At 3 pm: Melgunov, 185.
152   Nicholas summoned Fedorov: Gilliard, 148–149; Shavelsky, II, 289–290.
152   Guchkov and Shulgin at the *Stavka*: Shulgin, *Days*, 183–190; Melgunov, 192; Steinberg and Khrustalev, 97.
154   "Now that I am about": Grabbe, 123.
154   "All around": *Dnevniki imperatora*, 625.
154   On March 3rd: HI, Tal.
154   The imperial train: *ibid.*
154   "Read a lot": Steinberg and Khrustalev, 108.
154   "The sovereign": *Otrecheniye*, 73.

154 Michael and Bimbo: Melgunov, 240.
155 At dawn: Katkov, 405.
155 The fateful meeting: Melgunov, 225.
155 Shulgin had undergone: Shulgin, *Days*, 194–195.
155 Miliukov talks to Shulgin: *ibid.*, 195–199.
156 The day was cold: *ibid.*, 201.
156 Meeting at Millionnaya: Shulgin, *Days*, 202–209; Paleologue, *Tsarskaya*, 255–257; Katkov, 407–409; Melgunov, 225–236.

Chapter Seven
The First Week of the Republic:
March 3–March 11, 1917

159 "Lord knows": *Dnevniki imperatora*, 625; Steinberg and Khrustalev, 108.
159 Allies and Nikolasha: "Romanovy i soyuzniki v pervye dni revolutsii," 50–51.
160 "Untimely": *ibid.*, 48.
160 Revolutionaries meanwhile: Steinberg and Khrustalev, 113.
160 Discipline everywhere was collapsing: *Otrecheniye*, 76.
160 Sergei Mikhailovich called Sandro: *Rossiiskii imperatorskii dom*, 190.
160 "The sovereign": HI, Tal, 62.
160 On March 4th: *Dnevniki imperatora*, 625–626; *Otrecheniye*, 129–130.
161 In a letter: *Rossiiskii imperatorskii dom*, 189.
161 Nicholas and the dowager: *Otrecheniye*, 130–131; Voyeikov, 152.
161 "When are you going": *Otrecheniye*, 131–132.
162 Dinner: *Dnevniki imperatora*, 626; *Otrecheniye*, 131–132.
162 March 5th: *Otrecheniye*, 133.
162 In the morning of March 6th: "Romanovy i soyuzniki," 48–51.
162 But the British government: Whittle, 284.
163 In 1918: Bokhanov, 267.
163 The Duke of Windsor related: Windsor, 131.
163 On March 8th: Steinberg and Khrustalev, 120.
163 In the morning of March 8th: *Dnevniki imperatora*, 626; *Otrecheniye*, 136.
163 "Russia without a tsar": *Otrecheniye*, 130–136.
164 "The absence": Alexander, *Once*, 291.
164 Nicholas, in a simple khaki blouse: *Otrecheniye*, 136; Alexander, *Once*, 292.
164 The old empress: *Rossiiskii imperatorskii dom*, 190.
164 The Empress Alexandra Fedorovna: Melnik, 177.
164 "I don't believe it!": Paleologue, *Tsarskaya*, 257.
164 Paul and his wife were very busy: "Romanovy v pervye dni revolutsii," 208.

165   On March 2nd: *ibid.*, 209.

165   Bimbo in Petersburg: Paleologue, *Tsarskaya*, 271.

165   Bimbo and his brother Sergei Mikhailovich: *Rossiiskii imperatorskii dom*, 190–191.

166   Bimbo also took the initiative: *ibid.*, 191.

166   George Mikhailovich and Kyril on succession rights: *ibid.*; "Romanovy v pervye dni revolutsii," 14.

166   On March 9th: Paleologue, *Tsarskaya*, 272.

166   Kyril was quoted: ibid, 274.

166   "After that, the end": *Rossiiskii imperatorskii dom*, 190.

166   Miliukov and the British: Steinberg and Khrustalev, 120.

167   "Would be strongly resented": Rose, 212.

167   "We must be allowed": *ibid.*, 213.

167   Nikolasha and the Provisional Government: "Verkhovnoye komandovaniye," 219–220.

167   In a conversation: "Iz dnevnika A.V.Romanova," 196–198.

168   On March 5th: *The New York Times*, 23 March 1917.

168   On March 6th: "Verkhovnoye komandovaniye," 221.

168   Nikolasha arrived at Moghilev: HI, Chasovoi, Box 3.

168   Nikolasha gave an oath: *Otrecheniye*, 81.

168   Nikolasha dismissed: "Uvolneniye N.N.Romanova," 343.

168   Nikolasha left for the Crimea: *Otrecheniye*, 84.

169   Diaghilev in Rome: Buckle, Richard, 325–326.

169   Madame de Chevigne: *ibid.*, 324.

169   Sandro on Marie-Antoinette: Alexander, *Once*, 219.

Chapter Eight
"The Mood Smells of Blood," March–October 1917

171   "Delicate chest": Buchanan, *Victorian Gallery*, 60.

172   Grand Duke Boris: BA, Shevich, 92.

172   Kislovodsk remained: BA, Manukhin, Box 2, Autobiography.

172   Andrew's train stopped: BA, Shevich, 94.

173   Miechen's villa searched and she herself confined: *ibid.*, 96–97; *The New York Times*, 31 March 1917; "Iz dnevnika A. V. Romanova", 201.

173   Miechen and Stopford: Stopford, 162.

173   Kerensky's permission: *The New York Times*, 9 June 1917.

173   Stopford at Kislovodsk: Stopford, 183.

173   On August 4th: *ibid.*, 189.

174   Stopford and the jewels: *ibid.*

175   "It was a bitter night": Vorres, 154.

175   "When we left": *ibid.*, 154.

175   The Yusupovs's journey: GARF, f.670, op.1, d.176, Irina Yusupova to Nicholas Mikhailovich, April 1917.

176   "It was spring": Vorres, 154–155.

176   "Colony of grand dukes": HI, Georgii Mikhailovich, Box 2, George Mikhailovich to Xenia Georgievna, 25 March 1917.

176   "Quiet life": GARF, f.670, op.1, d.176, Xenia Alexandrovna to Nicholas Mikhailovich, 13/27 April 1917.

177   "So dear Mimka": Vorres, 155.

177   A group of sailors: Alexander, *Once*, 300–301.

177   "We transferred": Vorres, 157.

178   Minnie's Bible: Alexander, *Once*, 304.

178   "I brought": Poliakoff, 305.

178   Minnie herself wrote: Bing, 302.

178   "Wiener schnitzel": Alexander, *Once*, 309.

178   "To hear of the harsh": RA/PS/G V/M 1180/13, telegram, King to Buchanan, 23 August 1917.

178   Buchanan replied: RA/PS/GV/M 1180/20, Buchanan to Stamfordham, 3 September 1917.

178   Sandro understood: GARF, f.670, op.1, d.178, Felix Yusupov to Nicholas Mikhailovich, 11 May 1917.

178   His son, Fedor, noted: *Rossiiskii imperatorskii dom*, 194.

179   On August 1st: *Dnevniki imperatora*, 646; Steinberg and Khrustalev, 168–169.

179   Kyril: Alexander, *Once*, 333.

179   But the legend grew: *ibid.*

180   Kyril himself had to go: RA/VIC Add. C 22/206, Margaret of Sweden to Lady Egerton, 24 January 1918, Stockholm.

181   "My dearest soul": HI, Georgii Mikhailovich, Box 2, George Mikhailovich to Xenia Georgievna, 29 June 1917; also 1 July 1917.

181   Buchanan's instructions: RA/PS/GV/M 1067/73, Telegram, 5 September 1917.

181   George Mikhailovich pointed out: HI, Georgii Mikhailovich, George Mikhailovich to Xenia Georgievna, 1 July 1917.

182   Ambassador Buchanan was reporting to London: RA/PS/GV/M 1067/74, Buchanan to Balfour, 8 September 1917.

182   Bimbo: Blok, VIII, 482.

182   "A Russian is so uncivilized": *Rossiiskii imperatorskii dom*, 193.

182   "If I am elected": Gray, 82–83.

183   "God help us": GARF, f.614, op.1, d.98, Dmitri Pavlovich to Vladimir Paley, 19 March 1917.

183   Those who met Dmitri in Persia:" HI, Baratov, Box 3, Borba v Persii vo vremya revolutsii v Rossii.

183   Sometimes soldiers: GARF, f.644, op.1, d.170, Dmitri Pavlovich to Paul Alexandrovich, 23 April 1917.

183   Order #1: Voyeikov, 143–144.

183   Disorder spread: Fatemi, 485–486.

183   Dmitri moved to Teheran: HI, Baratov, Box 3, Borba v Persii vo vremya revolutsii v Rossii.

184   Dmitri on Rasputin's murder: *ibid.*.

184   Paul had made Dmitri swear: Houghton Library, *Dmitri Diaries,* 16 December 1917.

184   Delegation visited Teheran: HI, Baratov, Box 3, Borba v Persii vo vre-mya revolutsii v Rossii.

184   Marling became a father-figure: Houghton Library, Dmitri's Diaries, 6 October 1917.

184   Dmitri on meditating: *ibid.*, 9 January 1918.

184   Dmitri's wishes: *ibid.*, 9 January 1918.

185   "As before": GARF, f.614, op.1, d. 98, Dmitri Pavlovich to Vladimir Paley, 18 September 1917.

185   "Only God knows": Houghton Library, Dmitri's Diaries, 16 September 1917.

185   "What an awful": GARF, f.614, op.1, d.4, *Dnevnik knyazya Paley Vladimira Pavlovicha,* 21 June 1917.

185   Thin and intense: Paustovsky, III, 573–574.

185   Kerensky's speaking: *ibid.*

186   "Finally, here is a man": GARF, f.644, op.1, d.170.

186   September and October in Petrograd: John Reed, 33–44.

187   Lenin on October 24th: Pipes, 482, 490–491.

187   "The eyes of a lemur": writer Alexander Kuprin quoted in *Vozhd,* 110–111.

188   "Fencer": *ibid.*, 97.

188   Arrest of the Provisional Government: John Reed, 100.

189   The mob began to loot: *ibid.*, 99–100.

189   A great drinking frenzy: Malkov, 72–76.

189   On October 25th: GARF, f.614, op.1, d.4, *Dnevnik knyazya Paley Vladimira Pavlovicha,* 25 October 1917.

189   "Lord, save and forgive us!": *ibid.*, 30 October 1917.

189   Paul arrested: *ibid.*, 31 October 1917.

Chapter Nine
Firestorm, October 1917–January 1919

191   In the Crimea: HI, Rerberg, *Istoricheskiye zagadki v russkoi revolut-sii,* part 1, 25–26.

191   On one day: HI, Gopstein, Box 1. This collection is worth some ex-planation. It consists of the writings of an amateur historian, E.E. Gopstein, who lived in Simferopol, the capital of the Crimea, and wrote a detailed chronicle of the peninsula from the revolution of 1917 until the end of World War II, he himself being a witness to all periods he described.

191   On May 1, 1918: Malkov, 127–128.

192   "The Revolutionary": *ibid.*, 290.

193   "There might not be": Steinberg and Khrustalev, 288.

193   On July 17th: *ibid.*, 351–365.
193   In early July: *ibid.*, 291.
193   On July 16th: *ibid.*, 331.
194   Execution of Michael and Johnson: Massie, *The Romanovs*, 255–256.
194   "The strongest": HI, Smolin.
195   The Romanovs at Alapayevsk: HI, Smolin.
195   Execution at Alapayevsk: *ibid.*; Miller, Liubov, 210–211; Massie, *The Romanovs*, 256–257; Scott, 91.
196   "Darling Georgie boy": RA/PS/GV/M 35/19, Sandringham, 15 June 1918.
196   The Romanovs moved to Dulber: Alexander, *Once*, 305.
196   "He was a murderer": Vorres, 159.
197   "In his colorful way": Alexander, *Once*, 307.
197   When a group of Bolshevik inspectors: Poliakoff, 306.
197   Minnie's emotions: GARF, f.670, op.1, d.178, Felix Yusupov to Nicholas Mikhailovich, 11 May 1917.
198   When the Bolshevik government: Wrangel, Alexis, 95.
199   Stana and a German general: Poliakoff, 322.
199   Nikolasha and the Germans: Wrangel, *General*, 95–96.
199   Patrols on the roads: RA/PS/GV/M 1344A/49, 22 November 1918.
199   "Here we were": Vorres, 161.
199   "All that is dead": Gerhard, 461.
199   "A man of": *ibid.*, 460.
199   "A plague bacillus": Whittle, 286.
200   Two peripheral Romanovs: Williams, 76–78.
200   "Who would have thought": Bing, 301.
201   "With base comments": Kokovtsov, 522.
201   Figes: Figes, 349–350.
201   By October, 1918: Williams, 75.
201   The Leuchtenbergs: Williams, 76–78.
201   Russia embarked: Paley, 198; Interview with Kyra Volkova Robinson.
202   "Veal": Chukovsky, 101.
202   At the Kremlin: Malkov, 133.
203   In 1917–1920, Kiev: Sokolov, 239–240.
204   Old Countess Kleinmichel: Obolensky, 153.
205   A brooch sewed into a teddy bear: Horsbrugh-Porter, 101.
205   Kshesinskaya hid her money: Romanovsky-Krassinsky, 181.
205   Ladies soon learned: Horsbrugh-Porter, 65–66.
206   A commissar on the border: Paustovsky, III, 662.
206   "Farsighted old chambermaid": Nabokov, 186.
206   Finland offered: Viroubova, 377.
207   "Any way you look at it": *ibid.*

207   "My machine": Paley, 123.
207   A Danish diplomat: *ibid.*, 212.
208   "Every one of us": *Rossiiskii imperatorskii dom*, 197.
208   "For their [own] safety": RA/PS/CV/M 1344A/26, 17 August 1918.
208   "The want of food": *ibid.* RA/PS/GV/M 1344A/43, 16 October 1918.
208   Book about duck hunting: Gavriil Constantinovich, 366.
208   "On what His Imperial Highness": RA/PS/GV/M 1344A/43. 16 October 1918.
208   "Petrograd. Jail": HI, *Georgii Mikhailovich,* George Mikhailovich to Xenia Georgievna, 25 Novermber 1918.
208   "While I am sleeping": *ibid.*, 20 October 1918.
208   Gorky and Brassova: BA, Manukhin, Box 2.
208   Princess Paley and Gorky: Paley, 241.
209   Gorky and Lenin: BA, Manukhin, Box 2; Scott, 101.
209   On 28 January 1919: Scott, 101.

Chapter Ten
"Open the Gates!" February 1919–February 1920

211   Several groups: *Beloye dvizheniye*, 127–128.
212   Father Shavelsky at Dulber: Shavelsky, II, 315–321.
212   The Jassy Conference: "K istorii Yasskogo soveshchaniya," 107.
213   Lukomsky and Nikolasha: *Beloye dvizheniye*, 128.
213   "The Russian soldiers": Fatemi, 486.
213   On 10 June 1918: HI, Baratov, Box 3, Prikaz otdelnomu kavkazskomu kavaleriiskomu korpusu #85.
213   The British became: Fatemi, 486–498.
214   Radical newspapers on Dmitri: Buranov, 318.
214   Marling said: WRA, GEO V Q 745/47, Sir Charles Marling to King George V, 11 May 1918.
214   But London brushed off: WRA, GV Q 745/40, FO to Marling, 20 May 1918.
214   Marling retorted: *ibid.*WRA, GV Q 745/50, 23 May 1918.
214   Dmitri was shocked: Houghton Library, Dmitri's Diaries, 12 May 1918.
214   "As a mother": *ibid.*, 5/18 November 1918.
215   "In a very fast vessel": WRA, GEO V M 1344A/48, 19 November 1918.
215   Minnie asked: *ibid.* WRA, GEO V M 1344A/47, 23 November 1918.
215   "Her Imperial Majesty": *ibid.*
215   Negotiating with Minnie: *ibid.* WRA, GEO V M 1344A/55, 28 November 1918.
216   "Please ask Mama": *ibid.* RA/PS/GV/M 1344A/68, 17 December 1918.
216   Sandro left: *ibid.* RA/PS/GV/M 1344A/70, 26 December 1918.

216   "Not to facilitate": RA/PS/GV/M 1344A/76, Adm Sir E. Wemyss to Sir R. W. Graham, 14 January 1919.

217   "It was a sad and bitter": Vorres, 163.

217   "Whatever may be": RA/PS/GV/M 1344A/90, 8 April 1919.

217   Minnie and the Russian refugees: HI, Rerberg, Istoricheskiye zagadki v russkoi revolutsii, part 2.

217   The dowager's visit to the church: HI, Tarsaidze, Box 15.

217   "It was a sad sight": Stone and Glenny, 165.

217   "Like a mother": *ibid.*

218   Minnie's journey: Countess Ekaterina Kleinmichel in *ibid.*

218   "One fine evening": Battiscombe, 297.

218   Olga was perhaps the only Romanov: Marie, *Education*, 52.

218   "At every halt": Vorres, 164.

219   Olga went to Novorossiysk: *ibid.*, 166.

219   Typhus in Novorossiysk: Teffi, 412–415; Vorres, 166.

219   The British cruiser: Vorres, 166.

220   "We got on Good Friday": *ibid.*, 168.

220   "Indecent": When Prince Gavriil Constantinovich was hospitalized and his wife came to visit him and gave her last name to the nurse, the nurse reacted: "What an indecent name you have!": Gavriil Constantinovich, 356.

220   Marie leaves Soviet Russia: Marie, *Education*, 368–380.

223   "All through the summer of 1918": Bulgakov, 117.

224   A witness wrote: Teffi, 329.

225   Once, sailors searched: Vladimir Kirillovich, *et al.*, 14–15.

226   In June 1918: Williams, 76.

227   Ducky's letter to King George V: RA/PS/GV/Q 1550/XIX/319, Victoria Melita to King George V, 29 January 1919.

227   The king replied: *ibid.*, RA/PS/GV/Q 1550/XIX/320, 13 March 1919.

228   "He could not": Pipes, 92–93.

228   "I was very much struck": RA/PS/GV/P 1569/1, Lord Acton to King George, 8 December 1919.

228   "To proceed to France": RA/PS/GV/P 1569/1, Lord Acton to King, 1 March 1920.

229   Shkuro: Luckett, 184.

229   The Red Terror: BA, Bashmakov, Box 15, Perezhitoye, 139.

229   "What a wonderfully picturesque": Romanovsky-Krassinsky, 190.

229   The Vladimirovichi reached Anapa: *ibid.*, 191.

230   "Not too dirty": *ibid.*, 192.

230   She told a British officer: *ibid.*, 195.

230   Dmitri was getting Kyril's letters: Houghton Library, Dmitri's Diaries, 9 June 1918.

230   Miechen and Andrew in the North Caucasus: Romanovsky-Krassinsky, 195–199.

230   Evacuation from Novorossiysk: Teffi, 412–415; *Beloye dvizheniye*, 334–336.
231   But Miechen and Andrew: Romanovsky-Krassinsky, 200.
231   Fabergé cufflinks: Faberge, 146.
231   Andrew in Venice: Romanovsky-Krassinsky, 202.

PART THREE
Chapter Eleven
Stateless

236   The British were still reluctant: Interview with Marusya Chavchavadze; Interview with Paul Grabbe.
236   At times Paris had been home: Johnston, 17.
236   "An archaeological museum": *ibid.*, 15.
236   Nabokov on a dead civilization: Nabokov, 209.
236   "Nostalgia, fatalism": Johnston, 4.
237   "We lived": Marie, *Exile*, 331.
238   Russians in Constantinople: Loukomsky, 258–259.
239   Olga at Prinkipo: Vorres, 166–167.
239   "A very inferior document": Nabokov, 204.
239   Even Romanovs had to carry: Interview with Grand Duchess Leonida.
240   "No one should be": RA/PS/GV/M 1344A/125, Stamfordham to Col Sir Arthur Davidson, 2 May 1919.
240   Grand Duchess Marie: Marie, *Exile*, 99–100.
241   "I am more than sorry": RA/PS/GV/CC 45/544, Aunt Minnie to May, ND.
242   "Hvidore is quite perfect": Hvidore, 29.
242   "Warm one's hands": *ibid.*, 14.
242   Olga complained: BA, Sviatopolk-Mirskii, Box 3, Olga Alexandrovna to Princess Sviyatopolk-Mirskii, 1 April 1928.
243   Fake "Anastasia": Volkov, A. A., 188; HI, Botkin, Box 8, Grand Duke Andrew Vladimirovich to Baron Osten Saken, 11 October 1927, 26 September 1927; also to Botkin, 15 June 1927, 17 May 1927, 25 May 1927, 2 August 1927, 4 August 1927, 28 October 1926, 2 September 1927; Andrew to Botkin, 6 February 1928; Andrew to Botkin, 6 May 1928; *Pamyatnaya zapiska S.D.Botkina*.
243   Yurievskaya's death: Bakhrakh, 118–119.
244   "Can't you keep those boys": Interview with Princess Tatiana Ladyzhenskaya; Vorres, 173.
244   Xenia at Windsor: HI, Tarsaidze, Box 15.
244   Minnie in a Russian church: Interview with Princess Tatiana Ladyzhenskaya.
245   Olga was terrified: Vorres, 172–173.

245 The Soviet government requested: *The New York Times*, 7 November 1924.

245 "Her Imperial Majesty": Vorres, 172.

246 The dowager's funeral: BA, Rozen, Box 1; *The London Times*, 20 October 1928.

247 Olga wrote from Hvidore: BA, Sviatopolk-Mirskii, Box 3, Olga Alexandrovna to Princess Sviatopolk-Mirskii, 26 October 1928.

247 Xenia to Queen Mary: RA/PS/GV/CC 45/729, Xenia to May, Hvidore, 1 November 1928.

247 Dowager looking at her jewel box: Vorres, 180.

247 Christian X had started hinting: *ibid.*, 180–181.

247 Sandro wrote to the dowager: *ibid.*

248 King George V wrote: *ibid.*

248 Queen Mary's jewels: Edwards, 225.

248 "Fourteen tiaras": Field, 10.

249 Minnie would not sell: Vorres, 180–181.

249 Olga did not care: Interview with Olga Kulikovsky.

249 Xenia allowed a British agent: Vorres, 182–183.

249 Peter Bark: Ponsonby, 470.

249 The box was opened: Field, 60, 101.

250 Fate of the jewels: Vorres, 182–183; Interview with Olga Kulikovsky; Ponsonby, 172, 471; Clarke, 169–170. Mrs. Kulikovsky (Olga's daughter-in-law) insists that the book by Clarke was commissioned by Buckingham Palace: Interview with Olga Kulikovsky.

251 "Here you are": Alexander, *Always*, 4.

251 Sandro's clothes: *ibid.*

251 "Travelling under British protection": PRO, FO 371/3989 #2755, January 1919.

251 "Of the opinion": *ibid.*, 5 January 1919.

251 "In the most friendly manner": WRA, GEO V M 1394A/79, Lord Hardinge of Penhurst to King, Paris, 13 January 1919.

252 "I cannot say": *ibid.*

252 "Continued to believe": Alexander, *Always*, 5–6.

252 "I stand and fall with Russia": *ibid.*, 37.

252 "The revolution had taught me": *ibid.*, 41.

253 Sandro and Balfour: Stephan, 3.

253 Sandro's collection of coins: Alexander, *Always*, 54.

253 "Just think": *ibid.*

254 "The very idea of hiring": *ibid.*, 121.

254 "I am afraid": *ibid.*, 122.

254 On arriving in New York: *The New York Times*, 27 March 1931.

254 Sandro told the New York reporters: *ibid.*

255 On the question of vodka: *ibid.*

255 After a dinner speech: *The New York Times*, 14 May 1933.

255   Biography of the two sisters: Alexander, *Always*, VIII.
256   Sandro's death: *The New York Times*, 14 May 1933.
256   "Gleaning the admiration": Alexander, *Always*, 42.
256   Dmitri's journey to Europe: Houghton Library, Dmitri's Diaries, 16 November 1918; Marie, *Exile*, 74–75.
256   Dmitri in Paris: Houghton Library, Dmitri's Diaries, 29 November 1918.
256   Dmitri for the first time grasped: *ibid.*, 8 December 1918.
256   "I feel": *ibid.*, 12 January 1919.
256   "Real sympathy": Marie, *Exile*, 13.
256   "With the single": *ibid.*, 29.
257   "Often when speaking": *ibid.*, 30–31.
257   "To be brilliant is not always": *ibid.*, 17.
257   "We had outlived": *ibid.*, 47.
258   Before the revolution: *ibid.*, 67.
258   Reunion with Dmitri in London: *ibid.*, 69.
258   Sapphire tiara: Nadelhoffer, 114.
259   "Each time that I was obliged": Marie, *Exile*, 82.
259   "Either too big or too small": *ibid.*, 83.
259   Death of Roman: *ibid.*, 85.
259   Marie's second marriage: *ibid.*, 261.
260   "Feverish idleness": Houghton Library, Dmitri's Diaries, 13/31 June 1920.
260   Dmitri at Monte Carlo: Ktorova, 92.
260   "Nobody has had an easier": Marie, *Exile*, 71.
261   "He had not looked": *ibid.*, 72.
261   Felix's couture house and restaurant: King, *Man*, 229.
262   "Extremely attractive": Youssoupoff, *Lost*, 95.
262   In February 1920: Houghton Library, Dmitri's Diaries, letter from Felix Yusupov to Dmitri, 26 February 1920.
262   Dmitri felt so angry: *ibid.*, letter from Dmitri to Felix Yusupov, 27 February 1920.
262   Dmitri fell in love: Baillen, 32–33; Kennet, 45; Houghton Library, Dmitri's Diaries, April–May 1921.
263   "These grand dukes": Baillen, 33.
263   Long before the deluge: Buckle, Richard, 112.
264   Miechen's jewels: Clarke, 161.
264   Boris was his mother's favorite: Interview with Grand Duchess Leonida.
264   Andrew owned a villa: Interview with Grand Duchess Leonida.
264   Andrew and Kshesinskaya gamble: *The New York Times*, 2 June 1928; Ktorova, 93.
264   Nijinsky insane: Nijinsky, 7–19.
265   Diaghilev and the European royals: Garafola, 348.
265   Diaghilev's homosexuality: *ibid.*, 374.

265   Zinaida Rashevskaya: Interviews with Grand Duchess Leonida and Andrei Shmeman.
265   Queen Marie: Interview with Grand Duchess Leonida.
265   Boris: *The New York Times*, 10 January 1925.
265   LaGuardia: *ibid.*, 15 January 1925.
266   "Except to the comparatively": *ibid.*, 19 June 1924.
266   Boris's interview: *ibid.*, 18 January 1925.

Chapter Twelve
"We Should Act!"

267   Nikolasha in Italy and France: Danilov, 342–347.
267   Nikolasha granted a pension: Wrangel, Alexis, 237–238.
268   The house: *ibid.*, 352.
268   Kyril described by an unfriendly observer: Alexey Tolstoy, IV, 236.
268   Semenov wrote to Kyril: Williams, 214.
268   Semenov: Luckett, 210–211, 388; Pipes, 46; Borisov, 15, 36.
269   Zemsky Sobor: HI, Lampe, Box 2, letter to Miller, 3 July 1922.
269   Gippius on monarchism: Robert Frost Library, Gippius and Merezhkovsky, Box 3, Folder 88, Gippius to Andrei Beloborodov, 9 December 1921.
270   Charles I: Brooke-Shepard, 263.
270   On August 8, 1922: HI, Wrangel, Box 143, Kyril's manifesto.
271   On the same day: HI, Wrangel, Box 143, Kyril's address to Russian soldiers.
271   Duke of Leuchtenberg: Williams, 215.
271   Some wealthy: *Memoirs of Alfred Rosenberg*, 62; Williams, 212–213.
271   Ducky photographed with Hitler: Interview with Zakatov; Zakatov's pictorial collection; also Museum of the Imperial Family, Moscow.
271   Hitler visited the couple: King, *Man*, 235.
271   Ducky was believed to be the driving force: Williams, 212; Epanchin, 497.
271   "You should be": BA, Bashmakov, Perezhitoye, 164.
271   Kyril particularly sought out: HI, Wrangel, Box 143, cable from Kyril to Wrangel.
272   Wrangel did believe: HI, Wrangel, Box 143.
272   Top secret document: HI, Wrangel, Box 143, Svodka informatsion-nykh soobshchenii, 28 August 1922.
272   Munich and Budapest supported Kyril: *ibid.*
272   As the monarchists: HI, Wrangel, Box 143, unsigned letter, 17 January 1923.
273   Kyril met the representatives of Wrangel: *ibid.*
273   Meanwhile Nikolasha: HI, Wrangel, Box 144, Vypiska iz pisma starshego Lionskoi gruppy, podpolkovnika Prokopenko.

274   "There can be no doubt": PRO, FO 371/4061 #211896, Memo of 17 August 1920.

274   Nikolasha on succession and intervention: *The New York Times*, 18 June 1924 and 20 July 1924.

274   In August 1924: HI, Wrangel, Box 143, Kyril to Nicholas Nikolaevich, August 1924.

274   Council for Building Imperial Russia: BA, Bentkovskii.

274   Kyril's representatives: BA, Bashmakov, Box 18.

274   Kyril wrote to Minnie: HI, Wrangel, Box 143, Kyril to Maria Fedorovna.

275   "My heart": HI, Wrangel, Box 143, Obrashcheniye E.I.V. Gosudaryni Imperatritsy k V.K. Nikolayu Nikolayevichu.

275   "Son-like love": HI, Wrangel, Box 143, Kyril to Maria Fedorovna.

275   "Painfully": HI, Wrangel, Box 143, Obrashcheniye E.I.V. Gosudaryni Imperatritsy k V.K. Nikolayu Nikolayevichu.

275   In a brief commentary: *ibid.*

275   He told several people: HI, Baratov, Box 2, Dnevnik.

275   Dmitri at Choigny: *ibid.*

275   "I recognize": BA, Kozlianinov, Box 1, Dmitri Pavlovich to Metropolutan Antony.

275   Dmitri argued: HI, Baratov, Box 2, Dnevnik.

276   Dmitri talked to Baratov: *ibid.*

276   Baratov felt sad: *ibid.*

276   Disgusted by Kyril's behavior: HI, Wrangel, Box 147, Obrashcheniye v.k.Nikolaya Nikolayevicha, 16 November 1924; also see: HI, Wrangel, Box 147, Nicholas Nikolaevich to Wrangel, 18 July 1925, Anastasia Nikolaevna to Wrangel.

276   Kyril's supporters: HI, Chasovoi, Box 3, Kutepov's letter.

276   Russian gold: HI, Wrangel, Box 150, Otkuda dengi u "nikolaevtsev"?

276   "Devourer": HI, Wrangel, Box 150, letter to Wrangel, 8 February 1925.

276   "The army": HI, Lampe, Box 2, Miller to Lampe, 30 June 1928.

277   Nikolasha's political platform: HI, Tarsaidze, Box 15, *Zayavleniye velikogo knyazya Nikolaya Nikolayevicha; The New York Times*, 11 October 1925.

277   Wrangel in Berlin: Williams, 286.

277   Herriot on Soviet Russia: Johnston, 62.

278   Princess Paley to Nansen: Library, University of Oslo, Nansen, Ms.flo. 1988, F2Z, Paley to Nansen, 26 June 1920.

278   A rumor circulated: Interview with Olga Kulikovsky.

278   Kyril on "grannies and aunties" and the British: Interview with Grand Duchess Leonida.

278   The Romanovs and the Windsors: Interview with Grand Duchess Leonida; Interview with Olga Kulikovsky; Vorres, 54.

278   Royal refuges in Britain: Edwards, 313.

278 Charles I and the British: Van der Kiste, *Windsor*, 156.
279 On 9 March 1923: *General*, 147.
279 Nikolasha decided to create an underground: *General*, 291–292; Pryanishnikov, 41–42.
279 Wrangel disliked the idea: Pryanishnikov, 42.
279 Fighting Group: Pryanishnikov, 47, 80.
279 Nikolasha began to spend: Interview with Andrei Shmeman.
280 Security measures at Choigny: HI, Wrangel, Box 144, Vypiska iz pisma starshego Lionskoi gruppy, podpolkovnika Prokopenko.
280 Nikolasha's popularity in France: Interview with Andrei Shmeman.
280 Kutepov and the security measures: *General*, 293–294; HI, Wrangel, Box 150, Kak zhivet i rabotayet b.v.k.N.N.Romanov.
280 The CIA study: HI, U.S. CIA, The Trust.
281 Yakushev in 1921: Pryanishnikov, 47–49.
281 Artamonov: Leggett, 295–298; Andrew, 68–74.
281 Polish and Finnish General Staffs: Voitsekhovsky, 10.
281 Code: HI, Voitsekhovsky, Box 2, letter from Yu.A.Artamonov, 9 May 1923.
281 Some pointed out: HI, Voitsekhovsky, Box 2, letter from Prince Shirinsky-Shakhmatov, 5 June 1923.
281 The Kremlin even sacrificed: Voitsekhovsky, 130.
281 The naïve emigres: HI, Voitsekhovsky, letter from Yu.A.Artamonov, 9 May 1923.
282 To surround Nikolasha with "Trest" people: *ibid*.
282 To induce Dmitri: *ibid*., 22 April 1923.
282 In late 1922: *ibid*., 6 February 1923; Pryanishnikov, 70.
282 In 1923: Pryanishnikov, 88, 91–92, 106–107; Nikulin, 130–131. Nikulin's book *Mertvaya zyb'* is a chronicle of the operation published by a Soviet author in 1963. Obviously, Nikulin had been using many authentic KGB documents. Experts in the field, like the CIA people who have done research on Trest, find this book convincing.
283 "It's time to pack": Nikulin, 130.
284 Many small monarchist groups: Saparov, 11.
284 "The British": Dobronozhenko, 96.
284 "All Communists": *ibid*., 118.
285 "And then Russia": *ibid*.
285 "There is one": Okunev, 437.
285 In April 1924: Sokolov, 55.
285 In the summer of 1921: HI, Miller, Box 16, Antibolshevistskoye dvizheniye v Rossii po svedeniyam k kontsu fevralya 1922 g.
285 The Cossack areas: HI, Miller, Box 17, Povstancheskoye dvizheniye na Severnom Kavkaze i Donskoi oblasti vo vtoroi polovine 1921 g.
285 350,000: HI, Miller, Box 17, Terror v Sovetskoi Rossii.
285 "Has not reached": HI, Miller, Box 16, Oslableniye deyatelnosti pravitelstvennogo apparata kak odno iz posledstvii "novogo kursa."

285   "People say": HI, Miller, Box 16, Vyderzhka iz pisma komissara.
285   They dispatched: Pryanishnikov, 85.
285   "At any rustle": HI, Wrangel, Box 150, Informatsiya ot P.Dolgo-
       rukova.
286   "The name": BA, Kutepov, Box 3, agent to Kutepov, 20 September
       1923.
286   "Moscow is the key": BA, Kutepov, Box 3, Zapiska o rabote po pod-
       gotovke, rukovodstvu i osushchestvleniu sverzheniya Sovetskoi vlasti
       v Rossii.
287   "The things": BA, Kutepov, Box 3, report from an agent.
287   "Not to deprive us": *ibid.*
287   Yakushev sardonically promised: *ibid.*
287   Intelligence reports: BA, Kutepov, Box 3, report no. 15.
287   Kutepov agreed to represent Trest: Voitsekhovsky, 11.
287   5 November 1924: Nikulin, 191; Pryanishnikov, 91–92.
287   Immediate use of terror: Voitsekhovsky, 11.
287   Yakushev did his best: Pryanishnikov, 91.
288   "This strange and sinister man": Bailey, 15.
288   "One of the most": BA, Kutepov, Box 3, letter from Trest.
288   "We have reasons": *ibid.*, another letter (no exact date).
288   Wrangel intensely disliked: Voitsekhovsky, 141–142.
288   "You": BA, Kutepov, Box 3, letter from Trest.
288   Trest agents proposed: *ibid.*
289   Marked the place: Kutepov's map at BA, Kutepov, Box 3.
289   The Kremlin did not despair: BA, Kutepov, Box 3, agent to Kutepov.
289   "Let Kutepov": BA, Kutepov, Box 3, letter to Kutepov from Choigny,
       15 July, 1924.
289   Nikolasha did not believe: *ibid.*
289   "I trust only": Voitsekhovsky, 98.
289   Yakushev's visit: Nikulin, 236–237.
289   Shulgin's visit: Pryanishnikov, 100–104.
291   In 1926: Nikulin, 324–325.
291   The shocking truth: Leggett, 295–298.
291   Their "Fighting Group": *General*, 325–329.
291   Kutepov's people in Russia: Pryanishnikov, 142, 151; Voitsekhovsky,
       12–13; *General Kutepov*, 325–329.
292   Provocateur Yakushev was so frightened: Nikulin, 358.
292   On the morning: *Ustami Buninykh*, 192–193.
292   "Everyone who admires": *The New York Times*, 24 November 1922.
292   Requiem for Nikolasha: *Ustami Buninykh*, 192–194.
292   "Lying in the coffin": Odoevtseva, 287.
293   "When I saw him": *Ustami Buninykh*, 192.
293   Obituary: *The New York Times*, 18 December 1930.
294   "With him dies": Knox, II, 539.
294   *Spring*: Sokolov, 424.

294 Kutepov's people: BA, Bashmakov, Box 15, Perezhitoye, 185.

295 Kutepov's kidnapping: Johnston, 101–102; Interview with Andrei Shmeman; *General*, 330, 333, 363; Pryanishnikov, 172–175; Andrew, 115–117.

295 "The worst thing": BA, Bashmakov, Box 15, Perezhitoye, 185.

296 Grand Duke Peter's: Interview with Prince Nicholas Romanov.

296 Tardieu: BA, Benseman.

296 Miller dispatched agents: HI, Arkhangelsky, Box 2, letter to Miller, 15 January 1936.

296 In the summer of 1930: BA, Bashmakov, Box 1, Miller to Bashmakov, 10 February, 1934.

297 Miller kidnapped: Johnston, 141; Pryanishnikov, 326–416; Andrew, 126–127.

297 French police helping the Romanovs: Interview with Grand Duchess Leonida.

297 Peter's family decided to leave France: Interview with Prince Dmitri Romanov; interview with Prince Nicholas Romanov.

Chapter Thirteen
"Always Be Visible"

299 Kazem-Bek: Hayes, 258–259.

300 In 1923: HI, Miller, Box 16, letter to Miller, August 2, 1923.

300 Kazem-Bek and Kyril: HI, Wrangel, Box 150.

300 "Careerist," "smart boy": HI, Voitsekhovsky, Box 2, Shirinsky-Shakhmatov to Artamonov, February 1, 1923.

300 "We believe in Russia": BA, Kartashov.

301 "Glava!": Johnston, 93–94.

301 Blue shirts: Interview with Andrei Shmeman.

301 "The predominance": HI, Bunin family.

301 "Reconciliation": *ibid.*

301 "At that point everyone was": Interview with Grand Duchess Leonida.

301 The Young Russians: Interview with Andrei Shmeman.

301 Dmitri's marriage: Ferrand, 110–112.

302 Baratov about Dmitri: HI, Baratov, Box 2, *Dnevnik*.

302 Dmitri in America: BA, Kozlianinov, Dmitri to Kozliyaninov, 8 January 1932.

302 Dmitri's divorce: Ferrand, 110–112; Intervew with Paul Ilyinsky.

302 Funeral of George V: Edwards, 393.

303 "Horrible blow": Ronchevsky, 32.

303 The Romanov charisma: Interview with Andrei Shmeman.

303 Dmitri in the 1930s: Interview with Andrei Shmeman.

303 "For me": Interview with Paul Ilyinsky.

303 Dmitri kept a distance: Interview with Andrei Shmeman.

303   Kazem-Bek would stand at the grand duke's back: Interview with Andrei Shmeman.
304   Kyril's New Year appeal: BA, Bashmakov, Box 18.
304   Red Army songs: Interview with Andrei Shmeman.
304   Shkuro's letter: HI, Shkuro.
305   At four p.m.: Ronchevsky, 39–40.
305   Kazem-Bek's explanation: Hayes, 266.
306   Three weeks before: *Pravda*, 13 June 1937.
306   Analyzing: HI, Arkhangelsky, Box 2, Provokatsiya.
306   Kazem-Bek: Interview with Andrei Shmeman; Pryanishnikov, Box 2; Connecticut College Archives, File of Alexander Kasem-Beg.
306   The KGB-infested: see evidence in: GARF, Sovet po delam religii.
307   Kazem-Bek's papers: Interview with Rev. Nikon; Interview with Zakatov.
307   Kyril and Ducky in St.Briac: Interview with Angela Winthrop.
307   "Difficult": Interview with Angela Winthrop.
308   Wedding anniversary: BA, Bashmakov, Box 15, Perezhitoye, 165.
308   "Court circular": BA, Bashmakov, Box 18.
309   "The would-be Emperor of Russia": Alexander, *Twilight*, 163.
309   Ducky's death: HI, Tarsaidze, Box 15.
309   Kyra and Lulu: *Daily Telegraph*, 28 September 1994.
309   Kyril died: Vladimir Kirillovich *et al.*, 50–51.
310   In his diary: Houghton Library, Dmitri's Diaries, 8 March 1938.
310   Dmitri and his son: Interview with Paul Ilyinsky; Ferrand, 116.
310   "He is an asshole": BA, Kozlianinov, Box 1, Dmitri to Kozlianinov, 22 April 1940.
310   "I think he will not": *ibid.*
310   Andrew wrote to Dmitri: *ibid.*, 27 March 1940.
310   Dmitri instructed his friends: *ibid.*
310   Dmitri's postcard: *ibid.*, 12 January 1940.
311   Wagnerian photograph: *ibid.*, 30 March 1940.
311   Small chateau: *ibid.*
311   "Our life here": *ibid.*, 10 February 1940.
311   "Everything starts": *ibid.*, 10 April 1940.
311   Churchill sent a message: Palmer, 244.
311   Dmitri's illness and death: BA, Kozlianinov, Box 1, Gavriil Constantinovich to Kozlyaninov, 20 March 1941.

Chapter Fourteen
"Escape Contact with Allies at Any Cost"

313   Coco collaborating: Garafola, 377.
313   Ivan Bunin: *Ustami Buninykh*, 96.
313   Vladimir Kirillovich's proclamation: HI, Chasovoi, Box 1.
314   Vladimir later insisted: Vladimir Kirillovich *et al.*, 59–61.
314   "Russia did not exist": Interview with Prince Nicholas Romanov.

314 Russians setting their forests afire: *Ustami Buninykh*, 100.

314 Hitler on Leningrad: Shirer, 1020.

314 Nazi bigwigs and the Crimea: Shirer, 1121.

314 Russians in the resistance: Johnston, 169–171.

314 Andrew and Maklakov: HI, Maklakov, Box 22, letter from Andrew to Maklakov, n/d, letter from Maklakov to Andrew, 26 June 1941.

315 Boris died: HI, Tarsaidze, Box 15.

315 Militsa in Rome: Interview with Prince Dmitri Romanov; Interview with Prince Nicholas Romanov.

316 The Romanovs and the Vatican: Gavriil Constantinovich, 196.

316 "It hurts to think": RA/PS/GV/CC 45/1374, Xenia to May, Balmoral, 29 February 1944.

317 Vladimir Kirillovich's education: Vladimir Kirillovich, *et al.*, 31; Fenyvesi, 253–254; *The New York Times*, 22 April 1992.

317 In December 1938: HI, Tarsaidze, Box 15.

318 Rosenberg on Ukraine: Nova, 43.

318 The Romanov made it known: HI, Tarsaidze, Box 15.

318 "A plausible legal claim": PROFO 371/22301 N 6026, Sir Alexander Cadogan to Sir Alexander Hardinge, 14 December 1938.

318 "The banks": *ibid.*

319 "Some purely private": *ibid.*

319 Vladimir went to England: Vladimir Kirillovich, *et al.*, 57.

319 Andrew on Vladimir: Vladimirov, *Moskva*, 1971, no. 8, 183. The source is the memoir of a former Gestapo officer of Russian origins, published in the Soviet magazine under the pseudonym of S.Vladimirov. The introduction to the memoir said the author lived in South America and that all the facts had been checked by editors.

320 "When the time comes": HI, Arkhangelsky, Box 3, Vladimir to Arkhangelsky, 6 February 1939.

320 "I do not exclude": Vladimirov, 183.

320 "[Vladimir] Romanov": *ibid.*, 183.

321 "A great deal of trouble": PROFO 371/24854 N 4951, Hardinge to Cadogan, 13 May 1940.

321 "Even in the event": *ibid.*

321 Vladimir's letter: BA, Lampe, Box 8, Vladimir to Peter Skarzhinsky, Head of the Supreme Monarchist Council, 21 September 1942.

321 Smyslovsky's army: Holmston-Smyslovsky, 6, 12, 174; Hoffman, 70–71.

322 Vladimir Kirillovich brought to Germany: Vladimir Kirillovich, *et al.*, 62.

322 Hitler and the Windsors: Allen, 107, 108, 227.

322 Duke of Saxe-Coburg-Gotha: *ibid.*, 56–59.

322 Rosenberg in the Crimea: *Memoirs of Alfred Rosenberg*, 281; Nova, 49.

323 Felix and Hitler: King, *Man*, 261.

323 "When in spring of 1945": Vladimir Kirillovich, 62–63.

323   This was Feldkirch: Frelikh, 301.
323   "All roads": BA, Tal, notebook 18–19, p.22.
323   On April 14: HI, Voitsekhovsky, Box 1, list of Vladimir's addresses.
323   Vladimir crosses the border: HI, Voitsekhovsky, Box 11, Report of Voitsekhovsky to Vladimir Kirillovich; Frelikh, 301–302; Bethouart, 291–292; Holmston-Smyslovsky, 12–13, 35–36.
323   Voitsekhovsky's background: Andreyev, 56; Voitsekhovsky, *Episody*, 27.
323   Holmston on the run: Hoffman, 71; Frelikh, 301.
324   The French troops: Bethouart, 288.
324   "Make a decision!": Holmston-Smyslovsky, 154.
325   The French zone of occupation: Balfour and Mair, 288; Bethouart, 17–18, 283.
325   SOE: West, 1–2.
325   SOE in Austria: *ibid.*, 241–244.
326   Kesselring decided to surrender: Bethouart, 288.
326   Soviets cruising: Frelikh, 302.
326   The British turned over the Russians to Soviet custody: Hoffman, 241, 236–237.
326   Shulgin arrested: Ioffe, 77.
326   Soviet secret services kidnapping people: Voitsekhovsky, *Episody*, 116–124.
327   Vladimir would not be allowed: Vladimir Kirillovich, *et al.*, 64.
327   "Everywhere is": *Dnevniki imperatora*, 625.

Chapter Fifteen
The End of the Line

329   Militsa in Egypt: Interview with Prince Dmitri Romanov.
330   "With one privilege": *The London Times*, 21 April 1960.
330   "Has a bad duodenal ulcer": WRA, GEO V CC 53/1462, 2 March 1946.
330   "Oh, & here comes": WRA, GEO V CC 45/1411, Xenia to May, Wilderness House, 5 March 1945.
330   Xenia's death: HI, Tarsaidze, Box 15.
330   Xenia's funeral: *The London Times*, 27 April 1960.
330   Xenia's estate: HI, Tarsaidze, Box 15.
331   Olga in Denmark: Vorres, 185–187; Interview with Olga Kulikovsky.
331   One hundred kronor: HI, Ivanov, Box 5, File 265.
331   Olga hiding people: Vorres, 188; Interview with Olga Kulikovsky.
331   Cossacks at Lienz: Hoffman, 236–237; Interview with Olga Kulikovsky.
331   Olga and the Cossacks: Interview with Olga Kulikovsky.
332   "What a foolish thing": Hoffman, 238.
332   Soviet defector: Interview with Princess Tatiana Ladyzhenskaya.
332   Scotland Yard and Armstrong: Vorres, 189–192; Interview with Olga Kulikovsky.

332 Olga at Queen Mary's birthday party: Vorres, 192.

332 "We have got": WRA, GEO V CC 45/1599, Olga to May, 3 September 1948.

333 "A tiny bungalow": WRA, GEO V CC 45/1756, Olga to May, Christmas 1951.

333 "There are but few houses": *ibid.*

333 Olga wrote Queen Mary: WRA, GEO V CC 45/1812, 5 December 1952.

333 Kulikovsky dies: HI, Tarsaidze, Box 15.

334 Olga's last months: HI, Odintsov, Box 2, correspondence between Martemianov and Odintsov.

335 Olga's funeral: HI, Odintsov, Box 2; Tarsaidze, Box 15.

336 "I was filled with exhilaration": Marie, *Exile*, 293.

336 Marie's book: *ibid.*, 296.

336 Marie moved to the US: *ibid.*, 297.

337 Marie working for Bergdorf Goodman: Interview with Betty Tobias.

337 Marie in America: *ibid.*

337 "She made a most agreeable": Phelps, 851–853.

338 "The usual agency": BA, J. O. Brown, Bye to Marie, 28 January 1930.

338 "I hope very much": *ibid.*, Marie to Bye, 4 November 1931.

338 "I do not know": *ibid.*, Bye to Marie, 5 November 1931.

339 In 1941: Bernadotte, 159; Ferrand, 68–69.

339 Marie in Buenos Aires: Bernadotte, 161, 171–172.

339 Marie in Europe: *ibid.*, 158, 171–172.

340 Audrey sold Dmitri's belongings: BA, Kozlianinov, Box 1, Kozlianinov to Gavriil Constantinovich, 27 July 1949.

340 In his old age: Interview with Andrei Shmeman.

340 Andrew's death: Romanovsky-Krassinsky, 271.

340 Andrew's funeral: *ibid.*

341 Vladimir in Spain: Vladimir Kirillovich *et al.*, 64, 85; Interview with Grand Duchess Leonida.

341 Leonida's past: BA, Lampe, Box 13; HI, Nikolaevsky, Box 788; on Sumner Kirby: *Memories, the Story of the Kirby Family,* 231 ff.

342 Vladimir and Leonida: *ibid.*

342 Vladimir's marriage: HI, Voitsekhovsky, Box 2.

342 "Men marry": BA, Lampe, Box 13, Shinkarenko to Orekhov, 14 June 1953.

343 "Poor soul": BA, Kozlianinov, Box 15, Gavriil to Kozlianinov, 26 August 1948.

343 Vladimir's supporters: BA, Lampe, Box 8, Lampe to Leonida, 11 October 1953.

343 "The dynasty in Russia": BA, Kozlianinov, Box 1.

343 Vladimir's appeal: HI, Vladimir Kirillovich.

344 After a while: Vladimir Kirillovich *et al.*, 64–65.

344   "Create an executive body": BA, Lampe, Box 8, D.Oznobishin to Lampe, 31 July 1950.

344   Incident with Gune: HI, Voitsekhovsky, Box 2, Dvorzhitsky to Gune, 23 May 1953; Gune to Dvorzhitsky. The letter did cause some stir indeed: BA, Kozlianinov, Box 1.

345   "Stop performing": HI, Voitsekhovsky, Box 2.

345   Nikita argued: HI, Voitsekhovsky, Box 2.

345   Vladimir proclaimed Maria regent: HI, Voitsekhovsky, Box 3.

345   Maria's marriage: HI, Voitsekhovsky, Box 3; Vouytch, 26–27.

Chapter Sixteen
"Eternal Memory"

347   Natalia Androsova: Interviews with Princess Natalia Iskander.

347   "Top Secret": Iskander's personal archive, Alexander Iskander's birth cerificate.

352   She retired: Iskander's personal archive, trudovaya knizhka.

353   The Ipatiev house destroyed: Yeltsin, 81.

353   Vladimir made a trip to Russia: Vladimir Kirillovich *et al.,* 130; Interview with Grand Duchess Leonida.

354   Vladimir's funeral: Interview with Grand Duchess Leonida.

354   "His faith and long patience": *The New York Times,* 30 April 1992.

354   Kyril and Ducky: Their reburial was arranged by Grand Duchess Leonida with the consent of President Yeltsin. Interview with Grand Duchess Leonida.

354   Supreme Monarchist Council: Interview with Zakatov; Interview with Rev. Nikon.

354   Twenty-six trips: Interview with Grand Duchess Leonida.

355   George: Interview with Grand Duchess Leonida; Interview with Zakatov.

355   The monarchist movement: Interview with Zakatov; Interview with Rev.Nikon.

356   Paul Ilyinsky: Interview with Paul Ilyinsky.

356   "She has a lot of people": *Miami Herald,* 9 February 1997.

356   Kiselyev: *Argumenty i fakty,* #33, 1997.

357   Lipman: *International Herald Tribune,* 14 January 1997.

357   The Queen's visit to Russia: WRA, Acc 1568, Vickers.

358   "Bearing your mission": *Majesty* 15:2 (December 1994), 20.

358   At Sts. Peter and Paul: *The Herald* (Glasgow), 21 October 1994.

359   Leonida not sure: Interview with Grand Duchess Leonida.

359   "The shooting of the Romanov family": *Izvestiya,* 18 July 1998.

SELECTED
BIBLIOGRAPHY

Primary Sources

UNPUBLISHED

Bakhmetieff Archive, Columbia University, New York.

Bashmakov, Aleksandr A. and Maria N.
Benseman, Gleb
Bentkovskii, Alfred Karlovich
Brown, J. O.
Chechulin family
Danilchenko, Petr V.
Epanchin, Nikolai Alekseevich
Gavriil Konstantinovich, Grand Duke
Iskander, Aleksandr Nikolaevich
Kartashov, Petr Vasilievich
Kozlianinov, Vladimir Fedorovich
Kutepov, Alexander
Lampe, Aleksei
Manukhin, I. I.
Meshcherskii, V. P.
Romanov, Elena Petrovna
Rozen, Konstantin Nikolaevich
Sakhno-Ustimovich, Yury Konstantinovich
Shevich, Maria Kirillovna
Shvarts, Alexei Vladimirovich
Silin, Vladimir A.
Sviatopolk-Mirskii, Maria A. and Nikolai V.
Tal, Georgy
Vereshchagin, Vladimir Alexandrovich

Connecticut College Archive, New London, CT

File on Alexander Kasem Beg (Kazem-Bek)

Gosudarstvenny arkhiv Rossiiskoi Federatsii
(State Archives of the Russian Federation),
Moscow, Russia

Emperor Alexander III. Fond 677.
Empress Maria Fedorovna. Fond 642.
Grand Duchess Maria Pavlovna Sr. Fond 655.
Grand Duke Alexander Mikhailovich. Fond 645.
Grand Duke Andrew Vladimirovich. Fond 650.
Grand Duke Boris Vladimirovich. Fond 654.
Grand Duke Nicholas Mikhailovich. Fond 670.
Grand Duke Nicholas Nikolaevich Jr. Fond 671.
Grand Duke Pavel Alexandrovich. Fond 644.
Grand Duke Sergei Alexandrovich. Fond 648.
Prince Vladimir Paley. Fond 614.
Sovet po delam religii pri Sovete Ministrov SSSR. Fond 6991.

Hoover Institution on War, Revolution and Peace,
Stanford University, Stanford, CA

Arkhangelsky, Alexey
Baratov, Nikolai Nikolaevich
Botkine, Serge
Bunin family
Chasovoi
Dolgorouky, Princess Barbara
Georgii Mikhailovich, Grand Duke of Russia
Gopstein, E. E.
Gramotin, Alexander Alexandrovich
Ivanov, Nikolai
Kaulbars, Alexander Vasilievich
Lampe, Alexei
L'Escaille
Livingstead, Ivor M. V. Z.
Maklakov, Vasily
Miller, Eugeny
Mukhanov, Mikhail Georgievich
Narodno-trudovoi soiuz
Nikolaevsky, B.
Odintsov, Gleb Nikolaevich
Olga, Consort of George I, King of the Hellenes
Pryanishnikov, B.
Rerberg, Fedor Petrovich
Russia, Ministerstvo imperatorskogo dvora
Shebeko, Boris Konstantinovich
Shkuro, Andrei Grigorievich

Smolin, I. S.
Soudakoff, Peter
Tal, Georgii Alexandrovich
Tarsaidze, Alexander Georgievich
United States Central Intelligence Agency
Vitkovsky, Vladimir K.
Vladimir Kirillovich, Grand Duke of Russia
Voitsekhovskii, Sergei Lvovich
Wrangel Collection

Houghton Library,
Harvard University, Cambridge, MA

Kilgour Collection.
Russian Imperial Family, correspondence of Tsar Alexander II, Tsaritsa
   Maria Alexandrovna, Grand Duke Vladimir Alexandrovich and letters to
   him, Diaries of Grand Duke Dmitri Pavlovich

Library, University of Oslo, Norway

Fridjof Nansen Papers

Public Record Office, London, United Kingdom

Correspondence relating to Romanov Family, 1917–

Robert Frost Library, Amherst College, Amherst, MA

Zinaida Gippius and Dmitrii Merezhkovsky Papers

Rossiiskii gosudarstvenny arkhiv voenno-morskogo flota (Russian State Naval
Archives), St. Petersburg, Russia

Fond 17.
Fond 406.
Fond 418.
Fond 467.
Fond 469.
Fond 763.

Royal Archives, Windsor Castle, United Kingdom

The Queen's State Visit to Russia, 17 to 20 October, 1994
Correspondence with and relating to Romanov Family, 1917–

Princess Natalia Iskander
Private Papers

PUBLISHED

Alexander II, St. Petersburg: Pushkinskii fond, 1995.

Alexander, Grand Duke of Russia, *Always a Grand Duke*, New York: Farrar & Rinehart, 1933.

———, *Once a Grand Duke*, Garden City and New York: Garden City Publishing, 1932.

———, *Twilight of Royalty*, New York: Ray Long & Richard R. Smith, Inc., 1932.

Alice, Her Royal Highness Princess, Countess Athlone, *For My Grandchildren*, Cleveland and New York: World Publishing Company, 1967.

Almedingen, E. M., *I Remember St. Petersburg*, London: Longmans Young, 1969.

Averchenko, Arkadii, *Zapiski prostodushnogo. "Ya v Evrope,"* Berlin: Sever, 1923.

Baddeley, John F., *Russia in the 'Eighties': Sport and Politics*, London: Longmans, Green and Co., 1921.

Bakhrakh, Alexander, *Bunin v khalate*, New York: Tovarishchestvo zarubezhnykh pisatelei, 1979.

Balsan, Consuelo Vanderbilt, *The Glitter and the Gold*, New York: Harper, 1952.

Beloye dvizheniye: nachalo i konets, Moscow: Moskovskii rabochii, 1990.

Benckendorf, Count Constantine, *Half a Life, The Reminiscences of a Russian Gentleman*, London: The Richards Press, 1954.

Bernadotte, Graf Lennart, *Gute Nacht, Kleiner Prinz*, Munich: Wilhelm Heyne Verlag, 1977.

Bethouart, Marie Emile, *La bataille pour l'Autriche*, Paris: Presses de la cité, 1966.

Between Paris and St. Petersburg. Selected Diaries of Zinaida Gippius, Urbana: University of Illinois Press, 1975.

"Bezobrazovskii kruzhok letom 1904 g.," *Krasny arkhiv*, 1926, 4 (17).

Bing, Edward J., ed., *Letters of the Tsar Nicholas and Empress Marie*, London: Ivor Nicholson and Watson Limited, 1937.

Blok, Alexander, *Sobraniye sochinenii*, Moscow: GOKhL, 1963.

Blucher, Evelyn, Princess, *An English Wife in Berlin*, New York: E. P. Dutton, n.d.

Bogdanovich, A. V., *Tri poslednikh samoderzhtsa. Dnevnik A. V. Bogdanovich*, Moscow-Leningrad: Frenkel, 1924.

Brusilov, A. A., *Moi vospominaniya*, Moscow: Voenizdat, 1983.

Brussilov, General A. A., *A Soldier's Note-Book, 1914–1918*, Westport, CT: Greenwood, 1971.

Bubnov, A., *V tsarskoi stavke*, New York: Izdatelstvo imeni Chekhova, 1955.

Buchanan, Sir George, *My Mission to Russia*, Boston: Little Brown, 1923, 2 vol.

Buchanan, Meriel, *The Dissolution of an Empire*, London: John Murray, 1932.

Buckle, George Earle, ed., *The Letters of Queen Victoria*, New York: Longmans, Green, 1926, 2 vol.

Bulgakov, Mikhail, *The White Guard*, New York: McGraw-Hill, 1971.

Bunin, Ivan, *Memories and Portraits*, London: John Lehnmann, 1951.

_____, *Okayannye dni*, London, Canada: Zarya, 1973.

_____, *Pod serpom i molotom*, London, Canada: Zarya, 1975.

Cantacuzene, Princess, *Revolutionary Days, Recollection of Romanoffs and Bolsheviki, 1914–1917*, Boston: Small, Maynard & Co, 1919.

_____, *Russian People, Revolutionary Recollections*, New York: Charles Scribner's Sons, 1923.

Chavchavadze, David, *Crowns and Trenchcoats, A Russian Prince in the CIA*, New York: Atlantic International Publications, 1990.

Chekhov, Anton, *Polnoye sobraniye sochinenii*, 30 vols. Moscow: GIKhL, 1949.

Christopher, Prince of Greece, *Memoirs*, London: Hurst & Blackett, 1938.

Chukovsky, Kornei, *Dnevnik, 1901–1929*, Moscow: Sovremenny pisatel, 1997.

Churchill, Winston, *The World Crisis*, New York: Charles Scribner's Sons, 1927.

Cyril, Grand Duke, *My Life in Russia's Service, Then and Now*, London: Selwyn & Blount, 1939.

Davydov, Alexander, *Vospominaniya*, Paris: Albatros, 1983.

Dehn, Lili, *The Real Tsaritsa*, London: Thornton Butterworth, 1922.

Dnevnik A. N. Kuropatkina, Nizhnii Novgorod, 1923.

Dnevnik imperatora Nikolaya II, 1890–1906, Moscow: Polistar, 1991.

Dnevniki imperatora Nikolaya II, Moscow: Orbita, 1991.

"Do Tsusimy," *Krasny arkhiv*, 1934, 6 (67).

Dolgorukov, Petr, *Peterburgskiye ocherki*, Moscow: Novosti, 1992.

Epanchin, N. Λ., *Na sluzhbe trekh imperatorov*, Moscow: Nashe naslediye, 1996.

Fabritsky, S. S., *Iz proshlogo. Vospominaniya fligel-adjutanta gosudarya imperatora Nikolaya II*, Berlin: n.p., 1926.

Ferro, Marc, *Nicholas II: Last of the Tsars*. Oxford University Press, 1995.

Figes, Orlando, *A People's Tragedy: The Russian Revolution, 1891–1924*. New York: Penguin Books, 1997.

Fisher, H. H., ed., *Out of My Past: The Memoirs of Count Kokovtsov*, Stanford: Stanford University Press, 1935.

Francis, David R., *Russia from the American Embassy, April 1916–November 1918*, New York: Charles Scribner's Sons, 1922.

Freilina Ee Velichestva Anna Vyrubova, Moscow: Orbita, 1993.

Gautier, Theophile, *Russia: Descriptive and Illustrative*, Philadelphia: John Winston, 1905, 2 vol.

Gavriil Konstantinovich, *V mramornom dvortse: iz khroniki nashei semyi*, New York: Izdatelstvo imeni Chekhova, 1955.

General Kutepov, Paris: Izdaniye Komiteta imeni generala Kutepova, 1934.

George, Grand Duchess, *A Romanov Diary*, New York: Atlantic International, 1988.

Gering, A.A., ed., *Sbornik pamyati Velikogo Knyazya Konstantina Konstantinovicha, poeta K.R.*, Paris: n.p., 1962.

Gilliard, Pierre, *Thirteen Years at the Russian Court*, London: Hutchinson, 1922.

Gippius, Zinaida, *Stikhotvoreniya. Zhivye litsa*, Moscow: Khudozhestvennaya literatura, 1991.

Gorky, Maxim, *Sobraniye sochinenii*, Moscow: Goslitizdat, 1951.

Grabbe, Paul, *Windows on the River Neva*, New York: Pomerica Press, 1977.

Gurko, Vladimir Iosifovich, *Features and Figures of the Past, Government and Opinion in the Reign of Nicholas II*, Stanford: Stanford University Press, 1939.

Gurko, V.I., *Tsar i tsaritsa*, Paris: Vozrozhdeniye, 1927.

Hamilton, Lord Frederic, *The Vanished Pomps of Yesterday, Some Random Reminiscences of a British Diplomat*, London: Hodder and Stoughton, n/d.

Hanbury-Williams, Major General Sir John, *The Emperor Nicholas II As I Knew Him*, London: Arthur L. Humphreys, 1922.

Hibbert, Christopher, ed., *Queen Victoria in Her Letters and Journals*, New York: Viking, 1985.

Hindenburg, Marshal Paul von, *Out of My Life*, New York: Harper, 1921.

Holmston-Smyslovsky, Boris, *Izbrannye rechi i statyi*, Buenos Aires: Rossiiskoye voenno-osvoboditelnoye dvizheniye im. gen. A. V. Suvorova, 1953.

Horsbrugh-Porter, Anna, ed., *Memories of Revolution: Russian Women Remember*, London: Routledge, 1993.

Hough, Richard, ed., *Advice to a Grand-daughter: Letters from Queen Victoria to Princess Victoria of Hesse*, London: Heinemann, 1975.

Ignatyev, Lieutenant-General A. A., *A Subaltern in Old Russia*, Ivan Montagu, trans., London: Hutchinson & Co., 1944.

"Iz dnevnika A.V.Romanova za 1916–1917 gg," *Krasny arkhiv*, 1930, 6 (43); 1931, 1 (44); 2 (45).

"Iz dnevnika Konstantina Romanova," *Krasny arkhiv*, 1928, 1 (26).

Iz dnevnika V.M.Purishkevicha, Moscow: Interprint, 1990.

"Iz perepiski Nikolaya i Marii Romanovykh v 1907–1910 gg.," *Krasny arkhiv*, 1932, 1–2 (50–51).

"Iz perepiski Nikolaya Romanova s V.A.Romanovym," *Krasny arkhiv*, 1926, 4 (17).

"Iz perepiski S.M. i N.M. Romanovykh v 1917 g.," *Krasny arkhiv*, 1932, 4 (53).

Izvolsky, Helene, *No Time to Grieve: An Autobiographical Journal*, Philadelphia: Winchell, 1985.

"K istorii poslednikh dnei tsarskogo regima (1916–1917)," *Krasny arkhiv*, 1926, 1 (14).

"K istorii ubiistva Grigoriya Rasputina," *Krasny arkhiv*, 1923, 4.

"K istorii Yasskogo soveshchaniya," *Krasny arkhiv*, 1926, 5 (18).

Kalmykow, Andrew D., *Memoirs of a Russian Diplomat, Outposts of the Empire, 1893–1917*, New Haven, CT: Yale University Press, 1971.

Kerensky, Alexander, *The Crucifixion of Liberty*, New York: John Day, Kraus Reprint, 1972.

Kleinmichel, Countess (Marie Edouardovna), *Memories of a Shipwrecked World*, London: Brentano's Ltd., 1923.

Knox, Major-General Sir Alfred, *With the Russian Army, 1914–1917*, London: Hutchinson, 1921, 2 vol.

Kokovtsov, Count V.N., *Out of My Past*, Stanford: Stanford University Press, 1935.

"L. N. Tolstoy i N.M. Romanov," *Krasny arkhiv*, 1926, 1 (14).

Lamsdorf, V.N., *Dnevnik (1886–1890)*, Moscow: Gosudarstvennoye izdatelstvo, 1926.

———, *Dnevnik (1891–1892)*, Moscow: Gosudarstvennoye izdatelstvo, 1934.

———, *Dnevnik (1894–1896)*, Moscow: Mezhdunarodnye otnosheniya, 1991.

Lensen, George Alexander, *Revelations of a Russian Diplomat, the Memoirs of Dmitrii I. Abrikossow*, Seattle: University of Washington Press, 1964.

Letters of the Tsar to the Tsaritsa, 1914–1917, London: John Lane, 1929.

Letters of the Tsaritsa to the Tsar, 1914–1916, Stanford, CA: Hoover Institution Press, 1973.

Lettres des Grand-Ducs a Nicolas II, Paris: Payot, 1926.

Liberman, Anatoly, *Mikhail Lermontov, Major Poetical Works*, Minneapolis: University of Minnesota Press, 1983.

Lockhart, Bruce R. H., *British Agent*, New York: G. P. Putnam's Sons, 1933.

Loukomsky, Alexander S., *Memoirs of the Russian Revolution*, Westport, CT: Hyperion Press Inc., 1975.

Maclean, Fitzroy, *Eastern Approaches*, London: Penguin Books, 1991.

Majolier, Nathalie, *Step-Daughter of Imperial Russia*, London: Stanley Paul, 1940.

Malkov, P., *Zapiski komendanta Kremlya*, Moscow: Molodaya gvardiya, 1967.

Marie, Grand Duchess of Russia, *Education of a Princess*, New York: Viking Press, 1931.

———, *A Princess in Exile*, New York: Viking Press, 1932.

Mayakovsky, Vladimir, *Polnoye sobraniye sochinenii*, Moscow: Goslitizdat, 1955.

Maylunas, Andrei, and Sergei Mironenko, *A Lifelong Passion: Nicholas and Alexandra, Their Own Story*, London: Weidenfeld & Nicolson, 1996.

Melnik, Tatiana, *Vospominaniya o tsarskoi semye i ee zhizni do i posle revolutsii*, Moscow: Ankor, 1993.

Memoirs of Alfred Rosenberg, Chicago: Ziff-Davis Publishing Company, 1949.

Mikhailovsky, G.N., *Zapiski. Iz istorii rossiiskogo vneshnepoliticheskogo vedomstva, 1914–1920*, Moscow: Mezhdunarodnye otnosheniya, 1993, 2 vol.

Miliukov, Pavel N., *Vospominaniya*, Moscow: Sovremennik, 1990, 2 vol.

Mosolov, A. A., *Pri dvore poslednego rossiiskogo imperatora*, Moscow: Ankor, 1993.

Mossolov, Alexander A., *At the Court of the Last Tsar*, ed. by A. A. Pilenko, London: Methuen, 1935.

"N.N.Romanov i amerikanskaya kontsessiya na zheleznuyu dorogu Sibir-Alyaska v 1905 g.," *Krasny arkhiv*, 1930, 6 (43).

Nabokov, Vladimir, *Speak, Memory*, London: Victor Gollancz Ltd., 1951.

"Net spokoistviya ni fizicheskogo, ni moralnogo. Pisma Aleksandra III imperatritse Marii Fedorovne, 1891–1892 gg.," *Istoricheski arkhiv*, 1994, #3.

Nicholas of Greece (Prince of Denmark), *My Fifty Years*, London: Hutchinson & Co, 1926.

Nijinska, Bronislava, *Early Memoirs*, New York: Holt, Rinehart and Winston, 1981.

Nijinsky, Pomola, ed., *The Diary of Vaslav Nijinsky*, Berkeley: University of California Press, 1968.

Obolensky, Serge, *One Man in His Time*, New York: McDowell, Obolensky, 1958.

Odoevtseva, Irina, *Na beregakh Seny*, Paris: La press libre, 1983.

Okunev, Nikita, *Dnevnik moskvicha (1917–1924)*, Paris: YMKA-PRESS, 1990.

Otrecheniye Nikolaya II: Vospominaniya ochevidtsev, Moscow: Sovetskii pisatel, 1990.

Paleologue, Maurice, *An Ambassador's Memoirs*, London: Hutchinson, 1923, 2 vol.

_____, *Roman imperatora*, Moscow: TsGA SSSR, 1991.

_____, *Tsarskaya Rossiya nakanune revolutsii*, Moscow: Mezhdunarodnye otnosheniya, 1991.

Paley, Princess (Olga), *Memories of Russia, 1916–1919*, London: Herbert Jenkins Ltd., 1924.

Pares, Bernard, *My Russian Memoirs*, London: Jonathan Cape, 1931.

Pasternak, Boris, *Stikhotvoreniya i poemy*, Leningrad: Sovetskii pisatel, 1976.

Paustovsky, Konstantin, *Sobraniye sochinenii*, Moscow: Goslitizdat, 1958.

"Perepiska Nikolaya II i Marii Fedorovny," *Krasny arkhiv*, 1927, 3 (22).

Phelps, William Lyon, *Autobiography*, New York: Oxford University Press, 1939.

"Pisma K.P.Pobedonostseva k Aleksandru III," *Krasny arkhiv*, 1923, 4.

"Pisma V.V.Vereshchagina Nikolayu Romanovu v 1904 g.," *Krasny arkhiv*, 1931, 2 (45).

Ponsonby, Sir Frederick, first Lord Sysonby, *Recollections of Three Reigns*, New York: E. P. Dutton, 1952.

Port-Artur: sbornik vospominanii uchastnikov, New York: Izdatelstvo imeni Chekhova, 1955.

Pridham, Admiral Francis, *Close of a Dynasty*, London: Wingate, 1958.

Purishkevich, V. M., *The Murder of Rasputin*, Ann Arbor, MI: Ardis, 1985.

"Rasputin v osveshchenii okhranki," *Krasny arkhiv*, 1924, 5.

Reed, John, *10 dnei, kotorye potryasli mir*, Moscow: Gospolitizdat, 1957.

Rodzyanko, Mikhail, *The Reign of Rasputin: An Empire's Collapse*, Academic International Press, 1973.

The Romanov Family Album, New York and Paris: Vendome Press, 1982.

Romanovsky-Krassinsky, Princess (Kshesinskaya, Mathilda Feliksovna), *Dancing in Petersburg, The Memoirs of Kschessinska*, Garden City and New York: Doubleday & Company, 1961.

"Romanovy i soyuzniki v pervye dni revolutsii," *Krasny arkhiv*, 1926, 3 (16).

"Romanovy v pervye dni revolutsii," *Krasny arkhiv*, 1927, 5 (24).

Rosen, The Baron, *Forty Years of Diplomacy*, New York: Alfred Knopf, 1922, 2 vol.

Rossiiskii imperatorskii dom, Moscow: Perspectiva, 1992.

Russkiye narodnye pesni, Moscow: Khudozhestvennaya literatura, 1957.

Sazonov, Sergei, *Fateful years, 1909–1916*, London: Jonathan Cape, 1928.

_____, *Vospominaniya*, Moscow: Mezhdunarodnye otnosheniya, 1991.

Semennikov, V. P., ed., *Dnevnik b. velikogo knyazya Andreya Vladimirovicha*, Leningrad-Moscow: Gosudarstvennoye izdatelstvo, 1925.

_____, *Monarkhiya pered krusheniyem imperii, 1914–1917*, Moscow-Leningrad: Gosudarstvennoye izdatelstvo, 1927.

_____, *Nikolai II i velikiye knyazya*, Leningrad-Moscow: Gosudarstvennoye izdatelstvo, 1925.

_____, *Romanovy i germanskiye vliyaniya vo vremya mirovoi voiny*, Leningrad: Krasnaya gazeta, 1929.

_____, *Za kulisami tsarisma. Arkhiv tibetskogo vracha Badmaeva*, Leningrad: Gosudarstvennoye izdatelstvo, 1925.

Shavelsky, Georgy, *Vospominaniya poslednego protopresvitera russkoi armii i flota*, New York: Izdatelstvo imeni Chekhova, 1954, 2 vol.

Shchegolev, P. E., ed., *Padeniye tsarskogo rezhima*, Moscow-Leningrad: Gosudarstvennoye izdatelstvo, 1924–1927, 7 vol.

Shulgin, V. V., *Days of the Russian Revolution. Memoirs from the Right, 1905–1917*, Academic International Press, 1990.

_____, *The Years. Memoirs of a Member of the Russian Duma, 1906–1917*, New York: Hipocrene Books, 1984.

Smirnova-Rosset, A. O., *Vospominaniya, pisma*, Moscow: Pravda, 1990.

Speer, Albert, *Inside the Third Reich*, New York: Collier Books, 1970.

Steffens, Lincoln, *Autobiography of Lincoln Steffens*, New York: Harcourt Brace, 1968.

Steinberg, Mark D., and Vladimir M. Khrustalev, *The Fall of the Romanovs*, New Haven, CT: Yale University Press, 1995.

Stone, Norman, and Michael Glenny, *The Other Russia*, London: Faber and Faber, 1990.

[Stopford, The Hon. Bertie] *The Russian Diary of an Englishman*, Petrograd, 1915–1917, London: William Heinemann, 1919.

Svyatoi Ioann Kronshtadskii v vospominaniyakh sovremennikov, Moscow: Bratstvo vo imya vsemilostivogo Spasa, 1994.

Teffi, *Nostalgia*, Leningrad: Khudozhestvennaya literatura, 1989.

Tiutcheva, A. F., *Pri dvore dvukh imperatorov*, Moscow: Mysl, 1990.

Tolstaya, A. A., *Zapiski freiliny*, Moscow: Entsiklopedia rossiiskikh dereven, 1996.

Tolstoi, Alexey, *Sobraniye sochinenii*, 10 vols., Moscow: Izdatelstvo khudozhestvennoi literatury, 1958.

Twain, Mark, *The Innocents Abroad or the New Pilgrim's Progress, Being Some Account of the Steamship Quaker City's Pleasure Excursion to Europe and the Holy Land*, New York: Heritage Press, 1962.

Ustami Buninykh. Dnevniki, Frankfurt am Main: Posev, 1982.

"Uvolneniye N.N.Romanova ot dolzhnosti verkhovnogo glavnokomanduyushchego," *Krasny arkhiv*, 1925, 3 (10).

Vassili, Count Paul, *Behind the Veil at the Russian Court*, New York: John Lane Company, 1914.

"Verkhovnoye komandovaniye v pervye dni revolutsii," *Krasny arkhiv*, 1924, 5.

Viroubova, Anna, *Memories of the Russian Court*, New York: Macmillan, 1923.

Vladimir Kirillovich, Velikii Knyaz, Leonida Georgievna, Velikaya Knyaginya, *Rossiya v nashem serdtse*, St. Petersburg: Liki Rossii, 1995.

Vladimirov, S., *Zapiski sledovatelya gestapo* in *Moskva*, 1971, nos. 6, 8.

Voitsekhovsky, S. L., *Episody*, London, Canada: Zarya, 1978.

_____, *Trest. Vospominaniya i dokumenty*, London, Canada: Zarya, 1974.

Volkov, A. A., *Okolo tsarskoi semyi*, Moscow: Ankor, 1993.

Von Dreyer, V., *Na zakate imperii*, Madrid, 1965.

Voronovich, N. V., *Vsevidyashchee oko. Iz byta russkoi armii*, New York, 1951.

Vorres, Ian, *The Last Grand Duchess*, London: Hutchinson of London, 1964.

Vospominaniya o Vladimire Iliyche Lenine, Moscow: Politizdat, 1979, 5 vol.

Voyeikov, V. N., *S tsarem i bez tsarya*, Moscow: Rodnik, 1994.

The War in the Far East, 1904–1905, by the Military Correspondent of The Times, London: John Murray, 1905.

William II, *My Early Life*, London: Methuen & Co, 1926.

Windsor, *Memoirs of the Duke of Windsor, A King's Story*, New York: G. P. Putnam's Sons, 1947.

Witte, Sergei Y., *Vospominaniya*, Moscow: Sotsekgiz, 1960, 3 vol.

Wrangel, General Baron Peter N., *Always With Honor*, New York: Robert Speller & Sons, 1957.

_____, *Vospominaniya*, Moscow: Terra, 1992, 2 vol.

Youssoupoff, Felix, *Konets Rasputina*, Paris, 1927.

_____, *Lost Splendour*, London: Jonathan Cape, 1953.

_____, *Rasputin*, New York: The Dial Press, 1928.

"Zagovor monarkhicheskoi organizatsii V.M.Purishkevicha," *Krasny arkhiv*, 1928, 1 (26).

"Zapiski N. M.Romanova," *Krasny arkhiv*, 1931, 4–5 (47–48), 6 (49).

"Zaveshchaniye Nikolaya I synu," *Krasny arkhiv*, 1923, 3.

Zhevakhov, N. D., *Vospominaniya*, Moscow: Rodnik, 1993, 2 vol.

Zhilyar, P., *Imperator Nikolai II i ego semya*, Moscow: Megapolis, 1991.

Zhukov, Georgy K., *Vospominaniya i razmyshleniya*, Moscow: APN, 1971.

Secondary Sources

Allen, Peter, *The Windsor Secret. New Revelations of the Nazi Connection*, New York: Stein and Day, 1984.

Almedingen, E. M., *The Emperor Alexander II*, London: The Bodley Head, 1962.

_____, *The Empress Alexandra, 1872–1918, A Study*, London: Hutchinson, 1961.

_____, *An Unbroken Unity, A Memoir of Grand-Duchess Serge of Russia, 1864–1918*, London: The Bodley Head, 1964.

Andrew, Christopher, and Oleg Gordievsky, *KGB: the Inside Story*, London: Hodder and Stoughton, 1990.

Andreyev, Catherine, *Vlasov and the Russian Liberation Movement: Soviet Reality and Emigre Theories*, Cambridge: Cambridge University Press, 1987.

Aronson, Theo, *Crowns in Conflict: The Triumph and Tragedy of the European Monarchy, 1910–1913*, London: J. Murray, 1986.

_____, *A Family of Kings, The Descendants of Christian IX of Denmark*, London: Cassell, 1976.

_____, *Grandmama of Europe. The Crowned Descendants of Queen Victoria*, Indianapolis and New York: Bobbs-Merrill Company, 1973.

Ashdown, Dulcie M., *Victoria and the Coburgs*, London: Robert Hale, 1981.

Auchincloss, Louis, *Persons of Consequence, Queen Victoria and Her Circle*, London: Weidenfeld and Nicolson, 1979.

Bailey, Geoffrey, *The Conspirators*, New York: Harper, 1960.

Baillen, Claude, *Chanel solitaire*, Paris: n.p., 1971.

Bakh, E., *Rezidentsiya poslednikh Romanovykh. Opyt istoriko-bytovoi kharakteristiki*, Leningrad: Krasnaya gazeta, 1927.

Balfour, Michael, *The Kaiser and His Times*, London: Cresset Press, 1964.

Balfour, Michael, and John Mair, *Four-Power Control in Germany and Austria, 1945–1946*, London: Oxford University Press, 1956.

Battiscombe, Georgina, *Queen Alexandra*, Boston: Houghton, Mifflin, 1969.

Belyakova, Zoya, *The Romanov Legacy: The Palaces of St. Petersburg*, London: Hazar, 1994.

Benson, E. F., *Queen Victoria's Daughters*, New York: D. Appleton Century, 1938.

Berberova, Nina, *Lyudi i lozhi: russkiye masony XX stoletiya*, New York: Russika, 1986.

_____, *Tchaikovsky. Istoriya odinokoi zhizni*, Berlin: Petropolis, 1936.

Bergamini, John D., *The Tragic Dynasty, A History of the Romanovs*, New York: G. P. Putnam's Sons, 1969.

Billington, James H., *The Icon and the Axe, An Interpretive History of Russian Culture*, New York: Vintage, 1970.

Blake, French R. L. V., *The Crimean War*, Archon Books, 1972.

Bokhanov, Alexander; and Manfred Knodt, Vladimir Oustimenko, Zinaida Peregudova, Lyubov Tyutyunik, *The Romanovs: Love, Power & Tragedy*, London: Leppi Publications, 1993.

Borisov, B., *Dalny Vostok*, Vienna: n.p., 1921.

Botkin, Gleb, *The Real Romanovs*, New York: Fleming H. Revell, 1931.

Brayley Hodgetts, E. A., *The Court of Russia in the Nineteenth Century*, London: Methuen, 1908.

Brooke-Shepard, Gordon, *The Last Habsburg*, London: Weidenfeld & Nicolson, 1968.

Buchanan, Meriel, *Queen Victoria's Relations*, London: Cassell, 1954.

_____, *Victorian Gallery*, London: Cassell, 1956.

Buckle, Richard, *Diaghilev*, New York: Atheneum, 1979.

Buranov, Yu., and V. Khrustalev, *Gibel imperatorskogo doma, 1917–1919*, Moscow: Progress, 1992.

Cannadine, David, *The Pleasures of the Past*, New York: Norton, 1989.

_____, "Splendor out of Court: Royal Spectacle and Pageantry in Modern Britain, c. 1820–1977," in Sean Wilentz, ed., *Rites of Power: Symbolism, Ritual and Politics since the Middle Ages*, Philadelphia: University of Pennsylvania Press, 1985.

Cecil, Lamar, *Wilhelm II. Prince and Emperor, 1859–1900*, Chapel Hill: The University of North Carolina Press, 1989.

Charques, Richard, *The Twilight of Imperial Russia*, Fairlawn, NJ: Essential Books, 1959.

Chavchavadze, David, *The Grand Dukes*, New York: Atlantic International Publications, 1990.

Cherkasov, P., and D. Chernyshevsky, *Istoriya imperatorskoi Rossii*, Moscow: Mezhdunarodnye otnosheniya, 1994.

Cherniavsky, Michael, *Tsar and People, Studies in Russian Myths*, New Haven and London: Yale University Press, 1961.

Chernukha, V. G., "Alexander III," *Voprosy istorii*, 11–12, 1992.

Chudakov, A., "'Neprilichnye slova' i obraz klassika. O kupiurakh v izdaniyakh pisem Chekhova," *Literaturnoye obozreniye*, 1991, 11.

Chulkov, Georgy, *Imperatory*, Moscow: Moskovskii rabochii, 1991.

Clarke, William, *The Lost Fortune of the Tsars*, New York: St. Martin's Press, 1994.

Corti, Count Egon, *The Downfall of Three Dynasties*, London: Methuen, 1934.

Cowles, Virginia, *The Romanovs*, London: Collins, 1971.

Crawford, Rosemary & Donald, *Michael and Natasha. The Life and Love of Michael II, the Last of the Romanov Tsars*, New York: A Lisa Drew Book/Scribner, 1997.

Danilov, Yu. N., *Velikii Knyaz Nikolai Nikolaevich*, Paris: Imprimerie de Navarre, 1930.

Dobronozhenko, G. F., *VChK-OGPU o politicheskikh nastroyeniyakh severnogo krestyanstva, 1921–1927*, Syktyukar: Syktyvkarsky Gosudarstvenny universitet, 1996.

Dom Romanovykh, Moscow: Zhivaya voda, 1991.

Edwards, Anne, *Matriarch. Queen Mary and the House of Windsor*, New York: William Morrow and Company, Inc., 1984.

Engelstein, Laura, *The Keys to Happiness: Sex and the Search for Modernity in Fin-de-Siecle Russia*, Ithaca, New York: Cornell University Press, 1992.

Faberge: pridvorny yuvelir, St. Petersburg: Gosudarstvenny Ermitazh, 1993.

Fatemi, Nasrollah Saifpour, *Diplomatic History of Persia, 1917–1923. Anglo-Russian Power Politics in Iran*, New York: Russell F. Moore Company, 1952.

Feis, Herbert, *The Spanish Story: Franco and the Nations at War*, New York: W. W. Norton, 1966.

Fenyvesi, Charles, *Splendor in Exile. The Ex-Majesties of Europe*, Washington, DC: New Republic Books, 1979.

Ferrand, Jacques, *Le grand-duc Paul Alexandrovich de Russie*, Paris: n.p., 1993.

Field, Leslie, *The Jewels of Queen Elizabeth II*, New York: Harry Abrams, 1992.

Flanner, Janet (Genet), *Paris Was Yesterday, 1925–1939*, San Diego, CA: Harcourt Brace, 1972.

Florinsky, Michael T., *The End of the Russian Empire*, New York: Howard Fertig, 1973.

Fol, Jean-Jacques, *Acession de la Finlande a l'independence, 1917–1919*, Paris, 1977.

Frelikh, Sergei, *General Vlasov. Russkiye i nemtsy mezhdu Gitlerom i Stalinym*, Tenafly, NJ: Hermitage, 1990.

Friedlander, Saul, *Pie XII et le III-e reich*, Paris: Editions du seuil, 1964.

Fusi, J. P., *Franco. A Biography*, New York: Harper and Row, 1987.

Garafola, Lynn, *Diaghilev's Ballets Russes*, New York, Oxford: Oxford University Press, 1989.

Gerhard, William, *The Romanovs: Evocation of the Past as a Mirror for the Present*, New York: G. P. Putnam's Sons, 1939.

Golovine, Lieutenant-General Nicholas N., *The Russian Army in the World War*, New Haven, CT: Yale University Press, 1931.

Goroda Rossii. Entsiklopedia, Moscow: Bolshaya Sovetskaya Entsiklopediya, 1994.

Gorokhov, Dmitri, "Kuzina imperatora," *Ekho planety*, 11, 1993.

Grabbe, Paul and Beatrice, eds., *The Private World of the Last Tsar, in the Photographs and Notes of General Count Alexander Grabbe*, Boston and Toronto: Little, Brown & Co., 1984.

Grant, Natalie, "Deception on a Grand Scale," *Journal of Intelligence and Counterintelligence*, Vol I (1986–88), No. 4.

Gray, Pauline, *The Grand Duke's Woman*, London: Macdonald and Janeís, 1976.

Grebelskii, P., *Dom Romanovykh: biograficheskiye svedeniya o chlenakh tsarstvovavshego doma, ikh predkakh i rodstvennikakh*, St. Petersburg: LTO Redaktor, 1992.

Greenhill, B., Giffard A., *The British Assault on Finland, 1854–1855*, London: Naval Institute Press, 1988.

Gul, Roman, *Krasnye marshaly*, Moscow: Molodaya gvardiya, 1990.

Harcave, Sidney, *Years of the Golden Cockerel: The Last Romanov Tsars, 1814–1917*, New York: Macmillan, 1968.

Hayes, Nicholas, "Kazem-Bek and the Young Russians' Revolution," *Slavic Review* 39:2 (June 1980).

Hibbert, Christopher, *The Royal Victorians: King Edward VII, His Family and Friends*, Philadelphia and New York: J. B. Lippincott Company, 1976.

Hoffman, J., *Istoriya vlasovskoi armii*, Paris: YMCA-PRESS, 1990.

Hull, Isabel V., *The Entourage of Kaiser Wilhelm II, 1888–1918*, Cambridge: Cambridge University Press, 1982.

Hvidore—An Historical Treasure Trove, Novo Nordisk A/S, September 1993.

Ioffe, Henrikh, *Revolutsiya i sudba Romanovykh*, Moscow: Respublika, 1992.

Jagerskiold, Stig, *Mannerheim, Marshal of Finland*, Minneapolis: University of Minnesota Press, 1986.

Johnston, Robert H., *New Mecca, New Babylon—Paris and the Russian Exiles, 1920–1945*, Kingston, Montreal: McQuill-Queen University Press, 1988.

Jones, Daniel, "Imperial Russia's Forces at War," in Allan R. Millett and Murray Williamson, eds., *Military Effectiveness*, Vol. I, Boston: Allen & Unwin, 1988.

Kann, *Progulki po Peterburgu*, St. Petersburg: Palitra, 1994.

Karlinsky, Simon, "Russia's Gay Literature and Culture: the Impact of the October Revolution," *Hidden from History: Reclaiming the Gay and Lesbian Past*, ed. by Martin Duberman, Martha Vicinius & George Chauncey, Jr., New York: NAL Books, 1989.

Kasvinov, Mark, *Dvadtsat tri stupeni vniz*, Moscow, Sovetskii pisatel, 1982.

Katkov, George, *Russia, 1917. The February Revolution*, New York: Harper and Row, 1967.

Keep, John, "The Military Style of the Romanov Rulers," *War and Society* 1:2(1983).

Kennet, Frances, *Coco: The Life and Loves of Gabrielle Chanel*, London: V. Gollancz, 1989.

King, Greg, *The Last Empress. The Life and Times of Alexandra Fedorovna, Tsarina of Russia*, New York: Birch Lane Press, 1994.

_____, *The Man Who Killed Rasputin*, New York: Birch Lane Press, 1995.

Kobylin, Viktor, *Imperator Nikolai II i general-adjutant M.V.Alexeev*, New York: Vseslavyanskoye izdatelstvo, 1970.

Kornilov, N. I., and Yu. P. Solodova, *Yuvelirnye kamni*, Moscow: Nedra, 1983.

"Korona rossiiskoi imperii," *Ogoniok*, 1990, 2.

Krivoshlyk, M. G., *Istoricheskiye anekdoty iz zhizni russkikh zamechatel-nykh liudei*, Moscow: ANC-Print, 1991.

Ktorova, Alla, *Poteryannye rossiyane*, Tver: Alba, 1996.

Kurenberg, Joachim von, *The Kaiser. A Life of Wilhelm II, Last Emperor of Germany*, London: Cassel & Co, 1954.

Lebina, N. B., and M.V. Shkarovsky, *Prostitutsiya v Peterburge*, Moscow: Progress, 1994.

Leggett, George, *The CheKA: Lenin's Political Police*, Oxford: Clarendon Press, 1981.

Lehovich, Dmitry, *White Against Red, The Life of General Anton Denikin*, New York: Norton, 1973.

Lenyashin, V. A., *Portretnaya zhivopis V.A.Serova 1900-kh godov: osnovnye problemy*, Leningrad: Khudozhnik RSFSR, 1980.

Liddell Hart, Captain B. H., *The Real War, 1914–1918*, Boston: Little, Brown, 1930.

Lieven, Dominic C., *Nicholas II: Twilight of the Empire*, New York: St. Martin's Press, 1996.

_____, *Russia's Rulers Under the Old Regime*, New Haven, CT: Yale University Press, 1991.

Lincoln, Bruce, *The Great Reforms: Autocracy, Bureaucracy, and the Politics of Change in Imperial Russia*, Dekalb, IL: Northern Illinois University Press, 1990.

_____, *Nicholas I: Emperor and Autocrat of All the Russias*, Dekalb, IL: Northern Illinois University Press, 1989.

_____, *The Romanovs: Autocrats of All the Russias*, Anchor, 1983.

Longford, Elizabeth, *Queen Victoria, Born to Succeed*, New York: Harper & Row, 1964.

Lotman, Yu.M., and E. A. Pogosian, *Velikosvetskiye obedy*, St. Petersburg: Pushkinskii fond, 1996.

Lowe, Charles, *Alexander III of Russia*, New York: Macmillan & Co., 1895.

Luckett, Richard, *The White Generals. An Account of the White Movement and the Russian Civil War*, London: Longman, 1971.

Ludwig, Emil, *Poslednii Gogentsollern (Wilgelm II)*, Moscow: Moskovskii rabochii, 1991.

Lyons, Marvin, *Russia in Original Photographs, 1860–1920*, New York: Charles Scribner's Sons, 1977.

Malcolm Smith, E. F., *Patriots of the Nineteenth Century*, London: Longmans Green, 1928.

Malinin, V., *Starets Eleazarova monastyrya Philophei i ego poslaniya*, Kiev, 1901.

Massie, Robert K., *Nicholas and Alexandra*, London: Gollancz, 1968.

_____, *The Romanovs: The Final Chapter*, New York: Random House, 1995.

Massie, Suzanne, *Land of the Firebird*, Hearttree Press, 1980.

Melgunov, S., *Na putyakh k dvortsovomu perevorotu*, Paris: Rodnik, 1931.

Memories, The Story of the Kirby Family, Volume Six, privately printed.

Menkes, Suzy, *The Royal Jewels*, London: Grafton Books, 1985.

Michael of Greece, *Crown Jewels*, New York: Crescent Books, 1983.

Miller, J. Martin, *Thrilling Stories of the Russian-Japanese War*, Chicago: n.p., 1904.

Miller, Liubov, *Sviataya muchenitsa rossiiskaya Velikaya Kniaginya Elizaveta Fedorovna*, Moscow: Stolitsa, 1994.

Monarkhii Evropy. Sudby dinastii, Moscow: Respublika, 1996.

Morris, Edwin T., *Fragrance*, New York: Charles Scribner's Sons, 1984.

Nadelhoffer, Hans, *Cartier, Jewelers Extraordinary*, New York: Thames and Hudson, 1984.

Nicolson, Harold, *George V, His Life and Reign*, London: Constable, 1952.

Nikulin, L.V., *Mertvaya zyb*, Moscow: Voenizdat, 1965.

Nova, Fritz, *Alfred Rosenberg. Nazi Theorist of the Holocaust*, New York: Hippocrene Books, 1986.

Occleshaw, Michael, *The Romanov Conspiracies*, London: Chapmans, 1993.

Pakula, Hannah, *The Last Romantic: A Biography of Queen Mary of Romania*, New York: Simon & Schuster, 1984.

Palmer, Alan, *The Kaiser, Warlord of the Second Reich*, New York: Charles Scribner's Sons, 1978.

Pares, Bernard, *The Fall of the Russian Monarchy, A Study of the Evidence*, London: Cassell, 1988.

Pavlov, A. P., *Khramy Sankt-Peterburga*, St. Petersburg: Lenizdat, 1995.

Pavlova, Zhermena, *Imperatorskaya biblioteka Ermitazha, 1762–1917*, Tenaffy, NJ: Ermitazh, 1988.

Pearson, Raymond, *The Russian Moderates and the Crisis of Tsarism, 1914–1917*, New York: Barnes and Noble, 1977.

Pervaya mirovaya v zhizneopisaniyakh russkikh voenachalnikov, Moscow: Elakos, 1994.

Petropavlovskaya (Sankt-Peterburgskaya) krepost, St. Petersburg: Musei istorii Sankt-Peterburga, 1993.

Pipes, Richard, *The Russian Revolution, 1888–1919*, London: Collins Harvill, 1990.

Poliakoff, V. (Augur), *Mother Dear. The Empress Marie of Russia and Her Times*, New York: D. Appleton & Co, 1926.

Pope-Hennesy, James, *Queen Mary*, New York: Alfred A. Knopf, 1960.

Popov, A. R., *Romanovy na yuzhnom beregu Kryma*, Simferopol: Gosizdat, 1930.

Popov, N.V., "Dinastiya Romanovykh v semye evropeiskikh monarkhov," *Novaya i noveishaya istoriya*, 1994, 2.

Poznansky, Alexander, "Tchaikovsky's Suicide: Myth and Reality," *19th Century Music*, vol. 11, no. 3, Spring 1988.

Pryanishnikov, Boris, *Nezrimaya pautina*, St. Petersburg: Chas pik, 1993.

Pryce-Jones, David, *Paris in the Third Reich, A History of the German Occupation, 1940–1944*, New York: Holt, Rinehart & Winston, 1981.

Putevoditel po Peterburgu, St. Petersburg: n.p., 1886.

Raeff, Marc, "The Romanovs and Their Books: Perspectives on Imperial Rule in Russia," *Biblion: The Bulletin of the New York Public Library*, Fall 1997.

_____, *Russia Abroad. A Cultural History of the Russian Emigration, 1919–1939*, New York: Oxford University Press, 1990.

Rayfield, Donald, *The Dream of Lhasa: the Life of Nikolai Przevalsky, Explorer of Central Asia*, Columbus: Ohio University Press, 1977.

Reed, T. J., *Death in Venice. Making and Unmaking a Master*, New York: Twayne Publishers, 1994.

Romanovy i Krym, Moscow: Kruk, 1993.

Ronchevsky, R. P., *Mladorossy. Materialy k istorii smenovekhovskogo dvizheniya*, London, Canada: Zarya, 1973.

Rose, Kenneth, *King George V*, London: Weidenfeld and Nicholson, 1983.

Rossiiskaya diplomatiya v portretakh, Moscow: Mezhdunarodnye otnosheniya, 1992.

Rossiiskie samoderzhtsy, 1801–1917, Moscow: Mezhdunarodnye otnosheniya, 1993.

Russkii literaturny anekdot kontsa XVIII-nachala XIX veka, Moscow: Khudozhestvennaya literatura, 1990.

Saparov, A., "Opasnye komedianty," *Zvezda*, 1972, no. 4.

Sayers, Michael, and Albert E. Kahn, *The Great Conspiracy against Russia*, New York: Boni and Gaer, 1946.

Scott, Stephan, *Romanovy*, Ekaterinburg: Larin, 1993.

Segel, Harold B., *Turn-of-the-century Cabaret: Paris, Barcelona, Berlin, Munich, Vienna, Cracow, Moscow, St. Petersburg, Zurich*, New York: Columbia University Press, 1987.

Shirer, William L., *The Rise and Fall of the Third Reich*, London: Pan Books, 1960.

Shtakelberg, N. S., "Zagadka smerti Nikolaya I", *Russkoye proshloye*, vol.1, 1923.

Smith, G. Jay, *Finland and the Russian Revolution, 1917–1922*, Athens: University of Georgia Press, 1958.

Sokolov, Boris, *Bulgakovskaya entsiklopediya*, Moscow: Lokid-Mif, 1996.

Sole, Kent M., "The Fate of the Romanovs: The Survivors," *Imperial Russian Journal* 2:1.

Solovieva, T. A., *Paradnye rezidentsii Dvortsovoi naberezhnoi*, St. Petersburg: Evropeiskii dom, 1995.

Somin, Ilya, *Stillborn Crusade, The Tragic Failure of Western Intervention in the Russian Civil War, 1918–1920*, New Brunswick, NJ: Transaction Press, 1996.

Spoto, Donald, *The Decline and Fall of the House of Windsor*, New York: Simon & Shuster, 1995.

Stearman, William Lloyd, *The Soviet Union and the Occupation of Austria*, Bad Godesberg: Verlag fur Zeitarchive, 1961.

Stephan, John J., *The Russian Fascists, Tragedy and Farce in Exile, 1925–1945*, New York: Harper & Row, 1978.

Strakhovsky, Leonid I., *Intervention at Archangel, The Story of Allied Intervention and Russian Counter-Revolution in North Russia, 1918–1920*, New York: Howard Fertig, 1971.

Sullivan, Michael John, *A Fatal Passion: The Story of Victoria Melita, the Uncrowned Last Empress of Russia*, New York: Random House, 1997.

Sykes, Percy, *A History of Persia*, London: Macmillan & Co, 1921, 2 vol.

Tisdall, E. E. P., *The Dowager Empress*, London: Stanley Paul, 1957.

Tolstoy, Leo, *Great Short Works of Leo Tolstoy*, New York: Harper and Row, 1967.

Tomich, V. M., *Warships of the Imperial Russian Navy*, San Francisco: B.T. Publishers, 1968.

Troyat, Henri, *Catherine the Great*, New York: E. P. Dutton, 1980.

Tuchman, Barbara W., *The Guns of August*, New York: Ballantine Books, 1994.

Van der Kiste, John, *George V's Children*, Stroud, Gloucestershire: Alan Sutton, 1991.

_____, *Princess Victoria Melita, Grand Duchess Cyril of Russia, 1876–1936*, Stroud, Gloucestershire: Alan Sutton, 1991.

_____, *Queen Victoria's Children*, Stroud, Gloucestershire: Alan Sutton, 1986.

_____, *Windsor and Habsburg*, Stroud, Gloucestershire: Alan Sutton, 1987.

_____ and Bee Jordann, *Dearest Affie . . . Alfred, Duke of Edinburgh, Queen Victoria's Second Son, 1844–1900*, Stroud, Gloucestershire: Alan Sutton, 1984.

Velikoknyazheskaya usypalnitsa v Petropavlovskoi kreposti, St. Petersburg: Arsis, 1993.

Viereck, George Sylvester, *The Kaiser on Trial*, The Greystone Press, 1937.

Voleyu Bozhiei: albom o pretendente velikom knyaze Vladimire Kirilloviche, ego predkakh i potomkakh, Paris: n.p., 1957.

Volkov, Solomon, *St. Petersburg, A Cultural History*, New York: The Free Press, 1995.

Vouytch, Dmitry N., *Pamyatka dlya russkikh liudei*, Moscow: Riurik, 1993.

Vozhd, Lenin, kotorogo my ne znali, Saratov: Slovo, 1992.

Weintraub, Stanley, *Victoria, An Intimate Biography*, New York: Truman Talley Books, E. P. Dutton, 1987.

West, Nigel, *Secret War. The Story of SOE, Britain's Wartime Sabotage Organization*, London: Hodder and Stoughton, 1992.

Wheeler-Bennett, John W., *King George VI, His Life and Reign*, New York: St. Martin's Press, 1958.

Whittle, Tyler, *The Last Kaiser, A Biography of Wilhelm II, German Emperor and King of Prussia*, London: Wm. Heinemann, 1977.

Williams, Robert C., *Culture in Exile—Russian Emigres in Germany, 1881–1941*, Ithaca, NY: Cornell University Press, 1972.

Wortman, Richard S., "Power and Responsibility in the Upbringing of the Nineteenth Century Tsars," *Newsletter* (of the Group for the Use of Psychology in History), Springfield, IL, 4:4 (March 1976).

_____, *Scenarios of Power, Myth and Ceremony in Russian Monarchy, Volume I, from Peter the Great to the Death of Nicholas I*, Princeton, NJ: Princeton University Press, 1995.

_____, "The Russian Empress As Mother," in David L. Ransel, ed., *The Family in Imperial Russia: New Lines of Historical Research*, Urbana: University of Illinois Press, 1978.

Wrangel, Alexis, *General Wrangel. Russia's White Crusader*, New York: Hippocrene Books Inc., 1987.

Interviews

Marusya Chavchavadze, Cape Cod, MA, 5/20/95

Custodian of the Vladimir Palace, St. Petersburg, 10/23/94

Paul Grabbe, Cape Cod, MA, 5/20/95

Paul Ilyinski, by phone 8/6/96

Princess Natalia Iskander (Androsova), Moscow, 9/19/97, 10/11/97, 12/25/97

Rosemary Kerry, Manchester, MA, 7/97

Vladislav Kostin, Moscow, 12/20/95

Olga N. Kulikovsky, by phone, 4/1/96

Princess Tatiana Ladyzhenskaya, Copenhagen, 12/11/95

Grand Duchess Leonida Georgievna, Paris, 10/20/95

Mikhail Moliukov, Moscow, 12/16/95

Rev. Nikon, Moscow, 9/19/97

Prince Alexander Romanov, by phone, 9/15/97

Prince Dmitri Romanov, Copenhagen, 12/12/95

Prince Nicholas Romanov, Rome, 10/16/97

Andrei Shmeman, Paris, 10/21/95

Betty Tiemann Tobias, New York, 4/11/96

Kyra Volkova Robinson, Annisquam, MA, 8/14/95

Angela Winthrop, Hamilton, MA, 7/97

Alexander Zakatov, 7/96

Periodicals

Daily Telegraph
Evening Standard
The Herald (Glasgow)
Imperial Russian Journal
The Independent
International Herald Tribune
Izvestiya
The Japan Weekly Mail
Komsomolskaya pravda
The (London) *Times*
Majesty
Miami Herald
Moskovsky komsomolets
Moscow News
The New York Times
Novoye russkoye slovo
Pravitelstvenny vestnik
Pravda

INDEX